הגדה של פסח
THE HERITAGE HAGGADAH

הגדה של פסח

THE HERITAGE HAGGADAH

WITH LAWS, CUSTOMS, TRADITIONS, AND COMMENTARY FOR THE SEDER NIGHT

ELIYAHU KITOV

Translated from the Hebrew by
GERSHON ROBINSON

JERUSALEM FELDHEIM PUBLISHERS NEW YORK

Originally published in 1961 in Hebrew as
Seder Leil Pesach.

First published 1999

Copyright © 1999 by Yad Eliyahu Kitov

ISBN 0-87306-868-8

All rights reserved.
No part of this publication may be translated,
reproduced, stored in a retrieval system or transmitted,
in any form or by any means,
electronic, mechanical, photocopying, recording, or otherwise,
without permission in writing from the publishers.

FELDHEIM PUBLISHERS
POB 35002 / Jerusalem, Israel

200 Airport Executive Park
Nanuet, NY 10954

Printed in Israel

About the Author

Rabbi Avraham Eliyahu Kitov (Mokotovsky), of blessed memory, was born in Warsaw, Poland in 5672 (1912). His childhood and youth were spent in a nearby small town, where he attended the local *cheder* and later learned in the *beis midrash*. The essence of his Jewish education, however, was imparted to him by his father, R' Michael, of blessed memory, whose Chasidic roots and way of life greatly influenced his developing character. At the age of 17, he returned to Warsaw where his days were spent in physical labor, Torah study in the *beis midrash*, and active involvement in *Agudas Yisrael*, especially in the field of Jewish education. During this period, he taught regular classes in Talmud, *Tanach*, and Jewish thought, and also did volunteer teaching in secular institutions for homeless Jewish children.

In 1936, he came to Eretz Yisrael and found employment as a construction worker. He and his colleagues, distressed by the plight of the religious laborer, founded a religious Jewish workers' union under the acronym PAGI, which successfully addressed the issue of workers' conditions, and also established workers' cooperatives in industry and construction. In the years that followed, he headed a religious boys' school, engaged in communal activity, and edited the PAGI newspaper, in which he wrote hundreds of articles on various subjects. In these early writings one can see the seeds which flourished in his later works.

When Eliyahu Kitov was in his forties, he turned seriously to writing. The four decades of life behind him had given him sagacious wisdom, a profound knowledge of the Written and Oral Torah, and a consummate command of Chasidic thought and lore.

Two things above all made him leave other interests aside at last, and devote the final part of his life to writing. Through all his adult years he had been an educator. Even when he entered the arena of politics and public affairs he retained his abiding love of teaching.

His other motive was the strong wish to reach beyond the confines of the classroom.

How could a master teacher reach far beyond his classroom? With the power of the pen. He founded a small publishing house called "A" — today Yad Eliyahu Kitov — through which he published the books that he wrote.

From 1955 to 1966, he produced five modest books of stories and lore from the vanished world of *Chasidim* that he knew so well, in which great Chasidic rabbis of bygone years sprang vividly to life.

In 1957, he published *Ish u'Beiso — A Jew and His Home*, a guide to Jewish home life, as our people have known it through the centuries. This work appeared in English as well, and a revised, expanded edition is in preparation at the time of this writing.

His next published work was *Sefer haToda'ah*, which appeared in two volumes, in 1958 and 1961, the Hebrew original of *The Book of Our Heritage*. A revised, expanded, and annotated three-volume edition was published in 1996. Here his theme is the Jewish calendar. Month by month, he takes up the special days and times of the Jewish year, and gives new meaning and richness to their historic significance.

In 1961, *Seder Leil Pesach* was published. This book, like Eliyahu Kitov's other works, has been overwhelmingly popular and has become an essential part of the family library. This edition, *The Heritage Haggadah*, is its first appearance in English as a complete work.

Eliyahu Kitov's final work, *Sefer haParashiyos*, is a wide-ranging and comprehensive commentary on the Torah. This multi-volume project is in essence a compilation of Midrashic literature, interpretations of the Early Authorities, and Chasidic sources. This work, which reflects the author's unique character, occupied him for the last years of his life. He died on Shabbos Kodesh, the sixth of Adar I, 5736 (1976).

Preface to the Hebrew Edition

The Pesach Haggadah is a beloved and classical Jewish work, an integral part of our treasured heritage. Over the centuries, an untold number of commentaries have been written on it, and the Haggadah has appeared in an untold number of different editions.

Nevertheless, there is much in the commentary of R. Eliyahu Kitov, *zt"l*, that is new and unique. First, the book before you is much more than a Haggadah. It is a guide that takes one step-by-step through the days that lead up to the Seder night, explaining what one needs for the Seder and how to prepare for the holiday in general. R. Kitov's work elucidates the significance of all the laws and customs, the special foods, and everything else that is connected to Pesach. It also serves as a practical guide for observance, providing many details as to how the different mitzvos of Pesach are properly fulfilled. Thus the author has provided us with an invaluable tool, not only for helping us to conduct the Seder and observe Pesach, but also for helping us to understand and appreciate the significance of the things that we do, so that we truly enjoy this beautiful holiday, deriving full benefit from its external lessons.

The extensive commentary on the Haggadah itself comprises the majority of this volume. Regarding almost every passage of the Haggadah, readers will find several insightful explanations collected from Jewish history's most illustrious commentators. There also are informative discussions about the Haggadah's design and structure — these, too, from the best-known of our commentators. Throughout, the author adds his own delightful and learned insights and explanations as well.

The book's final section comprises various subjects which are connected to the Seder night. For example, there is a chapter devoted exclusively to the Ten Plagues, drawing upon se-

Preface to the Hebrew Edition

lected *midrashim* and other Rabbinic teachings. Readers also will find a separate chapter about the origin and significance of *Shir haShirim*, the Song of Songs, which by custom is read after the Seder is completed. A number of other interesting and related topics are discussed in the book's final pages.

Much in the opening chapters — those that precede the collected commentaries on the Haggadah — is taken from the author's magnum opus, the popular and well-loved *Sefer haToda'ah (The Book of Our Heritage)*. This acknowledged masterpiece covers the entire Jewish calendar year, describing and explaining all the holidays, customs, and observances of Judaism, in a clear, enjoyable, and unique style, drawing upon the author's profound love and knowledge of the Written and Oral law. In our generation, simply to have read the vast amount of material that the author consulted for *The Book of Our Heritage*, would be considered a major accomplishment. R. Kitov fully grasped this material as well, and was able to bring it all together under one cover, in a way that is pleasing, stimulating, and inspiring to contemporary readers.

As a result, *Sefer haToda'ah* is not simply eloquent, enjoyable reading; it also supplies today's audience with a satisfying, sweeping understanding of our rich Jewish heritage, in all its breadth and depth.

In the original edition of *Sefer haToda'ah*, R. Kitov felt it necessary to devote an entire section to the Pesach Seder itself, not only to explain the meaning and significance of the Seder, but also to simply set out all the different things that a person at the Seder is supposed to do. The details of the Seder night are many, and not everyone could easily retain all these details at once, in order to properly perform the customary and obligatory practices smoothly and comfortably. Thus the author decided to provide helpful instructions, explaining the Seder in a systematic, organized way, so that all the different elements and practices could easily be remembered and followed.

In the chapter entitled "The Structure of the Haggadah," the author provides brilliant and original explanations for why different parts of the Haggadah are arranged as they are. In a reverent way, he shows the masterful planning behind the Haggadah, explains its contents, and interweaves a delightful commentary on the many mitzvos that are performed in the course of the Seder.

From the vast treasure house of the commentary on the Haggadah, the author generally selected those explanations which follow the simple reading of the text. However, when it was relevant and timely, he also occasionally quoted more poetic interpretations that are on the level of *derash*. A sizable number of quotes are from renowned Chassidic luminaries, whose interpretations add an additional dimension to the volume, particularly their writings about our Nation's enslavement in Egypt and our Exodus to freedom.

In preparing the commentary on the Haggadah, R. Kitov took great care in selecting which particular explanations and interpretations to include, for as noted, an enormous amount has been written on the Haggadah, by a very large number of different commentators. He struggled long hours making his choices, and then had to make additional efforts to assure that the resulting commentary would flow, despite the fact that the styles and approaches of the different commentators often varied greatly. R. Kitov sometimes slightly edited the texts of the original works that he cited, so that the commentary as a whole would read more smoothly. At the same time, he restrained himself so that, as much as possible, the style and flavor of the original commentaries would be retained.

Many of these selected commentaries on the Haggadah were originally printed in *Sefer haToda'ah*. R. Kitov wanted *Sefer haToda'ah* to accompany a person through the entire Jewish year, as an aid to achieving deeper understanding of everything that we do from one season to the next. Regarding the chapters connected to Pesach and the Seder, it was his feeling that what these commentators had written on the actual Haggadah was truly indispensible, if in fact *Sefer haToda'ah* was to achieve its goal. Thus, in the first edition of *Sefer haToda'ah*, to complement the chapters that he wrote on Pesach and the Seder, R. Kitov included these choice explanations of the Haggadah, adding his own interpretations and explanations as well.

However, after the first edition was published, R. Kitov decided that this particular part of such an extensive work would be much more useful if it were printed separately under its own cover. Therefore, he placed the selected commentaries alongside the text of the Haggadah itself, and as an introduction, he attached the chapters from *Sefer haToda'ah* which deal with Pesach and the Seder. In the second and later editions of *Sefer haToda'ah*, the selected commentaries on the Haggadah which appear in this volume do not appear at all.

It was known that in the eyes of the author, the more important component of the separate, special Pesach volume was the section containing his collection of selected commentaries on the Haggadah. Thus, he entitled this volume *Yalkut Tov* — "A good collection," to hint that the main feature of the volume was the *Yalkut* — the "collection" — and that he, *Kitov*, was simply the "collector." As a result, he never even put his name on the Pesach volume's title page. We find his name only on one of the inside pages, at the beginning of one of the chapters. There, too, he refers to himself as merely the one who gathered together the different commentaries.

We, however, are permitted to look at this impressive work quite differently. In truth, the most precious component may well be the chapters that accompany the collected commentaries on the Haggadah. There is such a great wealth of material contained in these chapters, culled from the greatest authorities, skillfully arranged in the author's distinctly eloquent literary style. R. Kitov, an exceptional scholar, also adds several of his own explanations and comments. Accordingly we have taken the liberty to change the name of the [Hebrew] volume, and we have entitled it *Seder Leil Pesach*, for as explained, it is much more than simply a high-quality collection of commentaries on the Haggadah.

In this volume, some additional laws and customs were noted, along with some supplementary points of explanation about the Haggadah. Instrumental in the completion of this work were R. Mordechai Ben Eliyahu, and my brother-in-law, R. Oded Kitov, the author's son, who clarified many legal aspects, cited sources for the author's statements, and quoted additional commentaries on the Haggadah. May Hashem continue to strengthen them and give them His blessings.

When the author was actually working on his Haggadah, he spoke in gratitude of haRav Raphael Katzenelenbogen, zt"l, and haRav haGaon Shlomo Zalman Auerbach, zt"l, who aided him greatly with their sound advice and insightful comments.

We have made great effort to publish this volume in a way that befits the honor and stature of its author.

May the pleasantness of God be upon us, and our deeds be pleasing in His Eyes.

Chanoch Ben Arza

Publisher's Preface to the English Edition

The works of R. Eliyahu Kitov, *zt"l*, are unique, each one a reflection of the author's vast knowledge of Torah and Jewish tradition and his great love for the Almighty, the People of Israel, the Torah of Israel, and the Land of Israel.

It was our great privilege to recently publish a revised and expanded edition of the author's classic *Sefer haToda'ah — The Book of Our Heritage*; in preparation is a new English translation of *Ish u'Beiso — A Jew and His Home*; and now it is with great pleasure that we present to our readership another popular Kitov classic, for the first time in English translation: *Seder Leil Pesach — The Heritage Haggadah*.

The book opens with preparations for the Seder night and detailed explanations and commentary on the structure of the Haggadah and its significance; proceeds to the Haggadah itself, accompanied by extensive, rich and varied commentary; and concludes with a wealth of *midrashim* on our slavery in Egypt and the miracle of our redemption. Unique in scope and depth, Eliyahu Kitov's writings open a window onto the treasure-house of Halachah, Aggadah, and tradition, by whose radiant light the entire Seder night is illuminated.

This book could not have come to fruition without the devoted assistance, talents, and skills of the following people: Chanoch ben Arza of Yad Eliyahu Kitov; Rabbi Gershon Robinson, translator of the book; Rabbi Yaakov Lavon, translator of parts of the Haggadah text and of *Seder Amiras Korban Pesach*; Rabbi Binyamin Moore, translator of *Shir haShirim*; R. Dovid Landesman, who translated the sections from *The Book of Our Heritage* included here; Mrs. Bracha Steinberg, for her design and production work on the book; Mrs. Joyce Bennett, editor; Michael Silverstein, for his design of the cover; Mrs. Hannah Hartman, English typesetter; Yosi ben Shachar,

Hebrew typesetter; and all the members of the editorial and production staffs at Feldheim Publishers.

It has been our privilege to have a part in the publication of this important and all-encompassing work on the redemption from Egypt; may *Am Yisrael* merit the final Redemption of our People speedily and in our days, Amen.

Yaakov Feldheim
Jerusalem
Tu bi-Shevat 5759
February 1999

Contents

Preface to the Hebrew Edition   vii
Publisher's Preface to the English Edition   xii

Before the Holiday

CHECKING FOR CHAMETZ, 3
   "Chametz" in One's Character, 6

EREV PESACH, 7
   Eruv Tavshilin, 7
   Needs for the Seder, 8
      10 The Seder Plate

HOW THE PESACH SACRIFICE WAS DONE, 15
   Seder Amiras Korban Pesach, 16

THE NIGHT THE FESTIVAL IS SANCTIFIED, 23
   Ma'ariv — the Evening Prayer, 23
   The Correct Time for the Seder, 25
   The Night the Festival Is Sanctified, 26
   Customs of the Rabbis, 28
   Wearing White at the Seder, 29
   Candle Lighting, 30

UNDERSTANDING THE SEDER, 31
   The Order of the Seder, 31
   The Mitzvos of the Seder Which Apply Today, 34
   Rules for Conducting the Seder, 36
      36 Kiddush and the Shehecheyanu blessing
      36 Mitzvos should not be performed in "bundles"
      37 Telling the story of the Exodus
      37 Matzah is eaten before maror
      38 The Afikoman

Contents

A Short Summary of the Seder, *38*
Simanim — Aids for Remembering
 the Seder's Structure, *40*
The Alshich on Rashi's Simanim, *43*
Making Kiddush, *43*
The Obligation of Reclining, *46*
The Four Cups, *48*
Red Wine, *53*
The Mitzvah of the Four Cups Needs No Blessing, *54*
The Fifth Cup, *55*
The Three Matzos, *56*
Haste, *59*
Maror and Charoses, *61*
Karpas, *64*
Korech, *66*
The Roasted Bone and the Egg, *68*
Eggs in Salt Water, *70*
The Afikoman, *72*
  74 Afikoman Customs
  76 The Meaning of the Word Afikoman
The Structure of the Haggadah, *77*
Start with Shame, End with Glory, *80*
An Overview, *83*
Dividing the Haggadah into Parts, *83*
  84 Part One
  84 Part Two
  84 Part Three
  85 Part Four
  87 Part Five
  87 Part Six
  92 Part Seven
  92 Part Eight

xvi

93 Part Nine
93 Part Ten
The Haggadah in Any Language, *93*

The Pesach Haggadah

KADESH — THE PESACH KIDDUSH, *96*

U'RECHATZ — WASHING, *100*

KARPAS, *100*

YACHATZ — DIVIDING THE MATZAH, *102*

MAGGID — THE PESACH STORY, *102*
    The Four Questions, *110*
    The Four Sons, *126*
    The Ten Plagues, *192*
    Dayenu, *208*
    Pesach, Matzah, and Maror, *216*
    The Second Cup of the Four Cups, *240*

RACHTZAH — WASHING FOR THE MEAL, *242*

MOTZI, *244*

MATZAH, *244*

MAROR, *246*

KORECH — MATZAH & MAROR TOGETHER, *246*

SHULCHAN ORECH — THE SEDER MEAL, *248*

TZAFUN — EATING THE AFIKOMAN, *248*

BARECH — GRACE AFTER MEALS, *249*

HALLEL, *268*

NIRTZEH — ACCEPTANCE, *304*

Appendices

1/ SHIR HASHIRIM — THE SONG OF SONGS, *331*
    Shelomo haMelech and Israel, *332*
    The Parable of the Lovers, *337*

Reading Shir haShirim on Pesach, *339*
    339 Comments from the Zohar on Shir haShirim
Shir haShirim, *342*

2/ THE MIRACLES IN EGYPT:
A COMPENDIUM OF MIDRASHIM, *356*

Come, Let Us Be Clever with Him, *357*
And God Heard Their Cries, *360*
The Signs, *365*
The Plague of Blood, *366*
The Plague of Frogs, *367*
The Plague of Lice, *369*
The Plague of Mixed Beasts, *370*
The Plague of Pestilence, *370*
The Plague of Boils, *371*
The Plague of Hail, *372*
The Plague of Locusts, *374*
The Plague of Darkness, *377*
The Fourteenth of Nisan in Egypt, *379*
And It Came to Pass, at Midnight, *382*
Taking Spoils from Egypt, *385*
"With a Soft Mouth" — Measure for Measure, *388*
The "Spoils" that Moshe Rabbenu Took, *390*
On the Wings of Eagles, *391*
The Secret Is Finally Revealed, *393*

3/ THOSE WHO WOULD DEVOUR YAAKOV:
PERSECUTION AND BLOOD LIBELS, *397*

The Jealousy of Slaves toward Free Men, *399*
The First Libels, *400*

4/ A NIGHT THAT IS GUARDED, *411*

Four Nights, *412*

Before the Holiday

Checking for Chametz

On the 14th of Nissan (the night before the Seder) after nightfall, one searches and inspects his property, using the light of a candle, checking for *chametz*. (If the 14th is Shabbos night, the search is done the night of the 13th.) Every room of one's house must be checked, as well as one's yard, car, office, store, etc. The rule is that checking is required for every place that is considered one's own, and in these places, one must check everywhere that there is reason to suspect that there may be *chametz*. One should not forget to carefully check closets, briefcases, children's schoolbags, purses, baby carriages and the pleats and pockets of one's clothing.

It is advisable to sweep and clean up on the afternoon of the 13th of Nissan, so that later, at the time of the search, one does not get dirty and does not find an overabundant amount of *chametz*. After the afternoon clean-up, it is customary for someone who will not be conducting the search to hide small bits of *chametz* around the house, remembering where he put them (today, the small pieces of *chametz* are usually wrapped in separate plastic bags). This is to guard against the possibility that the afternoon's prior clean-up was too thorough, and removed all of the *chametz*. Once the pieces of *chametz* are "planted" around the house, it is certain that the search will turn up at least these pieces of *chametz*, so that the one who said the blessing beforehand will not have made a blessing in vain. Some follow the custom, based on Kaballah, of hiding away exactly ten pieces of *chametz* for this purpose.

The search must begin immediately after the *Ma'ariv* evening prayers, without delay. A person should not eat a meal or do anything else before he performs this mitzvah. It is best for the head of the household to conduct the search, but he is allowed to appoint others to help him. Women and children can be his helpers, but it is preferable that the search be done only by males of at least the age of bar mitzvah. When the blessing

Checking for Chametz

on the search is said, the one who says the blessing must be careful to start checking for *chametz* immediately, without any delay whatever, for if he says or does anything in between, he must say the blessing again.

Before the blessing which is said prior to the search, one washes his hands. At this point, some say the following:

הִנְנִי מוּכָן וּמְזוּמָן לְקַיֵּם מִצְוַת עֲשֵׂה וּמִצְוַת לֹא תַעֲשֶׂה שֶׁל בְּדִיקַת חָמֵץ.

Here I am, ready and willing to fulfill the positive and negative commandments associated with the search for chametz.

Then the blessing on the search is said:

בָּרוּךְ אַתָּה יְהֹוָה אֱלֹהֵינוּ מֶלֶךְ הָעוֹלָם אֲשֶׁר קִדְּשָׁנוּ בְּמִצְווֹתָיו וְצִוָּנוּ עַל בִּעוּר חָמֵץ.

Blessed are You, Hashem our God, King of the Universe, who made us holy by means of His commandments, and commanded us to remove chametz.

Once the search is under way, one should try to complete it without stopping to do anything else, though he is allowed to drink something, if he really must, in order to continue. While the search is in process, neither should anyone who is searching say anything which is not directly related to the mitzvah.

As soon the search is completed, one disowns his chametz, making the following declaration, with a sincere heart (the Sephardic custom is to say this three times). If he does not understand the Aramaic declaration, he should state the declaration in a language that he knows:

כָּל חֲמִירָא וַחֲמִיעָא דְּאִכָּא בִרְשׁוּתִי דְּלָא חֲמִתֵּהּ וּדְלָא בְעַרְתֵּהּ וּדְלָא יְדַעְנָא לֵיהּ לִבָּטֵל וְלֶהֱוֵי הֶפְקֵר כְּעַפְרָא דְאַרְעָא.

All chametz, leaven, and leavened bread in my possession, which I did not see and did not remove, and that of which I am not aware — is all null and ownerless, as dust of the earth.

At this stage, *chametz* still may be eaten. That is, after the search on the night of the 14th, people usually save some *chametz* for breakfast on the following morning. In the morning, however, before the end of the fifth hour of daylight, one physically must remove all *chametz* from one's possession, by burning it.

> *After doing so, he again disavows ownership of his chametz, by saying (three times, according to the Sephardic custom):*

כָּל חֲמִירָא וַחֲמִיעָא דְּאִכָּא בִרְשׁוּתִי, דַּחֲמִתֵּהּ וּדְלָא חֲמִתֵּהּ, דְּבִעַרְתֵּהּ וּדְלָא בִעַרְתֵּהּ, לִבָּטֵל וְלֶהֱוֵי הֶפְקֵר כְּעַפְרָא דְאַרְעָא

All chametz, leaven, and leavened bread in my possession, whether I have seen it or not, and whether I have removed it or not, is all null and ownerless, as dust of the earth.

In the *Zohar*, we find the following about the search and removal of *chametz*:

> Man's evil inclination is called "the leaven in the dough" for as leaven, when it is put into dough, makes it ferment and become chametz, the evil inclination in man is what entices him to sin. Our Sages taught: Chametz symbolizes the evil inclination, which is a foreign god, while matzah symbolizes the good inclination ... The Blessed One said: All those years a foreign nation [Egypt] enslaved you, and forces of evil controlled you. Now, though, you are free [for I have lifted your bondage]!
>
> When the Torah states, Remove leaven from your homes. You shall not eat anything that is *leavened* [and] leaven shall not

be seen in your possession — it hints that Pesach and matzah stand for freedom, from the forces of evil which chametz symbolizes. At Pesach time — the festival of freedom and redemption — while a Jew carefully rids himself of his chametz, he also should be thinking about how he can rid himself of his evil inclination. *(Zohar, Shemos 40, Riya Mehemna)*

In fact, some have the custom of saying a special prayer which incorporates this idea at the time that they burn their *chametz*:

Just as we have merited to rid ourselves of this chametz, may we also merit to rid our hearts of our evil inclination, and may we also see impurity and evil uprooted from the world. (Sefer Zikaron l'Tziyon and Haggadah of Chasam Sofer)

According to the book *Bnei Yissachar*, destroying *chametz* particularly represents the destruction of idolatry and false religions. The Scriptures substantiate this, for in *Sefer Melachim II*, it says that the Jewish King Yoshiyahu cleared the Land of Israel of all idol worship, and that year, *It was a Pesach unlike any other one since the days of the Judges (23:22-24)*. It says in *Shemos*, as well, *You shall not make graven images* and immediately afterwards *Observe the festival of matzos* is written. The *Bnei Yissachar* states that if the nation of Israel, when destroying its *chametz*, were to intend also to be destroying idolatry, the terrible strain of our nation's exile would be greatly eased.

When we check for *chametz*, our pockets need checking, too (i.e., for *chametz*; see *Rabbenu* Yerucham, cited by the Rema in *Shulchan Aruch, siman* 434). Similarly, one also should check his "pockets" before Pesach to make sure they do not contain money that may have been obtained dishonestly, by means of theft, cheating, or unfair business practices *(Sefer haShelah)*.

"Chametz" in One's Character

The numerical value of the Hebrew word *chametz* (חמץ) is 138, while that of *matzah* (מצה) is 135. The difference (3) represents the three bad character traits that, according to *Pirkei Avos, remove a person from this world* — jealousy (קנאה), desire for physical pleasures (תאוה), and the thirst for honor (כבוד). Just as during the course of the year, we do not keep ourselves at a distance from *chametz*, we are not sufficiently careful to distance ourselves from these three negative character traits. Another similarity is that on Pesach, if a Jew eats *chametz*, his punishment is כרת, a Divine "cutting off" or "removal" from the world. Thus, a person must set aside time to carefully check himself for these traits, searching out and destroying them completely, just as he does regarding *chametz* before Pesach (*Chasam Sofer*).

Erev Pesach

Eruv Tavshilin

If the second day of Pesach falls on a Friday, (outside of Israel) one must prepare an *eruv tavshilin*, a halachic device which makes it permissible to prepare for Shabbos on the holiday. So, too, when the seventh day of Pesach falls on a Friday.

Before the holiday begins, one sets aside on a plate some matzah (no less than the volume of a large egg) along with a cooked food (such as an egg, meat, or fish, no less than the volume of two present-day olives), saying the following blessing:

בָּרוּךְ אַתָּה יְהֹוָה אֱלֹהֵינוּ מֶלֶךְ הָעוֹלָם אֲשֶׁר קִדְּשָׁנוּ בְּמִצְוֹתָיו וְצִוָּנוּ עַל מִצְוַת עֵרוּב:

Blessed are You, Hashem our God, King of the world, Who has made us holy with His mitzvos and commanded us about the mitzvah of eruv.

Erev Pesach

Then he says:

בַּהֲדֵין עֵרוּבָא יְהֵא שָׁרֵי לָנָא לְמֵיפָא וּלְבַשָּׁלָא וּלְאַטְמָנָא וּלְאַדְלָקָא שְׁרָגָא וּלְמֶעֱבַד כָּל צָרְכָנָא מִיּוֹמָא טָבָא לְשַׁבַּתָּא, לָנוּ וּלְכָל יִשְׂרָאֵל הַדָּרִים בָּעִיר הַזֹּאת.

Through this eruv we shall be permitted on Yom Tov to prepare for Shabbos — to bake, cook, fry, and to insulate food for the sake of preserving its warmth, to kindle lights, and do any other necessary acts for the sake of Shabbos, we and all Jews who live in this city.

Needs for the Seder

These are the items which must be obtained before the holiday for the sake of the Seder:

- ☑ Wine (enough for four cups for each participant)
- ☑ Matzos
- ☑ Seder plate and its contents

    A ROASTED BONE: An animal shank with meat on it
    AN EGG: Roasted or boiled, or boiled and then roasted
    MAROR: Horseradish, endive, or Romaine lettuce
    CHAROSES: A mixture of grated apples, nuts, red wine, cinnamon and other spices and fruits
    KARPAS: Celery, parsley, radish, carrot, or potato, but not a bitter vegetable that can be used for *maror*
    CHAZERES: Usually defined as Romaine lettuce [also horseradish]

- ☑ Salt water
- ☑ Candles (ready to be lit)
- ☑ Cups (for each participant, even children. Also, a large cup for the cup of Eliyahu)

The mitzvah of the Four Cups should be performed with wine of the highest quality that one can afford, as long as it does not bring on drunkenness, or cause one to fall asleep before he can complete the Seder. Preferably, the wine should be red, unless one can obtain white wine that is better.

Regarding matzah, those who want to perform the mitzvah in the optimal fashion should use only *shemurah matzah*, made from wheat that was guarded especially for Pesach not only during its growth, but also after its harvest. There also is a preference for matzos that were made by hand, as opposed to machine, and some are particular to use only hand-made *shemurah* matzah that was prepared the afternoon before the Seder.

If *challah* has not been separated from the matzah, it must be separated before the holiday begins. All the matzos are gathered together in a cloth. The cloth is then draped to cover them all. Next, the blessing is said. Immediately, one matzah is taken out of the pile and *challah* is taken from it for the sake of the entire pile. Many have the custom of separating no less than the size of two modern-day olives (a *k'zayis*). *Challah* must be separated only in the case that, after it is separated, the amount of matzos remaining would itself be enough to require *challah* separation, or if the remainder came from a dough batch which was large enough to require it. Some say that this minimum measure is 1.68 kilograms of flour, but others maintain that while 1.68 kilograms does obligate that *challah* be separated, no blessing should be said on less than 2.25 kilograms.

When doubt exists as to whether separating *challah* is required, the separation should be done without the blessing. If the original dough contained less than 1.2 kilograms of flour, there is no obligation to separate *challah* at all.

Preferably, the woman of the home should perform the mitzvah of separating *challah*. Some place the matzos one atop the other in a container which is specially designated for this mitzvah. Otherwise, as described above, a cloth can serve as the "container" with the separation being done on an ordinary table or counter.

Erev Pesach

The Seder Plate

The Seder Plate should be large enough to hold the six different items that need to be on it, so that the items do not touch one another and cannot mix with each other. Some have the custom of having a place for the matzos on the Seder Plate, as well.

THE ROASTED BONE, preferably a shank, should have meat on it. If an animal shank containing a bone is not available, one simply roasts some meat, over a fire, before the holiday starts. The roasting cannot be done once Pesach begins, for on the Seder night, eating roasted meat is forbidden, and thus roasting is forbidden, too (lest someone think that the meat is from the Pesach offering, and the offering was unlawfully slaughtered outside the Temple. Roasting meat on the Seder night is permitted only if one intends to serve the meat for a meal on Pesach day). The animal shank is placed on the Seder Plate on the upper right.

THE EGG is boiled or roasted, or roasted after it is boiled, and is placed on the left side of the Seder Plate, opposite the animal shank.

The roasted bone is in remembrance of the Pesach offering, while the egg is in remembrance of the *Chagigah* or Holiday offering, both of which were brought in the days of the Temple and were eaten on the Seder night, the *Chagigah* on the left, the *Pesach* on the right.

MAROR, or "bitter herbs," is usually lettuce or endive — their leaves and stalks, but not their roots. Horseradish also is used, or any other local vegetable that is sufficiently bitter. Some use lettuce leaves for *maror* for the time in the Seder that *maror* is eaten alone, while stalks of the lettuce are used for when the *maror* is eaten between matzos as part of a "sandwich" (i.e., for the *Korech*). The *maror* must be thoroughly washed and carefully checked to see that there are no insects or worms in it. On the Seder Plate the *maror* is placed between the egg and the roasted bone, slightly below them, because the Torah states (*Bemidbar 9*), *You shall eat the Pesach sacrifice with matzos and maror*, indicating that *maror* is eaten for the sake of the Pesach offering, and is secondary to it. Thus, the *maror* is placed near the roasted bone — which commemorates the Pesach offering — but slightly below it.

CHAROSES is a sauce or dip composed mainly of grated apples (some use mashed dates with honey as the main ingredient). Chopped almonds and other nuts are mixed in, along with cinnamon, ginger, and red wine, so that in the end, *charoses* resembles the wet, clay-like building material made of straw, mud, and water. *Charoses* also should be prepared before the holiday begins. If one forgot, it can be made at night (but with a "change," i.e., in some unusual fashion) using the same ingredients. It should be kept paste-like, though. That is, not all the wine should be mixed in until the Seder, when the *charoses* is needed as a dip. In the case where one forgot to add wine or some other liquid to the *charoses* before the holiday, and the Seder falls on Shabbos, halachic authorities differ as to whether he is allowed to add the wine (or other liquid) on the Seder night at all, even with a "change."

On the Seder Plate, the *charoses* is placed near the *maror*, to the right of it and below it, for *charoses* is a dip for the *maror*, and being secondary to it, it is placed below it. Accordingly, the *charoses* lies opposite the roasted bone, which also is on the right on the Seder Plate.

Charoses is an Aramaic term for a mixture of this sort, and the term closely resembles the Hebrew word *cheres*, which means "something made of clay." As a result, not only does the food itself remind us of the bricks the Jews made in Egypt, but so does the Aramaic term for the food.

KARPAS means "celery," but one can also use other vegetables which, unlike *maror*, are not bitter, for example, cooked potato or carrot, or fresh radish. The *karpas* is placed on the left side of the Seder Plate beneath the *maror*, below the egg and parallel to the *charoses*. Like *charoses*, *karpas* is only for the sake of the *maror*, and is secondary to it (see explanation later), and this is why it is placed below it.

CHAZERES is Romaine lettuce leaves, or horseradish, or any other vegetable that can be used for *maror*. In fact, the vegetable which is used for *maror* at the Seder also can be used for *chazeres*. *Chazeres* is placed at the very bottom of the Seder Plate, between the *charoses* and the *karpas*, but beneath them. *Maror* and *chazeres* really mean the same thing, but *maror* is mentioned in the Torah and on the Seder night is used for a mitzvah, while *chazeres* is not mentioned in the Torah and is only a remembrance (see explanation later).

Thus the arrangement of the six items on the Seder Plate resembles the Hebrew vowel *segol* — one *segol* atop the other (i.e., the points of two triangles, each pointing downwards, one atop the other). The upper *segol* is made of the roasted bone, the egg, and the *maror*, while the lower *segol* is made of the *charoses*, the *karpas*, and the *chazeres*. The items in the upper *segol* are rooted in actual Torah mitzvos of the Seder, while those in the lower *segol* serve to accompany these items (see illustration).

The *Ari, z"l* wrote:

THE 3 MATZOS *correspond to* חכמה *(Wisdom),* בינה *(Understanding), and* דעת *(Knowledge).*

THE ROASTED BONE, *on the right, represents Hashem's trait of* חסד *(Kindness).*

THE EGG, *on the left, represents Hashem's* גבורה *(Strength).*

THE MAROR, *between the bone and the egg, stands for* תפארת *(Glory) which mediates between* חסד *(Kindness) and* גבורה *(Strength).*

THE CHAROSES, *below and on the right, corresponds to* נצח *(Eternity).*

THE KARPAS, *below and on the left, corresponds to* הוד *(Honor).*

THE CHAZERES, *at the bottom, corresponds to* יסוד *(Foundation).*

THE SEDER PLATE, *containing all its components, represents* מלכות *(Kingship).*

These are the ten sefiros of חכמה (Wisdom). Thus, one must not deviate from this arrangement, and happy is the one who arranges his Seder Plate with these deeper meanings in mind!

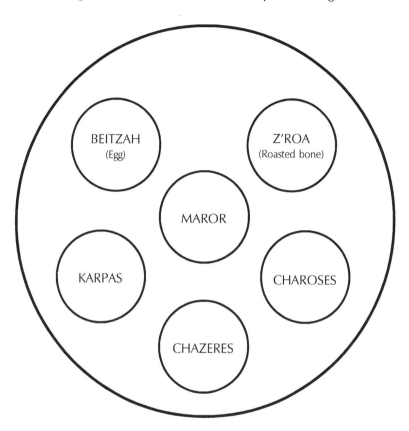

The Seder Plate, with this arrangement, is placed above the three matzos, which are covered by a special cloth. Today, now that we do not have the Temple, matzah is the only item that the Torah obligates us to eat on the Seder night. Everything else on the Seder Plate is eaten either as a Rabbinic mitzvah or as a remembrance. It therefore has become a custom to make a separate place for the matzos, and not to put them on the Seder Plate at all. Some, however, do have the custom of putting the matzos on the Seder Plate.

Erev Pesach

One also prepares the salt water before the holiday begins, for the sake of dipping the *karpas* into it during the first part of the Seder (and those whose custom is to eat the egg during the Seder also use the salt water for dipping the egg). The salt water should be made of two parts salt and one part water. If one forgot to prepare this mixture before the holiday, it can be done at night but it should be made weaker, with just a small amount of salt compared to the water. If the Seder night falls on Shabbos and one forgot to prepare salt water beforehand, not only should it be made weak, but the amount which is made should be no more than is necessary for the Seder.

Instead of salt, some use a mixture of lemon juice and water, while others mix vinegar with water. These mixtures also should be prepared the previous day.

Before the night arrives one should also rinse the cups that will be used for the four cups of wine. The cups then should be placed on the table, which should be set with one's finest silverware and dishes. Pillows for reclining also should be prepared ahead of time.

If the day before Pesach is Shabbos, on Shabbos one cannot prepare for the Seder at all, even if the acts would be permitted for the sake of Shabbos itself. One must wait for nightfall, and then prepare in the ways described above.

Once everything is ready for the Seder, one goes to the synagogue for the afternoon and evening prayers (*Minchah* and *Ma'ariv*). On this day, some have the custom of praying *Minchah* earlier than usual, so that after *Minchah* they have time to read the order of the Pesach sacrifice, and also so that in case they are troubled by last-minute preparations, they do not allow the time of *Minchah* to pass.

For details of candle lighting, see p. 30.

How the Pesach Sacrifice Was Done
(Based on the version of R. Yaakov Emden)

[Said the Holy One, blessed be He, to the Jewish people: "Even though the Beis haMikdash will someday be destroyed and the sacrifices cease, do not let yourselves forget the way to bring the sacrifices; be careful to read and review their laws. If you study them, I will count it as if you are actually making the sacrifices."

"This is the Torah of the burnt-sacrifice; that is the burnt-sacrifice...." [Vayikra 6:2]

Said R. Acha in the name of R. Chanina bar Pappa: [The Torah equates the laws of sacrifice with the sacrifice itself, to tell you that] "The Jewish people must not say, 'In the past we used to bring sacrifices and study their laws; now that there are no more sacrifices, why should we study their laws?' [In answer to this,] God says to them: 'Seeing as you study their laws, I count it to your credit as if you were making the sacrifices.'"

R. Huna said: "The Diaspora will be regathered by the merit of the Mishnah [which teaches about sacrifices]. What is the proof for this? '... in every place sacrifice and incense is made in My name, and pure offering; for My name is great among the nations.' [Malachi 1:11] Are sacrifices made in the Diaspora? [No,] but God says, 'Seeing as you study the Mishnayos [of the sacrifices] it is as if you were making the sacrifices.'"]

How the Pesach Sacrifice Was Done
סֵדֶר אֲמִירַת קָרְבַּן פֶּסַח
(כפי שהעלה הגאון רבי יעקב עמדין זצ"ל בסידורו "בית יעקב")

רִבּוֹן הָעוֹלָמִים, אַתָּה צִוִּיתָנוּ לְהַקְרִיב קָרְבַּן פֶּסַח בְּמוֹעֲדוֹ בְּאַרְבָּעָה עָשָׂר לַחֹדֶשׁ הָרִאשׁוֹן, וְלִהְיוֹת כֹּהֲנִים בַּעֲבוֹדָתָם וּלְוִיִּם בְּדוּכָנָם וְיִשְׂרָאֵל בְּמַעֲמָדָם קוֹרְאִים אֶת הַהַלֵּל. וְעַתָּה בַּעֲווֹנוֹתֵינוּ חָרַב בֵּית הַמִּקְדָּשׁ וּבָטַל קָרְבַּן הַפֶּסַח. וְאֵין לָנוּ לֹא כֹּהֵן בַּעֲבוֹדָתוֹ וְלֹא לֵוִי בְּדוּכָנוֹ וְלֹא יִשְׂרָאֵל בְּמַעֲמָדוֹ, וּנְשַׁלְּמָה פָרִים שְׂפָתֵינוּ. לָכֵן יְהִי רָצוֹן מִלְּפָנֶיךָ יְהֹוָה אֱלֹהֵינוּ וֵאלֹהֵי אֲבוֹתֵינוּ שֶׁיִּהְיֶה שִׂיחַ שִׂפְתוֹתֵינוּ חָשׁוּב לְפָנֶיךָ כְּאִלּוּ הִקְרַבְנוּ אֶת הַפֶּסַח בְּמוֹעֲדוֹ וְעָמַדְנוּ עַל מַעֲמָדוֹ וְדִבְּרוּ הַלְוִיִּם בְּשִׁיר וְהַלֵּל וְהוֹדוֹת לַיהֹוָה. וְאַתָּה תְּכוֹנֵן מִקְדָּשְׁךָ עַל מְכוֹנוֹ וְנַעֲלֶה וְנַקְרִיב לְפָנֶיךָ אֶת הַפֶּסַח בְּמוֹעֲדוֹ כְּמוֹ שֶׁכָּתַבְתָּ עָלֵינוּ בְּתוֹרָתֶךָ עַל יְדֵי מֹשֶׁה עַבְדֶּךָ כָּאָמוּר.

שמות יב ג דַּבְּרוּ אֶל־כָּל־עֲדַת יִשְׂרָאֵל לֵאמֹר בֶּעָשֹׂר לַחֹדֶשׁ הַזֶּה וְיִקְחוּ לָהֶם אִישׁ שֶׂה לְבֵית־אָבֹת שֶׂה לַבָּיִת: ד וְאִם־יִמְעַט הַבַּיִת מִהְיוֹת מִשֶּׂה וְלָקַח הוּא וּשְׁכֵנוֹ הַקָּרֹב אֶל־בֵּיתוֹ בְּמִכְסַת נְפָשֹׁת אִישׁ לְפִי אָכְלוֹ תָּכֹסּוּ עַל־הַשֶּׂה: ה שֶׂה תָמִים זָכָר בֶּן־שָׁנָה יִהְיֶה לָכֶם מִן־הַכְּבָשִׂים וּמִן־הָעִזִּים תִּקָּחוּ: ו וְהָיָה לָכֶם לְמִשְׁמֶרֶת עַד אַרְבָּעָה עָשָׂר יוֹם לַחֹדֶשׁ הַזֶּה וְשָׁחֲטוּ אֹתוֹ כֹּל קְהַל עֲדַת־יִשְׂרָאֵל בֵּין הָעַרְבָּיִם: ז וְלָקְחוּ מִן־הַדָּם וְנָתְנוּ עַל־שְׁתֵּי הַמְּזוּזֹת וְעַל־הַמַּשְׁקוֹף עַל הַבָּתִּים אֲשֶׁר־יֹאכְלוּ אֹתוֹ בָּהֶם: ח וְאָכְלוּ אֶת־הַבָּשָׂר בַּלַּיְלָה הַזֶּה צְלִי־אֵשׁ וּמַצּוֹת עַל־מְרֹרִים יֹאכְלֻהוּ: ט אַל־תֹּאכְלוּ מִמֶּנּוּ נָא וּבָשֵׁל מְבֻשָּׁל בַּמָּיִם כִּי אִם־צְלִי־אֵשׁ רֹאשׁוֹ עַל־כְּרָעָיו וְעַל־קִרְבּוֹ: י וְלֹא־תוֹתִירוּ מִמֶּנּוּ עַד־בֹּקֶר וְהַנֹּתָר מִמֶּנּוּ עַד־בֹּקֶר בָּאֵשׁ תִּשְׂרֹפוּ: יא וְכָכָה תֹּאכְלוּ אֹתוֹ מָתְנֵיכֶם חֲגֻרִים נַעֲלֵיכֶם בְּרַגְלֵיכֶם וּמַקֶּלְכֶם בְּיֶדְכֶם וַאֲכַלְתֶּם אֹתוֹ בְּחִפָּזוֹן פֶּסַח הוּא לַיהֹוָה.

Lord of the universe, You commanded us to make the Pesach sacrifice in its proper time, the fourteenth of Nissan, and You commanded the Kohanim to be at their work, and the Leviyim to be on their platform singing, and the Jewish people to be present saying the Hallel.

But now, for our sins, the Beis haMikdash is destroyed and the Pesach sacrifice cannot be made; we have neither Kohanim at their work nor Leviyim with their song nor the people with their sacrifices, so we must offer our sacrifices with our lips.

Therefore may it be Your will, God our Lord and Lord of our fathers, to account what we say as if we had brought the Pesach sacrifice in its proper time and had been present at its offering, and the Leviyim had sung the Hallel to thank You. For Your part, may You re-establish Your Mikdash; and we will go up and make the Pesach sacrifice before You in its proper time, as You wrote for us in Your Torah by the hand of Your servant Moshe (Shemos 12:3-11):

Speak to the whole Jewish people thus: On the tenth of this month they shall each of them take a lamb for his family, a lamb for each household. If the household are too few for a lamb, he and the neighbor who is closest to his house shall take [a lamb together] according to the number of people; you shall assess the lamb according to each person's eating.

Your lamb must be an unblemished male in its first year; you may take it from the sheep or from the goats. It must be guarded by you until the fourteenth day of this month, and then the whole assembled Jewish people shall slaughter it in the afternoon. They shall take some of its blood and put it on the two doorposts and on the lintel of the houses where they will be eating it. They shall eat the meat that night roasted over the fire; with matzos and bitter herbs they shall eat it. Do not eat any of it half-cooked or boiled in any way with water: only roasted over the fire with its head, its feet, and its innards. You shall not [deliberately] leave any of it until morning, and what is left of it until morning you shall burn in the fire. This is how you shall eat it: your belt tied around your waist, your shoes on your feet, and your staff in your hand; you shall eat it hastily — it is a Pesach for Hashem.

[*This is how the sacrifices were made in the Holy Temple each day:*

The Temple day was divided into twelve hours, each of them lasting one-twelfth of the time between sunrise and sunset. In the morning, after the altar was cleared of ashes, the fire was laid again and a lamb was brought for the Tamid sacrifice, the "perpetual sacrifice" that was made every morning and evening. After it was slaughtered and its blood thrown on the altar, the great golden Menorah was cleaned and refilled with new oil and wicks, and then the limbs of the Tamid were put up on the altar to burn.

How the Pesach Sacrifice Was Done

כָּךְ הָיְתָה עֲבוֹדַת קָרְבָּן פֶּסַח בְּאַרְבָּעָה עָשָׂר בְּנִיסָן. אֵין שׁוֹחֲטִין אוֹתוֹ אֶלָּא אַחַר תָּמִיד שֶׁל בֵּין הָעַרְבַּיִם, עֶרֶב פֶּסַח בֵּין בְּחוֹל בֵּין בְּשַׁבָּת הָיָה הַתָּמִיד נִשְׁחָט בְּשֶׁבַע וּמֶחֱצָה וְקָרֵב בִּשְׁמוֹנֶה וּמֶחֱצָה. וְאִם חָל עֶרֶב פֶּסַח לִהְיוֹת עֶרֶב שַׁבָּת, הָיוּ שׁוֹחֲטִין אוֹתוֹ בְּשֵׁשׁ וּמֶחֱצָה וְקָרֵב בְּשֶׁבַע וּמֶחֱצָה, וְהַפֶּסַח אַחֲרָיו.

כָּל אָדָם מִיִּשְׂרָאֵל אֶחָד הָאִישׁ וְאֶחָד הָאִשָּׁה, כָּל שֶׁיָּכֹל לְהַגִּיעַ לִירוּשָׁלַיִם בִּשְׁעַת שְׁחִיטַת הַפֶּסַח, חַיָּב בְּקָרְבָּן פֶּסַח. מְבִיאוֹ מִן הַכְּבָשִׂים אוֹ מִן הָעִזִּים. זָכָר תָּמִים בֶּן שָׁנָה. וְשׁוֹחֲטוֹ בְּכָל מָקוֹם בָּעֲזָרָה, אַחַר גְּמַר עֲבוֹדַת תָּמִיד הָעֶרֶב וְאַחַר הֲטָבַת הַנֵּרוֹת. וְאֵין שׁוֹחֲטִין הַפֶּסַח וְלֹא זוֹרְקִין הַדָּם וְלֹא מַקְטִירִין הַחֵלֶב עַל הֶחָמֵץ.

שָׁחַט הַשּׁוֹחֵט וְקִבֵּל דָּמוֹ כֹּהֵן שֶׁבָּרֹאשׁ הַשּׁוּרָה בִּכְלִי שָׁרֵת וְנוֹתֵן לַחֲבֵרוֹ וַחֲבֵרוֹ לַחֲבֵרוֹ, כֹּהֵן הַקָּרוֹב אֵצֶל הַמִּזְבֵּחַ זוֹרְקוֹ זְרִיקָה אַחַת כְּנֶגֶד הַיְסוֹד. וְחוֹזֵר הַכְּלִי רֵיקָן לַחֲבֵרוֹ וַחֲבֵרוֹ לַחֲבֵרוֹ, מְקַבֵּל אֶת הַמָּלֵא וּמַחֲזִיר אֶת הָרֵיקָן. וְהָיוּ הַכֹּהֲנִים עוֹמְדִים שׁוּרוֹת וּבִידֵיהֶם בָּזִיכִים שֶׁכֻּלָּן כֶּסֶף אוֹ כֻלָּן זָהָב, וְלֹא הָיוּ מְעֹרָבִים, וְלֹא הָיוּ לַבָּזִיכִין שׁוּלַיִם שֶׁלֹּא יַנִּיחוּם וְיִקְרֹשׁ הַדָּם.

אַחַר כָּךְ תּוֹלִין אֶת הַפֶּסַח בְּאוּנְקְלָיוֹת, וּמַפְשִׁיט אוֹתוֹ כֻּלּוֹ וְקוֹרְעִין בִּטְנוֹ וּמוֹצִיאִים אֵמוּרָיו. הַחֵלֶב שֶׁעַל הַקֶּרֶב וְיוֹתֶרֶת הַכָּבֵד וּשְׁתֵּי הַכְּלָיוֹת וְחֵלֶב שֶׁעֲלֵיהֶן וְהָאַלְיָה לְעֻמַּת הֶעָצֶה, נוֹתְנָן בִּכְלִי שָׁרֵת וּמוֹלְחָן וּמַקְטִירָן הַכֹּהֵן עַל הַמַּעֲרָכָה' חֶלְבֵי' כָּל זֶבַח וָזֶבַח לְבַדּוֹ, בְּחוֹל, בַּיּוֹם וְלֹא בַּלַּיְלָה שֶׁהוּא יוֹם טוֹב. אֲבָל אִם חָל עֶרֶב פֶּסַח בְּשַׁבָּת מַקְטִירִין וְהוֹלְכִין כָּל הַלַּיְלָה וּמוֹצִיא קָרְבָיו וּמְמַחֶה אוֹתָן עַד שֶׁמֵּסִיר מֵהֶן הַפֶּרֶשׁ. שְׁחִיטָתוֹ וּזְרִיקַת דָּמוֹ וּמִחוּי קָרְבָיו וְהֶקְטֵר חֲלָבָיו דּוֹחִין אֶת הַשַּׁבָּת, וּשְׁאָר עִנְיָנָיו אֵין דּוֹחִין.

בְּשָׁלֹשׁ כִּתּוֹת הַפֶּסַח נִשְׁחָט, וְאֵין כַּת פְּחוּתָה מִשְּׁלֹשִׁים אֲנָשִׁים. נִכְנְסָה כַּת אַחַת נִתְמַלְּאָה הָעֲזָרָה נוֹעֲלִין אוֹתָהּ. וּבְעוֹד שֶׁהֵן שׁוֹחֲטִין וּמַקְרִיבִין וְכֹהֲנִים תּוֹקְעִין, הֶחָלִיל מַכֶּה לִפְנֵי הַמִּזְבֵּחַ. הַלְוִיִּים קוֹרִין אֶת הַהַלֵּל. אִם גָּמְרוּ קֹדֶם שֶׁיַּקְרִיבוּ כֻּלָּם, שָׁנוּ. אִם שָׁנוּ שִׁלֵּשׁוּ. עַל כָּל קְרִיאָה תָּקְעוּ וְהֵרִיעוּ וְתָקְעוּ. גָּמְרָה כַּת אַחַת לְהַקְרִיב, פּוֹתְחִין הָעֲזָרָה, יָצְאָה כַּת רִאשׁוֹנָה נִכְנְסָה כַּת שְׁנִיָּה. נָעֲלוּ דַּלְתוֹת הָעֲזָרָה. גָּמְרָה יָצְאָה שְׁנִיָּה נִכְנְסָה שְׁלִישִׁית. כְּמַעֲשֵׂה הָרִאשׁוֹנָה כָּךְ מַעֲשֵׂה הַשְּׁנִיָּה וְהַשְּׁלִישִׁית.

Afterwards every man might bring his sacrifices. Every sacrifice has four mitzvos: slaughtering, catching the blood and bringing it to the altar, throwing the blood on the altar, and burning its eimurim on the altar: its organ fat, its kidneys, and the protruding lobe of its liver. Every Jew is allowed to do the first mitzvah himself, but the mitzvos from there on are only for the Kohanim.

The last work of the day was to offer the afternoon Tamid and light the golden Menorah. Afterwards no more sacrifices might be brought that day. But the Pesach sacrifice is unlike any other: it may only be slaughtered after the afternoon Tamid-sacrifice.]

Every Jew, whether man or woman, who is able to get to Yerushalayim in time for the slaughtering is obligated to bring the Pesach sacrifice. It may be a lamb or a kid: an unblemished male in its first year. It may be slaughtered anywhere in the Temple Court, after the offering of the afternoon Tamid is finished and the Menorah has been lit for the night.

[All year long, the Tamid was slaughtered at eight-and-a-half hours of the day and offered on the altar at nine-and-a-half hours.] But on Erev Pesach, whether Shabbos or a weekday, the Tamid was slaughtered at seven-and-a-half hours and offered at eight-and-a-half hours [to allow time for everyone to offer his Pesach sacrifice]. And if Erev Pesach fell on Erev Shabbos, then they would slaughter it as early as possible, at six-and-a-half hours, and offer it at seven-and-a-half hours, with the Pesach sacrifice coming after it. The Pesach may not be slaughtered, nor its blood caught and thrown on the altar, nor its eimurim burned, as long as its owners and certain Kohanim have any chametz in their possession.

This is how the Pesach sacrifice was offered on the fourteenth of Nissan:

The Pesach was slaughtered in three groups, with never less than thirty men in each. The first group would go in to the middle courtyard, which was called the Court of Am Yisrael, because no one but Kohanim could go in any further. When the courtyard was full the gates were locked. As the people began to slaughter their sacrifices and the blood and eimurim were passed along to the altar, the Kohanim blew the shofar, the Levite musicians began to play before the altar, and the Leviyim of the choir sang the Hallel.

The Kohanim stood in rows, stretching all the way across the inner courtyard to the altar, while the people entered with their sacrifices. Each man came up to the head of a line of Kohanim and slaughtered his sacrifice. The Kohen at the head of the line caught its life-blood in a holy vessel and passed it to the next Kohen, and he to the next, and the Kohen closest to the altar would throw it, all in one go, towards the base of the altar. Then the empty vessel was passed back from hand to hand: each one would pass a full vessel forward and an empty one back. The Kohanim stood thus in rows with vessels all of silver or all of gold in

How the Pesach Sacrifice Was Done

אַחַר שֶׁיָּצְאוּ כֻּלָּן רוֹחֲצִין הָעֲזָרָה מִלִּכְלוּכֵי הַדָּם וַאֲפִלּוּ בַּשַּׁבָּת. אַמַּת הַמַּיִם הָיְתָה עוֹבֶרֶת בָּעֲזָרָה, כְּשֶׁרוֹצִין לְהָדִיחַ הָרִצְפָּה סוֹתְמִין מְקוֹם יְצִיאַת הַמַּיִם וְהִיא מִתְמַלְּאָה עַל כָּל גְּדוֹתֶיהָ, עַד שֶׁהַמַּיִם עוֹלִין וְצָפִין וּמְקַבְּצִין אֲלֵיהֶם כָּל דָּם וְלִכְלוּךְ שֶׁבָּעֲזָרָה. אַחַר כָּךְ פּוֹתְחִין הַסְּתִימָה וְיוֹצְאִין הַמַּיִם עִם הַלִּכְלוּךְ. נִמְצֵאת הָרִצְפָּה מְנֻקָּה, זֶהוּ כְּבוֹד הַבַּיִת.

יָצְאוּ כָּל אֶחָד עִם פִּסְחוֹ וְצָלוּ אוֹתָם. כֵּיצַד צוֹלִין אוֹתוֹ, מְבִיאִין שַׁפּוּד שֶׁל רִמּוֹן, תּוֹחֲבוֹ מִתּוֹךְ פִּיו עַד בֵּית נְקוּבָתוֹ, וְתוֹלֵהוּ לְתוֹךְ הַתַּנּוּר וְהָאֵשׁ לְמַטָּה, וְתוֹלֶה כְּרָעָיו וּבְנֵי מֵעָיו חוּצָה לוֹ. וְאֵין מְנַקְּרִין אֶת הַפֶּסַח כִּשְׁאָר בָּשָׂר.

בַּשַּׁבָּת אֵינָן מוֹלִיכִין אֶת הַפֶּסַח לְבֵיתָם, אֶלָּא כַּת רִאשׁוֹנָה יוֹצְאִים בְּפִסְחֵיהֶם וְיוֹשְׁבִין בְּהַר הַבַּיִת. הַשְּׁנִיָּה יוֹצְאִין עִם פִּסְחֵיהֶם וְיוֹשְׁבִין בַּחֵיל. הַשְּׁלִישִׁית בִּמְקוֹמָהּ עוֹמֶדֶת. חֲשֵׁכָה יָצְאוּ וְצָלוּ אֶת פִּסְחֵיהֶן.

כְּשֶׁמַּקְרִיבִין אֶת הַפֶּסַח בָּרִאשׁוֹן מַקְרִיבִין בְּיוֹם י"ד זֶבַח שְׁלָמִים מִן הַבָּקָר אוֹ מִן הַצֹּאן גְּדוֹלִים אוֹ קְטַנִּים זְכָרִים אוֹ נְקֵבוֹת. וְהִיא נִקְרֵאת חֲגִיגַת אַרְבָּעָה עָשָׂר. עַל זֶה נֶאֱמַר בַּתּוֹרָה וְזָבַחְתָּ פֶּסַח לַה׳ אֱלֹהֶיךָ צֹאן וּבָקָר. וְלֹא קְבָעָהּ הַכָּתוּב חוֹבָה אֶלָּא רְשׁוּת בִּלְבַד. מִכָּל-מָקוֹם הִיא כְּחוֹבָה מִדִּבְרֵי סוֹפְרִים כְּדֵי שֶׁיְּהֵא הַפֶּסַח נֶאֱכָל עַל הַשֹּׂבַע.

אֵימָתַי מְבִיאִין עִמּוֹ חֲגִיגָה, בִּזְמַן שֶׁהוּא בָּא בְּחוֹל בְּטָהֳרָה וּבְמוּעָט וְנֶאֱכֶלֶת לִשְׁנֵי יָמִים וְלַיְלָה אֶחָד. וְדִינָהּ כְּכָל תּוֹרַת זִבְחֵי הַשְּׁלָמִים, טְעוּנָה סְמִיכָה וּנְסָכִים וּמַתַּן דָּמִים שְׁתַּיִם שֶׁהֵן אַרְבַּע וּשְׁפִיכַת שִׁירַיִם לַיְסוֹד.

זֶהוּ סֵדֶר עֲבוֹדַת קָרְבַּן פֶּסַח וַחֲגִיגָה שֶׁעַמּוֹ בְּבֵית אֱלֹהֵינוּ שֶׁיִּבָּנֶה בִּמְהֵרָה בְּיָמֵינוּ אָמֵן.

יִהְיוּ לְרָצוֹן אִמְרֵי פִי וְהֶגְיוֹן לִבִּי לְפָנֶיךָ יְהוָה צוּרִי וְגוֹאֲלִי.

their hands, only one kind in each row. The vessels had no feet so that they could not be put down, for if the blood of one of the sacrifices were allowed to clot it would no longer be fit to throw and that Pesach would be forbidden to eat.

Next the Pesach was hung on a hook and skinned. The belly was slit open and the eimurim, that go on the altar, were removed: the belly fat, the protruding lobe of the liver and a bit of the liver with it, the two kidneys and their fat, and (if it was a sheep) the fat tail with a bit of the spine. The Kohanim put the parts in a holy vessel, salted them, and burned them in the fire on the altar, the parts from each sacrifice separately. When Erev Pesach falls on a weekday they are burned right away, and all the parts must be put up on the altar fire before nightfall, for by then it would be Yom Tov. But things made holy on Shabbos are an exception to this rule, so when Erev Pesach falls on Shabbos, if any of the parts were forgotten and not put up on the altar right away they may be put up and burned all night long, even though it is Yom Tov.

After this the intestines are pulled out and squeezed to remove the excrement from them. Slaughtering the Pesach, throwing its blood, cleaning its intestines, and burning its parts override Shabbos, but the other things that need to be done must wait until the night.

If the Leviyim finished singing the Hallel before everyone was finished with his sacrifice, they would sing the Hallel again, and a third time, too, if necessary. Every time they began to sing, a Teki'ah-Teru'ah-Teki'ah was blown. When the first group was all finished, the gates were opened; one group went out and the next came in, and the gates were locked again. When they were finished, they went out and the third group came in. Everything was done in the second and third groups the same as in the first.

After everyone had left, the Kohanim would wash the Inner Court clean of the blood, even if it was Shabbos. It was done like this: an aqueduct passed through the Court, and whenever the Kohanim wanted to wash the floor they would stop up the exit, and the water would overflow into the Court and mix with all the blood and dirt. Then they would open the exit and the water would rush out with all the blood and dirt, and there would be a clean floor in honor of Shabbos.

As soon as he left the Court of Am Yisrael, each man hurried home with his Pesach and roasted it. This is how it is roasted: a spit of pomegranate wood is passed from the mouth to the anus, and the Pesach is hung on it in the oven with the fire below. The feet and innards are hung on the spit away from the body. The Pesach is not cut open and cleaned in the same way as other meat, so as to keep it whole. Pomegranate wood is used for the spit because other woods exude sap when heated, which "boils" the Pesach, but pomegranate wood does

How the Pesach Sacrifice Was Done

not. *A metal spit cannot be used because it becomes hot enough to cook the meat around it, and the Torah says "roasted over the fire", not with heated metal; but a grill of metal bars over the fire may be used.*

On Shabbos the Pesach was not brought home right away: instead, the first group would come out of the Court of Am Yisrael with their sacrifices and sit on the Temple Mount, then when the second group came out they would sit in the Outer Court, and the third would just sit where they were. When it was dark and Shabbos was over they would all go home and roast their sacrifices.

All those who bring their sacrifice on the fourteenth of Nissan also offer a Shelamim-sacrifice: any kind of sheep, goat, or cattle, young or old, male or female. This kind of Shelamim is called a Chagigah, a Festival-sacrifice, and the Torah calls this one a "Chagigah of the Fourteenth [of Nissan]." And where is it mentioned in the Torah? "You shall slaughter a Pesach sacrifice to God your Lord, sheep and cattle." (Devarim 16:2). The Pesach itself can never be cattle, so we learn that a Chagigah must come with it. According to the Torah this sacrifice is voluntary, but the Rabbis made it almost an obligation, so that the Pesach should be eaten when the company are already full.

However, the Chagigah is not always brought with the Pesach. When Erev Pesach falls on a weekday, and the company eating this particular sacrifice are all purified, and their Pesach is too small to satisfy all of them, then they bring a Chagigah too. But if Erev Pesach falls on Shabbos, or the company are not purified, or there is enough meat on their Pesach to satisfy them all completely, then they do not bring a Chagigah.

The Chagigah may be eaten for two days and the night in between them. It comes under the laws of a regular Shelamim sacrifice: the one who brings it must lay his hands on its head, wine for the nesachim must be brought with it and poured over the horn of the altar, and the blood must be thrown on the altar "twice that makes four times": the Kohen goes over to one corner of the altar and throws half the blood, making it run along two sides of the altar at once. Then he goes to the opposite corner and does the same, so that in two throws the blood has touched all four sides. The blood left in the vessel must be poured out at the base of the altar.

This is how to offer the Pesach sacrifice and the Chagigah sacrifice with it in the House of our Lord, may it be built soon, in our days, Amen.

May my mouth's speech and my heart's thought be pleasing before You, God, my Rock and my Redeemer.

The Night the Festival Is Sanctified

Ma'ariv — the Evening Prayer

Basically, the *Ma'ariv* prayer on Pesach night is no different from that of the other festivals, for the special mitzvos of the night are performed in the home, at one's table, rather than in the synagogue. Nevertheless, there are some variations in the *Ma'ariv* service, so that the special character of the Seder night is discernible in the synagogue as well.

If the first night of Pesach falls on Shabbos, many communities omit the *Magen Avos* prayer that normally is recited on Shabbos at *Ma'ariv* after the silent *Amidah*. This prayer was added for the sake of "people of the fields" who could not get to Shabbos *Ma'ariv* on time, to allow them to finish their prayers with the congregation, so that afterwards, they would not have to walk home from the synagogue alone, which could be dangerous. On *Erev Pesach*, however, work is prohibited after midday, and everyone is home and can arrive at the synagogue with plenty of time to spare. Furthermore, as we noted, everyone tries to begin the Seder as early as possible, so that the children do not fall asleep and are able to participate. In addition, *Hallel* is recited after *Ma'ariv* on the Seder night, and this makes *Ma'ariv* longer anyway. What is more, the night of the Seder is a "night that is guarded" (*Shemos* 12:42) — each Jew is protected from harm. Nevertheless, some communities, when Pesach falls on Shabbos, do say *Magen Avos* after *Ma'ariv*, as usual.

While it is customary in many communities, on Shabbos and festivals, to recite Kiddush over wine in the synagogue after *Ma'ariv*, this is not done on the Seder night, for the cup of Kiddush is the first of the four obligatory cups of wine of the Seder, and Kiddush must be at home with the other three cups. Moreover, the whole reason behind the custom of reciting Kiddush in the synagogue was so that strangers who had no place to eat, and would remain in the synagogue, would be able to have Kiddush. On the Seder night, however, everyone eats at someone's table. Finally, the custom of reciting Kiddush also arose as a means to make the Kiddush text familiar to those who recite it at home by heart. On the Seder night, however, Kiddush is read from the Haggadah.

The most obvious special thing in the synagogue on Pesach night is the recital of *Hallel*. It is customary in almost all communities to recite *Hallel* after *Ma'ariv* on the night of the Seder [and in the Diaspora, on the second night, too]. The custom dates back to Talmudic times (see Talmud Tractate *Sofrim* 20a). Although normally, *Hallel* is said only by day, the Seder night, which marks the birth of the Jewish Nation, is considered to be "as lit up" as day, and *Hallel* is said in its entirety, with its blessings before and after. *Hallel* should be sung in a spirit of great rejoicing, in sweet melodies, so that the congregants "exalt together" the Name of God *(Tehillim* 34:4). Although some of the major authorities took issue with this custom (e.g., Rama on *Orach Chayim* 487:4) it nevertheless has become very widespread, including the reciting of both blessings, as mentioned above.

The custom arose as a means of exempting us from saying a blessing on the *Hallel* that is said later, at home, as part of the Seder, upon which no blessing is said. This, though, raises another question: Why, in fact, is there no blessing recited over the *Hallel* which is said at home? Is not the main *Hallel* of Pesach night the one that is said at home at the Seder, and not the one said in the synagogue? The reason is that the *Hallel* at home is said as part of the Haggadah, i.e., as part of the mitzvah of speaking about the Exodus from Egypt, and over the saying of the Haggadah the Sages ordained no blessing at all. This, though, raises a further question. Why did the Sages not institute a blessing over the saying of the Haggadah?

One explanation, a particularly beautiful one, is that on the Seder night, every Jew is so filled with joy over his spiritual lot, over God's having redeemed him from Egypt, that the entire Haggadah is essentially a blessing of thanks, where we express our recognition and gratitude to God for allowing us to taste this spiritual "satiety." As a result, the Torah's mitzvah of saying the Haggadah is actually a requirement to say a blessing on being "full," just as the Torah requires us to say a blessing after eating bread, when we feel physical satiety. Thus just as no blessing need be said before Grace after Meals, no blessing need be said before saying the Haggadah, for blessings are not said on blessings!

Some maintain that Kiddush serves as a blessing over *Hallel*, for the Exodus from Egypt is mentioned in Kiddush. Others say that the blessing "Who has redeemed us" (recited after *Hallel* at the Seder) is considered a blessing over *Hallel*. Finally, some maintain that no blessing is required over the *Hallel* said at the table, for that *Hallel* is interrupted — part of it being said before the meal, and part of it after.

The Correct Time for the Seder

Although it is usually considered meritorious to spend much time making preparations to carry out a mitzvah, so that the mitzvah is done well, if things are not so well-prepared for the Seder, one nevertheless does not delay, because the main mitzvah of saying the Haggadah is to say it to the children, and one must hurry to begin so that the children remain awake for the entire Haggadah.

On the other hand, one may not make Kiddush — and surely not eat matzah — before nightfall. Usually, one is permitted to "add," that is, to accept a festival or Shabbos early, and make Kiddush before night, but Pesach is different, for the time of the Torah mitzvah of eating matzah is night, when the Pesach offering was eaten. The verse states (*Shemos 12:8*): *And you shall eat the meat on this night*, and the Torah later says (*Bemidbar 9:11*): *It [the meat of the offering] shall be eaten with matzah and maror*, so that the time of eating matzah must be at night. This being so, the Rabbinic obligations ordained to accompany the mitzvah of eating matzah — e.g., the drinking of the four cups of wine — also cannot be fulfilled except at night. As said above, the wine at Kiddush is the first of the Four Cups, and thus Kiddush for the Seder cannot be made until after nightfall.

The Night the Festival Is Sanctified

The Holy One, blessed is He, wanted to bring joy to the hearts of Israel, and breathe hope into us about the Final Redemption, by giving us a feeling for how great those Final Days will be. Therefore, through prophecy (*Yeshayahu 30:29*), God tells us, *The song shall be for you like the night when the festival is sanctified* — the song of the future will be very much like the night of Pesach.

That is, the verse does not say that the song of the future will resemble *"the song"* that was sung at Pesach, when the Jews left Egypt. Rather, the verse says that the song of the future will resemble the night of Pesach, for every year, this particular night of the Jewish calendar is by essence like a song.

You see, the verse cannot be referring specifically to the night that God split the sea, and that the Jews, emerging on the other side, sang praises to Him, for when God split the sea, that night was not yet even considered a festival. Neither can the verse in Yeshayahu be referring specifically to the actual night when the Jews left Egypt, a week earlier. Regarding the mitzvos of the seventh day of Pesach, and also those that the Jews had been commanded to do on the Seder night in Egypt, the Torah states explicitly that the mitzvos are *for all generations* (*Shemos 12:14*), not just for the generation that was freed from Egypt. Thus, when Yeshayahu said that the song of the future will resemble *the night when the festival is sanctified*, meaning Pesach, he did not mean a night that is long passed and is already a part of history. Rather, the reference is to Pesach night every year, in all generations, in every Jewish home where there is a Seder. When Jews gather together to retell all the great and mighty deeds that God performed for us in Egypt, and we praise Him and thank Him, the night "sings" — the song of the Final Redemption in the End of Days.

As Jews perform the Seder, here on earth, all those in Heaven join us, and just as our homes are filled with song — even the very walls, and everything they contain — so, too, all of the Heavens fill with song, together with the earth and the seas, and every thing in them. All Creation sings praise to the Living God, until the entire night is a song and the night of the holy festival is sanctified.

The song of this night — song in which all Creation joins, is not always heard by the human ear. There are ears which are not attuned to this music, and do not hear it at all. There are other ears that are attuned, and do hear, but the sound is muffled, and what the ears hear is not comprehended. Preoccupation with things mundane can block out the glorious music entirely. The greater the preoccupation, the thicker is the wall that blocks out the song. Were a person to achieve purity of heart and repose of soul, then he would hear this beautiful song clearly, for it emanates from within himself, as well as from within everything around him, until it fills the universe: *Halleluyah, praise the name of God! (Tehillim 135:1)*

On this night, one's very soul must echo: *May the Name of God be blessed, now and forever. (Ibid)*

Would that our hearts be so open at all times! Would that we could feel the reverberations of this song constantly, that no barriers conceal it and no preoccupations confuse us! Would that we see always how: *From the rising of the sun until it sets, the Name of God is praised (Ibid)*!

Yeshayahu has told us that in the End of Days, when the world will be filled with the Knowledge of God, and all voices will sing His praise, that song which is heard then will be no more glorious than the one that is sung now, every year, on the night of the Seder, when *the festival is sanctified*. When the Final Days finally come, all hearts will be opened, and all ears will hear, and everything will be clear — as clear as it should be on the night of Pesach!

Therefore, before the Seder night, a person should try his best to purify his heart. Once he has succeeded in freeing himself from all that is mundane, his ears will be able to discern the special song of this holy night, and both his body and soul will join in the song, with praises to the Living God.

The Shelah ha-Kadosh (R. Yeshayahu Horowitz) writes:

After the Ma'ariv evening prayers, one should return home.

He and his wife should behave in the manner of a king and queen, and the children as royal offspring. They should eat from vessels of silver and gold, and they should be dressed in silk and embroidered garments, using all the beautiful things and finery that God has granted them, to show how they rejoice in God's kindnesses. This night, with all of its attendant laws, has very great sanctity, for this was the night when God chose us as His, from out of all the nations, and sanctified us by means of His commandments. It therefore is fitting that one take special care to not speak of anything mundane on this night, and one should instruct one's children not to do so either, so that each and every Jew's closeness to God on this night be retained. One should devote oneself totally to the special mitzvos of the Seder, teaching them to his household, and discussing at length the miracles that God did for us when He freed us from Egypt.

It is said of the Maharil (R. Yisrael Isserlein) that non-Jews would deposit valuable gold and silver vessels with him for safekeeping. All year long, he would never touch them, but on the Seder night, he would take them out and place them on a special table, so that he could look at them and take pleasure in their beauty. He did so to help himself get into a happy mood for the Seder, for once one is in a good frame of mind, his heart can sing, and his soul can attain tremendous spiritual heights.

Customs of the Rabbis

In many Jewish communities, it was customary for rabbis and other halachic authorities to delay the start of their own Seders, until long after the rest of the townspeople had begun theirs. Compared to other nights of the year, many more questions of law are liable to arise on the Seder night, for the laws forbidding *chametz* are more stringent than the laws regarding other types of forbidden foods, and punishment for violations of these laws is more serious, too. Were the rabbis to have begun their own Seders along with everyone else, they would not have been able to issue halachic rulings. Once they had made

Kiddush over wine, they would be prohibited from ruling, since anyone who drinks a *revi'is* (86 grams) of wine is considered not to be in complete control of his faculties.

It is told of two of Jerusalem's great rabbis, Rabbi Shemuel Salant and the Saba Kadisha, Rabbi Shelomo Eliezer Alfandi, *zt"l*, that they came up with a brilliant way of helping to deal with this problem. They would pray *Ma'ariv* at the earliest possible time, quickly begin and finish their Seders, and then would rest for half an hour, in order to free themselves of the influence of the wine they had drunk. Then they would make themselves available for questions from their congregants, though at that time, practically everyone in town would just be starting to recite the Haggadah. Congregants who had questions earlier, while the two rabbis were rushing to complete their Seders, would take them to other rabbis who had delayed their Seders!

Here, it is appropriate to say that whether the rabbi was one who hurried his Seder, or whether he was one who delayed, surely, each one's intent was for the sake of Heaven!

Wearing White at the Seder

Although we mentioned that it is fitting to wear silk or some other colorful and expensive garment on this night, in Ashkenazic communities, those who lead the Seder customarily wear a white garment, called a *kittel*. Some maintain that the basis for this custom lies in the fact that the *kittel* resembles the garment that a person wears when he is buried, and thus it serves as a solemn reminder to avoid frivolity at the Seder. These commentators maintain that it is for the same reason that many eat hard-boiled eggs at the Seder, for eggs are served to mourners. In the same vein, the white *kittel* also serves to remind us of Tishah b'Av, the day that the Temple was destroyed, for we also wear white on Tishah b'Av, which every year falls on the same day of the week as the first day of Pesach.

Others interpret the custom quite differently — that the white garment serves to remind us of what the *Kohen Gadol* would wear in the Temple on Yom Kippur, when he entered the Holy of Holies. That is, every Jew who leads the holy service of the Seder should see himself as being like the *Kohen Gadol*, when he performed the most sublime service in the Temple, on the holiest day of the year!

Sephardic communities do not have the custom of wearing a white garment at the Seder.

Candle Lighting

Before Kiddush, the woman of the house lights candles, saying two blessings:

בָּרוּךְ אַתָּה יְיָ אֱלֹהֵינוּ מֶלֶךְ הָעוֹלָם, אֲשֶׁר קִדְּשָׁנוּ בְּמִצְוֹתָיו וְצִוָּנוּ לְהַדְלִיק נֵר [שֶׁל שַׁבָּת וְ] שֶׁל־יוֹם טוֹב:

Blessed are You, Hashem, our God, King of the universe, Who has sanctified us with His commandments, and has commanded us to light the candles of [Shabbos and of] the Festival.

בָּרוּךְ אַתָּה יְיָ אֱלֹהֵינוּ מֶלֶךְ הָעוֹלָם, שֶׁהֶחֱיָנוּ וְקִיְּמָנוּ וְהִגִּיעָנוּ לַזְּמַן הַזֶּה:

Blessed are you, Hashem, our God, King of the universe, Who has kept us alive, sustained us, and brought us to this season.

If Pesach falls on a weekday, she can wait until after *Ma'ariv* to light the candles, or she can light at sunset, or even earlier. She says the blessings first, and then she lights. If she is lighting after sunset, however, she must remember not to strike a match, as she is accustomed to do when she is lighting candles for Shabbos, which is always done before sunset. Rather, she lights the Festival candles from an existing flame.

If Pesach falls on Shabbos, she lights the candles as she normally lights for Shabbos — before sunset — and says the blessings after lighting. In her blessing, she mentions Shabbos, as well: "and has commanded us to light the candles of Shabbos and of the Festival." Then she says the *Shehecheyanu* blessing.

While saying *Shehecheyanu*, she should have in mind that her blessing refer to all the mitzvos of Pesach, just as the leader of the Seder has this in mind when he recites the *Shehecheyanu* after reciting Kiddush.

Understanding the Seder

The Order of the Seder

For several reasons, the rabbis ordained a special order for the Seder. There are many mitzvos to be performed this night. Some of them are of Torah origin, some of them are Rabbinic, and still others are traditions or customs. It is an accepted rule that mitzvos should not be performed "in bundles" — meaning that each should be performed separately, in its proper time and place, so that two mitzvos are not performed simultaneously in one act and, if one mitzvah is supposed to performed after another, the sequence should not be switched. Accordingly, for all generations, the great rabbis of old established for Israel a particular order for the mitzvos of this night, and we should carefully keep this order, and not deviate from it even slightly.

Today, because of our sins, we no longer have the *Beis ha-Mikdash*, our Holy Temple, which means that the special Pesach and *Chagigah* sacrifices are no longer offered. Thus a number of obligatory mitzvos associated with these offerings can no longer be performed. Nevertheless, several mitzvos remain that we can perform at the Seder table, to which the Sages added others, in order to commemorate those mitzvos that cannot be performed without the Temple.

Although the Seder performed today is different from the one performed in the ancient days, the order which was established after the Temple's destruction will remain unchanged until the Temple is rebuilt, may it be speedily in our days.

The Maharil writes:

Let all be filled with fear and trembling when they come to fulfill the mitzvos that the Sages ordained concerning the Seder and the Haggadah. Let no one take this matter lightly. Even if one feels that there are elements that are of little significance, he nevertheless should fulfill them, and realize that, in truth, every element is significant.

In the *Zohar* we find:

The next mitzvah is to speak in praise of the departure from Egypt. Everyone is obligated to recall those events, at all times. It has been said that he who joyfully recounts the departure from Egypt will also merit to rejoice with the Divine Presence in the World-to-Come, which is the greatest joy possible. Even the Holy One, blessed is He, delights in the telling of the story of the Exodus, and as the events in Egypt are told at the Seder table, God gathers together all of His Heavenly hosts and says to them, "Go and listen to My children praising My greatness and rejoicing over My redeeming them!" The Heavenly hosts all go together to join with Israel, and listen at the Seder table to the Jews happily telling of all the miracles that their God wrought for them, to bring them out of Egypt. Afterwards, the Heavenly hosts give thanks for those miracles and mighty deeds, and give praises that God has this holy nation on earth, which rejoices in His Might and His salvation. Thus the glory of God is magnified on high.

The Jewish People, as well, by speaking of the Exodus, greatly magnify the glory of their Master, just as an earthly king's glory and strength are magnified when his subjects speak glowingly of his powers, and happily acknowledge his greatness. It creates awe of the king until his glory is manifest to all. For this reason, one is obligated to exalt and extol God, for all that He did for us in Egypt. It is written that one should accustom himself to speak of God's greatness always, and at every opportunity one should publicize the miracles that He does.

You might ask, "Why should a person be obligated as such?

> *After all, God knows everything — all that ever occurred and all that will ever be. Why then should it be obligatory to say again and again what God does, and what He did in the past, and already knows? Why does God want us to speak of these things?"*
>
> *[The answer is, that] nevertheless, we must publicize God's miracles and tell of His great and mighty deeds, for man's words rise to the Heavens, where the Heavenly hosts gather together to look down and listen, until they, too, give thanks to the Creator, and elevate His Glory, so that His greatness is acknowledged above and below, in Heaven and on earth, blessed is He, Amen.*

In establishing the order of the Seder, the rabbis inserted numerous mystical allusions and hidden secrets into every different act that we perform, each one in its proper sequence. Thus, whether it be a Rabbinic requirement or an adopted custom, everything must be done as prescribed, without variation, and no one should deviate from the customs of his community.

We Jews of today can understand the various elements of the Seder only at a simple level, and we are not able to comprehend the wealth of hidden, cosmic significance of the different things we do. Still, by simply following the instructions of our Sages, with the intent that our actions be in accordance with their knowledge, we can reach a sublimely high level of holiness and sanctity at the Seder, for these depend not so much upon intelligence as upon goodness, happiness, and purity of heart.

Thus, our Sages spoke of the great spiritual potential of the Seder night. They gave extravagant praise to the entire Jewish People, for sanctifying itself by means of careful performance of the mitzvos of the night, around the Seder table:

> *The Holy One leaves His celestial family and the righteous in Gan Eden, and comes to watch how Israel celebrates with the mitzvos of this night, and speaks of His Glory.*

Accordingly, although we know almost nothing about such hidden matters, we earn reward through our belief that

Understanding the Seder

everything that we do at the Seder is significant, and so, too, do we earn reward for learning about these matters even at a simple level. There are certain main elements of the Seder, and these have meanings that we can fathom. There also are interesting reasons for the various customs. All this is extremely satisfying to know, for every Jew, and every Jew should learn what he can.

The Maharal writes that the very word *seder* is an allusion to the miracles and wonders that God performed for us in Egypt, for *seder* means "order," and God's mighty deeds in Egypt serve as the root sources for all subsequent miracles and wonders that He did, and will continue to do — everything in a preordained order, with foresight, as part of a grand plan, culminating with the great Redemption that He will bring for His People at the End of Days.

Even the Jewish People's bondage and long exile are parts of the grand plan — everything put into motion by the First Cause of the Creation. *Seder* or "order" is a fitting term for what we do to start Pesach for another reason, for as we shall see, all the other Jewish holidays are fixed on the calendar according to when Pesach begins, so that Pesach serves as a reference and a prior sign, establishing when all the other special days will come in the "order" of the year.

The Mitzvos of the Seder Which Apply Today

Regarding the Seder, there remain two positive mitzvos of the Torah which are obligatory today — eating matzah, and telling the story of the Exodus from Egypt (the mitzvah of saying the Haggadah).

The Torah states (*Shemos 12:16*): *On the first day, on the fourteenth of the month [of Nissan] in the evening, you shall eat matzos.* Concerning telling the story of the Exodus, the verse says (*Shemos 13:8*): *And you shall tell your son on that day, "Because of this, did God do [great things] for me as I left Egypt."* Because the second verse says *on that day,* we might think that the mitzvah of telling the story of the Exodus should be performed during daylight, rather than at night. However, the verse states that the father should tell his son, *Because of this...* which refers to the matzah, *maror*, and the meat of the Pesach sacrifice. Thus the Sages derived that the mitzvah of telling about the Exodus should be performed when the mitzvah of eating matzah is performed, which is the night of the Seder, the night of the 15th of Nissan, when matzos and *maror* are before us, to be eaten (when the Temple is standing) along with the Pesach sacrifice.

What is more, even though the verse states: *And you shall tell your son*, the Sages taught that the verse simply is speaking about a usual case, but really, one must tell the story of the Exodus even if he does not have a son. He should recount the story of the Jews in Egypt to whomever shares his table; moreover, even if he is sitting alone he must say the Haggadah aloud, to himself!

Thus, matzah and Haggadah are the only mitzvos of the Torah that remain with us today, for lacking the Temple and its altar, we cannot offer the Pesach sacrifice or the *Chagigah*, and all the mitzvos which accompany these offerings are not applicable either, as mentioned. In our times, therefore, even the obligation to eat *maror* at the Seder is not a Torah requirement, for we have a Torah mitzvah to eat *maror* only when we eat it along with the Pesach offering. Thus eating *maror* is now a Rabbinic requirement. Another Rabbinic mitzvah of the Seder night is the drinking of the four cups of wine.

In summary, there are four separate special mitzvos of the Seder, two from the Torah (matzah and Haggadah) and two from the Rabbis (*maror* and the four cups). We are required to make Kiddush and say *Shehecheyanu*, as well, but these mitzvos are not unique to the Seder, for they are mandatory at other festivals and holidays as well.

In order that we fulfill the requisite mitzvos of the night in the best way possible, and commemorate those that are not applicable anymore, and for spiritual reasons known only to them, our Sages instituted many different practices and customs for the Seder night, such as reclining at the table; dipping the *karpas* in salt water, after having washed one's hands, and only then eating the *karpas*; breaking one of the three matzos and saving it for *Afikoman*, which must be eaten last; a set wording for the Haggadah, ending with the blessing "He Who redeems Israel"; a special blessing on the eating of matzah; dipping *maror* in *charoses*; making a "sandwich" out of matzah and *maror*; and the singing of *Hallel* and other praises.

Whether they be the mitzvos of the night, or the unique customs and practices, all have common themes — to remind us of our slavery in Egypt before God intervened, and to remind us of the miraculous redemption. The entire Seder is structured as such, as is the Haggadah itself, which "begins with dishonor and concludes with praise," starting with our slavery, and the causes for it, and ending with the redemption, and why we merited it.

Rules for Conducting the Seder

Kiddush and the Shehecheyanu blessing must be said first

The reason for this is that before Kiddush, we can neither eat nor drink, not even the things we are obligated to eat and drink at the Seder. One who makes Kiddush says three blessings — "Who has created the fruit of the vine"; "Who has sanctified Israel and the times of the festivals"; and *Shehecheyanu*. If the Seder night falls on Saturday night (*Motza'ei Shabbos*) two additional blessings are added to Kiddush, as will be explained. As noted, the cup of wine used at Kiddush is the first of the four required cups that are drunk at the Seder.

Mitzvos should not be performed in "bundles"

That is, each mitzvah should be performed separately, in its proper place and time. For this reason, the four cups are not drunk all at once. Rather, they are spread out throughout the Seder, each in its own special time in the course of the evening. The mitzvah of the four cups is especially dear to us, for the four cups correspond to the four expressions of redemption used in the Torah, in God's promise that He would free us from Egypt, and each term expresses a slightly different facet of the redemption. Therefore, it is fitting that each cup be ascribed individual importance, by reciting a series of blessings over it, or by praising God over it, thanking Him for His grace and His many kindnesses. Only then is the cup drunk. Only after these blessings and praises have filled one's heart, and the heart sings, has the proper moment arrived for drinking the cup of redemption.

The first cup, as mentioned above, is drunk after Kiddush, while the second is drunk after the recital of what is called the "Egyptian *Hallel*" — the first two psalms of *Hallel* (*Tehillim* 113-14), which are praises that refer to the Exodus. The third cup is drunk following the Grace after Meals, and the final cup is drunk following the completion of *Hallel* at the end of the Seder. Thus, the first and third cups are connected to blessings, while the second and fourth are connected to *Hallel*.

Telling the story of the Exodus: a son's questions are answered by his father

Being that the saying of the Haggadah is a Torah obligation, this mitzvah theoretically should be performed immediately after Kiddush. Instead, however, after Kiddush, we first wash our hands, dip *karpas* into salt water, eat the *karpas*, and then break the middle matzah. The Sages saw fit to delay the Torah mitzvah of reciting the Haggadah, in favor of these unusual ceremonies, precisely in order to stimulate the sons to ask their father the desired questions. The children are surprised and aroused by the Seder's unusual ceremonies. Their curiosity is pricked, and when they hear their father's explanations for what they see, they are drawn into the grand story which lies behind the ceremonies, and will pay close attention to everything else the father will say, absorbing the Haggadah's lessons deep into their hearts, and having no desire to sleep.

Matzah is eaten before maror

This was true even in the days of the Temple, when it was a Torah obligation to eat both. The Torah alludes to matzah's precedence, for where the verse commands us to eat matzah and *maror* on the Seder night (*Bemidbar* 9:11), matzah is mentioned first. Now that the Temple has been destroyed, and it no longer is a Torah mitzvah to eat *maror* (rather, *maror* is a Rabbinic obligation) all the more so must the matzah be eaten first, for eating matzah at the Seder remains a Torah mitzvah.

The Afikoman must be the last thing eaten at the Seder

The only thing that can be drunk afterwards is water, and the third and fourth cups of wine. This is to demonstrate that the mitzvah of eating matzah is so dear to us, that the last taste that we want to be left in our mouths when the meal is over is that of the matzah. The third and fourth cups of wine also would come before the *Afikoman*, but different considerations make this impossible.

A Short Summary of the Seder

Using the rules above, the Seder can be summarized as follows:

KIDDUSH AND ITS BLESSINGS: Includes the first of the four cups of wine, to be drunk while reclining (see details later).

WASHING OF THE HANDS (WITHOUT A BLESSING): This is for dipping the *karpas* in salt water Then we recite the blessing over vegetables and eat the *karpas*.

YACHATZ (BREAKING THE MIDDLE MATZAH): All of these rituals are for one purpose — to arouse the curiosity of the children and get them to ask questions. Thus, the rituals are performed at the very start of the Seder, to lead up to the Haggadah — *and you shall tell it to your son*. (Note that the rules for washing one's hands for the *karpas* are the same as for washing before a meal, except that no blessing is said.)

MAGGID (RECITING THE ENTIRE HAGGADAH): This mitzvah, the retelling of the story of the Exodus from Egypt, is the primary mitzvah of the night, and precedes even the eating of the matzah, though both obligations are from the Torah. In addition, the mitzvah of eating matzah is incumbent only upon adults, and does not include children at all, but the obligation on adults to tell the Haggadah does include the children, for it is mainly for their sake!

SECOND CUP OF WINE: It is drunk when the recital of the Haggadah is completed.

RACHTZAH (WE WASH OUR HANDS BEFORE THE MEAL): This is as we do during the year, before bread, with the blessing *Who commanded us regarding the washing of the hands.*

HAMOTZI AND AL ACHILAS MATZAH: In addition to the blessing *haMotzi*, which during the year is said on bread and tonight is said on matzah, we also say the blessing, "Who has commanded us regarding the eating of matzah." We eat the matzah while reclining. This is followed by:

MAROR: We dip the *maror* in *charoses*, shaking the *charoses* off, and reciting the blessing on *maror* (*Who has commanded us regarding the eating of bitter herbs*), and eating the *maror*, which is one of the main mitzvos of the Seder.

KORECH: We eat a sandwich of matzah and *maror*, dipping it in *charoses*. Although matzah and *maror* already have been eaten separately, we now eat them together, in remembrance of the opinion of Hillel the Elder, who said that when the Temple stood, this is how the matzah and *maror* had to be eaten, with the meat of the Pesach sacrifice in the "sandwich" too. In light of the fact that in the days of the Temple, the meat of the Pesach sacrifice was eaten at the end of the meal, we really should eat the *Korech* at the end of the meal, too. Today, lacking the Temple, we begin the meal with matzah, the one food which is a Torah obligation, and then we eat *maror* separately. Thus it is fitting that immediately thereafter we perform the remembrance that employs the two foods together.

THE CUSTOM OF EATING THE BOILED EGG: This is eaten after we dip it in salt water. Many follow the custom of eating it after the meal has begun. The egg is a remembrance of the *Chagigah* offering, which according to the Torah was actually a voluntary offering that the Rabbis made almost an obligation, so that when it came time to eat the meat of the Pesach offering, the Pesach offering would be eaten as required — on a full stom-

Understanding the Seder

ach, and not because of hunger, in the way of royalty. In that the *Korech* reminds us of the Temple and of how the Pesach offering was eaten, the egg, representing the *Chagigah*, which was eaten for the sake of the Pesach offering and before it, should be eaten as soon after the *Korech* as possible.

In Sephardic communities, some have the custom of eating the egg later in the meal, and some partake of it twice, once after the *Korech* and once later. Some, especially first-born males, eat the egg immediately after Kiddush, and others do not eat it at all.

SHULCHAN ORECH: The festive meal is eaten before the obligatory eating of the *Afikoman*.

TZAFUN: We eat the *Afikoman* last in order that the last taste in our mouths be the taste of matzah, in memory of the Pesach offering, which also had to be eaten last.

BARECH: Grace after Meals is recited, followed by the third cup of wine.

HALLEL: It is then completed, followed by the prayer *Nishmas*, both in order to conclude with praises to God, and to give a special place to the fourth cup of wine, which symbolizes the fourth expression of redemption.

THE FOURTH CUP: The wine is drunk, followed by an after-blessing (with intent that it cover all four cups).

PIYUTIM, SHIR HASHIRIM, PESACH SONGS: The evening is concluded with *piyutim*, the recital of *Shir haShirim*, and traditional Pesach songs, until we are overtaken by sleep.

Simanim — Aids for Remembering the Seder's Structure

In that there are many steps to the Seder, and they all must be performed in a definite order, it is helpful on the Seder night to use memory aids, so that the proper order is clear in one's mind. Our illustrious ancient Sages and more recent noted commentators, as well, have designed different sets of memory aids, to assist us in remembering the Seder's order. Once these *simanim* (literally, "signs") are memorized, it is much easier to conduct the Seder smoothly, without error or awkward pauses, exactly as the Sages wanted the Seder to be.

Systems of memory aids have been devised by great Torah scholars such as R. Meir of Rothenburg and R. Yom Tov Ilem. Above, in our brief description of the Seder, we mentioned some of these *simanim*, from the system attributed to Rashi. Rashi's method for recalling the Seder's order contains fifteen *simanim*, and is the most popular memory aid of all. The fifteen words correspond to fifteen basic steps to the Seder, and have a rhythm and rhyme to them, to make them very easy to remember.

Over the years, Rashi's system of memory aids has actually become a part of the Haggadah itself. Other memory aids sometimes are used to complement Rashi's, and in certain communities, these other *simanim* also are included in the Haggadah. Sometimes, it is not known who actually devised the system of *simanim*, but it is clear that many of these aids are ancient, for later authorities have found that they contain profound wisdom and hidden teachings, as sublime as those of the Haggadah itself. In truth, this is not very surprising, for the Haggadah is sacred, possessing several layers of meaning, so that something that is closely attached to it, such as a system designed to remember it, is likely to be the same.

Rashi's *simanim* are as follows:

Kadesh/U'rechatz;

Karpas/Yachatz;

Maggid/Rachtzah;

Motzi/Matzah;

Maror/Korech;

Shulchan Orech;

Tzafun/Barech;

Hallel/Nirtzah.

Understanding the Seder

Kadesh: Make Kiddush. *U'rechatz:* Wash hands.
Karpas: Dip and eat karpas. *Yachatz:* Break middle matzah.
Maggid: Recite Haggadah. *Rachtzah:* Wash hands.
Motzi: Blessing on two matzos. *Matzah:* Eat matzah.
Maror: Eat maror. *Korech:* Eat "sandwich."
Shulchan Orech: Eat meal.
Tzafun: Eat Afikoman. *Barech:* Say Grace after Meals.
Hallel: Say Hallel. *Nirtzah:* Praises.

During the Seder, when the time arrives to perform one of the fifteen steps, many have the custom to first say aloud Rashi's *siman* for that step, for as noted, Rashi's *simanim* have profound, hidden meanings behind them. Though few people today can perceive these meanings, Rashi's *simanim* retain their holy significance, and because of their sanctity, and also because of their great utility, they have established themselves as an integral part of the Seder.

One must take care to note, however, that Rashi's system mentions only one of the four cups of wine — that of Kiddush. Also, eating the egg is not mentioned, perhaps because it is not obligatory. Finally, Rashi does not provide a *siman* for the after-blessing on the fourth cup of wine.

Possibly, Rashi limited his number of *simanim* to fifteen as a reminder of the fifteen steps of Israel's spiritual elevation from the state of depredation that the Nation suffered in Egypt. These stages of spiritual growth, which are listed in the Haggadah, begin with God's freeing the Jews from Egypt, and they conclude with His giving us the Torah, His bringing us into the Land of Israel, and His resting the *Shechinah* — the Divine Presence — on the Temple in Jerusalem.

The number fifteen may be meant also to remind us of the fifteen expressions that are used to praise God in the daily prayer *Yishtabach*, which also was made part of the Haggadah.

The Alshich on Rashi's Simanim

A great Jewish commentator from Safed, R. Moshe Alshich, found that Rashi's "memory aids" have lessons to teach about mitzvos beyond the mitzvos of the Seder. The fifteen *simanim* particularly allude to mitzvos involving charity and acts of loving-kindness, and the rewards that are hidden away for the righteous who perform these mitzvos.

KADESH: Sanctify yourself with what is permitted to you.

U'RECHATZ: As it is written (*Yeshayahu* 1:16): *Cleanse yourselves and become pure.*

KARPAS: Be frugal regarding yourself but be generous to the poor. (Allusions to the connotations of the Hebrew letters involved.)

YACHATZ: Split the matzah — some you eat now, in this world, and some — what you give to the poor — is put away for you in the Next Life.

MAGGID, RACHTZAH: Tell others of this, and you shall help yourself and them, for in your merit, they will be moved to try to cleanse themselves, as you did.

MOTZI, MATZAH: Let what is good in you come out. This is "matzah" which stands for your good inclination.

MAROR, KORECH: Put the matzah together with the bitter herbs — the evil inclination — as our Sages explain the *Shema*'s words to *love Hashem your God with all your heart* — "with both of your inclinations."

SHULCHAN ORECH, TZAFUN: If you do so, your table will be set in Gan Eden...

BARECH, HALLEL, NIRTZAH: The blessings and praises that you give to God will protect you there, and will be pleasing to Him.

Making Kiddush

As we mentioned above, if Pesach falls on a weekday, there are three blessings said at the Seder night Kiddush. Before saying the third blessing, *Shehecheyanu*, one should have in mind to be thanking God for giving us life, and for bringing us to the Seder night, when we not only are able to make the blessings of Kiddush, we also are able to perform the mitzvos of Haggadah, matzah, *maror*, and the four cups of wine.

If the Seder night falls on Shabbos (Friday night), we begin the Kiddush with the recital of *vaYechulu* — *Thus the heavens and earth were finished* — as on Shabbos. Also, mention of Shabbos is added to the second blessing of Kiddush — "Who sanctifies the Shabbos, Israel, and the festive seasons."

If the Seder falls on Saturday night, Kiddush consists of five blessings, said in the following order: "Who creates the fruit of the vine"; "Who sanctifies Israel and the festive seasons"; "Who creates the light of the fire"; "Who distinguishes between the holiness of Shabbos and the holiness of the Festival"; and "*Shehecheyanu.*"

The cup used for Kiddush cannot be cracked or chipped, and it must be able to hold a *revi'is*, which is a measure of liquid volume. According to most authorities, a *revi'is* is about 86 cc. and this, therefore, is the minimum amount of wine that the Kiddush cup must hold. Interestingly, the numerical equivalent — or gematria — of the Hebrew letters of the word *kos* (cup) is 86!

According to the Chazon Ish, however, the minimum volume of the Kiddush cup is 150 cc. This numerical value is the gematria of the Hebrew words *kos hagun* — "a proper [or respectable] cup"!

When drinking the Kiddush wine (and also the other three cups of the four cups of wine) one should recline on his left side (see details of reclining below) and he must drink at least a *revi'is*. When drinking this *revi'is*, he also should be sure to drink at least the majority of the cup's contents. Preferably, he should drink this quantity from the cup all at once, without interruption. If his cup holds only a *revi'is*, he must drink the whole cup, and again, it preferably should be drunk all at once. Some say that at least a majority of the cup must be drunk, even if the cup contains much more than a *revi'is*.

Since some authorities say that most of the contents of the

cup must be drunk, no matter how big the cup is, anyone who wants to keep his drinking to a minimum should use a small cup containing only a *revi'is*.

Drinking a *revi'is* all at once is required not only for the sake of fulfilling the mitzvah of the Four Cups, but also in order to be able to say the after-blessing which is said after the fourth cup (for an after-blessing on a drink never is said unless one has drunk a *revi'is*). In the case of those who follow the Sephardic tradition and do not say the blessing over wine before the fourth cup, even if one does not drink a *revi'is* of the fourth cup, as required, he can and should say the after-blessing for wine after his fourth cup, because no after-blessing is said after the third cup (even according to Ashkenazim), and since, as all Sepharadim, he did not say any prior blessing on his fourth cup, his after-blessing will also count for what he drank of the third cup. As long as he drank from both cups a total of a *revi'is,* the after-blessing can and should be said.

In many Ashkenazic communities, every participant at the Seder makes Kiddush for himself. Women, however, do not do so, even though as all participants, each woman has a full cup of wine at her place when Kiddush is said. Women are included in the Kiddush recited by the man who conducts the Seder, and when he says the Kiddush, he should have in mind that he is making Kiddush not only for himself, but also for the women, and the women should intend to be included.

Some authorities maintain that women also do not say the blessing over wine before they drink the first cup, for they were exempted from that blessing as well, when it was said by the leader of the Seder, before he said the second blessing of Kiddush. Others maintain that they should say the blessing over wine, even though regarding the second blessing of Kiddush, women are included.

Regarding the size of her cup, and how much she must drink from it, the same rules apply to a woman as to a man. (For the laws regarding reclining while drinking the four cups, and whether women must do so too, see the following section.)

The Obligation of Reclining

At the Seder, whenever one drinks one of the four cups of wine, and almost every time that he is required to eat something, he is obligated to recline while doing so. Accordingly, the chair where he is sitting should be upholstered, or be equipped with pillows, so that he can recline comfortably. This is how royalty and nobility used to eat and drink, and on this night, it is fitting that the Jew conduct himself in this way as well.

In his *Mishneh Torah*, the Rambam writes about the Seder night:

> Each Jew is obligated to see himself this night as if he is actually in Egypt, having just been freed from bondage. Thus, while he is eating his meal, he is required to eat and drink in a manner that reflects this freedom.

In his commentary to *Mishnah Pesachim*, the Rambam adds: *...in the manner of kings and nobility.*

The Me'iri writes similarly:

> [The purpose of reclining] is to allude to the redemption, to our becoming free, and to stir our hearts to sing praises to the One Who bestowed upon us this good, Who extricated us from such a difficult and degrading oppression.

One should recline on his left side, eating and drinking with his right hand, even if he is left-handed.

Normally, a son would not eat or drink in a reclining position in the presence of his father [out of respect], but on the Seder night, he is required to do so, for fathers actually want their sons to recline on the Seder night. It is in the father's interest that his sons recline, for he wants them to attain the feeling that he is trying to attain — that they have actually been released from slavery in Egypt.

Regarding a student eating in the presence of his rabbi, however, the student is not allowed to recline unless the rabbi gives him explicit permission.

In a verse about the Exodus from Egypt, the Torah states

(*Shemos* 13:18): *And God made the people go around, towards the desert.* The Hebrew word for "to go around" is very similar to the Hebrew word for "to recline." Thus, the Sages saw this verse as a hint to the law that the head of every Jewish household should recline on the Seder night, even the most humble and poor, for the aforementioned verse applies to all Jews.

Usually, in Ashkenazic communities women do not recline, but in Sephardic communities they do.

When eating *maror*, one should not recline, however, because we eat *maror* in remembrance of the bitterness of our lives when we were slaves in Egypt, and reclining expresses the opposite of bitterness. *Karpas*, as will be explained, is somewhat connected to the mitzvah of *maror*, so that according to some authorities, one also should not recline when eating the *karpas*. Other disagree with this, however, saying that one should recline for the mitzvah of *karpas*.

When one is required to recline but failed to do so, the laws are as follows:

Regarding matzah, he should eat the required amount of matzah a second time, this time reclining, but without repeating the prior blessing. So, too, regarding the second cup of wine. Regarding Kiddush, and the third and fourth cups of wine, authorities argue whether it is necessary to drink them again (making sure to recline).

Accordingly, in most Ashkenazic communities, if someone forgets to recline when he is obligated to drink wine, the custom is not to drink the cup a second time (making sure to recline) except if he forgets to recline for the second of the four cups. Regarding the eating of the *Afikoman*, which also requires reclining, if one forgot to do so, the Ashkenazic custom is not simply that he is not required to eat the portion a second time; he is forbidden to do so.

The custom in Sephardic communities is quite different regarding this point. Regarding all four cups, the drinking must be repeated (without the prior blessing), this time reclining. The *Afikoman* should be eaten a second time, too, this time reclining, as long as one has not said the Grace after Meals.

Even according to those who say that one should recline for *karpas*, if he forgot, he need not eat the *karpas* again.

It is praiseworthy to recline for the entire Seder (except when one should not recline — see above). Reclining is obligatory, however, only for the mitzvos of eating matzah (including the *Afikoman*) and drinking the four cups of wine. We recline at the Seder, even though regarding the remainder of the year, the custom of reclining no longer exists. Our Sages decided to continue to require the practice, because it is an obvious sign of nobility and dignity, expressing our elevated status as free men, and thus is appropriate for the Seder night.

For the same reasons, the custom is that the Seder's leader does not pour his own cup of wine. Rather, someone else at the table takes care of this, for each of the four cups. Some have the custom that no one at the table pours his own cup. The same applies regarding the washing of one's hands, before *karpas* and before the mitzvah of eating matzah. One's hands are washed by someone else — all to express every Jew's royalty and nobility, and that this night is different from all other nights.

It also is praiseworthy to have many guests at the Seder table, as a remembrance of the days when the Temple stood, and each Pesach lamb was shared by many people, and had to be eaten under one roof. Some say that having many guests is actually a part of the mitzvah of reclining.

The Four Cups

As noted, every Jew is obligated to drink four cups of wine on the Seder night — each cup at its appropriate time (see above). If he drinks all four cups at once, or two or three at a time, he has not fulfilled the mitzvah at all. The Talmud states that this mitzvah is obligatory for men, women, and even children (to a certain extent) for all were redeemed from Egypt, and the four cups are so important, that even someone who lives off charity must obtain the necessary wine for them — even if he has to sell his clothing (*Pesachim* 108b).

One who does not normally drink wine because he does not like its taste, or because it makes him feel uncomfortable or ill, must force himself to drink it, in order to fulfill the mitzvah. Though wine is preferable, grape juice can be used for the four cups as well.

If wine makes one so sick that he must lie in bed, he is exempt from the mitzvah, unless he can force himself to drink grape juice. If one has no wine or grape juice, or if he is ill and fears that drinking wine or grape juice will be harmful to his health, he should consult a competent halachic authority as to what he should do.

As is true of all the elements of the Seder, the four cups of wine symbolize various phases of Israel's history, involving her descent into Egypt and into slavery, and her ascent into freedom. The four cups also allude to the four periods of bondage that Israel suffered after the Exodus from Egypt. Finally, the four cups allude to the fact that God will judge the nations that oppressed Israel, and make them drink four bitter "cups." At the same time, Israel will drink four "cups" of consolation.

So taught our Sages (*Talmud Yerushalmi, Pesachim* 10):

> *What is the source for our drinking four cups? R. Yochanan taught in the name of R. Benayah: It is derived from verses that mention four expressions of redemption (Shemos 6:6-7): Therefore, say to the Children of Israel, "I am the Lord, Your God, and I shall take you out from under the heavy burdens that Egypt has put upon you [so that even though you will remain in bondage, your work will be easier — first cup], and I shall save you from their tasks [you will no longer have to work for them at all — second cup], and I...shall redeem you with an outstretched arm and with wondrous deeds [I will punish the Egyptians so harshly, you no longer will have any fear of them — third cup], and I shall draw you close to Me, to be My nation, and I shall be your God [I will bring you near to Me, to completely liberate you, physically and spiritually — fourth cup]." Four expressions of redemption also are found in Prophecy, in a verse (Yechezkel 34:13) describing how God*

will liberate Israel in the End of Days: *I will bring them out...and gather them...and bring them...and pasture them.*

R. Yehoshua ben Levi taught:

The four cups symbolize the four cups of Pharaoh that are mentioned regarding the dream of Pharaoh's butler (Bereshis 40:11). This dream led to Yosef's being liberated from prison. And the cup of Pharaoh was in my hand...and I squeezed the grapes into the cup of Pharaoh...and I put the cup into Pharaoh's hand...and you shall put the cup of Pharaoh into his hand.

R. Levi taught:

The four cups allude to the four kingdoms that subjugated Israel (after the Exodus from Egypt) — Babylonia, Media (Persia), Greece, and Edom (Rome).

Our Sages also taught that the four cups symbolize the four cups of punishment that the Holy One, Blessed is He, will mete out to the nations of the world. As the verse states (*Yirmeyahu* 25:15):

For thus says God, the Lord of Israel: This wine, in a cup of wrath — take it from My Hand, and the nations to whom I send you — make them drink of it.

And the verse (*Ibid* 51:17) states:

For Babylonia is like a golden cup in the Hand of God, making all the nations intoxicated. From her wine the nations have drunk and therefore they have gone mad.

We also read (*Tehillim* 75:9):

For there is a cup in the Hand of God, with wine in it, red and mixed. The evil people of the world drink of it and suck its dregs.

And (*Ibid* 11:6):

Barrels of hot tar and fire He shall rain down upon the wicked, and their portion in the cup will be tempestuous winds.

In contrast, we learn that the Holy One, blessed is He, will give Israel to drink of four cups of consolation, for the verse states *(Tehillim* 16:5):

> *For God is my portion and my cup; You annoint my head with oil, my cup overflows (Ibid 23:5) ; and [two more cups], I shall raise aloft cups of salvation, and call out loud in the Name of God (Ibid 116:13).*

The Abarbanel writes that the four cups also allude to four redemptions which span almost the whole length of Jewish history. The first cup corresponds to God's choosing Avraham and his descendants, from whom He sowed the seed of our Nation. The second cup corresponds to God's delivering us from Egypt. The third commemorates God's having saved us from the hands of our enemies, throughout our long exile, and having kept us alive, despite repeated attempts to destroy us. The fourth cup corresponds to the future, when God will bring us the Final Redemption, putting an end to our exile.

The Gaon of Vilna sees a parallel between the four cups and the four worlds: the world of today, the world as it will be in the days of *Mashiach*, the world at the time of the Resurrection of the Dead, and the World-to-Come. Thus, if a Jew is careful to fulfill all of the Seder's requirements, he is assured that he will have a share in all of these worlds. Accordingly, it is fitting that we give thanks and praise to God, for granting us all of this kindness.

The Maharal finds a parallel between the four cups and the four Matriarchs — Sarah, Rivkah, Rachel, and Leah, for in their merit, and the merit of the Patriarchs, Israel was redeemed from Egypt. In fact, the names of the Patriarchs and the Matriarchs were inscribed on the staff that Moshe used in Egypt to bring forth God's miracles. *(Yalkut Shimoni)*

The Bnei Yissaschar writes that the four cups parallel the four sources of virtue that Israel had in Egypt: They did not change their Hebrew names and adopt heathen names instead; they retained their own language; they were careful not to engage in illicit relationships; and there were no informers among them. The Meshech Chochmah adds that this indicates the great importance of these virtues as safeguards, for though

Israel had become defiled by all the other impurities of Egypt, their care in these four areas kept them sufficiently apart from the Egyptians, so that they still could be called "distinguishable" — and in this merit they merited redemption.

Reference to the four cups can been found in a verse about the Pesach sacrifice (*Shemos* 12:4), in which the word for "shall you make your count" — תכסו — contains the same letters as the word for "cups" — כוסות.

The Shem Mi-Shemuel explains that when the Prophet Yirmeyahu praises Israel for *the kindness of your youth*, he is referring to Israel's leaving Egypt to enter the desert as God commanded. Though the desert was dry and barren, the Nation did a "kindness" and obeyed the command, without questioning it at all. As a result, the Jews who left Egypt were called "the generation of wisdom," for when someone puts his own way of thinking aside, in deference to the word of God, he truly is considered to be wise, and will be granted even more wisdom. In fact, the greatest wisdom is to realize that on one's own, one knows nothing. Therefore, on the Seder night we drink four cups of wine, for wine creates confusion and lack of understanding, and by our drinking the four cups, we demonstrate that we, too, are confused and lack understanding. We admit that we know nothing, except for what God commands and teaches us, and because we drink the four cups and thereby make this statement, we merit God's bestowing sublime wisdom upon us.

How great is the difference between Israel and the other nations of the world! Among other peoples, when someone drinks, he can see no farther than the rim of his glass! He forgets everything that he knows, and thinks about nothing but his drink. His world shrinks. He cannot remember what was once obvious to him, and certainly he is not able to see into the future!

Israel is not so! On the night of Pesach, the Jews eat and drink, and a great amount of wine is served. Yet precisely at that time, they see revealed before them the entire history of the world, from the time when the Holy One, blessed is He, renewed His world with the light of Avraham, into the future — the End of Days. They review their actions and past behavior, and that of the other nations, too. They see everyone's destiny before their eyes, as if everything had already transpired, and they offer praises and songs of thanksgiving.

How are they able to do this? Because they have supressed their own desires before the Will of their King in Heaven, because everything that they are doing this night is in fulfillment of His command. It is He Who has lifted them above all other nations, by sanctifying them with His commandments. The wine of this night is not the wine of merrymaking and drunkenness. Therefore, it does not cause intoxication or degradation of any sort. Rather, it is the wine of *mitzvah*, and it makes the Jew contemplate, and helps elevate him to higher levels of holiness and sanctity.

Regarding the drinking of wine, there is another fundamental difference between Israel and the rest of the nations. Among other peoples, when sadness befalls a person and he is full of anguish, he resorts to drink to dispel his misery, and he becomes happy for a while. His wine precedes his happy state of mind, and when he becomes sober again, his anguish returns. Israel is different, for the Jew drinks only after he is happy, and his happiness enters him by means of songs and praises that he sings to his God! Only then do the Jews drink wine. Thus, their happy state of mind precedes their drinking, and when the effect of the wine wears off, the happiness remains.

Red Wine

The mitzvah of the four cups is optimally fulfilled with red wine. This is based on the verse (*Mishlei* 23:31): *Do not look at the wine as it reddens*, which implies that the redder a wine is, the better it is.

Red wine also serves as a reminder of the blood of the Pesach offering, and the blood of circumcision, for Israel was told in Egypt that any male who was not circumcised would be forbidden from eating of the Pesach offering. The Torah states that Israel performed the circumcisions as commanded. The blood of the circumcision became mingled with the blood of the offering, and it is the merit of these two mitzvos that we commemorate by drinking red wine.

Red wine also serves to remind us of the blood that was smeared on the doorposts of Jewish homes in Egypt on the Seder night, the night of the tenth plague. The blood was a sign for the Jews that God was "passing over" them, so that while sitting in their homes, the Jews would realize that God was saving them from the destruction that He was bringing upon Egypt. Through the use of red wine at the Seder, we express our prayer that God continue to protect us, and deliver us from all our enemies.

Finally, red wine reminds us of the Jewish blood which was shed by Pharaoh. (Our Sages tell us that Jewish children were slaughtered by Pharaoh so that he could bathe in their blood, as a cure for his *tzara'as*.) May the blood of these Jews never be forgotten! Even today, after over 3,000 years have passed since this tragedy occurred, we still remember it. The eternal nation remembers eternally, and there is no forgiveness for those who sought to destroy her.

The Mitzvah of the Four Cups Needs No Blessing

Although one usually recites a blessing before the performance of a mitzvah, the Sages did not require a blessing for the mitzvah of the Four Cups, for two reasons. Firstly, the four cups are not drunk all at once, and it could happen that for some reason, one might not be able to drink every cup, in which case the blessing that was said before the first cup would have been in vain. Secondly, how to word the blessing would be problematic, for the proper wording would be "Who commanded us to drink the four cups." However, the first of the four cups is the cup of Kiddush, and is obligatory by itself. We cannot say, "Who commanded us to drink three cups," because the mitzvah is four cups! Thus, no blessing is said at all.

The Sephardic and Ashkenazic communities have two different customs regarding saying a prior blessing for wine. Sepharadim say the prior blessing only at Kiddush and on the third cup, which accompanies the Grace after Meals. Ashkenazim follow the ruling of the Rama and say the blessing on each of the four cups.

The Fifth Cup

When pouring the fourth cup, over which *Hallel* is said, it is customary to pour an additional cup, one that is larger than the others. This fifth cup is called the "cup of Eliyahu." Its basis is the Talmud — the opinion of R. Tarfon, who maintained that one must drink five cups of wine at the Seder: four to parallel the four expressions of redemption that are used in *Shemos* 6:6-7, as discussed above, and a fifth to parallel a fifth expression found in the verse that follows — *I shall bring you into the land.*

Although R. Tarfon's view was not accepted, still, our Sages ruled that we should recognize R. Tarfon's opinion, and pour a fifth cup, but we should not drink it. When the Prophet Eliyahu comes, he will adjudicate all unsolved questions of law, and this particular dispute will be settled, too. Thus, the fifth cup is called the "cup of Eliyahu."

According to the Sages of later generations, the fifth cup is an allusion to the Final Redemption, which will be announced by Eliyahu the Prophet, upon the fall of Gog and Magog (the fifth kingdom, which will follow Rome). This is in line with the fact that in the Torah (*Shemos* 12:42), the night of the Seder is called *leil shimurim l'Hashem* — *a night of watching for God*, and afterwards, in the same verse, the Torah seemingly repeats itself, saying that the night is *a night of watching for all Israel for all generations*. The Sages of old explain that the Torah is teaching us that the Seder night must deal with two redemptions — the one in the past, when we were saved from Egypt, and the one in the future, when we will be saved from Gog and Magog. Moreover, the word *shimurim* is plural, so that the Seder night is called, literally, a night of "watchings." Accordingly, the Seder is split into two — the first part (until the Grace after Meals) concentrates on the redemption of the past, from Egypt, and the second part concentrates on the Redemption to Come. In that the Redemption to Come will be heralded by Eliyahu, it is fitting that we remember him on this night, by pouring a fifth cup —the "cup of Eliyahu."

Others point out that Eliyahu has a special connection to the mitzvah of circumcision, as is evidenced by the teaching that every time a circumcision is performed, Eliyahu is said to be there, as the attending angel. As noted above, red wine is used at the Seder partly as a commemoration of the blood of two mitzvos that the Jews performed in Egypt — the Pesach offering and circumcision. By fulfilling these two mitzvos, the Jews merited to be redeemed from Egypt. On the Seder night, every year, Eliyahu testifies that the Jews fulfilled these mitzvos and continue to perform circumcisions to this day, and that through these mitzvos, we will merit the Ultimate Redemption, that he will usher in.

Near the end of the Seder, before we say *Pour out Your wrath*, it is customary to open the door of the house, to signal our desire that Eliyahu come in. The Maharal writes that as the door is being opened, it is fitting to say the following prayer:

> *May the Merciful One send us Eliyahu the Prophet, may he be remembered for good, to herald good news, salvation and comfort, as the verse states (Malachi 3:23): Behold, I send you Eliyahu the Prophet, before the great and awesome day of God's coming. And he will turn back hearts of fathers toward their sons, and hearts of sons toward their fathers.*

The Three Matzos

The three matzos of the Seder are called *Kohen*, *Levi*, and *Yisrael* [the three divisions of the Jewish People], as a means of distinguishing them from each other. *Kohen*, who is first and highest, is the top matzah; *Levi*, being second to *Kohen*, is the middle matzah; and *Yisrael* is at the bottom.

Levi, the middle matzah, is broken in two at the start of the Seder. The bigger piece, symbolizing the Ultimate Redemption, is hidden away for the *Afikoman*, for the Ultimate Redemption is "hidden" from us, too (as to when it will be). When the Haggadah is completed, the smaller piece of *Levi* is eaten with *Kohen*, in order to fulfill the mitzvah of eating matzah. *Yisrael* is used for *korech* — the "sandwich" with *maror* inside, so that all three matzos are used for mitzvos.

The question may be asked: During the year, on Shabbos and on festivals, the blessing on bread is said over two loaves, or two matzos. Why at the Seder do we require three?

One answer is based on the fact that in the Torah (*Devarim* 16:3) matzah is called *lechem oni* — "bread of poverty." When someone who is poor is able to gather together some bread for himself, it usually is only pieces, and not a full loaf. Even if he does get hold of a loaf, he fears for tomorrow, and he therefore breaks the loaf into pieces, eating only some today, and saving the rest for later.

On Shabbos and festivals during the year, one must eat from whole loaves, or whole matzos, as a sign of honor and respect for these holy days. Pesach, a festival, also requires two whole matzos, but in addition we must eat the "bread of poverty." Thus, for the sake of the blessing of *haMotzi* — *He Who brings forth bread from the earth*, we hold all three matzos in our hands, in order to include the two whole matzos (*Kohen* and *Yisrael*) in the blessing. Afterwards, before we say, *Who commanded us to eat matzah*, we put down one of the whole matzos (*Yisrael*), to emphasize that the idea of this blessing is the "bread of poverty," epitomized by the middle matzah (*Levi*) which is only a piece.

When eating the matzah immediately after these two blessings, it is best if everyone at the table eats not only from the middle matzah (*Levi*), but also from the upper one (*Kohen*).

Other commentators view the three matzos as alluding to the three Patriarchs. We take three matzos as a sign that, although we were enslaved, we were nevertheless of distinguished lineage, for our ancestors were the three pillars of the world. Even in bondage, we preserved our precious link to our forefathers, and retained our dignity and nobility, and this was part of the reason that we merited redemption.

Some see the three matzos as allusions to the three measures of flour that Avraham asked Sarah to bake for the angels who visited him after his circumcision. The Torah, in the verse where Avraham makes his request, says that he asked Sarah to hurry (*Bereshis* 18:6) — which parallels the haste in which Israel was forced to leave Egypt. Also, according to the oral tradition, the "cakes" that Sarah made were matzos, because the episode took place on *Erev Pesach*.

Others say that the three matzos allude to the days of the Temple, to the three types of matzos that were brought to accompany the thanksgiving offering. According to the Sages, there are four who are required to bring this offering: one who returns from a journey at sea; one who returns from a journey in the desert; one who recovers from a serious illness; and one who is released from prison. The Jews were released from bondage in Egypt — a type of prison. God split the sea for us, and we journeyed through to the other side. God also led us through the desert, and cured us of all our illnesses at Mount Sinai. Thus, we have every reason to bring an offering of thanksgiving, along with its three types of matzos, and it is fitting that on the Seder night, we remind ourselves of this offering.

The Gaon of Vilna had a different practice, however, based on the opinion of the *Rishonim* — the early authorities — that only two matzos should be used for the mitzvos of the night: Divide one and keep the other whole, and say two blessings on both.

The Gaon also maintained that it is a mitzvah to eat matzah not only on the Seder night, but throughout all the days of Pesach. To support this view, the Gaon cited the verse (*Shemos* 12:15): *For seven days you shall eat matzos.* He maintained that when the Sages said that eating matzah is an obligation only on the Seder night, while eating it *for seven days* is voluntary, they meant only to draw a contrast between the Seder night and the rest of Pesach, in that the mitzvah of eating matzah on the Seder night is greater than during the remainder of the holiday.

However, said the Gaon, the Sages did not mean to say that there is no mitzvah at all in eating matzah during the rest of Pesach. On the contrary, the verse indicates that throughout the seven days, every time one eats matzah, he indeed fulfills a mitzvah.

Haste

As the Haggadah deals explicitly with bondage and redemption, the matzah alludes to these two opposites. That is, the essence of matzah is that it is nothing more than flour and water, and it is made in great haste. It is simple, lowly, and also rushed, just as the Jews, lowly slaves, were rushed to work by their Egyptian taskmasters, and were rushed out of Egypt at the time of their redemption.

Before being freed, the Jews were under the rule of harsh Egyptian overseers, who forced them to toil incessantly. Even at night they were not allowed to rest. Their oppressors would rouse them out of bed before the sun came up, and the bread that the Jews would prepare was made in haste and had no time to rise. They would have to eat it as it was, and hurry off to their labors.

When the power of their oppressors was broken and the Egyptians chased the Jews out of Egypt, again the Jews had no time to wait for their bread to rise. Suddenly, the King of kings revealed Himself to them and redeemed them.

> *And they baked the dough which they would take from Egypt, and made it into matzah cakes, for it had no time to rise, for they were banished from Egypt. They were not allowed to tarry, and could not even gather provisions for themselves for the way (Shemos 12:39).*

This is the nation's character, and also its greatness. They do not seek respite. Rather, what they seek is to fulfill their mission. When they are humbled they do not despair, for they realize that their salvation is always near, and they never give up hope. On the contrary, they accept hardship with love, and in Egypt they knew that the harsh slavery was a means of bringing the date of their redemption closer. Thus, they ate their lowly bread as slaves, but recognized the taste of freedom in it.

When they enjoy good times, they do not become haughty, for they remember their past, that they were slaves in Egypt and that it was God Who freed them, explaining: So that you and your servant shall rest [on Shabbos] as you [were given rest from your Egyptian taskmasters]! (Devarim 5:14). Thus, they eat their bread in freedom, but they well recall the taste of bondage and exile.

This way of looking at things is reflected in the Torah itself. While the Jews were still in Egypt, and were commanded to eat matzah, they were to eat it with the Pesach offering, so the matzah then was a symbol of becoming free. Forty years after their redemption, God told Moshe to again teach them to eat matzah on the Seder night, and although now they were far from Egypt, matzah is called *the bread of poverty* (Devarim 16:3). Why? *In order that you shall remember the day that you left Egypt, all the days of your lives!* (Ibid).

In addition, when God redeemed them from Egypt, the Jews were freed from servitude to mortals, but they accepted upon themselves servitude to Heaven. Instead of being servants of Pharaoh, they were now servants of God. This is the greatest freedom of all, for by working hard to be a faithful servant, the Jew helps and elevates himself, and the entire world is elevated with him.

When they were in Egypt, they toiled and suffered, so that they could quickly pay off their obligation as slaves, and would merit to be freed. When they were redeemed, they immediately set to work again, hastening to rectify what had been done by the twenty-six generations that preceded them, so that the world would not be deprived of its King, and the Divine image in man would again appear.

God told the Jews: *You have seen what I did to Egypt* (Shemos 19:14). The Egyptians had been at ease, and their very tranquillity led to their downfall. *You, though, shall be for Me a kingdom of priests* — examples and representatives for all peoples, energetically fulfilling His Will, serving God, the Lord of Hosts.

Only the Jews said: *We shall do, and [only later] we shall hear.* Only the Jews hurry to fulfill God's Will, without questions, willing to act now and "hear" only later if there are explanations for the commands. *For you left Egypt in haste.* In the merit of this special trait [God says], and in the merit of your hurried departure from Egypt, may you never become haughty — may the leaven in your dough never have time to rise. May God's Presence be upon you always, and may others call you His servants, forever! *Praised are the servants of God! (Tehillim 135:1)*

Maror and Charoses

Both men and women must eat a *k'zayis* of *maror* at the Seder, for *maror*, the bitter herbs, symbolizes the bitterness of the Egyptian enslavement, and women, too, were forced to be slaves. The Torah states (*Shemos* 1:14): *And they embittered their lives with hard labor*, referring to all the Jews who were in Egypt, both men and women.

The Sages delineated the different vegetables which can be used for this mitzvah: Romaine lettuce, endive, horseradish, and bitter herbs. Optimally, lettuce should be used. Our Sages said that lettuce is especially appropriate, for it is reminiscent of what the Jews experienced in Egypt: at first it is sweet and then it becomes bitter, just as our servitude was at first "sweet" and only later became bitter.

At the beginning, the Egyptians talked to them nicely about working for their host nation, and the Jews went to work willingly, not knowing what was to follow. The verse says (*Shemos* 1:13): *And the Egyptians made the Jews work with* פרך — *parech*, which literally means they forced them to work "hard." However, the Hebrew letters can also suggest "with a soft mouth" (*peh rach*), meaning that initially, when the Egyptians enticed the Jews by talking to them softly and nicely, the bitterness was hidden.

Furthermore, the Hebrew word for "lettuce" is חסה (*chasah*), which is very similar to the word for "pity" — חס (*chas*), to remind us of the pity that God showed for us when He redeemed us.

Understanding the Seder

The Sages ordained that the *maror* be dipped into *charoses* at the Seder.* One should be careful, however, to shake most of the *charoses* off after the dipping, so that the bitterness of the *maror* can still be tasted.

Charoses also contains numerous allusions, one of them due to the fact that its main ingredient is apples. Our Sages explain that this reminds us of the apple trees under which, it is said, the Jewish women in Egypt would give birth, far from the notice of the Egyptians, who had decreed death on all newborn Jewish males, as is written (*Shir haShirim* 8:5): *Under the apple tree I stirred you. Your mother was in travail with you there. There, she who bore you suffered her pains.*

Why did the Jewish women choose to give birth specifically under apple trees? Unlike other fruit trees, which first produce leaves to protect their fruit, and only afterwards sprout their fruit, the apple tree first brings out its fruit, and the protective leaves come out later. In Egypt, as a result of the enslavement, the Jewish men had become discouraged, and therefore separated themselves from their wives, so that they would not bring any more children into the world, who also would have to suffer the enslavement. The women, however, did not agree to this. They wanted to continue to bear children. Thus, they persuaded the men, and encouraged them to continue with this important mitzvah. Their message was, "Let us first bear fruit, as does the apple tree, and let the protection for our fruit be provided later, by the Holy One, Who surely will redeem us."

The Jewish women concealed their pregnancies from the murderous Egyptians, and when it came time to give birth, the women went out to the fields, to the apple trees, in great pain and unprotected, but with faith and trust that God soon would reveal Himself and protect them as well as the children. The verse alludes to this (*Ibid*): *Who is this coming up out of the desert,*

---
* Commentators differ as to exactly why we do this. According to Rashi, the dipping is a precautionary measure, taken only on the Seder night, against the remote possibility of the presence of a harmful substance in the *maror*.

leaning on her beloved one? Under the apple tree...

This virtuous act of the women sweetened the bitterness that our forefathers suffered, and enabled them to withstand the Egyptian servitude. Thus, on the Seder night, when we commemorate the bitter servitude by eating *maror*, we sweeten it with a dip made of apples.

In *Shir haShirim*, which depicts the love that exists between God and Israel, the Jewish Nation is compared to other types of fruits — pomegranates (4:3), figs (2:13), dates, (7:9) and nuts (6:11). It is customary to put these fruits into the *charoses*, too. Each fruit, in its own way, expresses the praiseworthy behavior of Israel — how the Nation copes through times of stress. Precisely because of her special character, the bitter is made sweet for her, and she merits redemption.

On the Seder night, we do not simply retell the events that took place in Egypt. Rather, we try to actually experience those events personally, for when God redeemed our forefathers, He redeemed us with them. Every taste that they tasted, bitter or sweet, we taste, too.

As mentioned above, *charoses*, whose ingredients are mixed and ground, also is in remembrance of the mortar the Jews made in Egypt in order to produce bricks. Even the letters of *charoses* (חרסת) remind us of this clay-like material, for חרסת is like חרס (*cheres*), which means "vessels of clay." The cinnamon and other spices in *charoses* remind us of the straw that was in this building material. Thus, *charoses* should be made to be sticky, with a consistency which is similar to mortar.

We also noted previously that, on the Seder night, the different observances call contrasts to mind — redemption as opposed to slavery, glory as opposed to degradation. *Charoses* is sweet while *maror* is bitter, and thus we temper the bitterness of the *maror* by dipping it into the sweet *charoses*, just as our forefathers tempered the bitterness of their servitude by looking forward to the redemption.

Red wine is an ingredient in the *charoses*, too, and as stated, the redness is to remind us of blood, both the blood of Jewish children who were slaughtered by Pharaoh, and the blood of two mitzvos — circumcision and the Pesach lamb.

Thus, the underlying theme is that things that we consider bitter are not completely void of sweetness, and things that we consider sweet are not completely void of bitterness. Servitude is not automatically servitude, and freedom is not automatically freedom. Rather, if one subscribes to the ways of Pharaoh and Egypt, exposing himself to their defilement, then even sweetness becomes bitter, and even freedom becomes servitude. If one turns to God, however, trusting Him and following in His Ways, then even bitterness becomes sweetness, and even servitude becomes freedom.

The Haggadah says: *We were slaves to Pharaoh in Egypt.* That is, as long as we ascribed power and greatness to Pharaoh, and put stock in him, we actually were slaves in Egypt. But *God took us out* — as soon as we ascribed power and greatness to God, and we put our stock in Him instead, we became free, really free, even though physically we were still in chains.

Then, the Haggadah continues: *And if God had not freed our forefathers from Egypt* — that is, if our forefathers had thought that it was Pharaoh who had freed them, and not God; or that they had escaped from Egypt on their own power — *then we and our children and our children's children would still be slaves in Egypt.* Our freedom is based exclusively on our connection to God, Who chose us above all other nations, and constantly keeps us in His care. It was God Who redeemed us from Egypt, and always, we ascribe power and greatness only to Him. This is our freedom and our true salvation.

Karpas

Although *karpas* literally means "celery," any type of vegetable can be used, as long as it is not bitter. *Karpas* can be either a raw vegetable or a cooked one. If the vegetable normally is eaten raw, one should not cook it, and if it is normally cooked, one should not eat it raw.

Immediately after Kiddush we wash our hands, in preparation for eating the *karpas*. No blessing is said on this washing, however. One does say a blessing on the *karpas* — the blessing over vegetables — and before he does so, he should intend that his blessing cover also the *maror* that he will eat later. Less than a *k'zayis* is eaten of the *karpas*, so that no after-blessing is required.

On the simplest level, the eating of the *karpas*, preceded by the hand-washing, is simply a means to arouse the curiosity of the children, to make them ask questions which will lead to the telling of the Haggadah. Some say that the *karpas* is eaten so that later, when we come to perform the mitzvah of *maror*, we will not have to say two blessings: the specific blessing on the mitzvah (*Who has commanded us on the eating of maror*) and the general blessing on vegetables. Saying these two blessings together would be awkward, and contradictory in a way, because the normal blessing over vegetables is a blessing of thanks and praise and thus is a happy blessing, while the special blessing over *maror* (and the *maror* itself) is to remind us of the bitterness of the Egyptian enslavement.

It is customary to dip the *karpas* into salt water or vinegar. When the Temple stood, and for many years afterwards, it was customary for people to eat in a state of ritual purity. This required that before they could eat any moist food, they would have to wash their hands, for the Sages had decreed that moist foods (or liquids) that were touched by unwashed hands would become ritually impure. Nowadays, as we no longer have the custom to eat in ritual purity, we wash our hands only before eating bread (or matzah). On the Seder night, however, we remind ourselves of the practices associated with ritual purity, and wash before the *karpas* — and this departure from our norm serves to arouse the children's curiosity.

What is more, there is the requirement to recline at the Seder, in the way of royalty and nobility, and one also acts as the *kohanim*, serving in the Temple. The *kohanim* were obligated to eat according to the laws of ritual purity, and thus it is fitting that we, too, observe these laws on this night. Most authorities say, however, that the washing before *karpas* is not obligatory, so that the blessing over washing one's hands should not be

Understanding the Seder

said. The Gaon of Vilna maintained that the blessing should be said.

There are a number of allusions and mystical associations involving the eating of *karpas*. Eating a lot of *maror* can cause discomfort, and eating *karpas* is a remedy for the problem. We eat the *karpas* first, however, to signify that whatever the ill, God creates its remedy first. So, too, regarding the Egyptian slavery — God prepared Israel's redemption even before the slavery started.

When we reverse the letters of the word *karpas* (כרפס) the result is ס — whose numerical value is 60 — followed by פרך, "hard", the word used by the Torah (*Shemos* 1:14) to describe the rigorous labor that the Egyptians forced on our people. It is known through tradition that the number of Jewish males who were enslaved in Egypt totalled six hundred thousand. Thus the word *karpas* alludes to these six hundred thousand, who were forced into hard labor. The letters of *karpas* also are close to those of *ketones pasim*, the coat of many colors which Yaakov gave to Yosef, and which played a large part in bringing the Jews down to Egypt in the first place.

Korech

After the mitzvah of eating *maror* dipped in *charoses*, the leader of the Seder takes the remaining whole matzah — that is, the third (bottom) matzah (*Yisrael*) and breaks it, in order to place *maror* between the bottom matzah's two pieces, to make a sandwich called *korech*. The sandwich should be made of one *k'zayis* of matzah and one *k'zayis* of *maror*. Each participant at the Seder must have such a sandwich (usually the third matzah is not large enough to provide each participant with the required *k'zayis* of matzah, but each participant should be given at least a bit of the third matzah for this mitzvah. He should use other *shemurah* matzah to complete the *k'zayis*, the required amount.

The blessings over matzah and *maror* were made previously, when each was eaten separately, so that now, when the two are eaten together, no blessing is said. However, as noted above, we do make a short declaration before eating the *korech*, stating that what we are about to do is in accordance with the opinion of Hillel the Elder. It is a three-word statement, which is included in the Haggadah: *Zecher l'Mikdash k'Hillel* — In remembrance of the Temple, according to Hillel.

One should recline while eating the *korech*, for in the opinion of Hillel, the mitzvah of eating matzah in the days of the Temple was not to eat the matzah alone, but to make a sandwich with it, placing *maror* together with meat of the Pesach sacrifice, as the filling between two pieces of matzah. Because reclining is required for matzah (and also for the eating of the *Pesach* when the Temple is standing), reclining also is required when eating the *korech*.

In addition, it is best to not to speak or make any other type of interruption from the time that we first eat matzah, by itself, until we finish eating the *korech*. This way, the prior blessing that we made on the mitzvah of eating matzah also covers the matzah of the *korech*.

In the days of the Temple, when eating *maror* was an obligation of the Torah, one could eat matzah with *maror*, as Hillel prescribed, and thereby fulfill the two mitzvos at once. This was so because if the obligations to eat two different foods are Torah obligations, the taste of neither of the two foods can "nullify" the taste of the other. In the days of the Temple, both matzah and *maror* were Torah obligations, for the Torah states that the Pesach offering must be eaten with each. Thus, matzah could be eaten with *maror*.

Nowadays, however, lacking the Temple, eating matzah is a Torah obligation, but eating *maror* is not, so that we cannot eat the two together and gain credit for fulfilling both mitzvos, for the taste of matzah is nullified by the presence of the *maror* taste. Thus, even according to Hillel, matzah these days must be eaten by itself, and the *korech* can serve only as a remembrance.

Some dip the sandwich into *charoses*, in order to counteract its bitterness, while others feel that the presence of the matzah makes this unnecessary.

The Roasted Bone and the Egg

In the times of the Temple, the practice was that after Kiddush was made on the night of the Seder, the table would be brought in. On it would be the matzah, *maror*, *karpas* (a different vegetable from the *maror*), *charoses*, meat from the Pesach offering, and also meat from the *Chagigah*, or festival, offering. Earlier in the day, at the Temple, the Pesach and *Chagigah* offerings were slaughtered together, with the intention of eating the meat of both at the Seder table. The meat of the *Chagigah* had to be eaten prior to the meat of the Pesach offering, for, as noted above, the *Pesach* could not be eaten until the Seder participants were already satiated. Its taste had to be the last food taste in one's mouth at the night's end.

Because of our sins, however, the Temple was destroyed, and we no longer can bring the Pesach and festival offerings. To commemorate them, though, we use a roasted bone with some meat on it, to stand for the Pesach offering, and a cooked egg to stand for the *Chagigah*. In the days of the Temple, if the fourteenth of Nissan, *erev Pesach*, fell on Shabbos, there was no *Chagigah* meat on the Seder table, because slaughtering the *Chagigah* on Shabbos is prohibited. These days, when the egg stands simply as a remembrance of the *Chagigah*, it is placed on the Seder plate no matter when the fourteenth falls.

Today we are lacking these two precious mitzvos, and at the Seder table, we must satisfy ourselves with mere remembrances of them. Nevertheless our faith remains strong, and we are certain that God will redeem us, too, and rebuild the Temple, so that we will be privileged to partake of the sacrificial meat again, just as in the days of old.

In fact, the *Talmud Yerushalmi* says that the egg and the roasted bone symbolize God's desire to redeem us *with an outstretched arm* — the bone symbolizing the arm, and the egg, *beya* in Aramaic, which also means "desire," standing for God's desire. Just as our redemption from Egypt was not dependent upon our righteousness or merits, but took place only because it was God's desire, so too do we look forward to seeing the Ultimate Redemption, even if we do not deserve it. The Redemption is God's desire, and thus we are certain that it will come.

Some say that the egg carries another nuance involving the Redemption to Come. Other foods, such as fruits and vegetables, have a stem, an opening or "mouth" from where their growth begins. An egg, however, has no such "mouth." By putting an egg on the Seder plate, we ask God to seal the mouths of our detractors, who accuse and malign us — who say that since the Redemption has not come after so long, we should realize that we do not deserve it, and we should give up hope of its coming.

Throughout history, those who have plotted and planned to destroy us have always claimed that we are no better than they, and thus we have no reason to hope that God will save us. This is what the Egyptians said to us, until God redeemed us and silenced them. The egg on the Seder plate symbolically silences our enemies, for every year, despite being subjugated, Jews everywhere sit at the Seder table as kings, and jubilantly sing, "Our enemies have disappeared and we remain!" It is fitting, then, that an egg be seen on the Seder plate, to express our faith that the mouths of the nations will be closed.

Others say that the egg and the roasted bone also allude to Aharon and Moshe, who served as God's agents in redeeming the Jews from Egypt. In the Haggadah, Aharon and Moshe are not mentioned at all, so as not to detract from the praise given to God this night. The Haggadah notes that when Moshe retold the story of the Exodus, he said (*Devarim* 26:8): *And God took us out of Egypt...* — Himself, and not by means of any angel, or any messenger. Thus, the egg and the roasted bone mention, symbolically, Aharon and Moshe.

Another allusion provided by the egg and the bone is connected to the explanation of the Rambam, as to why God commanded us in Egypt to slaughter specifically lamb to eat on the night of our redemption. In his *Moreh Nevuchim*, the Rambam writes:

> ...to instill in us true faith in God, and to drive out the false beliefs in which we were immersed in Egypt, God commanded us to slaughter the Pesach lamb, for the Egyptians worshiped the lamb — i.e., the astrological sign of the lamb — and they forbade the slaughter of sheep. For this reason we were commanded to specifically slaughter this animal, and throw its blood on our doorposts, so that we would be cleansed of the erroneous beliefs of the Egyptians. When we fulfilled these commands, we declared that our belief is the opposite from theirs. According to them, the slaughter of sheep is a reason for plagues and suffering, while according to us, the slaughter of sheep saves us from these things.

Thus, it is fitting that we have meat of some sort on the Seder plate, and an egg, which also comes from an animal, since the Egyptians, in their false beliefs, would not eat animals, or anything that comes from animals. The *Kesser Shem Tov* writes:

> In my opinion, the Egyptians at the time of Moshe were like the Hindus of India today, who because of their beliefs, refrain from eating meat, milk, fish, or eggs. In order to distance ourselves from these foolish beliefs, we place an egg and a roasted bone on the Seder plate.

Eggs in Salt Water

After eating matzah, *maror*, and *korech*, it is customary to bring hard-boiled eggs to the table, which are dipped into salt water and eaten. As noted, some eat these eggs immediately after Kiddush.

The *Mishnah Berurah* (476:11) says that because the egg on the Seder plate is in remembrance (according to the Vilna Gaon) of the *Chagigah* offering, everyone at the table should be careful to eat of it at the Seder, while eating the other eggs is a matter of custom.

This custom is interpreted in several ways. The Darkei Moshe writes that it is a sign of mourning, for eggs are the food served to mourners, and every year, the Seder night falls on the same night of the week as does Tishah b'Av, which was when the Temple was destroyed. Thus eating eggs reminds us that now that we lack the Temple, we cannot bring the Pesach offering.

The Vilna Gaon supports this interpretation by noting a passage from *Midrash Eichah*. *Eichah*, which is read on Tishah b'Av, says (3:15): *You [God] have satiated me with bitterness, You have filled me with wormwood*. The Midrash comments:

> *"You have satiated me* במרורים *— with bitterness," this refers to the first night of Pesach, as it is written (Shemos 12:8): "You shall eat it [the offering] with matzos* ומרורים *— and maror"; "You have filled me with wormwood" refers to the night of Tishah b'Av. The first night of Pesach is [like the] night of Tishah b'Av.*

The Vilna Gaon explains that the Midrash means that God has us satiate ourselves on *maror* at the Seder (for we eat it once by itself and again in the *korech*) partly because He "satiated us with wormwood" — caused us sorrow — on Tishah b'Av. Thus, the custom of eating eggs at the Seder also is to remind us of Tishah b'Av.

The Chasam Sofer offers an alternative explanation for the custom of eating eggs:

> *With other foods, the longer they are cooked, the softer they become. Eggs become harder, though, which makes them much like Israel. The more that other nations oppress us, the harder we become — the more we resist them, and the less likely it is that we will become assimilated with them. The Jews are, as the Torah says (Bemidbar 23:9): a nation that dwells alone and (Shemos 1:12): the more they [the Egyptians] oppressed them, the more they multiplied.*

Because the Haggadah says that we dip foods twice at the Seder (*karpas* and *maror*), it is better that the hard-boiled eggs be dipped into the salt water by means of a fork or spoon, and not by hand, so that we do not wind up dipping three times at the Seder.

Some maintain that the eggs are dipped specifically into

salt water to remind ourselves of the destruction of Sedom, which is said to have taken place on the Seder night. The entire valley of Sedom, which originally was fertile and productive, was overturned, and became flooded water, which eventually became the salty waters of the Dead Sea. Lot's wife, who looked back to view the destruction of Sedom, was turned to a pillar of salt. Why a pillar of salt?

The Sages tell us that when the angels came to visit Lot, his wife went to neighbors, asking to borrow salt. By doing so, her intention was to inform on Lot, and let everyone know that there were guests in her house, which was a violation of the laws of Sedom. She wanted the citizens of Sedom to come and harm the guests, for she, as they, detested the idea of hospitality. Thus, even though she was allowed to flee before Sedom was destroyed, that was only in the merit of her husband, and she was told not to turn around to view the destruction. When she turned around to see what was happening to the people of Sedom, she was turned to salt, for she actually deserved the same fate that they suffered. (*Bereshis Rabbah*)

We, on the other hand, enjoy having guests, especially at the Seder table. In fact, at the start of the Haggadah, we extend an invitation: *Whoever is hungry, let him come and eat. Whoever is in need, let him come and join us!* We do not fear being punished by salt or its waters. Rather we eat these things and enjoy them, for what is a source of suffering for the wicked is a source of pleasure for the righteous.

The Afikoman

When the meal is finished, before we recite Grace after Meals, the matzah called *Afikoman* is taken from the place where it was hidden when we started to say the Haggadah, and everyone at the table eats a piece of it, while reclining on his left side. No blessing is recited. Each person should eat at least a *k'zayis* of the *Afikoman*, but some eat double this portion.

If the *Afikoman* is not large enough to provide every participant with the required amount, then at least the leader should eat the required amount from it, and the other participants should use other *shemurah* matzah. Similarly, if the *Afikoman* was eaten by mistake earlier, or if it simply cannot be found, the leader may take regular *shemurah* matzah, too. This is allowed because at the beginning of the Seder, when the matzah was hidden away, this did not designate that the particular matzah was the *Afikoman*. Rather, the hiding was simply to arouse the curiosity of the children, to make them ask, "Why are you hiding the matzah? We haven't eaten yet!" We answer their question by beginning to tell them the Haggadah.

One should be careful to finish eating the *Afikoman* before *chatzos*, i.e., before half the night has passed, for the *Afikoman* commemorates the Pesach offering, and this is when the eating of the Pesach offering had to be completed. *Chatzos*, it should be noted, is not necessarily twelve o'clock midnight. Rather, it is half the period between the onset of night and sunrise the following day.

What is more, it is preferable to eat the *Afikoman* soon enough so that afterwards, when we say the remainder of Hallel, the Hallel can be completed before *chatzos*.

After eating the *Afikoman*, we pour the third cup of wine and proceed with Grace after Meals. From then on, we are not allowed to eat anything, so that the last food taste in our mouths is the taste of the *Afikoman*. Except for the third and fourth cups of wine, all that we are allowed to drink is water.

As noted, the *Afikoman* symbolizes the Pesach offering, which at the meal had to be eaten last, when no one was hungry anymore. This is as kings eat — even though they are full. If the *Pesach* were to be eaten earlier, while the Seder participants still were hungry, they might come to break the bones of the Pesach offering, which is forbidden.

The Pesach offering was always eaten with great joy, as is described in the Talmud (*Pesachim* 85a): *They ate only a k'zayis of it, but their songs of praise as they ate it burst through the roof and climbed to Heaven.*

So, too, when we eat the *Afikoman*, it is fitting to do so with songs of praise and joy. Some maintain that the *Afikoman* commemorates the matzah that was eaten with the Pesach sacrifice, as was the opinion of Hillel the Elder. Many therefore observe the custom of eating a double portion for the *Afikoman* (two *k'zeisim*) — one to commemorate the meat of the sacrifice and the other to commemorate the matzah.

The Maharil writes that the basis for the custom of eating two *k'zeisim* of *Afikoman* is to demonstrate how beloved this mitzvah is to us, for all other mitzvos involving eating require only one *k'zayis*.

Afikoman Customs

In Rashi's memory aids for the Seder, the word which serves to remind us to eat the *Afikoman* is *tzafun*, which means "hidden," for the *Afikoman* has been hidden away since the start of the Seder, to be taken out to be eaten only when the meal is over. Some hide the *Afikoman* in the pillow or cushion which is used for reclining. *Tehillim 31:20* states: *How great is the goodness that you have hidden (*צפנת*, tzefanta) for those who fear you*, and according to the Rokeach, this may be the basis for the custom. *Shemos 12:17* says: *And you shall guard the matzos*, and *Minhagei Yeshurun* says that this verse may be the custom's source.

Many customs are associated with the *Afikoman*. Some eat it in great haste while holding a walking stick in hand, in fulfillment of the verse (*Shemos 12:11*): *And you shall eat it [the Pesach offering]: your loins girded, shoes on your feet and walking stick in hand*, expecting to have to leave at any moment.

Similarly, among Sepharadim, at the beginning of the Seder, when the middle matzah is broken, the larger piece to be the *Afikoman*, it is not hidden away at all. Rather, it is tied onto the shoulder of a child, who leaves the room and then knocks on the door. He is asked, "Who is there?" He responds, "Israel!" "From where have you come?" "From Egypt!" "Where are you going?" "To Jerusalem!" "What are you carrying?" "Matzah!" The child then enters the room, looks at the Seder table, and begins to ask the Four Questions, and the *Afikoman* stays on his shoulder until it is time to eat it.

In the Land of Israel, many have the custom of wrapping the *Afikoman* in a white cloth before hiding it. Then, while all are sitting, it is placed on someone's right shoulder, who transfers it to his left shoulder. Then the person next to him takes it and places it on his own right shoulder, etc., until it travels around the whole table. The last one to receive it recites the verse (*Shemos* 12:34): *Their kneading trays were bound in cloths on their shoulders*, and then he takes four steps with it. He is asked, "From where have you come?" He responds, "From Egypt!" "Where are you going?" "To Jerusalem!" he says, and then everyone calls out loudly, "Next year in Jerusalem!"

The Shelah writes that just as Jews have the custom of kissing the Torah scroll, *tefillin, mezuzos*, and other sacred objects, some have the custom of kissing not only the *Afikoman* and the other matzos, but even the *maror*.

Another custom is based on a statement in the Talmud (*Pesachim* 109a): *We learned (in a baraysa), R. Eliezer said:* חוטפין (chotfin) *matzos on the night of Pesach so that the little children will not fall asleep*. The word *chotfin* means "we snatch" or "we grab," and thus R. Eliezer's statement is the basis of the widespread custom of allowing little children to snatch the *Afikoman*, at the first chance, and to surrender it only for a ransom. Actually, R. Eliezer meant only to say that on the Seder night, the matzos are "eaten quickly" so that before the children fall asleep, they, too, will be able to have some. Nevertheless, the custom is ancient and widespread, so that some maintain that we should not object to such behavior.

Others disagree, saying that such "snatching" can cause the matzah to fall to the floor, making it unfit to eat, and that the children should be stopped from trying to grab the *Afikoman*. Also, since the whole night is so structured and organized, it does not make make sense that such a disorderly practice should be allowed, being that there are many other nicer and more polite ways to keep the children awake and interested.

Some have the custom of saving a piece of the *Afikoman* from the Seder and keeping it for the whole year, as a means of helping to guard oneself from the evil inclination. Although the mitzvah of eating matzah applies only on the Seder night (and, according to the Vilna Gaon, throughout Pesach), keeping one's *chametz* under control — his pride and other aspects of the evil inclination — is important at all times, the whole year round.

The Meaning of the Word Afikoman

The word *Afikoman* means different things to different commentators. The Mishnah says, in *Pesachim*:

אֵין מַפְטִירִין אַחַר הַפֶּסַח אֲפִיקוֹמָן

which means: *After we have exempted ourselves from [the mitzvos of eating different food items on the Seder night, and we have eaten the required amount of] the Pesach offering [when we were no longer hungry], we do not say Afikoman.* The word *afiku* means "let us take out" and what exactly the *man* means is where the commentators differ.

According to some, the Mishnah is saying that once the *Pesach* is eaten (during the days of the Temple, that is), we do not say afterwards, "Let us take out the food that has been on the table (*man*) and bring in desserts." Though eating desserts is the way of nobility and royalty, and would be fitting for us on the Seder night, the Mishnah teaches us that we cannot have dessert after eating the meat of the Pesach offering, for its taste must be the last food taste in our mouths this night.

Others say that *man* means "clothing," and the Mishnah is teaching us that we should not say, "Let us take out clothing," to change what we are wearing now and put on different clothes, to go to someone else's house to eat of their Pesach offering. Again, although to go visiting is the way of free men, we are not allowed to do so, for the only Pesach offering permitted to a person is the one that was slaughtered with him in mind, and he cannot eat of any other.

Thus, the last matzah of the Seder is called *Afikoman*, to remind us of the days that the Temple stood — of laws about the Pesach offering. Nowadays, it is after the last matzah that we do not have any dessert, and we do not change clothes and go visiting, while in the days of the Temple, these restrictions applied to after we had eaten the Pesach offering. Still, the word *Afikoman* brings to mind freedom — the ways of kings and nobility — and it also reminds us of the days of the Temple. Thus, it is a fitting name for the last taste in our mouths on the Seder night.

The Structure of the Haggadah

The Rambam writes (*Hilchos Chametz u'Matzah*, Chapter 7):

It is a positive mitzvah of the Torah, to relate on the night of the fifteenth of Nissan, the miracles and wonders that were done for our forefathers in Egypt. The verse states (Shemos 13:3): Remember this day on which you came out of Egypt, [an obligation that is] similar to, Remember the Shabbos day. (That is, just as there is a mitzvah to remember the Shabbos with words, and as the Sages ordained, this is done over wine at Kiddush, so, too, there is the mitzvah of Haggadah, to remember the Exodus from Egypt with words, and the Sages ordained that this remembering also be over wine, that of the Four Cups.) How do we know that the obligation[to speak of the Exodus] is on the night of the fifteenth? The verse says (Shemos 13:8): And you shall tell your son on that day, saying, because of this... — at the time that you have the matzah and maror in front of you (i.e., on the Seder night), and even if one does not have a son. Even great Sages are obligated to recount the Exodus from Egypt, and all who elaborate and tell the story at great length are worthy of praise.

It is a mitzvah to tell one's children even if they do not ask, for the verse states, And you shall tell your son. Also, the singular is used — "son," and not "sons" — to teach us that a father should explain to each child individually, at his own level of understanding. How is this accomplished? If a child is young, or simply lacking understanding, the father should say to him, "All of us were once slaves in Egypt, like the servants you see here (the father points to pictures). On this night, God, blessed is He, redeemed us, and took us out into freedom." If the child is older and more intelligent, the father should go into more detail about what happened in Egypt, and describe the many miracles that God did for us through Moshe and Aharon. The father should elaborate, as appropriate to the level of each child's understanding.

One also needs to do things differently on this evening, so that the children will take notice and ask, "Why is this night different from all other nights?" The child then can be answered, "Because this happened, and this happened, etc."

And what sort of changes does he make? He distributes nuts and sweets to the children, clears the table away (e.g., of food) before they have a chance to eat. They also grab matzos from one another and things of a similar sort.

If he has no children at the table, then his wife must ask him. If he is not married, then those sitting at the table must ask each other, even if they are the wisest of men. If he is alone, he must ask himself aloud, "Why is this night different from all other nights?"

[When retelling the story of the Exodus] he should begin with the shameful aspect [of our history] and conclude with the praiseworthy part. One begins by saying that first, in the days of Terach and beforehand, our forefathers were non-believers who subscribed to foolish and false ideologies, following in the ways of astrologers and idol-worshipers. One concludes by speaking of the true faith — and how the Omnipresent One brought us near to Him, and set us apart from all the other nations. Similarly [when speaking of Egypt], one begins by describing the slavery and all the evil done to us [all the different ways that we were oppressed in Egypt], and one concludes by describing all the wonders and miracles that were performed for us there, to give us our freedom...and the more that one elaborates, the more he is to be praised.

The mitzvah of relating this story has been fulfilled by our forefathers on the Seder night every single year, from the days of the generation that left Egypt, until the present. There was no set text for the Haggadah, however, until after the 40 years in the desert, and after Yehoshua brought the nation into the Land of Israel — until the days of the Second Temple. Though certain *Tehillim*, which are a part of Hallel, were said even in Egypt, about the Exodus, and others, composed by David and the Prophets who preceded him, were known prior to the Second Temple, the Haggadah text was not yet formalized, and the Seder night story was told by each father in the way that he felt was best, taking into account his own abilities and the levels of understanding of his children. Probably, the verses of the Torah about the Exodus were read, and the father would expound upon them.

This form of retelling the story continued until the days of the Second Temple, until the Sages of the Great Assembly formalized the Haggadah text, including all the different practices, blessings, and prayers. Thus, as early as the days of the Mishnah we find a fixed text for the four questions, as well as for other elements of the Haggadah. Over the generations, they added onto the basic text, selecting various *midrashim*, and quotes and anecdotes from noted Sages. The formalized text was called the *Haggadah* — the "telling" — after the verse (*Shemos* 13:8): *And you shall tell your son...*

After the destruction of the Second Temple, certain changes were made because of the changed circumstances. For example, one of the questions that the children used to ask at the Seder was why on this night only roasted meat was eaten, while on other nights the meat could be boiled. This question could no longer be asked, without the Temple, for we no longer were able to offer the Pesach sacrifice at all, and eating roasted meat at the Seder had become forbidden (see above). In place of this question, the Sages substituted a new one, about why we recline at the Seder table. The phrase that precedes the eating of the *korech* is also an addition made after the destruction, and it goes without saying that so is the statement, *This year we are here. Next year may we be in the Land of Israel.* Several songs as well were added later. By and large, however, the Haggadah that we use today is the same one that was composed by the Sages of the Great Assembly.

Start with Shame, End with Glory

According to the Talmud (*Pesachim* 116a), the most essential part of the mitzvah of Haggadah is: *to start with shame and end with glory.* That is, we must begin the narrative by telling about the shameful part of our history, describing the Nation's lowliness — its suffering before the redemption — and we should end the narrative by speaking of our exaltedness afterwards, which came about because God uplifted us, gave us His commandments, and made us His people.

The Talmud mentions two opinions about this basic structure of the Haggadah. Rav maintains that the denigration that we describe first is in the fact that our ancestors before Avraham were idol-worshipers, and the praise that we speak of which follows the denigration is God's "bringing us close," so that we now serve and worship Him. Shemuel maintains that we do not go so far back into our past. Rather, we speak first about our shameful state in Egypt as slaves, and we conclude by telling of how God freed us.

The Torah itself indicates that the Haggadah should be structured in this two-faceted way, for it states (*Devarim* 6:20): *When your son asks you in the future, "What are these symbols and statutes?" you shall tell him, "We were slaves to Pharaoh in Egypt, and God took us out of Egypt with a Mighty Hand."* The verse seems to be an explicit support for Shemuel, however. On what basis could Rav differ with Shemuel's opinion?

Quite possibly, Rav is not arguing with Shemuel at all. Rather, Shemuel tells us one way to begin with shame and end with praise, and Rav adds another way. The Haggadah, in fact, uses both approaches. The first approach taken in the Haggadah is Shemuel's, for the Haggadah begins, *We were slaves in Egypt*. Later, however, the Haggadah does tell of idolatry in our People's past, as Rav proposes.

We can understand that no argument really exists between

Rav and Shemuel, if we examine Torah verses that actually deal with the Seder night. These verses instruct us about how a father should speak on this night, to four different types of sons. First the Torah refers to a wicked son, then a son who does not know to ask, then a simple son, and finally to a wise son:

> SHEMOS 12:26 (WICKED SON): *And it will be, when your sons shall say to you, "What purpose do you see in this service?"*
>
> SHEMOS 13:8 (SON WHO IS INCAPABLE OF ASKING): *And you shall tell your son on that day saying, "Because of this did God do for me [great things] in Egypt."*
>
> SHEMOS 13:14 (SIMPLE SON): *And it shall be when your son asks you in the future, "What is this?"*
>
> DEVARIM 6:20 (WISE SON): *When your son asks you in the future, "What are these symbols and statutes?"*

Actually, the wicked and the wise sons constitute two general types of sons, and the other two types are sub-categories of these. That is, a son who does not know how to ask is associated with the wicked son, for the wicked son's rebellion against what is good is the cause for others not being interested in what is good. In turn, the simple son is grouped with the wise son, for though the simple son is easily influenced and can be led astray, he just as easily can be put upon the correct path.

Now, since the Torah spoke to different types of sons, and the Torah's answer to the wise son includes both denigration and praise (*We were slaves...and God took us out*) it follows that the Torah's answer to the wicked son also involves this duality. Each son has his own character and personality, however, and how the duality is presented to each one must differ, so that each son is taught something that is appropriate for him.

Thus, Shemuel would agree that the response to the wicked son should say that at first, our ancestors were idol-worshipers. We tell such a son that just as our ancestors were brought in the end to see what is right and true, he too can come around to the right way! Similarly, Rav would agree that for a wise son, who already is going on the right path, it is not

Understanding the Seder

necessary to begin the narrative by talking about the shamefulness of idol-worship. Rather, even Rav would agree that for the wise son, the Haggadah can start by saying that first, *We were slaves in Egypt, and then God took us out.* The wise son appreciates what a great salvation this was, that God freed us from Egypt in order to give us His commandments and make us His people. The wise son wants to learn more about God's commandments, for he knows that fulfillment of these commandments is the means by which we elevate ourselves further, and come even closer to God!

In short, all agree that the proper way to answer the wicked son is to say, "In the beginning, our ancestors worshiped idols, as you do!" This is the denigration to emphasize to this type of son! "But now, *the Omnipresent One has brought us close to Him, to serve Him* and you, in the end, also can come close to Him!"

Similarly, all agree what approaches should be taken regarding the two "sub-category" sons. In the Torah's verses regarding these sons, the answer is not made of two parts, for these two sons do not possess the capacity to listen to a "whole" Haggadah. The two are told only a "half"Haggadah — a half involving praise, one being told something found in the answer to the wicked son, and the other being told something found in the answer to the wise son.

The son who does not even think to ask is associated with the wicked son, so the Torah tells us part of what we answer the wicked son — *For the sake of this [the Pesach offering, representing mitzvos] did God do [great things] for me in Egypt.* This son, who is not stirred to ask questions at the Seder at all, is simply told that fulfilling mitzvos is praiseworthy. The simple son does ask a question, albeit a simple one, and he is told some of what we say to the wise son — *And with a strong arm did God take us out...*

Thus, the dispute between Rav and Shemuel is only over with which son we should begin the Haggadah. Rav maintains that we should begin with the wicked son, who is the first son mentioned in the Torah, and we should explain to him that it was our shameful beginnings that made the bondage and the redemption necessary. Our ancestors had to be purged of the impurities that were left in them from the idol-worship of their predecessors, and the wicked son needs to be purged of his impurities, too! On the other hand, Shemuel maintains that the Haggadah should begin with the wise son, though the wise son is the one that the Torah mentions last. In what merit did God redeem us from Egypt? In the merit of the mitzvos that we fulfilled there, and for the sake of the mitzvos that we would perform in the future — the ones whose details this son is so eager to learn!

In the end, the Haggadah employs Shemuel's approach as well as Rav's approach, intertwining both throughout its marvelous retelling of our unique past.

An Overview

The Haggadah is the means through which we fulfill the Torah mitzvah of retelling the story of the Exodus. All the practices of the Seder night are weaved into it. Furthermore, if one studies the Haggadah carefully, he becomes filled with wonderment, over its high level of structuring and precision, over its profound wisdom and deep insights, on one level after another — starting from the most basic and fundamental principles of Judaism, and reaching deeper and deeper, even into the realm of Jewish mysticism. Every word is holy and profound.

Dividing the Haggadah into Parts

The Haggadah can be divided into ten basic parts:

1. Acts and things which are said to arouse the curiosity of the children, to make them ask questions
2. The Four Questions
3. The answers given to the wise son, and also to the simple son
4. Blessings and thanks to God for granting us our four sons, for even the wicked one can be brought to the truth
5. The proof that the Seder night is the time for the mitzvah of

retelling the story of the Exodus
6. The detailed answer given to the wicked son
7. *Hallel*, its two parts
8. The blessings said at the end of each part of *Hallel*
9. The meal and its attendant mitzvos as part of the Haggadah
10. Concluding praises, including *Shir haShirim*

Part One

We begin with Kiddush, but unlike our normal procedure, we do not start the meal immediately afterwards. We wash our hands, dip the *karpas*, and then eat the *karpas*, separately from the meal. Then we take out one of the three matzos, break it into two, and put half of it away. We lift the remaining matzos, identifying them as *the bread of poverty*, and then we cover them up. The table is set, the Seder plate is ready, but we still do not eat, or even prepare to eat. Then we pour a second cup of wine, but we do not drink it. Hopefully, all this has aroused the curiosity of the children, and one of them will ask: "What is going on?"

Part Two

A son asks, *Why is this night different from all other nights?* No matter whether the son is capable of posing questions on his own, or whether he is not capable, the text of the questions is written out explicitly for him in the Haggadah, and all he needs to do is read it. The children and the other participants probably are full of questions by now, and all ears eagerly await the answers.

Part Three

The father responds, answering as if the questioner is the wise son of the Torah, for what father does not want to regard his son as wise! The father answers as the verse instructs him (*Devarim 6:20*): *When your son asks you in the future...you shall tell him that we were slaves in Egypt, and God took us out...* By doing so, the father fulfills a positive commandment of the Torah!

The Haggadah is not commanded simply for the sake of a wise son who lacks information and is seeking to learn. On the contrary, says the Haggadah: *Even if we are wise, understanding, and filled with Torah knowledge, we still have the mitzvah to retell the story of the Exodus from Egypt!* The Haggadah illustrates this point with a story that took place in Bnei Brak, where five Sages who knew every aspect of the Torah nevertheless sat at the Seder table speaking of the Exodus, and the night was not long enough to allow them to finish! Each one of these Sages had attended Seders in the past, every year, for sixty or seventy years, and had discussed the Exodus, but now, they were able to discover fresh insights and new ideas, and had it not been for their disciples coming to tell them that morning had arrived, they would not have noticed, they were so absorbed in their discussion. According to the Sages, even after the coming of the *Mashiach* it will be a mitzvah to relate the story of the Exodus from Egypt, for the redemption from Egypt was the root for all future redemptions, even the Ultimate Redemption, and he who elaborates on the Exodus from Egypt gains more and more insights from it.

Part Four

Even though not all of our children are wise, and there may be some who are simple, wicked, or so removed from the Seder that they do not think or know to ask — still, we bless God for giving us children, saying "Blessed" four times!

BLESSED IS THE PLACE — that is, *Blessed is the Omnipresent One* — for God is the "place" of the entire world, and because it has a "place" it is able to exist. No one, therefore, no matter how evil he is, can ever be that far from God, and this is a reason to give God praises and thanks.

BLESSED IS HE — We even thank Him for the son who is associated with the evil son, who is so disinterested in the night's special nature, he has already ceased to inquire.

BLESSED IS HE WHO GAVE THE TORAH TO HIS NATION, ISRAEL — All

Understanding the Seder

the more so do we thank God for giving us a wise son, who toils in Torah.

BLESSED IS HE — We also bless God for giving us a simple son, for though he may not be wise, he does perform mitzvos, even though he does so simply because he sees others performing them.

We thank God for all the sons, for when Moshe (*Devarim* 6:20) told the Jewish People: *When you shall come to the Land [of Israel] and your son shall ask you...*, this provided encouragement for that generation, for they knew not only that they would enter the Land of Israel, but also that they would bear sons there! Even though the verse spoke to them of a wicked son, still, he is a son! Our son!

That is, when the Torah speaks of the obligation to educate our children, it tells us that we have to educate all of our children! We must remember this especially on the Seder night, while we all sit around the Seder table, in peace, and discuss the Exodus together, as a family. The power of the Haggadah is so great, that a wicked son can suddenly turn into a wise son, and he who is too removed to even ask a question can suddenly be transformed to one who gets involved, simply because he sees others getting involved! Everyone can experience fulfillment at the Seder, until all four sons lift their voices high, together with their father, singing thanks and praises to God!

We relate that the Torah speaks of four types of sons, and briefly we tell how the Torah wants us to speak to them. The wise son is to be taught all the laws of the Seder, up to the laws governing the *Afikoman*. The wise son is first to be dealt with sternly, but then we soften our voice and start explaining things to him at great length. The simple son is given a simple response, for he asked a simple question, and a detailed response would be too hard for him to grasp. In our response to the son who is too removed to even inquire, we show how displeased we are with the ways of the evil son. The words we say to the son who is too removed to ask, actually serve as a lead-in to our lengthy attempt to appeal to the heart and mind of the evil son, and really, we are directing our words to both of these sons, in order to try to draw them near.

Part Five

Now that the Haggadah has mentioned the Torah verse about the son who does not even know to ask, we expound upon this verse, proving that only on the Seder night can he fulfill the mitzvah of telling about the Exodus from Egypt. He usually is distant and detached, but you stress to him that now is the time to get involved, now or never! No matter whom you invite to your table tonight, when he sees the matzah and *maror* there, when he gazes at the light of your countenance, when he listens to the melodies and the songs, he will listen to what you say, and surely understand.

Part Six

Now comes the time to deal with the most difficult son — the wicked one, the one that the Torah mentions first. Tell him that his ridicule and his estrangement from God are not original: Our ancestors worshiped idols and were far from God, too! Still, God drew the Jewish People close to Him, and you are of the Jewish People, too. In the future, you can draw close to God as well.

He challenges us, asking, "What do we gain from all these ceremonies?" We tell him that we will respond to his question later, but first we need to provide him with background information, to give him a broader perspective on what we are doing tonight.

Our early ancestors, who drew themselves close to God, were the finest of the fine. They were more pure than any of the righteous people who preceded them, but even they had impurities in them and needed further refinement. Avraham had many sons, but the only one who merited to continue in his father's tradition was Yitzchak. Yitzchak, a refinement of Avraham, underwent further refinement, and of his two sons, Esav was too coarse, and was sifted out, so that only Yaakov remained. You, my son, are a descendant of Yaakov! He was the purest of the three Patriarchs — sifted and clean. And you trace your lineage to him!

The sons of Yaakov, who were free of impurity, still needed to descend into Egypt, to suffer the slavery, and experience the redemption, and thereby become purified even more. Thus, they would be fit to undertake the service and the mitzvos whose worth you question.

When they descended into Egypt, they did not know how long they would be there. All they knew was that they had a debt that they needed to repay, and that God had made a promise about when they would complete the payments. Thus, when the time came, and God freed them, they declared, *Blessed is He Who is faithful to His Promise to Israel!*

In truth, even as slaves the Jews blessed God, for they accepted that the date of the redemption was unknown to them, and they left that determination to God. They knew that He would fulfill His promise, and give them not only their freedom, but much, much more. Just as He had kept His promise to Avraham (*Bereshis* 15:13): *Your children will be strangers...they will be enslaved...oppressed...* so, too, would He keep His other promises (Ibid), that *I shall judge the nation that they serve...afterwards they shall leave...with great wealth.*

As the Haggadah says, this faith that God would keep His promises *has stood our forefathers and us* throughout the generations. We have been oppressed and downtrodden, but because of our faith we have remained strong, whether we speak of Yaakov in his dealings with Lavan, the Jews during the Egyptian enslavement, or when they had their backs to the sea and Pharaoh was approaching. And all through our troubled history afterwards, through today and up until the End of Days — our faith keeps us strong and God keeps us alive.

This process of purification in the furnace that was Egypt — how awesome it was! For our forefathers were not thrust into that furnace briefly, refined a bit, and then removed. They were in the furnace around the clock, for over two hundred years, toiling and sweating. Lavan had tried to bring Israel into such subjugation, too, but just as Yaakov never despaired, neither did Israel under the Egyptians! Until finally, God "saw" our suffering and intervened. There were wicked Jews in Egypt, and they, too, went through this purification process. You were not among those who sank into oblivion, and failed to merit the redemption! No, you were saved with the others, and emerged from the furnace refined!

You witnessed the fulfillment of God's promises! You saw how He struck the Egyptians with two hundred and fifty plagues at the Red Sea. You joined those who were saved! And now, my son, come and learn just how grateful we all need to be — those of us who were saved. What do think that "great wealth" is that God promised you after you would leave Egypt? Listen to the Haggadah, and count the fifteen ways that God elevated you, from when you were taken from bondage until you witnessed the building of the Temple in Jerusalem! That Temple was to help us gain atonement for sins. It was for your atonement, too!

You ask: What is the purpose of what we do tonight, and what do we gain by it. Do you think that we will allow your question to remain unanswered?

Rabban Gamliel has already taught us, as the Haggadah says, that one has not fulfilled his obligation of telling about the Exodus unless he at least has spoken about three things: the Pesach sacrifice, the matzah, and the *maror*. Let me begin.

THE PESACH SACRIFICE: This was offered in remembrance of the fact that God passed over the homes of our fathers, as the verse states *(Shemos 12:27): And you shall tell him [the wicked son] it [the Pesach lamb] is an offering to God, Who passed over the homes of Israel in Egypt, when He struck the Egyptians [with the tenth plague, on the night of the Seder].* Could it be that God sent us down to Egypt simply to destroy us as He destroyed the Egyptians?! No, but many of the Jewish homes in Egypt could not be distinguished from Egyptian homes. Just as you, my son, have tried to blend in with non-Jews, and be exactly like them, many Jews in Egypt did the same. But God in His Kindness passed over even those homes, and that is why the verse about that "passing over" ends by saying, *and the people knelt and bowed.* Understand, my son, that God's "passing over" in Egypt, which we commemorate with this offering, was specifically for you and for those like you. Therefore, it is worthwhile for you to sit with us, so that you will understand this offering's meaning.

MATZAH: You question the worth and purpose of this mitzvah, as well. We use matzah to commemorate the fact that our ancestors' dough did not have time to rise before God appeared to them and took them out of Egypt. This is recorded in the continuation of the verse where the Torah says what a father should say to a son such as you (*Shemos* 12:28): *And they baked the dough which they would take out of Egypt, as matzah cakes, unleavened, for they were banished from Egypt and were not able to wait [for the dough to rise].* Isn't this strange? How could anyone rush the Jews out from Egypt if the Will of God were otherwise? The Master of the Universe had broken the laws of nature in Egypt, performing mighty miracles for His People. Why then did the Jews suddenly not have time even to allow their dough to rise?

Understand, my son, that if the Jews had tarried in Egypt even one moment longer, then you and all who speak and act as you, would have sunk so deeply into Egypt's impurity, it would have been impossible to distinguish you from the Egyptians themselves, and you would have been left there with them! It was for your sake, my son, that we were driven out of Egypt in such haste, and God wanted it that way, in order that you be saved! Just as the Pesach offering is meant especially for you, to remind you of God's mercy, so is the matzah! Come, say a blessing on the matzah, and we, too, will say the blessing, and remind ourselves of another miracle that God did for you!

MAROR: The Torah tells us that the Egyptians not only enslaved us, but also treated us with brutality. Consider this analogy: A King has a son and a servant, and the son takes care of the servant, providing him with food and all his other needs. One day, the son misbehaves, and the King orders this servant to punish him. Even though the servant is supposed to punish the son, would he beat him and torture him, after all the son had done for him? So, too, one should ask — Yosef had provided Egypt with all its needs, for many years. Had it not been for Yosef, the Egyptians would have died of starvation. Even though God wanted the Jews to be enslaved in Egypt, how could the Egyptians treat Yosef's descendants so harshly?

We can arrive at the answer by asking another question. The Torah states (*Shemos* 1:8): *And a new king arose in Egypt, who did not know Yosef.* According to *Midrash Rabbah*, this "new king" was actually the same Pharaoh that had appointed Yosef to rule over Egypt, and take care of her. Long after Yosef had died, the Midrash explains, the Egyptian people came to Pharaoh, to ask him if they could make war on the Jews. "You are fools!" Pharaoh told them. "Were it not for Yosef, we would not be alive today!" Hearing this, the people drove Pharaoh from his throne, for three months, until he finally agreed to allow the Egyptians to do as they pleased. Our Sages comment: This teaches you that when Yosef died, the Jews stopped fulfilling the mitzvah of circumcision. The Jews said, "Let us be like the Egyptians." Because they sought to become assimilated, and mix with the Egyptians, God entered the Egyptians' hearts, and transformed their love for the Jews into hatred.

Thus, when the Torah says that *a new king arose...who did not know Yosef,* it means that when Pharaoh, who actually did know Yosef, would look upon the Jews after Yosef passed away, he could not recognize Yosef in them. The Jews had changed dramatically, and as a result, Pharaoh had a dramatic change in attitude towards them, making him *a new king* who issued harsh decrees against them!

And now you see, my son, that most of the bitterness and suffering that we endured in Egypt were only because of Jews like you; and that the miracles that God performed, and other things that He did there, were for your sake only. Thus, you certainly should be at the Seder table. Say a blessing on the *maror*! Eat of it in its required amount, and thank God that He redeemed you from the bitterness in Egypt, so that you may taste bitterness only as a symbol, and not as fact!

Therefore, you and I, your brothers, your children — all of us are duty-bound to give thanks to God, to the One Who performed miracles for our forefathers and for us, and especially for you! Let us exalt His Name, and soon, when we complete the first half of *Hallel*, let us all praise Him together, and bless, *Blessed are You, God Who has redeemed Israel!* We do not say, "Who has redeemed the righteous of Israel," or "the wise" or "the simple" We say: *Who has redeemed Israel* — all of Israel. It is for the redemption of the whole people that we bless God — every type of Jew, and all his four sons.

Part Seven

Hallel follows — songs of praise that were sung by the Jews who left Egypt, by the Prophets throughout the generations, by David, the sweet singer of Israel, by Jews at the Seder table, year after year, throughout history, under all types of conditions and circumstances, whether we were free men or under the yoke of oppression. Having recited the Haggadah, which tells of God's love for us; after speaking at length of the many miracles He wrought for us because of that love; we attain such an exalted spiritual level that we sing with the same feelings that were felt by our ancestors, who actually experienced those miracles!

Normally, the recital of *Hallel* is not stopped in the middle, especially not for a meal! At the Seder, however, we do so, for the Seder meal is not an ordinary repast, but is itself a manner of praising God. Hence, the first part of *Hallel*, the second, and the meal in the middle, should be regarded as one continuous expression of praise and thanks.

Part Eight

After the first half of *Hallel*, we bless, as mentioned above, *Blessed are You, King of the world, Who has redeemed Israel*. After the second half of *Hallel*, we bless what is called *Birkas haShir*, the blessing which normally concludes the *Hallel*. All this, as if to say: Thank You for giving us our mouths, and for giving us hearts that can feel and understand, so that we can sincerely sing Your praises!

Part Nine

This consists of the festive meal, with the matzah, *maror, korech*, the egg, and all the other mitzvos, until the *Afikoman* and Grace after Meals — all the while continuing to discuss the Exodus and the holiday's laws.

Part Ten

The Haggadah concludes with a series of songs and *piyutim* — liturgical poems — which were added to the Haggadah after the period of the Great Assembly. After concluding the Haggadah, it is customary to recite *Shir haShirim*, the most sacred of songs, with great love and devotion to the One Who has exalted us, sanctified us, and has planted love for Him within our hearts — Whose great love for us is no less than that of a husband for his wife.

The Haggadah in Any Language

Since the Haggadah's primary purpose is to teach the children about the Exodus, and to publicize the miracles and wonders to all those attending the Seder, the leader must explain the Haggadah's different elements and supply additional explanations, in a way that is understandable to all those present. He must be especially careful to make sure that the children understand, as well as the Seder participants who are unfamiliar with the language and the expressions used by our Sages. Outside the Land of Israel, where Jews do not usually speak *lashon haKodesh* — Hebrew, the language of the Haggadah — one should recite the Haggadah in the language of that particular country, for that is the language which is familiar to everyone.

On this point, the Beis Yosef writes (*Orach Chayim* 473):

> *It should be recited in a language that the women and children understand, or it should be explained to them. This was the practice of R. Yitzchak of Londerres [one of the ba'alei ha-*

tosafos who lived in London], who would recite the entire Haggadah in English so that the women and children would understand.

It is said of the Chasam Sofer that he would recite the entire Haggadah in both Hebrew and German.

הגדה
של
פסח

The Pesach Haggadah

קַדֵּשׁ

Pour the first cup, pick it up with both hands, and hold it in the right hand. Before beginning to recite the blessings, some say aloud:

הִנְנִי מוּכָן וּמְזוּמָן לְקַיֵּם מִצְוַת קִדּוּשׁ וּמִצְוַת כּוֹס רִאשׁוֹן שֶׁל אַרְבַּע כּוֹסוֹת.

If the Seder falls on Shabbos, start here:

(*In an undertone:*) וַיְהִי עֶרֶב וַיְהִי בֹקֶר

(*Out loud:*)

יוֹם הַשִּׁשִּׁי. וַיְכֻלּוּ הַשָּׁמַיִם וְהָאָרֶץ וְכָל צְבָאָם: וַיְכַל אֱלֹהִים בַּיּוֹם הַשְּׁבִיעִי מְלַאכְתּוֹ אֲשֶׁר עָשָׂה וַיִּשְׁבֹּת בַּיּוֹם הַשְּׁבִיעִי מִכָּל מְלַאכְתּוֹ אֲשֶׁר עָשָׂה: וַיְבָרֶךְ אֱלֹהִים אֶת יוֹם הַשְּׁבִיעִי וַיְקַדֵּשׁ אֹתוֹ כִּי בוֹ שָׁבַת מִכָּל מְלַאכְתּוֹ אֲשֶׁר בָּרָא אֱלֹהִים לַעֲשׂוֹת:

When the Seder comes on a weekday, start here:

סַבְרִי מָרָנָן וְרַבָּנָן וְרַבּוֹתַי:

בָּרוּךְ אַתָּה יְהֹוָה אֱלֹהֵינוּ מֶלֶךְ הָעוֹלָם, בּוֹרֵא פְּרִי הַגָּפֶן:

Kadesh...U'rechatz — Kiddush and afterwards the washing of one's hands — this is not the normal order, for usually, as is written in *Tehillim* 34:15 and 37:27, one must first *turn from evil* (wash) before he can *do good* (make Kiddush). Tonight, however, the reversed order is ap-

KADESH — THE PESACH KIDDUSH

Pour the first cup, pick it up with both hands, and hold it in the right hand. Before beginning to recite the blessings, some say aloud:

Here I am, ready and willing to fulfill the mitzvah of Kiddush and drink the first cup of the Four Cups.

If the Seder falls on Shabbos, start here:

(In an undertone:) It was evening, and it was morning,

(Out loud:)
the sixth day. Heaven and earth were finished with all their legions. On the seventh day God finished His work that He had been doing, and He desisted on the seventh day from His work that He had been doing. God blessed the seventh day and made it holy, for on it He desisted from all His work that He had created and made.

When the Seder comes on a weekday, start here:
Your attention, gentlemen!

BLESSED ARE YOU, Hashem our God, King of the universe, Who creates the fruit of the vine.

propriate, for the redemption from Egypt was hurried as well, and God sanctified the Jews, making them holy, before they had been "washed" and cleansed of the impurities of Egypt. (*Avnei Nezer*)

בָּרוּךְ אַתָּה יְהֹוָה אֱלֹהֵינוּ מֶלֶךְ הָעוֹלָם אֲשֶׁר בָּחַר בָּנוּ מִכָּל עָם וְרוֹמְמָנוּ מִכָּל לָשׁוֹן וְקִדְּשָׁנוּ בְּמִצְוֹתָיו. וַתִּתֶּן לָנוּ יְהֹוָה אֱלֹהֵינוּ בְּאַהֲבָה (לשבת: שַׁבָּתוֹת לִמְנוּחָה וּ) מוֹעֲדִים לְשִׂמְחָה חַגִּים וּזְמַנִּים לְשָׂשׂוֹן (לשבת: אֶת יוֹם הַשַּׁבָּת הַזֶּה וְ) אֶת יוֹם חַג הַמַּצּוֹת הַזֶּה (וְאֶת יוֹם טוֹב מִקְרָא קוֹדֶשׁ הַזֶּה) זְמַן חֵרוּתֵנוּ (לשבת: בְּאַהֲבָה) מִקְרָא קֹדֶשׁ זֵכֶר לִיצִיאַת מִצְרָיִם. כִּי בָנוּ בָחַרְתָּ וְאוֹתָנוּ קִדַּשְׁתָּ מִכָּל הָעַמִּים. (לשבת: וְשַׁבָּת) וּמוֹעֲדֵי קָדְשֶׁךָ (לשבת: בְּאַהֲבָה וּבְרָצוֹן) בְּשִׂמְחָה וּבְשָׂשׂוֹן הִנְחַלְתָּנוּ. בָּרוּךְ אַתָּה יְהֹוָה מְקַדֵּשׁ (לשבת: הַשַּׁבָּת וְ) יִשְׂרָאֵל וְהַזְּמַנִּים:

If the Seder falls on Motza'ei Shabbos, add these two berachos before Shehecheyanu:

בָּרוּךְ אַתָּה יְהֹוָה אֱלֹהֵינוּ מֶלֶךְ הָעוֹלָם
בּוֹרֵא מְאוֹרֵי הָאֵשׁ:

בָּרוּךְ אַתָּה יְהֹוָה אֱלֹהֵינוּ מֶלֶךְ הָעוֹלָם הַמַּבְדִּיל בֵּין קֹדֶשׁ לְחֹל בֵּין אוֹר לְחֹשֶׁךְ בֵּין יִשְׂרָאֵל לָעַמִּים בֵּין יוֹם הַשְּׁבִיעִי לְשֵׁשֶׁת יְמֵי הַמַּעֲשֶׂה. בֵּין קְדֻשַּׁת שַׁבָּת לִקְדֻשַּׁת יוֹם טוֹב הִבְדַּלְתָּ. וְאֶת יוֹם הַשְּׁבִיעִי מִשֵּׁשֶׁת יְמֵי הַמַּעֲשֶׂה קִדַּשְׁתָּ. הִבְדַּלְתָּ וְקִדַּשְׁתָּ אֶת עַמְּךָ יִשְׂרָאֵל בִּקְדֻשָּׁתֶךָ: בָּרוּךְ אַתָּה יְהֹוָה הַמַּבְדִּיל בֵּין קֹדֶשׁ לְקֹדֶשׁ:

Sabbaths for rest and festivals for happiness — Do the words in this blessing mean that we rest only on Shabbos, and we are happy only on festivals? The explanation is:

SABBATHS FOR REST — The attribute of rest which God put into the world on the seventh day of Creation is what allows rest to be en-

BLESSED ARE YOU, Hashem our God, King of the universe, Who chose us out of all peoples and exalted us more than any tongue, and made us holy with His mitzvos. Hashem our God, You gave us with love [On Shabbos: Sabbaths for rest and] festivals for happiness, celebrations and times for joy: this [On Shabbos: Shabbos day and this] day of the Festival of Matzos, the time of our liberty, a hallowed day [On Shabbos: with love] in memory of the Exodus. For You chose us and made us holy out of all peoples, and gave us Your holy [On Shabbos: Shabbos and] Festivals [On Shabbos: with willing love and] with happiness and joy, to be our inheritance. Blessed are You, God our Lord, Who makes [On Shabbos: Shabbos and] the Jewish people and the times holy.

If the Seder falls on Motza'ei Shabbos, add these two berachos before Shehecheyanu:

BLESSED ARE YOU, Hashem our God, King of the universe, Who creates lights of fire.

BLESSED ARE YOU, Hashem our God, King of the universe, Who separates between holy and secular, between light and darkness, between the Jewish people and the gentiles, between the seventh day and the six days of activity. You made a separation between the holiness of Yom Tov and the holiness of Shabbos, and made the seventh day more holy than the six days of activity; You separated and hallowed Your people Israel with Your holiness. Blessed are You, Hashem, Who separates between one holiness and another.

joyed during the other days of the week, as well.

FESTIVALS FOR HAPPINESS — The happiness inherent in the holidays puts happiness into the rest of the year. So says the Torah (*Devarim* 16:14): *And you shall be happy on your festival* — That is, You will be happy all year long with happiness whose root is the happiness of the festival. (*Sefas Emes*)

When saying Shehecheyanu, have in mind that it covers the Yom Tov itself and all the mitzvos of this night. Women [and men, too] who made this berachah when lighting the candles should not make it again during Kiddush, and should not answer Amen to it.

בָּרוּךְ אַתָּה יְהֹוָה אֱלֹהֵינוּ מֶלֶךְ הָעוֹלָם, שֶׁהֶחֱיָנוּ וְקִיְּמָנוּ וְהִגִּיעָנוּ לַזְּמַן הַזֶּה:

Recline on the left side and drink the whole cup, or at least most of it, without pausing in the middle. Everyone should have in mind that they are doing the mitzvah of drinking the first of the Four Cups.

וּרְחַץ

Everyone washes his hands (some people's custom is that only the leader of the Seder washes); the berachah for hand-washing is not said.

כַּרְפַּס

Take less than a k'zayis, dipping it into salt water or vinegar, saying the following blessing. Have in mind that the blessing also will pertain to the maror which is eaten later. Eat without reclining, and distribute to all who are at the table.

בָּרוּךְ אַתָּה יְהֹוָה אֱלֹהֵינוּ מֶלֶךְ הָעוֹלָם, בּוֹרֵא פְּרִי הָאֲדָמָה:

When saying Shehecheyanu, have in mind that it covers the Yom Tov itself and all the mitzvos of this night. Women [and men, too] who made this berachah when lighting the candles should not make it again during Kiddush, and should not answer Amen to it.

*B*LESSED ARE YOU, Hashem our God, King of the universe, Who has given us life, sustained us, and brought us to this time.

Recline on the left side and drink the whole cup, or at least most of it, without pausing in the middle. Everyone should have in mind that they are doing the mitzvah of drinking the first of the Four Cups.

U'RECHATZ — WASHING

Everyone washes his hands (some people's custom is that only the leader of the Seder washes); the berachah for hand-washing is not said.

KARPAS

Take less than a k'zayis, dipping it into salt water or vinegar, saying the following blessing. Have in mind that the blessing also will pertain to the maror which is eaten later. Eat without reclining, and distribute to all who are at the table.

*B*LESSED ARE YOU, Hashem our God, King of the universe, Who creates the fruit of the earth.

יַחַץ

Break the middle matzah into two pieces. Place the larger half in a white cloth, and hide it for the Afikoman. Replace the smaller half between the two whole matzos.

מַגִּיד

While saying the Haggadah we need to have in mind that telling the Pesach story on the Seder night is one of the mitzvos of the Torah.

Before beginning the story, some say:

הִנְנִי מוּכָן וּמְזוּמָן לְקַיֵּם הַמִּצְוָה לְסַפֵּר בִּיצִיאַת מִצְרָיִם.

Some say:

בִּבְהִילוּ יָצָאנוּ מִמִּצְרָיִם.

Yachatz — The matzah symbolizes redemption. Part of the middle matzah, the larger half, is hidden away because the ultimate Redemption has not yet come. (*Sefas Emes*)

Our exit...was in haste — It may happen that the Seder leader finds himself rushing to get the proceedings under way, for he is worried about finishing the meal, in order to fulfill the mitzvah of *Afikoman* within the allotted time. It may happen that one of the children is confused by the fast pace of things, for on the Seder night, everyone at the table is supposed to behave in the manner of nobility, and rushing is inappropriate for nobility. If the child asks for an explanation,

Yachatz — Dividing the Matzah

Break the middle matzah into two pieces. Place the larger half in a white cloth, and hide it for the Afikoman. Replace the smaller half between the two whole matzos.

Maggid — the Pesach Story

While saying the Haggadah we need to have in mind that telling the Pesach story on the Seder night is one of the mitzvos of the Torah.

Before beginning the story, some say:

Here I am, ready and willing to fulfill the mitzvah of telling about the Exodus.

Some say:

Our exit from Egypt was in haste.

we tell him, *Our exit from Egypt was in haste,* and that haste is what led to our freedom. If we had tarried, and had not hurried to leave Egypt, we would not have been redeemed at all.

What was particularly praiseworthy in our hurrying? In Egypt, on the Seder night, we knew that we would be leaving at any moment for an unknown destination, yet we did not even prepare food for the way. We did not even ask where we were going. We did not even ask what our children would eat, for our one thought, our only desire, was to hear God's command to leave, and to heed His command as soon as He gave it. In the merit of our wanting to rush to fulfill the Divine Will, we were redeemed and left Egypt that very night. (*Eshel b'Rama*)

The head of the household lifts the Seder plate, with the matzos on it, and says together with everyone at the table, in a clear voice, happily:

הָא לַחְמָא עַנְיָא דִּי אֲכָלוּ אַבְהָתָנָא בְּאַרְעָא דְמִצְרָיִם. כָּל דִּכְפִין יֵיתֵי וְיֵיכוֹל. כָּל דִּצְרִיךְ יֵיתֵי וְיִפְסַח. הָשַׁתָּא הָכָא לְשָׁנָה הַבָּאָה בְּאַרְעָא דְיִשְׂרָאֵל. הָשַׁתָּא עַבְדֵי לְשָׁנָה הַבָּאָה בְּנֵי חוֹרִין:

This is the bread —This declaration, made when the matzos are uncovered, serves as an introduction, to begin the Haggadah, as well as an invitation to others to join us for the meal. The Torah calls matzah *lechem oni*, and though this is generally translated as "bread of poverty," or "bread of affliction," it is agreed that the term also means, "bread upon which many answers are said." Therefore, the matzah is now uncovered because it should be displayed to everyone during the questions and answers that are heard while the Haggadah is being said. (*Maharal*)

The Haggadah starts with these words, in order that poor people who have joined us at the table should not feel any embarrassment. One of the main joys of the holiday is to be able to help the poor to enjoy Pesach. Thus, it is as if we say to them, "Don't feel sad or downcast. We, too, come from poor ancestors. Some day, you will have means, and will eat at a fine table of your own!" (*Eshel b'Rama*)

Words such as these are found in the Talmud (*Ta'anis 20b*), where we read that all year round, before meals, Rav Huna used to say: *All who need, come and eat!* Thus, the declaration said on the Seder night seems to be rooted in an ancient custom that was preserved through the ages. (*Ha-Ri* of Narbona, in the name of the *Gaonim*)

This is the bread — This declaration also serves as a reminder of the destruction of the Temple, for in the days of the Temple, newly arriving guests could *not* join the Seder once it was under way, to eat the

The head of the household lifts the Seder plate, with the matzos on it, and says together with everyone at the table, in a clear voice, happily:

*T*HIS IS THE BREAD *of poverty that our forefathers ate in the land of Egypt. Whoever is hungry, let him come and eat! Whoever is in need, let him come and join in the Pesach! This year, we are here; next year, in the Land of Israel. This year, we are slaves; next year, free men!*

Pesach offering, for who exactly was allowed to eat the meat of a particular offering on the night of the Seder had to be pre-arranged the preceding afternoon, before the offering was slaughtered. While the one who did the ritual slaughtering was actually engaged in that mitzvah, he had to have in mind that he was performing the mitzvah for the sake of all those who were "counted" on the animal. Thus, by starting the Seder with an invitation that guests join us, we sadden ourselves momentarily, for we remind ourselves that these laws regarding the offering are not in effect today. Thus, we conclude with a statement of hope: *Next year in Jerusalem.* That is, may the Temple be rebuilt! (*Ma'asei Hashem*)

This is the bread of poverty — These words serve to explain why we broke one of the matzos, and hid away part of it — for the way of someone poor is to eat only a piece, saving the rest for later. (Rashbam on *Talmud Pesachim* 115b)

Bread of poverty (Lachma anya) — The Aramaic word *anya* connotes not only "poverty" or "affliction" (that matzah was the bread eaten by our forefathers while they were slaves); it also resembles the Hebrew word for "answer." The matzah is laid out in the open on the Seder plate, as if it is on display, and over it, we give answers to the many questions that are asked by the children, and also by others attending the Seder. (*Pesachim* 115b)

Bread of poverty — This symbolizes both subjugation and redemption. Before the Jews could merit the redemption, they first had to suffer subjugation. Therefore, we offer praise and thanks for both. (*Sefas Emes*)

📖

That our forefathers ate in the land of Egypt — The Egyptians did not allow our forefathers to eat normal bread which is quickly digested, because they did not want their slaves to become hungry afterwards, which would weaken them and slow them down in their work. Rather, the Egyptians allowed the Jews only matzah, which is difficult to digest, so that the slaves would be able to continue to work hard, for longer periods of time. (Abarbanel, *Orchos Chayim*, and others)

📖

In the land of Egypt — You may ask, "What did we gain by being freed from Egypt? After all, we have no Temple anymore, and again we are in exile!" There is a difference, however. When we were enslaved in Egypt, it was not in our hands to speed our redemption. Today, however, by giving charity, and by doing other good deeds, we can make our redemption come more quickly. Thus we say, at the start of the Seder, *Whoever is hungry, let him come and eat* and in the merit of our deed, *Next year in Jerusalem!* Bringing on the redemption is in our hands! (*Chasam Sofer*)

📖

Whoever is hungry — This applies even to the non-Jew, for it is a mitzvah also to feed the hungry people of other nations, so that we are not regarded as selfish, and can live in peace with them. (*Yavetz*)

📖

Whoever is hungry — The Jews said this even on their last night in Egypt, at the moment of their redemption, when they knew that at any moment, they would leave. Free men, not slaves, invite guests to their tables, and the Jews wanted to demonstrate that they already were free, even within the borders of Egypt! *Whoever is hungry, let him come and eat.* We and they are one, sharing the same lot, and as they looked forward to spending the next year in Jerusalem, so do we! (Based on *Rashbam* and others)

📖

Whoever is in need —Impoverished Jews need not only food; they also must have the opportunity to fulfill the mitzvos. Thus, no matter what type of Jew, upright or not, we invite them all to our Seder table. First we invite all people who are "hungry," which includes even non-Jews, while our invitation to our fellow Jews — all who are "in need," i.e., of the opportunity to fulfill the night's mitzvos — is extended only afterwards. We invite the non-Jews first, in order to keep peace with them (though if a Jew and a non-Jew need charity, the Jew comes first). Now that we have invited every type of Jew, even those of dubious character, we conclude with a prayer: "Today we are here, slaves. Next year, may we be in Jerusalem, free!" That is, just as we are not particular which type of Jews sit at our Seder table, You, too, our God, please do not be particular with us! Bring us to You, and redeem us, even if we are not worthy! (*Kol Yehudah and others*)

Let him come and join in the Pesach — That is, let him celebrate the holiday with us (*Mateh Moshe*). Some explain: Let him come and partake of what he needs to fulfill the mitzvos of Pesach. (*Machzor Vitry*)

And join in the Pesach — In the days of the Temple, as well, every household head was to regard himself as being in need of others. He was not supposed to sit by himself and partake of the meat of the Pesach offering. Rather, he was supposed to have guests who would partake of it with him, having others "counted in" with him ahead of time. (based on *Rashi* and others)

Next year — We say "Next year," but really, we hope at any moment to merit the Redemption.

In the Land of Israel — This is our first prayer for *next year*, and afterwards, *free men* is our second prayer for *next year*. This reflects the verse (*Yeshayahu* 1:27): *Zion [Jews in the Land of Israel] shall be redeemed in the merit of their good deeds, and [afterwards] those who return to her [those not in the Land of Israel will be freed] in the merit of charity.* (*Vilna Gaon*)

In the Land of Israel — Another explanation for the seeming redundancy of being *in the Land of Israel*, and also being *free men*, is as follows: One should not say to himself, "Why on the Seder night, in our time, should we do things to indicate that we are *free men*? After all, we are still in exile!"

To this question, the Haggadah responds: Our subjugation today is very different from what our forefathers suffered in Egypt. Today, though we may live outside of Israel, in lands which are not ours, our redemption is in our own hands, and we are not bound in chains as they were. We are *free men*, and by doing good deeds, we immediately can cause the Redemption to come, and be in Jerusalem even tomorrow.

Our forefathers, however, were captives, and no slave ever left Egypt on his own good deeds, and the Jews were able to come to the Land of Israel only after they were freed from their chains. Also, even if the time of the Redemption has not arrived, God forbid, still, the Land of Israel lies before us, and Jews are living there now. The Redemption, when it comes, will return the Land to these Jews in an instant, which was not the way it was for the Jews who were in Egypt. (*Yavetz*)

This year, we are slaves — Today, though we do perform the mitzvos, we perform them as slaves serve a master, without feelings of love for him. We hope, however, that by next year, we will be *free men*, redeemed, serving God as sons serve a father, out of love. (*Tiferes Shelomo*)

Next year — This is said in Hebrew, and not Aramaic, so that our overlords in Babylonia, who did not understand Hebrew, would not take offense at our desire to leave, and start to hate us. (*Riva, Orchos Chayim*)

Next year, free men — Freedom is something that is desired by every person, and by every nation. However, how Israel defines "freedom" differs greatly from how other nations define the term.

When someone seeks to rid himself of all work and responsibility, out of his desire to be "free," then even if he achieves his goal, he has not attained true "freedom." On the contrary — once the autonomy that he so selfishly seeks is actually his, he becomes a slave to his selfish longings, for he starts to desire more things, and more things. Never will he have rest from having new desires! Such a person cannot help himself from rebelling against authority, and also against the law of the land, for he sees such things as detracting from his beloved "freedom." In the end, therefore, his quest to be "free" can even lead him into prison. It can bring so many other sorrows upon him, that he completely loses the taste of his former "freedom."

So, too, if a nation seeks to throw off another nation's control. The rebelling nation may succeed, but that very success can easily cause it to become an aggressor nation itself, which selfishly lashes out to try to exploit other nations, just as it had been exploited. If it seeks its freedom and independence only in order to rid itself of responsibility to its overlord, then even if it succeeds in throwing off its yoke, it becomes a slave again — a slave to its own desire for control and domination. Its desire for mastery grows and grows, and consumes the nation, for it is a desire that cannot be satisfied. As a result, even the most powerful nations of the world can fail to attain the "freedom" that they seek for themselves, for they always are trying to increase the scope of their domination, and never have rest from their desire.

Israel, however, is different. True, we do not want to be under the control of other men, but the only reason is that control interferes with our struggle for true freedom — freedom from the "*chametz*" in us, freedom from our evil inclination.

Our Sages taught: "The only free man is the one who toils in Torah." Only Torah can cure a person of his evil inclination. Only Torah can weaken its hold on us, giving our souls the freedom to soar upwards and cling to God.

Thus, when God sent Moshe to Egypt to tell the Jews that He soon would set them free, He told Moshe (*Shemos 3:12*): *And this shall be the sign that I sent you, when you take them out of Egypt [the true freedom shall be when] you shall serve God on this mountain.* True, the Jews physically had to leave Egypt, to be released from their taskmasters, but true freedom would be theirs only because of God's promise to them — that they would receive the Torah, and thus be able to toil in it and cling to it, and thus come closer to God.

So it is now, and all the more so will it be in the days of *Mashiach*

Pour the second cup of wine, and remove the Seder plate from the table, as if the meal were finished, in order that the children see, and ask. Here, the youngest of those at the table asks:

מַה נִּשְׁתַּנָּה הַלַּיְלָה הַזֶּה מִכָּל הַלֵּילוֹת.

שֶׁבְּכָל הַלֵּילוֹת אָנוּ אוֹכְלִין חָמֵץ וּמַצָּה. הַלַּיְלָה הַזֶּה כֻּלּוֹ מַצָּה:

שֶׁבְּכָל הַלֵּילוֹת אָנוּ אוֹכְלִין שְׁאָר יְרָקוֹת. הַלַּיְלָה הַזֶּה (כֻּלּוֹ) מָרוֹר:

שֶׁבְּכָל הַלֵּילוֹת אֵין אָנוּ מַטְבִּילִין אֲפִילוּ פַּעַם אֶחָת. הַלַּיְלָה הַזֶּה שְׁתֵּי פְעָמִים:

שֶׁבְּכָל הַלֵּילוֹת אָנוּ אוֹכְלִין בֵּין יוֹשְׁבִין וּבֵין מְסֻבִּין. הַלַּיְלָה הַזֶּה כֻּלָּנוּ מְסֻבִּין:

when the Ultimate Redemption comes. For true freedom is the freedom of the soul, when it is released from the clutches of the evil inclination. A Jew cannot attain this freedom, however, as long as he is subjugated by other men, who put responsibilities on him which prevent him from toiling in Torah. Attaining true freedom is simply not possible as long as, in addition to God being our Master, there are men "over us" as well. But when we become free of human masters, then as individuals and as a nation, we are promised that we will have no other yoke upon us (no evil inclination controlling us), and we will be able to devote ourselves only to Torah, which we will freely accept upon ourselves with love, taking great pleasure from learning it and fulfilling it.

The Rambam writes *(Mishneh Torah, Laws of Kings, Chapter 12):*

The Sages and Prophets greatly looked forward to the coming of Mashiach, not because they would then become rulers of the world, and be able to exploit the non-Jews. They were not looking forward to be being honored or being lifted above everyone else, and neither were they looking forward to being able to eat, drink, and be merry.

Pour the second cup of wine, and remove the Seder plate from the table, as if the meal were finished, in order that the children see, and ask. Here, the youngest of those at the table asks:

*W*HY IS THIS NIGHT DIFFERENT FROM EVERY OTHER NIGHT?

Other nights we eat chametz and matzah; this night, only matzah.
Other nights we eat every kind of vegetable; this night, maror.
Other nights we do not dip [vegetables] even once; this night, twice.
Other nights we eat either sitting or reclining; this night we all recline.

Rather, they longed for the days of Mashiach because they wanted to be free to involve themselves in the Torah and its wisdom, without anyone over them, giving them other things to do, for they knew that Torah brings a person life in the World-to-Come.

When the days of Mashiach come, there will be no more war or hunger, no more jealously or competition, and goodness will be showered upon the world in plenty. Every fine food will be readily at hand, as the dust of the earth. Everyone thus will be totally occupied in only one thing — attainment of the knowledge of God; and the Jewish People will be regarded as the wisest of all, for we possess the hidden wisdom. The Jews will attain knowledge of God to the greatest extent that is humanly possible, as is written (Yeshayahu 11:9): "...The world shall be filled with the knowledge of God, as the waters cover the sea."

Pouring the second of the Four Cups, before the Four Questions — Four elements of the Seder come in groups of four: The four cups of wine, the four questions, the four different redemptions, and the four types of sons. These allude to the four who are obligated to give thanks: one who crosses the sea, one who travels through the desert, one who is released from prison, and one who has recovered from a serious illness. The Jews who left Egypt had to give thanks for all four reasons! (*Vilna Gaon*)

Removing the Seder plate after "This is the bread..." — In ancient days, it was the custom that everyone at the meal would have a small table of his own, and after *This is the bread...* was said, and before the recital of the Haggadah, the tables were taken away with everything on them. This was to arouse the curiosity of the children, to make them ask why this was done. These days, since everyone eats at one large table, it is very difficult to keep up the old custom. Instead, at this point in the Seder some try to arouse the children's curiosity by simply removing the Seder plate from the table, or by moving it away from its place in front of the leader. (*Shulchan Aruch, Orach Chayim* 473:6)

According to the Magen Avraham, Ashkenazic communities are no longer particular about this custom at all. Because the children know ahead of time that the Seder plate is mainly for holding remembrances and that it does not contain the meal, they hardly notice even if it is completely taken away. (*Magen Avraham* 473, *siman katan* 25)

Why is this night different — The difference between the Seder night and all other nights is very great. The verse states (*Tehillim* 139:12): *The night shall shine as day.* Moreover, the Torah itself refers to the Seder night as "day," for it says (*Shemos* 13:8): *And you shall tell your son on that day...* and the Sages prove that this means at night! Because it is called "day," we recite *Hallel* on the Seder night, even though normally *Hallel* is said only during the day. (*Sefas Emes*)

We do not dip [vegetables] even once — That is, with a blessing. During the year, vegetables are usually eaten together with the meal, or after the meal, so that the blessing which is said over bread at the start of the meal exempts them, and actually forbids us from saying a separate blessing over them.

This night, [we dip] twice — That is, we dip twice with a blessing. Over the *karpas*, we say the general blessing recited on vegetables, and on the *maror* we bless, *Who commanded us to eat maror*. (*Machzor Vitry*)

📖

This night, [we dip] twice — Even though before reciting the Haggadah, we dip only once, the children know that we will do so a second time, later — since the *maror* and *charoses* are already there on the Seder plate. Furthermore, it is clear from the *Mishnah* and *Talmud* that if none of the children ask the Four Questions, then the father must do so, even though he already knows the answers. (based on *Rashbatz*)

📖

Other nights we eat either sitting or reclining — This question was not asked in the days of the Temple, for at that time it was their norm to recline at all meals, even during the year. Instead, the question asked in those days was, "Other nights we eat roasted or cooked meat; tonight we eat only roasted meat (i.e., the meat of the Pesach and *Chagigah* sacrifices)." Once we lost our Holy Temple, however, and were no longer able to bring the offerings, we were not allowed to eat any roasted meat on the Seder night. Thus a new question had to be ordained, which asked about a different irregularity. (*Vilna Gaon*)

Return the Seder plate to its original place, uncover the matzos and say:

עֲבָדִים הָיִינוּ לְפַרְעֹה בְּמִצְרָיִם, וַיּוֹצִיאֵנוּ יְהֹוָה אֱלֹהֵינוּ מִשָּׁם בְּיָד חֲזָקָה וּבִזְרוֹעַ נְטוּיָה, וְאִלּוּ לֹא הוֹצִיא הַקָּדוֹשׁ בָּרוּךְ הוּא אֶת אֲבוֹתֵינוּ מִמִּצְרָיִם, הֲרֵי אָנוּ וּבָנֵינוּ וּבְנֵי בָנֵינוּ מְשֻׁעְבָּדִים הָיִינוּ לְפַרְעֹה בְּמִצְרָיִם. וַאֲפִילוּ כֻּלָּנוּ חֲכָמִים, כֻּלָּנוּ נְבוֹנִים, כֻּלָּנוּ זְקֵנִים, כֻּלָּנוּ יוֹדְעִים אֶת הַתּוֹרָה, מִצְוָה עָלֵינוּ לְסַפֵּר בִּיצִיאַת מִצְרָיִם. וְכָל הַמַּרְבֶּה לְסַפֵּר בִּיצִיאַת מִצְרָיִם הֲרֵי זֶה מְשֻׁבָּח:

We were slaves to Pharaoh...and Hashem our God took us out — Therefore we became servants of Hashem, instead of servants of Pharaoh, and we took upon ourselves to fulfill all of Hashem's commandments, even those that we do not understand. Thus, we answer the child that in fact, we *do* do things differently on this night, and even though we might not understand why, we make the changes anyway, for that is His Will. (*Ma'asei Nissim*)

📖

We were slaves to Pharaoh in Egypt — All the while that we were enslaved in Egypt, it was not possible for us to be servants of God. So says the *Zohar Vayikra* 108a: *Someone who is put in chains by another man cannot accept upon himself the yoke of Heaven.* However, God took us out of Egypt, and now, in fact, we are His servants. We are free of Pharaoh now, and we have the Torah, too, so although other nations may rule over us and oppress us, and rightly so, because of our sins, still, we are not their slaves, and never will we be their slaves. God says, speaking of Israel (*Vayikra* 25:55): *They are My servants, for I took them out of Egypt.*

Return the Seder plate to its original place, uncover the matzos and say:

WE WERE SLAVES to Pharaoh in Egypt, and Hashem our God took us out of there with a strong hand and an outstretched arm. And if the Holy One, blessed is He, had not taken our forefathers out of Egypt, then we, our children, and our children's children would still be enslaved to Pharaoh in Egypt. And even if we all were Sages, all wise, all elders, all learned in Torah, it would still be a mitzvah for us to tell about the Exodus from Egypt; and whoever elaborates on the story is to be praised.

On the Seder night, this is the source of our joy, for it was then, when God freed us, that we became His servants, forever.

That no ruler of any nation, no matter how powerful he may be, can enslave us again, can be deduced from logic: If while enslaved to mere flesh and blood, we could not become servants to God, then now that we are servants to God, can we again become enslaved to mere flesh and blood?! (*Sefas Emes*)

We were slaves — A slave is not simply someone who is obligated to work. He is someone else's property, and what he eats, where he lives, and everything he produces is not even his. He owes everything to his master. The Jews, too, were slaves, meaning that this was our essence. That is, according to the world's natural order, the Jewish People should not even exist. We owe everything to God. Is is said that Avraham saw, through astrology, which reflects the natural order, that he never would have children. Thus, *There is no mazal* — *astrological sign* — *that has power over Israel*. Avraham was able to have Yitzchak, only because God lifted Avraham "above" the natural order. Since, according to the natural order, Israel should not exist at all, we were indeed "strangers" in the world, from the time of Yitzchak's birth, and "slaves" in Egypt, as God had told Avraham (*Bereshis* 15:13): *Your seed will be strangers in a land that is not theirs, and there they will be worked and oppressed.*

There are twelve astrological signs. The Jews were "slaves" specifically to Pharaoh in Egypt, whose astrological sign is the sheep — the first astrological sign of the twelve. Egypt symbolizes the natural order in general, and God *took us out* from there, with miracles which shattered the natural order! Later, He gave us the Land of Israel, again by means of miracles, for according to astrology, we had no place of our own. (*Sefas Emes*)

Hashem our God took us out — We find this idea in what the Torah tells us to answer the wise son, who asks (*Devarim* 6:20): *What are these testimonies, chukim and statutes to you?* The "chukim" to which he refers are laws that God gave which we do not really understand. The Torah tells us to answer the wise son (*Devarim* 6:24): *Hashem commanded us to fulfill all these chukim in order to have awe of Him, for our good.* Here, even *"testimonies"* and *"statutes"* which are fully logical to us and we do understand are nevertheless referred to as "*chukim.*" This teaches us that these, too, are to be fulfilled simply because God commanded them, and not because we find them in accordance with our reason and logic.

With a strong hand — Our Sages explain that the Jews had been brought to such a low level, it was necessary for God to use a strong hand to bring them out of Egypt. (*Shochar Tov*, 114)

With a strong hand — But why did God allow things to reach such a state [that the Jews would have to be redeemed, *with a strong hand*]? The answer is as follows: It was always known and revealed to God, that after Egypt, the Jewish People would suffer other exiles. There would be other times in the future when God's "face" would be concealed from them. The difficult times would be tests for both individual Jews and for the Nation as a whole. God had promised Avraham that He would redeem the Jews from Egypt, and in His great wisdom and mercy, He saw fit to make the Jewish experience in Egypt a preparation for all the future trials and redemptions that the Jews would experience later. After Egypt, throughout history, no matter how difficult things might be, Jews would be able to look back at the Jewish suffering in Egypt, and gather strength, for that suffering was the worst of all, and God intervened in Egypt, because the Jews remained faithful, and trusted in Him. It was terrible for the Jews in Egypt, so much so that God had to use, so to speak, *a strong hand* to take them out. The Jews of the future would take comfort in this, for their suffering would not be as bad, and they would think that God's redeeming them would be "easier," so to speak, and would not require such *a strong hand*. Thus it would be easier for them to keep their faith.

Actually, God intervenes and saves us from our enemies in every generation, and even every day. The Haggadah says, *In every generation there are those who stand up to try to destroy us*. Even if we do not detect their efforts, we can be sure that their conspiracies are taking shape, and God is intervening to save us.

The *Zohar* finds this teaching in a verse (*Tehillim* 136:4): *He Who does great deeds alone*. That is, only the Almighty appreciates the greatness of His saving deeds, for often, the ones whom He saves do not even know that they were in danger, and are not even aware that God did miracles on their behalf!

In sum, were it not for God's having to use *a strong hand* in Egypt, Israel would have been, God forbid, destroyed by enemies which rose up against her afterwards, during the frequent periods of concealment of God's "face" throughout history. After all, God promised Avraham only that He would redeem the Jews from Egypt. What about the suffering in the exiles that would follow? However, it is because He brought about the redemption from Egypt, and with *a strong hand*, and He freed us of that terrible suffering — total concealment of His "face" — that we always have felt that our redemption is near, for all we needed to do was look upon the light of that first redemption. (*Sefas Emes*)

📖

We were slaves...and [He] took us out...and if [He] had not taken our forefathers out — The Haggadah begins by saying that God took "us" out, and afterwards it says He took out our "forefathers." While our forefathers were enslaved to Egypt, in fact all Jewish souls were enslaved, but the souls of Jews who were not born yet were enslaved to Egypt on high (just as all Jewish souls were present at Mount Sinai for the giving of the Torah). At the same time that the Jews of that generation were liberated from the Egypt on earth, the souls of all future generations were liberated from the Egypt on high.

However, if God had not taken out that particular generation from Egypt, there could never have been a redemption from Egypt later, God forbid, for that generation was close to the Patriarchs, and even closer to the sons of Yaakov. Only that generation was able to descend into Egypt and leave, and when they left, they were able to take us and every other generation out with them. (*Sefas Emes*)

And if [He] had not taken our forefathers out of Egypt — Rather, if Pharaoh had freed them willingly, or if Hashem had given the Jews the power to free themselves, *we...would still be enslaved to Pharaoh in Egypt*. If Pharaoh had been the one to free us, we still would owe him a debt of gratitude, and thus would still be "enslaved" to him. So, too, if we thought that our redemption was our own doing, rather than an act of God, we still would be slaves to Egypt, in the spiritual and ideological sense. Whenever we put our trust in our own strength, and not God's, and we ascribe greatness to ourselves, we are truly "slaves" to Pharaoh in Egypt. So, too, when we "put stock" in anyone other than God.

We, our children, and our children's children — Every father, by nature, has pity not only on his children, but also on his grandchildren. Thus, when he expresses his overflowing happiness and gratitude that he and his children are not enslaved, he also mentions his grandchildren.

And even if we all were Sages — And among us there was no one evil who was asking, "What purpose do these ceremonies serve you?"

All wise — And we already had been taught everything by our fathers, and much we understood on our own.

All elders — And we had told and retold the story of the Exodus year after year, and had been involved in Torah study all those years, which every day brings the Exodus to mind.

All learned in Torah — This was the purpose of the redemption in the first place. Since we would be constantly occupied in Torah, why would it still be a mitzvah for us to speak about the redemption from Egypt?

It would still be a mitzvah for us to tell — For God gave us the Torah so that we would be able to fulfill His commandments. Once the Torah tells us that it is a mitzvah to speak about the redemption from Egypt, we fulfill the mitzvah, even when we do not understand the reason for it. (based on *Rashbatz, Abudraham* and others)

📖

And whoever elaborates — Adding his own insights, in addition to what is written in the Haggadah — *is to be praised*. (*Vilna Gaon*)

📖

Even if we were all Sages...all wise...all elders — The Jews in Egypt had knowledge, understanding, the power of speech, and all other intellectual attributes associated with mitzvos and good deeds, but as long as Pharaoh held the Jews as his slaves, all these attributes were more in the realm of the potential than the actual. When God intervened and freed the Jews from Egypt, there was a redeeming miracle regarding our intellectual faculties as well, causing each one to emerge from potential and be realized. When we recite the Haggadah, we should have in mind these important "redemptions" as well. (*Tiferes Shelomo*)

📖

It would still be a mitzvah for us to tell about the Exodus — Performance of this mitzvah produces three important things:

1. It strengthens our belief in God, that He can do anything that He desires, and that everything is in His Hands.

2. It increases our trust in Him, so that we are better able to serve Him, and be happy, even when times are hard, and the exile is dark.

3. In the merit of our recalling the great miracles of Egypt, we awaken God's desire to perform miracles for us now, and bring the Final Redemption, for His Mercy is forever. (*Tiferes Shelomo*)

To tell about the Exodus — When a person tells the story of the Exodus aloud, it brings him knowledge, increasing his understanding of God, for God told Israel that He would save them from Egypt by means of great miracles (*Shemos* 10:2): *In order that you shall relate it to the ears of your son and your grandson.* The verse says immediately afterwards: *And you shall know that I am God.*

Our Sages taught that God "looked into" the Torah and then He created the world. God performed every act of creation only through the strength of the verses which speak about those acts of creation. So, too, regarding the redemption from Egypt. It came about only on the strength of the verses in the Torah which speak about it. The Torah was given to Israel, and by saying these verses about the redemption from Egypt, Israel, too, can awaken the powers of redemption that are hidden in these verses. The Jewish People uses its powers of speech to uncover the Torah's hidden wisdom, which can be revealed only by means of verbalization, and by so doing, Israel, like God Himself, can effect concrete changes on the world at large.

This is what the Sages meant when they said that one should elaborate when telling the story of the redemption from Egypt, for by so doing, one helps bring redemption to the world.

So, too, for the Final Redemption to come — all the hidden mysteries which remain concealed regarding the Exodus from Egypt will be revealed, for the redemption from Egypt is the source of all redemptions, including the final one. When Israel, through the power of speech, finally reveals all the hidden mysteries connected to the Exodus from Egypt, the world will contain everything that is necessary for the last, ultimate Redemption, which will then burst forth in full in the End of Days.

Our Sages hinted at this, by saying that it will be a mitzvah to speak about the Exodus from Egypt even after the coming of *Mashiach*. Thus, when sitting at the Seder table and reciting the Haggadah, one should intend that the mitzvah he is doing should help to bring *Mashiach*, as we have explained. (*Sefas Emes*)

And whoever elaborates — It also is praiseworthy to speak of the miracles in Egypt on other nights of the year, and in the daytime as well. God freed the Jews from Egypt in order to give them the Torah, and in the merit of speaking about the events in Egypt, even not on the Seder night, God increases our powers of comprehension, so that we, too, can receive the Torah. In the Haggadah, there is a story about the Sages in Bnei Brak who spoke about the Exodus all night long, almost until daybreak. Possibly, this incident did not take place on the Seder night at all — for on the night of the Seder, it is commonplace [and would not have been noteworthy] for Jews to stay up all night talking about the Exodus, even simple Jews. (*Sefas Emes*)

And whoever elaborates — Compared to the Haggadah, no other component of the Torah has had so many books and commentaries written on it, in order to explain it and expound upon it. In every generation, Torah scholars expound both its simple meaning and its deeper meanings, and continue to find new insights. The Haggadah is expounded also by those who are not Torah scholars — contemporary thinkers who search this ancient work looking for insights into things happening in the present, even in specific places. They find, in fact, even using their approaches, that the Haggadah does contain allusions and insights about the present day, for in the Exodus from Egypt, and in the slavery that preceded it, everything was contained — all the miracles that would be necessary, and all the other essential elements of redemption, from the days of Pharaoh until *Mashiach*, and the Sages wrote the Haggadah with Divine inspiration. Thus, the Haggadah is an overflowing well for all the generations, and for every individual who applies himself to it.

Is to be praised — That is to say, *this* is praiseworthy, elaborating on the Haggadah. But if a person, while saying his prayers, elaborates and goes on and on saying praises to God, beyond those praises that the Sages instituted in the prayers, he is not to be praised. (See *Berachos* 33b, the *Etz Chayim* in the name of the *Esh Das*, *Parashas Ki Tavo*, and others)

מַעֲשֶׂה בְּרַבִּי אֱלִיעֶזֶר וְרַבִּי יְהוֹשֻׁעַ וְרַבִּי אֶלְעָזָר בֶּן עֲזַרְיָה וְרַבִּי עֲקִיבָא וְרַבִּי טַרְפוֹן שֶׁהָיוּ מְסֻבִּין בִּבְנֵי בְרַק וְהָיוּ מְסַפְּרִים בִּיצִיאַת מִצְרַיִם כָּל אוֹתוֹ הַלַּיְלָה עַד שֶׁבָּאוּ תַלְמִידֵיהֶם וְאָמְרוּ לָהֶם רַבּוֹתֵינוּ הִגִּיעַ זְמַן קְרִיאַת שְׁמַע שֶׁל שַׁחֲרִית:

אָמַר רַבִּי אֶלְעָזָר בֶּן עֲזַרְיָה, הֲרֵי אֲנִי כְּבֶן שִׁבְעִים שָׁנָה, וְלֹא זָכִיתִי שֶׁתֵּאָמֵר יְצִיאַת מִצְרַיִם בַּלֵּילוֹת, עַד שֶׁדְּרָשָׁהּ בֶּן זוֹמָא, שֶׁנֶּאֱמַר, לְמַעַן תִּזְכֹּר אֶת יוֹם צֵאתְךָ מֵאֶרֶץ מִצְרַיִם כֹּל יְמֵי חַיֶּיךָ. יְמֵי חַיֶּיךָ הַיָּמִים. כֹּל יְמֵי חַיֶּיךָ

In Bnei Brak — This probably was where Rabbi Akiva lived and served as Rabbi (see *Sanhedrin* 32a), for Rabbi Akiva was a student of Rabbi Eliezer and Rabbi Yehoshua. If the story had taken place in the town of one of his teachers, Rabbi Akiva might not have been allowed to recline, for even at the Seder, a student cannot recline in his teacher's presence unless the teacher gives him explicit permission. If, however, Bnei Brak was where Rabbi Akiva served as Rabbi, he could recline, and could assume that his teachers permitted it. (*HaRama mi-Pano*)

All that night — Even though they had eaten the *Afikoman* and had fulfilled all the other mitzvos of the Seder night before half the night had passed. This is similar to how it had been in Egypt on that night. The first half of the night they were involved with their mitzvos, and during the second half they were occupied with leaving the land of their bondage. (based on *Rashbam, Ritva, Zevach Pesach*)

Until their students came — The Sages did not intend to stay up all night speaking about the Exodus, for on holidays, one is supposed to go to sleep at night, as part of the mitzvah of enjoying oneself on the holiday. Rather, they were so happy to be performing the mitzvah of speaking about the Exodus, and were so absorbed in it, that they did

THIS IS TOLD OF R. ELIEZER, R. Yehoshua, R. Elazar ben Azaryah, Rabbi Akiva, and R. Tarfon: They sat once in Bnei Brak and told about the Exodus all that night, until their students came and told them, "Rabbis, the time has come to say the morning Shema!"

Said R. Elazar ben Azaryah: I am like a man of seventy years, and yet I was never able to say that the Exodus should be mentioned at night until Ben Zoma explained it: The Torah says, "So that you may remember the day you left the land of Egypt all the days of your life." "The days of your life" — daytime; "all the days of your life" — the nights [too].

not feel any fatigue, and the night passed them by without their noticing it. (*Maharal*)

I am like a man of seventy years — Rabbi Elazar ben Azaryah only appeared to be that old, but really, he was not even twenty. The Talmud tells us (*Berachos 27b*) that the Sages appointed him to head the Sanhedrin because of his great knowledge of Torah, and because of his other superior qualities. For his part, however, the young Sage felt unworthy, because he was so young. The day he was appointed, in order to make his appearance fitting for his exalted position, a miracle occurred, and his hair turned completely white. But even though he had great wisdom, and deserved the position he was given, still he did not succeed in convincing his colleagues about saying the *Shema* at night, until Ben Zoma explained it.

Rabbi Elazar says: "I toiled in Torah with such effort, I learned as much in eighteen years as is usually learned in seventy!"

He put all his strength into his learning, day and night, until he became weak, and he was given the appearance of a man of seventy. (*Rambam on Mishnah Pesachim*)

Until Ben Zoma explained — "Explained," not "said," for Ben Zoma was regarded as having no equal in terms of his power to expound

הַלֵּילוֹת. וַחֲכָמִים אוֹמְרִים, יְמֵי חַיֶּיךָ הָעוֹלָם הַזֶּה. כֹּל יְמֵי חַיֶּיךָ לְהָבִיא לִימוֹת הַמָּשִׁיחַ:

בָּרוּךְ הַמָּקוֹם, בָּרוּךְ הוּא, בָּרוּךְ שֶׁנָּתַן תּוֹרָה לְעַמּוֹ יִשְׂרָאֵל. בָּרוּךְ הוּא.

and explain, as is stated in the Talmud (*Sotah*): *When Ben Zoma died, the power to expound the Torah died with him.* (*Makor haBerachah*)

All the days of your life — This includes the times of *Mashiach* too. We are obligated, for all time, to state aloud that God took us out of Egypt, to remind ourselves of those events, even in the days of *Mashiach*. God's freeing us from Egypt gave us our first lessons in how to serve Him and follow His ways, and in a person's struggle to become truly righteous, his first steps provide him his greatest measure of strength. Thus, the Torah obligates us to constantly remind ourselves of these first steps, and by so doing, we are better able to serve God with the same strength and enthusiasm that we had then. (*Shem mi-Shemuel*)

All the days of your life — All of one's life, whatever he is doing, a person should be hoping for *Mashiach*, and must be thinking of how he can merit to help make *Mashiach* come more quickly. (*HaRash mi-Rodomsk*)

Blessed is the Everpresent One. Blessed is He! Blessed is He Who gave... Blessed is He! — This passage is connected to the one preceding it. That is, if one already is wise and learned, etc., and already knows all about the Exodus from Egypt, there is room to think that he is exempt from praising God through telling about the Exodus on the Seder night — yet he is not exempt. We all should praise God and tell about the Exodus!

The Rabbis say: "the days of your life" — this world; "all the days of your life" — including the Era of Mashiach.

*Blessed is the Everpresent One.
Blessed is He! Blessed is He
Who gave the Torah to His People, Israel.
Blessed is He!*

We bless God four times, for earlier we heard four questions, corresponding to the four types of sons that are mentioned in the Torah. These include the wicked son and the son who is too detached to even ask questions. Now that we are giving thanks and praise, we do not want to seem ungrateful about anything. Therefore, we give four praises, for all of our sons, even though at present, one or two of them might not be on the correct path. We are thankful that we have them, for they, too, can come to the correct way; for they, too, are descended from the Patriarchs, and their souls are essentially pure.

Blessed is the Everpresent One (literally, "the Place") — This is said for the sake of the wicked son, for despite his wickedness, he is not "outside" of God's world. Such a thing is impossible, because God is the world's "place" and therefore is everywhere. Thus, even the wicked are never "far" from God, and if they mend their ways God forgives them.

Blessed is He — This is said for the sake of the son who is associated with the wicked son, in that he is close to becoming wicked, for he is too detached from everything, and so uninterested he does not ask questions.

Blessed is He Who gave the Torah to His People, Israel — This refers to the wise son, who occupies himself in Torah, and becomes wise because of it.

Blessed is He — This refers to the simple son, who is associated with the wise son, for he simply needs direction.

כְּנֶגֶד אַרְבָּעָה בָנִים דִּבְּרָה תוֹרָה: אֶחָד חָכָם. וְאֶחָד רָשָׁע. וְאֶחָד תָּם. וְאֶחָד שֶׁאֵינוֹ יוֹדֵעַ לִשְׁאֹל:

Blessed is He Who gave the Torah — We are about to expound the verses in the Torah about the four different types of sons. Thus, we say a blessing on the Torah, or at least something that resembles one. We praise the One Who gave us the Torah, as if to declare, "Let us now expound upon the Torah, in the Name of God!" (*Rashbatz*, Rabbi Yeshaya Ditrani)

Blessed is He — According to the Malbim, *Blessed is He* is a choral response that is twice given to the Seder's leader by the others at the Seder table — once after the leader says *Blessed is the Everpresent One* and once after he says, *Blessed is He Who gave the Torah*.

Blessed — It has been suggested that all the statements of blessing refer to the Torah:
> BLESSED IS THE PLACE — This is in praise of the place *where* the Torah was given — Mount Sinai — for this location was inherently holy. As soon as the Jewish People arrived there, all of their inner impurities completely disappeared. (*Shabbos* 146a)
> BLESSED IS HE — This is in praise of *Who* gave the Torah.
> BLESSED IS HE WHO GAVE THE TORAH — This is in praise of *what* God gave.
> TO HIS PEOPLE, ISRAEL — This is in praise of *who* received the Torah. (*Eshel b'Rama*)

The Torah speaks of four sons — This is so that we make efforts regarding all four, to see that they devote their lives to God, to answer their questions and remove their doubts, so that they all travel the path that is correct and true.

The Torah speaks of four sons — The Torah contains four separate

THE TORAH SPEAKS OF FOUR SONS: one who is wise, one who is wicked, one who is simple, and one who doesn't know to ask.

verses about four sons:
SHEMOS 12:27: *When your sons shall say to you, "What is this service..."*
SHEMOS 13:8: *And you shall tell your son on that day...*
SHEMOS 13:14: *When your son asks you..., "What is this?"*
DEVARIM 6:20: *When your son asks you, "What are these testimonies..."*

📖

One who is wise, one who is wicked, etc. — The Haggadah uses the word "one" for each son to teach us that all four are "one" regarding the mitzvah to speak of the Exodus from Egypt. (*Yerios Shelomo*)

📖

Four sons — Pharaoh's evil decrees on the Jews in Egypt were directed mainly against "sons": *And God saw our ill treatment* — that is, Pharaoh forbade the Jewish men to return to their homes after their work, in order that no sons be born to Jewish families. In case this failed, and they went home to their wives, and their wives became pregnant, there was another decree, in which Pharaoh ordered the Jewish midwives (*Shemos* 1:16): *If the child is a boy, you shall kill him.* If that failed, and baby boys were born, there was a third decree, which Pharaoh gave to his entire nation (*Shemos* 2:22): *Every son born to the Jews shall be cast into the river!*

If that failed, and the sons survived, Pharaoh had them murdered, and the bodies were used as filler in the walls of the buildings that the Jews were building. Also, our Sages tell us, Pharaoh contracted *tzara'as*, and in his attempt to cure the disease, he had Jewish sons killed, and washed his skin in their blood. Thus, the Haggadah's account of the miracles in Egypt begins with questions that are posed by sons, and continues with the four types of sons mentioned by the Torah. (*Toldos Moshe*)

חָכָם מַה הוּא אוֹמֵר.
מָה הָעֵדֹת וְהַחֻקִּים וְהַמִּשְׁפָּטִים אֲשֶׁר צִוָּה יְהֹוָה אֱלֹהֵינוּ אֶתְכֶם. וְאַף אַתָּה אֱמָר־לוֹ כְּהִלְכוֹת הַפֶּסַח, אֵין מַפְטִירִין אַחַר הַפֶּסַח אֲפִיקוֹמָן:

רָשָׁע מַה הוּא אוֹמֵר.
מָה הָעֲבוֹדָה הַזֹּאת לָכֶם. לָכֶם וְלֹא לוֹ. וּלְפִי שֶׁהוֹצִיא אֶת עַצְמוֹ מִן הַכְּלָל כָּפַר בָּעִקָּר. וְאַף אַתָּה הַקְהֵה אֶת שִׁנָּיו וֶאֱמָר־לוֹ. בַּעֲבוּר זֶה עָשָׂה יְהֹוָה לִי בְּצֵאתִי

What does the wise son say? "What are these testimonies, chukim, and statutes that Hashem our God commanded you?" — For your part, you acknowledge his question, teaching him, according to the laws of the Pesach offering, that after one eats of it, one is not allowed to eat anything else! (*Chasam Sofer*)

📖

Testimonies — These are the mitzvos that we perform tonight as commemorations. Matzah and *maror* are examples of this. *Chukim* are laws such as those governing the eating of the Pesach offering — laws whose reasons are not known to us, such as: its meat must be eaten under the roof of one house, and cannot be taken out of the house, and one is not allowed to break any of its bones. *Statutes* is a general term for all the laws of Pesach, whether they are of Torah or Rabbinic origin. (*Ritva, Avudraham* and others)

📖

That Hashem our God commanded you — He says *commanded you* simply because he personally did not hear the command, and not because he thinks (as does the wicked son) that the command applies only to "you" and not to him. (*Rashi*)

📖

That Hashem our God commanded you — Although it sounds as if the wise son is like the wicked son, and is excluding himself from being commanded, the Haggadah here is simply using the same word-

WHAT DOES THE WISE SON SAY? *"What are the testimonies, chukim, and statutes that Hashem, our God, commanded you?"* Tell him the laws of the Pesach offering: *"An Afikoman may not be served as a last course after the Pesach lamb."*

WHAT DOES THE WICKED SON SAY? *"What is this service to you?"* He says *"to you"* but not to him! And because he has disassociated himself from what the community does, he has denied God. And [for your part] you acknowledge [the tone of] his question, and set his teeth on edge by quoting the verse (Shemos 13:8): *"Because of this [very service] did Hashem do [wonders] for me as I was leaving Egypt."* [You emphasize] *"for me"* and

ing that the Torah uses when telling us what the wise son will ask (Devarim 6:20): *And it shall be, when your son asks you, What are these testimonies, chukim, and statutes that Hashem, our God, has commanded you.* (Beis Vaad l'Chachamim)

That Hashem our God commanded you — Because the wise son is referring to the giving of the command, it is proper for him to say these words for this reflects the fact that at first, only those who heard the command knew of it, and God commanded "you" and not him. The wicked son, however, is speaking about the performance of the mitzvah, so that when he says, *What is this service to you,* he must be corrected, for he should have said "What is this service to us." (Ma'asei Nissim)

Tell him the laws of the Pesach offering — That is, explain to him all the laws governing the Pesach offering, until you reach the last law, that after we eat of it, we are not allowed to eat anything else. (Emes l'Yaakov)

The wicked son — The Torah says (Shemos 12:25): *When you shall come into the Land...and when your sons shall say unto you, "What is this service to you..."* *and the Nation bowed down in gratitude.* Our Sages explain that the Jews were bowing in gratitude for three good things that God had promised with these words: that they would be freed from Egyptian bondage; that they would enter the Land of Israel; and that they would be blessed with sons. On the other hand, this verse is speaking about wicked sons! What good is there in having wicked sons?

The answer lies in the words of the holy *Zohar*, about Tzelofchad, one of the Jews who died in the desert after leaving Egypt, and never merited to enter the Land of Israel. Also, he never had any sons, only daughters. Moshe *Rabbenu* had doubts about whether Tzelofchad would merit the World-to-Come. It happened, however, that long after his death, Tzelofchad's daughters posed a question to Moshe *Rabbenu*, and made a request. Moshe *Rabbenu*, however, could not answer the question, and thus was not certain he could grant the request, which had to do with giving the daughters property in Israel, as if they were sons. Moshe referred the problem to God, and God said that their request should be granted: *The daughters of Tzelofchad spoke correctly*, and thus did have rights to land. When Moshe heard these words — that God mentioned the father's name — he knew that, in fact, Tzelofchad had merited the World-to-Come, for if he had not, God would not have mentioned his name.

So, too, regarding the wicked son. Because the Torah speaks about this son, and even tells us how to respond to him, this is good news for us, for we know that despite his words and his behavior, he is still one of us, and there is hope for him. (*Shem mi-Shemuel*)

📖

What is this service to you? — We see this son's wickedness, for in truth, he is not asking a question. Rather, he is making fun, downgrading those who are involved in the mitzvah. In the Torah, in fact, regarding the wise son and the simple son, it is written that he shall "ask"; regarding the wicked son, however, it is written that he shall "say." (*Malbim, Chukkas haPesach*)

📖

When your sons shall say [What is this service, etc.] — Regarding the wise son and the simple son, the Torah writes in the singular — *When your son asks*. Here, however, the Torah writes in the plural — *When your sons shall say*. We see that the wise and the simple son each ask because they truly want to know, and therefore neither has any worry about coming by himself to ask. The wicked son, however, is coming only to make fun and argue. Therefore, afraid to come by himself, he brings along someone else who is like him to be at his side!

Neither does the wicked son mention the Name of God when he speaks, and this is an indication that he does not even acknowledge that God exists. In fact, when he says, *What is this service to you,* he seems to be explicitly denying a fundamental principle of our faith, as if the things we do at the Seder are not done because God commanded us to do them, but that we made up *this service* on our own.

📖

He has denied God — For if one denies that he gains from performing the mitzvos, he is denying the One Who gave the mitzvos. (*Machzor Vitry*)

📖

You...set his teeth on edge — Your response to his ill-considered speech strikes him squarely in his mouth, making his teeth feel as if he had just eaten unripe fruit.

Rabbi Moshe Alshich explained that the wicked son is asking a question of sorts, about the purpose of bringing the Pesach offering every year, even long after the Exodus from Egypt. That is, he could understand the Jews in Egypt slaughtering the Pesach offering, for the purpose of smearing its blood on the doorposts of their homes, so that the Jews inside would be saved from the tenth plague. "But you are no longer in Egypt! What purpose does the Pesach offering serve for you?" The Torah tells us to reply (*Shemos* 12:27): *And you shall say, "This is the Pesach offering to Hashem, Who passed over the houses of the Children of Israel in Egypt [just as you say]...and He saved our houses."* If Hashem had not taken our forefathers out of Egypt, then we, our children, our grandchildren — and everyone in our houses — would still be enslaved.

Another explanation is as follows: The evil son is asking, "What do you gain from this service?" That is, what profits accrue "to you"? Our answer to him is in what we say to the son who does not know to ask: *For the sake of this [the Pesach offering, a mitzvah] did Hashem do [wonders] for me* — God took us out of Egypt only in order that we observe His commandments, simply because they are His commandments, and not because there may be benefits for us in doing so. We

מִמִּצְרָיִם. לִי וְלֹא לוֹ. אִלּוּ הָיָה שָׁם לֹא הָיָה נִגְאָל:

תָּם מַה הוּא אוֹמֵר.
מַה זֹּאת. וְאָמַרְתָּ אֵלָיו בְּחֹזֶק יָד הוֹצִיאָנוּ יְהֹוָה מִמִּצְרַיִם מִבֵּית עֲבָדִים:

do not do the mitzvos of the Seder for our own personal gain; in Egypt, as well, if our forefathers had done the mitzvos for selfish reasons, they would not have been redeemed.

📖

[You emphasize] "for me" and not for him...if he had been there he would not have been redeemed — The Haggadah uses the third person (he) and not the second (you). When the Torah tells us to respond: *And you shall say, "It is a Pesach offering to Hashem,"* note that it does not say "And you shall say to *him.*" Why not? Because the wicked son is not asking a question! His words are meant only to deride us and create an argument. Thus, the manner of response is such that his words do not enter our ears and cause our hearts to doubt. Really, we are not speaking to him at all! We are speaking to ourselves, and automatically, when he hears what we are saying, his "teeth" are set on edge. (based on *Malbim* and *Ma'asei Nissim*)

📖

If he had been there — We do not speak directly to the wicked son. Rather, we speak about him, to his brother —the son who does not know to ask. We say that if the wicked brother had been in Egypt, he would not have been redeemed. (*Vilna Gaon*)

📖

If he had been there — We could not say directly to the wicked son, "If you had been in Egypt, you would not have been redeemed," for when God took the Jews out of Egypt, He simultaneously redeemed the soul of every Jew to be born in every generation afterwards, and the soul of the wicked son went out of Egypt, too! Rather, we mean to not for him! [You imply] that if he had been there, he would not have been redeemed.

WHAT DOES THE SIMPLE SON SAY? "What is this?" (Shemos 13:14) "And you shall say to him, 'With a strong hand God took us out of Egypt, from the house of bondage.'"

say that if a Jew in Egypt had spoken as this son speaks now, that Jew in Egypt would not have been redeemed. As for the wicked son himself, however, inside he is good, and therefore there is hope for him.

We do not give him his answer immediately, however, because we want to make him think that we are angry with him. On the other hand, we do not ignore him either. When we turn to address the son who does not know to ask, what we say is intended for the ears of the wicked son as well, as will be explained.

How does the Torah teach us that the wicked son does not get his answer immediately? The verses say, regarding the other three sons, that we should say "*to him*," which implies that we are to respond to their questions immediately. Regarding our response to the wicked son, however, the Torah says only, *And you shall say*, and this carries no implication regarding when we answer him.

The simple son — The simple son is associated with the wise son; the two are different only in terms of their intelligence. Thus, the answer the Torah tells us to give to him is much like the answer we are told to give the wise son, but it is only half as long. The wise son is told not only that *God took us out...with a strong hand,* which is the glorious part of the Exodus; he also is told, *We were slaves* — which was the shame that preceded the glory. The simple son is not as intelligent, and thus we tell him only part of the story — the glorious part.

וְשֶׁאֵינוֹ יוֹדֵעַ לִשְׁאֹל
אַתְּ פְּתַח לוֹ. שֶׁנֶּאֱמַר, וְהִגַּדְתָּ לְבִנְךָ בַּיּוֹם הַהוּא לֵאמֹר בַּעֲבוּר זֶה עָשָׂה יְהֹוָה לִי בְּצֵאתִי מִמִּצְרָיִם:

Does not know to ask — In this verse, the Torah writes simply, *You shall tell your son,* even though it is not stated that he asked anything! This verse is about the son who does not even want to talk with those who do mitzvos. As such, this son is associated with the wicked son, and is an outgrowth of him. The evil son does interact with those who do mitzvos, though he argues and makes fun. The son who does not know to ask, however, is one step beyond the wicked son, having distanced himself so far from those who perform mitzvos that he does not even trouble himself to argue or make fun of them. We cannot give up hope for him, however. When he does not approach us, we approach him!

📖

You open [the dialogue] for him — For despite everything, he remains your son.

📖

You open — The Hebrew word for "you," when one is addressing a male, is אתה (*attah*), and את (*at*) when addressing a female. Twice in the Torah (*Bemidbar* 11, *Devarim* 5) God addresses Moshe *Rabbenu* using the feminine form, and our Sages explain that He did so because Moshe *Rabbenu* had become weak, as a woman, on account of sins that had been committed by Israel. Here, too, the Haggadah uses the feminine "you" because it is a sign of our weaknesses that such a son is found in our homes at all. He did not reach such a state all at once, however. You neglected him, and now the time has come for you to "open" to him.

📖

You shall tell your son — Here, the Torah uses the word "tell"; regarding how we address the other sons, the Torah uses the word "say," which has a softer nuance and sound. The *Talmud* (*Shabbos* 57) says that the term used here is *as hard as sinews* and that this can be under-

AS FOR THE SON WHO DOES NOT KNOW TO ASK, you open [the dialogue] for him, as the Torah says (Shemos 13:18): "You shall tell your son on that day, saying: Because of this [the Pesach offering, a mitzvah] did God do [great things] for me when I went out of Egypt."

stood in two ways: This son is "harder" than all the others, for he is even more distant from us than is the wicked son. Thus the words that we use in order to reach him must be just as "hard" as he is. Or, *hard as sinews* refers not to our words, but to our efforts. Because he is so far away, we must work harder and make greater efforts to bring him back.

Because of this [the Pesach offering, a mitzvah] did God do [great things] for me — On condition that I would fulfill His commandments. Never is a Jew exempt from fulfilling the mitzvos, even if his father is wicked and never taught him about the Torah and mitzvos at all. In fact, the Torah here is addressing fathers and grandfathers, as well as the elders of every town: *You shall tell your son.* You must teach this boy that he is obligated in the mitzvos, for the mitzvos are why God freed us from the Egyptian bondage.

Because of this — Just as the answer given to the simple son is only half the answer that is given to the wise son, the answer given to the son who does not know to ask, is only half the answer given to the wicked son. We answer the wicked son at length, beginning with the shameful part of our history, as background, and ending with the glory of the redemption. Here, to the son who is even farther removed from mitzvos, we omit the background, for he does not have the patience for it. We tell him only the praise and the glory — that *because of this [the Pesach offering, a mitzvah] did God do [great things] for me when I went out of Egypt.*

The order of the Four Sons

The Haggadah mentions the four sons in a different order from the Torah. In the Torah, the verses about the four sons appear in the following order: wicked, does not know to ask, wise, simple. In the Haggadah, however, the order is: wise, wicked, simple, does not know to ask. Let us explain the reason for this.

When the Jews were in Egypt, and were told by God that soon they would be freed and would receive the Torah, they so looked forward to these things and so desired to become servants of God, it did not even enter their minds that sons who are wicked could come out of them. At that very time, however, Moshe *Rabbenu* informed them that, in fact, they would bear such sons. At the same time, he assured them that not all of their sons would be wicked, and even the wicked ones could be brought back to the straight way, for the Torah provides instructions as to what approach a father should use to correct the problem. This is why the Torah mentions the wicked son first.

Next, Moshe *Rabbenu* warned them that if they do not use the Torah's approach, they will fail in bringing the wicked son back — which will lead them, God forbid, to have another type of son, the son who does not even know to ask. This son does not even associate with those who do mitzvos, and does not even bother to argue or make fun of them. Moshe warned the people that if they did not follow the Torah's recommendation about how to handle their wicked sons, then the nation could become two nations — the wicked and the disinterested on the one side, and the wise and the simple on the other!

Moshe *Rabbenu* continued, saying that if the Nation did not take the proper steps to repair these ills, something even worse could happen: Those who previously had served God out of simple faith, might begin to have doubts about God, Torah, and mitzvos. Seeing the Nation split in half, the simple sons could find their faith shaken. "What is this?" they will ask. Seeing two camps, one opposed to the other, they will begin to wonder, "Which camp is the mistaken one? Could it be that it really is not worthwhile to serve God and strive for holiness?"

Before his death, Moshe *Rabbenu* revealed to the Nation that things would deteriorate to a worse state of affairs, where even the wise among them would begin to have doubts, and even they would start asking questions. With the best intentions, hoping to reunite the torn nation, the wise would begin to investigate (*Devarim* 6:20): *What are these testimonies, chukim, and statutes?* That is, maybe there is a difference between these three categories, and one category may be less important than the other. If so, maybe leniencies are possible, and Jews can be exempted from the less important parts of the Torah, so that they can concentrate on fulfilling the more important parts.

Such a thought, however, only would show that the plague of weakness had struck the wise among us, too. The wise, however, have become weak and thus even they have to relearn the lessons of Egypt. They, too, must set it firmly in their hearts that we are the nation that was chosen, and we are not the nation that chooses! Surely, it is not for us to choose to do some things that God wants us to do, and to not do others, simply because we have questions in our minds. Just as we were once Pharaoh's servants, now we are God's, and it is not the nature of a servant to choose to follow one command that his master gives him, and not follow another, simply because the servant is troubled by doubts!

Thus, Moshe *Rabbenu* warned (*Devarim* 6:21-24): *We were slaves to Pharaoh in Egypt, and Hashem our God took us out...and commanded us to do all these chukim...* Moshe *Rabbenu* called the entire Torah *chukim*! He also emphasized that God commanded us to fulfill all the Torah, because the time would come when even the wise among us would want to make distinctions between mitzvos — between those that have reasons, and those that do not (*chukim*). They would think, even where the Torah explicitly states a reason for a mitzvah, that after all, times change, and the reason can become less compelling, so maybe the mitzvah changes, too! Maybe the mitzvah itself is less compelling, and maybe its fulfillment is no longer even necessary! Against these dangerous thoughts, Moshe *Rabbenu* called the entire Torah *chukim* — to teach us that no part of Torah changes at all! In the end, even the wise among us need this lesson.

This is the order found in the Torah — a chronological one, describing spiritual deterioration over the course of time, beginning with the wicked son, and what would happen, step-by-step, when we fail to bring him back to the way of truth.

On the Seder night, however, we are gathered together to do what we can in order to educate our children properly, as the Torah commands us, and all four types of sons are already with us. Among them are sons who cause us pain, as Moshe *Rabbenu* prophesied. Our

Sages advised us that on this night, we should begin with the wise son, to strengthen his faith, so that he can join us in our efforts to educate the others. Therefore, the wise son is mentioned first in the Haggadah.

The best way to strengthen the wise son's faith is to cause him to cling to the mitzvos, by discussing and explaining them to him in depth, from the first mitzvah of the night to the last. After this, he can do the same for his brothers. He can teach them the verse about doing all the *chukim*, concluding with the law that after the *Afikoman*, one does not eat anything else.

Once you have strengthened the wise son's faith, have him join you when you turn to the challenge of the wicked son, so that together you can bring the wicked son to the truth, in order that he may live. To reach the wicked son, you first must shake his confidence in himself, by showing that your self-confidence is even greater than his. Hopefully, this will make him think twice before he haughtily opens his mouth again. In the meantime you are patient, and hope for his sake that now he will not open his mouth, but will open his ears and his heart, so that what is said at the Seder to the other sons, can work its effect on him, and heal him.

You have strengthened the wise son, but you also have weakened him by using him as a shield against the wicked son. The wicked son is now quiet, his haughtiness subdued, for you have delivered a blow straight to his teeth. Now you must turn your attention to the simple son, who keeps the faith because he sees that this is what the wise son does. You must speak to him clearly, because the opening challenge from the lips of the wicked son has shaken hi m. You must return his faith to him, and firmly restore him to the side of the wise son. The wise son has been speaking and the wicked son has been silent, and now you tell the simple son, *With a strong hand God took us out.* You spoke clearly, and the simple son understood the point that you made: God's strength today is the same as it was in Egypt! Rebel against God? God forbid! I will never rebel!

The wise son now has an ally again, and he rejoins you in educating the others. The wicked son remains silent, for his teeth are still ringing, but his ears and heart are opening more and more. At this point, it is time for the walls of estrangement to crumble! There sits the son who does not even know to ask, who has totally disassociated himself from God, Torah, and mitzvos, involving himself instead in the ways of the non-Jewish world. To him, our words ring out: "Our Nation exists today not because of the ways you have adopted. Rather, because of this — the mitzvos — have we survived!" Now he, too, begins to understand, for his faith in his life style has been weakened. Neither has he done evil deeds which would have blemished his soul and thus would block him from seeing the truth. You have managed to create a small opening in his heart, the size of a needle, and as the night's discussion continues, the opening will grow and grow, so that the light of truth enters, like sunlight rushing in through the open door of a fortified castle.

By means of the order prescribed by the Haggadah, you are able to reach the most difficult son of all!

More about the Four Sons

As mentioned above, some explain that the four sons correspond to the four expressions of redemption that God employed when He promised us the redemption from Egypt. These four expressions, recorded in the Torah, allude to the four different exiles that our Nation suffered afterwards: Babylonia, Persia, Greece, and Rome (Rome includes all our subjugations until the future fall of Gog and Magog in the days of *Mashiach*). The Sefas Emes writes that all four kingdoms subjugated our People physically and spiritually, similar to what Egypt was able to do. They taxed, governed, and controlled us, and they also were able to undermine our faith to a certain extent. They succeeded in creating doubts in our minds, and caused us to make mistakes of a spiritual sort. Through the confusion in us that arose because of these four kingdoms, our sons have their questions — questions which have cropped up in the minds of all Jews.

As a Jew acquires more and more knowledge, his evil inclination causes him to wonder about those mitzvos which the Torah does not explain and which human reason cannot grasp. His evil inclination makes him ask, "What is the reason for this mitzvah?" Every wise Jew must be prepared to deal with such thoughts as soon as they arise. The answer to them must be set in one's heart: Doing the Will of God is the true satisfaction in life, and no other activity gives a "taste" as good or as sweet. Performing the mitzvah gives us much more pleasure than what we would feel if we were to simply "understand" the mitzvah. Thus, "once one performs the mitzvah of *Afikoman*, one does not eat anything else." That is, the taste of this matzah is the best taste of all, precisely because the taste comes to us through the performance of a mitzvah. There is no tasting anything else afterwards, because no other taste can compare.

When a Jew's evil inclination gains control over him, it places the question in his mouth: *What is this service to you?* That is, the evil inclination tells him, The human being is so small and insignificant. Why should I think that what I do on earth goes up to Heaven and is noticed by God at all?" He wonders, "Why should it matter to God whether I do mitzvos or not?"

What is the truth of the matter? *Because of this!* Precisely because you are mere flesh and blood! Precisely because you live in the physical world and lack understanding — this is what makes your performance of mitzvos more important to God, and very significant! Praises rising to God from those who dwell in the lower realms are more beloved to God than the praises rising to Him from higher realms. Do not listen to your evil inclination! Strengthen yourself in the performance of the mitzvos, and do not let yourself weaken!

There are Jews who live lives of simple faith, their hearts happy and satisfied that they are servants of God. The path ahead of them is clear, for God has put a spark in their souls which makes them realize that they were made in His Image. Regarding these Jews, the evil inclination works by making them start to feel haughty, until they say to themselves, "What is this?" That is, such a Jew may begin to wonder, "Perhaps I am one of the most beloved of our People — one of the few who is truly righteous!" He must realize, however, that no matter what advantage or superiority that he may enjoy over others, whether it be physical or spiritual, he enjoys it only because God has chosen to be exceptionally kind to him, and not because he is deserving of it. *With a strong hand* God extracted you from your lowliness in Egypt. The Nation had sunken into the Egyptian mire, and God lifted them out of it because of His Kindness — not because of the Nation's merits. And you, as well, were given gifts, and did nothing beforehand to earn them.

The condition of the son who does not know to ask, is unfortunate enough on its own, without the evil inclination having to whisper in his ear. He is a victim of our Nation's long and tortuous exile. Circumstances have caused his heart to become so closed that he cannot ask questions, because he cannot even begin to speak! *You open [the dialogue] for him!*

One Jew helps the other, brother supports brother, saying, "Stay strong!" We, too, are suffering from the long exile, and even though we, too, may feel weak, we still do our best to try to help others. If we do, then our strength, too, will revive! *(Sefas Emes)*

Elsewhere, the Sefas Emes provides an additional insight. The subjugation in Egypt was the root of the subsequent subjugations to the four different kingdoms. Similarly, the redemption from Egypt was the root of all the redemptions to follow. In turn, subjugation itself arises from four particularly serious sins: idolatry, illicit relations, murder, and, finally — baseless hatred of one's fellow and derogatory speech against him. It is said that the last of the four sins is as bad as all the other three combined.

It would seem that the purpose of the four exiles is to rectify these four terrible sins, each exile rectifying one in particular. Rectifying the first three sins was the purpose of the first three exiles, and by means of the whole process are the questions of the first three sons at the Seder answered. Moreover, the different aspects of the evil inclination which cause these sins are also rooted out — jealousy, desire for physical pleasure, and desire for honor.

The present-day exile is due to the sin of baseless hatred, which is the cause of derogatory speech against one's fellowman. It follows then, that the questions and doubts of the fourth son are regarded as belonging to one *who does not know to ask*, for what he asks is not even a question, is without basis, and results only from confusion.

יָכוֹל מֵרֹאשׁ חֹדֶשׁ, תַּלְמוּד לוֹמַר בַּיּוֹם הַהוּא. אִי בַּיּוֹם הַהוּא יָכוֹל מִבְּעוֹד יוֹם, תַּלְמוּד לוֹמַר בַּעֲבוּר זֶה. בַּעֲבוּר זֶה לֹא אָמַרְתִּי אֶלָּא בְּשָׁעָה שֶׁיֵּשׁ מַצָּה וּמָרוֹר מֻנָּחִים לְפָנֶיךָ:

You might think that one can [relate the Haggadah] from Rosh Chodesh Nisan — In Egypt, on *Rosh Chodesh*, God told Moshe and Aharon the part of the Torah in which Nisan is called *the head of the months*, i.e., the first month of the Jewish calendar. In these passages, the mitzvos regarding Pesach are found as well. In addition, the redemption is considered to have started on *Rosh Chodesh*. (*Rashbam, Orchos Chayim, Rashbatz*)

📖

So the Torah says, "on that day" — The day of the actual redemption (*R. Yeshaya Ditrani*), when the Jews slaughtered the Pesach offering. (*Rashi and others*)

📖

If "on that day," then you might think...while it is still daylight — It says "day" and the Pesach offering is slaughtered in the afternoon. Also, prohibitions regarding *chametz* begin that day, even before the *Pesach* is slaughtered.
So the Torah says, "because of this" — "This" refers to matzah, which is mentioned in the previous verse. (based on *Rashi, Machzor Vitry* and others)

📖

Because of this — When the father performs the mitzvah of retelling the story of the Exodus, it should not be simply with words. Rather,

You might think that one can [relate the Haggadah] from Rosh Chodesh Nisan onwards; so the Torah says, "on that day." If [it can be told] "on that day," then you might think that you can [tell it] while it is still daylight; so the Torah says, "because of this." I cannot say "because of this" except when matzah and maror are placed in front of you.

he should make the story come alive, and actually become a part of it. Here, therefore, he is speaking about the matzah, and he has laid the matzah in front of him, for all of the listeners to see. This is the way it must be regarding all the mitzvos of the Torah — we do not simply talk about them; we do them. When we speak about the mitzvos, we show that we also fulfill them. We illustrate what we say, and we speak in a way that everyone can understand.

When matzah and maror are placed in front of you — That is, at night. If so, why does the Torah say "on that day"? To teach us that the Seder night gives off light, as if it were day. (*Vilna Gaon*)

One might ask, "Why didn't the Torah fix the time of saying the Haggadah to be in the afternoon, while the Pesach offering is being slaughtered?" The answer: Because then, everyone is occupied with that mitzvah, and with other preparations for the Seder, so that they do not have peace of mind to dwell upon the story and elaborate. (*Shelah haKadosh*)

When matzah and maror — In the days of the Temple, they would say, "When the *Pesach*, matzah, and *maror*." The Mechilta, in its interpretation of the verse, states explicitly: "When the meat of the Pesach offering is to be eaten."

מִתְּחִלָּה עוֹבְדֵי עֲבוֹדָה זָרָה הָיוּ אֲבוֹתֵינוּ. וְעַכְשָׁו קֵרְבָנוּ הַמָּקוֹם לַעֲבוֹדָתוֹ. שֶׁנֶּאֱמַר, וַיֹּאמֶר יְהוֹשֻׁעַ אֶל כָּל הָעָם כֹּה אָמַר יְהוָֹה אֱלֹהֵי יִשְׂרָאֵל, בְּעֵבֶר הַנָּהָר יָשְׁבוּ אֲבוֹתֵיכֶם מֵעוֹלָם תֶּרַח אֲבִי אַבְרָהָם וַאֲבִי נָחוֹר וַיַּעַבְדוּ אֱלֹהִים אֲחֵרִים: וָאֶקַּח אֶת אֲבִיכֶם אֶת אַבְרָהָם מֵעֵבֶר הַנָּהָר וָאוֹלֵךְ אוֹתוֹ בְּכָל אֶרֶץ כְּנָעַן וָאַרְבֶּה אֶת זַרְעוֹ וָאֶתֵּן לוֹ אֶת יִצְחָק, וָאֶתֵּן לְיִצְחָק אֶת יַעֲקֹב וְאֶת עֵשָׂו, וָאֶתֵּן לְעֵשָׂו אֶת הַר שֵׂעִיר לָרֶשֶׁת אוֹתוֹ, וְיַעֲקֹב וּבָנָיו יָרְדוּ מִצְרָיִם:

At first — The telling of the story of the Exodus actually begins here. Up to now, everything in the Haggadah was stated in brief. Even regarding the wise son, whose question was to be answered in detail, the Haggadah simply outlined that answer. The Haggadah only hinted how the other sons were to be answered, mentioning only the main idea of the response to be given to each one. Elaboration on those answers begins now, so that everyone at the table can hear the wondrous account.

Up to this point, the wicked son, whom we surely want to reach, was hardly given any answer at all, though the Torah commands us to speak to him on this night. In fact, the Torah mentions the wicked son first! From this point in the Haggadah and onwards, much will be told that will open the heart of even the wicked son, and sink in deeply, so that he, too, will come to say, with everyone else at the table: "Therefore all of us must give thanks and praises to God!"

At first...but now — As noted, the Haggadah's basic format is to begin with the shameful part of our history, and to conclude with the part that is glorious. The Haggadah quotes several verses, dividing them

*A*T FIRST OUR FOREFATHERS were idol-worshipers, but now the Everpresent One has brought us close, to serve Him, as it is written (Yehoshua 22:2):

"And Yehoshua said to the entire Nation, 'Thus says Hashem, the God of Israel: Your fathers in olden times dwelt beyond the River [Euphrates], and [there] Terach, who was the father of Avraham and Nahor, served other gods. But I took your father Avraham from across the river, and had him walk the entire land of Canaan. I multiplied his seed, and gave him Yitzchak. To Yitzchak I gave Yaakov and Esav. To Esav, as his inheritance, I gave Mount Seir, and Yaakov and his sons descended into Egypt.'"

into three different groups. These verses outline the general sequence of events and focus on four major elements to this grand story:

1. God's selecting Avraham — one man out of all others, to be the Patriarch of the People who would receive the Torah. However, "sifting" had to be done regarding Avraham's offspring, until all impurities were removed.

2. The Covenant between the Pieces which God made with Avraham, containing a prophecy of the future, a condition, and a promise.

3. The Jewish People's fulfillment of the condition.

4. God's fulfillment of His promise.

The Haggadah expounds upon these verses until the story is completed.

At first, our forefathers were idol-worshipers — So it was until Avraham *Avinu*. The world was desolate, for mankind subscribed to foolish beliefs, and was ignorant of the importance of serving God. Shem and Ever were different, and did know the correct way, but they left no children, and very few students who could carry on these teachings and spread them. Their few students served God quietly, while the world around them was steeped in evil and idolatry.

But now, the Everpresent One has brought us close, to serve Him — We did not draw close to God on our own; rather, God brought us close. Even Avraham *Avinu* did not come to God on his own. From his very birth, Avraham had a special purity and other superior qualities, and afterwards, God brought him closer and elevated him even more. Thus, we must realize that everything comes from God, out of the kindness and mercy He has shown to our People. Therefore, it is fitting that we thank and praise Him.

At first...but now — If the evil son says he is tired of what is "old-fashioned," we show him that his is actually the old-fashioned way! What is new is that *God has drawn us close*. And just as the sons of idol-worshipers were brought to the truth, all the more so he can he experience the same thing, for he is descended from the Patriarchs, and if someone wants to mend his ways, the door is always open.

At first — before the giving of the Torah — *our forefathers were idol-worshipers, but now* — because we have accepted the Torah, we are no longer considered to be their descendants, for God said, *But I took your father, Avraham,* that is, only Avraham is considered your father, and you are not regarded as descendants of his fathers. (*Emes l'Yaakov*)

To Esav, as his inheritance, I gave Mount Seir — To remove him from the family, so that only Yaakov would inherit the legacy of Avraham, and neither would Esav inherit any part of Canaan. (*Vilna Gaon*)

At first, our forefathers were idol-worshipers

This, in essence, is the answer to a general question: Why did God send us down into Egypt — just to redeem us later? Then don't send us into slavery in the first place, and let us be free, as we were previously! To answer this, the Haggadah teaches: "The way of life of Terach and those before him was not true freedom." That is, if a person is subservient to another person, his situation is certainly not ideal, but he is worse off if he has made himself subservient to idols — to wood and to stone. If he does that, he is a servant to a servant! In one case he is like a whole utensil, and in the other case he is like a broken one.

In His Mercy, God implanted in the hearts of our forefathers the desire to completely abandon idol-worship. This was a great act of mercy. In order to get away from the worship of wood and stone, it is even worthwhile to enter fire or water, and even if one knows that he will not be saved. It is better to die than to live in such error! Once we feel gratitude to God for helping our forefathers abandon the worship of wood and stone, it is easier for us to cope with our being subjugated to other men, no matter how long such subjugation might last. We can cope, because we realize that enslavement of one's body with freedom of the soul is preferable to enslavement of one's soul with freedom of the body!

In truth, however, God had in mind much greater things for us: to bestow upon our souls eternity and grandeur, and to give our bodies strength and glory, so that we would be His messengers, and restore beauty and peace to the entire world. We, as His People, would correct the harm that was caused to the world by generation after generation of idol-worship and evil. Through us, the world would return to the pristine state in which it existed when God first created it. The descendants of Avraham would be the priests and leaders of humanity, who would hold the rod that would strike down the evil ones who would destroy themselves and the whole world with them. In His Mercy, God sought to purge our forefathers of the impurities that had entered them due to the evil doings of the many generations that preceded them. The previous generations caused nothing but anger to God, and now, He wanted to cleanse us of the effects of that shameful past, so that we could rise above it, and stand upright; and if momentarily we fell, we would have the strength to stand up again.

The King of Creation desired us, desired to dwell within us and among us, so that every human being who would ever be born, until the end of time, would have us as a bridge and pathway, leading creation to the Final Redemption, when all will turn to serve God, and attribute Kingship to Him, crowning Him in His Home on the Holy

Mountain in Jerusalem.

Avraham was one lone man in the world, and his wife Sarah was one lone woman. How would two individuals working alone bring about such a monumental change in the world? Through their offspring? But what about the twenty generations that preceded Avraham and Sarah — generations who all had angered God? All those previous generations were evil, and were riddled with the impurities of corruption and idol-worship. How could the offspring of Avraham and Sarah be cleansed of these impurities, so that they would have the spiritual strength which would enable them to accomplish the holy task?

A new start was needed. Avraham and Sarah had to be born without the natural ability to have children, so that when they did have children, it would be only by means of a miracle. In this way God put something completely new into Creation, specifically for His exalted purpose. In this way, Avraham and Sarah would bring offspring into the world, but offspring with no link to the evil of the past.

(Later in Jewish history, as well, we find Rivkah, Rachel, and Leah all coming from homes where idols were worshiped, and in the case of all three, it was God Who "opened their wombs," by means of a miracle, so that their offspring were totally disconnected to the past.)

Although Avraham's and Sarah's ability to have children was a new creation, Avraham and Sarah themselves were not new creations, and thus some of the blemish of the twenty previous generations of evil remained in them. Evil was mixed with good, and the seed of the Chosen People had to be free of the stain of evil. What would become of these traces of evil?

The seed of Avraham would be cleansed by means of a sifting process. God said, "Among your children, one will be My gift to you — Yitzchak, who will be holy at birth." That is, before Avraham and Sarah had Yitzchak, Sarah gave Avraham her maidservant Hagar as a wife. Hagar bore Avraham a son — Yishmael — and all the impurities in the seed of Avraham were passed to him, so that when Yitzchak was born, the only impurities in him were those that were passed to him from his mother Sarah, for Yitzchak was her first (and only) child.

In turn, Rivkah bore Esav and Yaakov to Yitzchak. When the two boys were born, the small amount of impurity in Yitzchak from Sarah, and the small amount of impurities in Rivkah, were both passed down exclusively to Esav, and Yaakov was free of any trace of the evil of the past. Thus, God said, "I will give to Yitzchak (as a gift) Yaakov and Esav." Even Esav was considered a "gift" to Yitzchak, for were it not for Esav, the impurities from Rivkah and those that had been left in Yitzchak from Sarah, would have been passed down to Yaakov! Rivkah was worthy of having only one son, but in her husband's merit, she had a second son — Esav — who acted as a sieve which collected all the impurities of the past, so that Yaakov would be born pure.

In the words of our Sages, "Yaakov's bed was whole." That is, he was absolutely clean of impurities from the previous generations, and his sons contained no trace of these impurities either. Yaakov's twelve sons were descended only from Yitzchak and Avraham. Avraham had been barren, and God gave him Yitzchak — thus the sons of Yaakov had no connection whatever to Avraham's father, Terach. They traced back their lineage no farther, and neither were they considered to be related to Avraham's brothers, Nahor and Haran. The holiness that began with Avraham had continually strengthened itself, culminating in Yaakov, for all three Patriarchs constantly clung to God, until the holiness of the seed of Yaakov was intact — for a thread woven of three strands does not come undone.

All of Yaakov's sons were born holy and free of impurity. Certainly we realize this regarding the sons born to Yaakov from Rachel and Leah, for Rachel and Leah were born barren and thus the previous generations' impurities could not possibly be passed on by them. God performed a miracle and "opened their wombs." Thus the only impurity that could be found in their offspring could be traced back to the fact that Rachel and Leah were raised in Lavan's house. Happily, this small amount of uncleanliness in the two sisters was completely nullified by the awesome holiness of Yaakov, and by the inherent holiness of Rachel and Leah themselves.

It is also the case that there was a unique purity to the sons born to Yaakov by Zilpah and Bilhah, the maidservants of Leah and Rachel. These women were not barren, and thus they could pass on impurities from the previous generations, and any impurities of their own as well. However, Zilpah and Bilhah both were such devoted servants of God that their inherent holiness, combined with the awesome holiness of Yaakov, erased all that was untoward, so that their children, too, were born completely free of blemish.

Thus all the sons of Yaakov were born in a state of purity, completely clean of stains which could have been left on their souls due to the sins of past generations. Later in their lives, if they would sin, causing new defilement to enter them, God would send fires of purification to consume the impurity, as furnaces refine metal. Afterwards, the sons would be clean and pure again, as free of stain as they were at birth, fully prepared for the monumental task that awaited them.

Lavan, Rivkah's brother, was descended from Shem, the most righteous of the sons of No'ach. Lavan, however, went in the ways of Nimrod, son of Kush and grandson of Cham, the wicked son of No'ach. As a result, Lavan was wicked, and also an idol-worshiper.

In the days of Avraham, the family of Shem was probably the most respected family in the world, for its lineage remained clear all the way back to before the flood. The members of this family were good-looking, strong, and tall. They reached maturity quickly, our Sages tell us, bearing children even at the age of six or seven. They also lived longer than other people, usually for hundreds of years. Although the family of Shem did not chase after idols, many were drawn to them, for this was the practice in Canaan, and the land of Shem was conquered by the other sons of Cham, who dominated the world in those days. Most of the family of Shem went the way of the rest of the conquered peoples, and willingly accepted the ways of their rulers.

Even though the family of Shem distinguished itself with its clear lineage lines, and had a tradition dating back to the days of No'ach that the great of mankind would be descended from Shem, the family found itself under the rule of Nimrod, and followed in his ways.

When Avraham's light began to shine, and God saved him when Nimrod had him thrown into a fiery furnace, everyone began to say, "He is the one who will overthrow Nimrod, and restore rulership to the family of Shem." If, in fact, Nimrod had not continually pursued Avraham, then Avraham's family, the family of Shem, would have joined with Avraham against Nimrod. It was dangerous, however, so his family abandoned him and followed Nimrod. Worse still, everyone in the family of Shem became Avraham's enemy, except for his brother Haran. As did Nimrod, they pursued Avraham, but they were motivated by jealousy, because the belief arose that Avraham would accomplish his goals, and thereby take all the grandeur that they had foreseen for themselves. They knew that when this happened, it would be too late for them to join ranks with him. Thus, they threw in their lot with Nimrod.

Nimrod's aggression, and the jealousy of the family of Shem, subsided as the years went by and everyone saw that Avraham had no inheritors. By the time that Avraham and Sarah, late in life, begot Yitzchak, Nimrod and the family of Shem did not see Avraham as much of a threat, and thus they left him alone. When Yaakov and Esav were born, however, and strife began between them, the family of Shem sided with Esav, and hoped for the day that Yaakov would be destroyed.

Thus, when Yaakov arrived in Aram at the house of Lavan, he entered the house of a man who hated him and everything that he stood for. Lavan was steeped in idolatry and he practiced his false religion with the strength and fervor which were inherent in the family of Shem. Our Sages taught: Why was he called Lavan ["white"]? Because he was "white" with evil! That is, in those days, until Lavan, everyone realized that Nimrod's way, the way of sin, was ugly, "black," and low. Lavan, however, succeeded in clothing Nimrod's sins "in white." He gave them a shine of legitimacy, by connecting them to the respected family of Shem.

Lavan, an Aramean, said to himself, "It is good that Yaakov has come to live with me, for here I can keep my eye on him, and any children that he will have will be mine! This spells the end to everything that Avraham dreamed! Those dreams are now in my hands!"

Thus, Lavan the Aramean already felt that everything was in his possession, that in a quick turn of events he had gained control, would be able to destroy Yaakov, and Avraham's legacy would be his. Thus, Moshe *Rabbeinu* recounted, *My father* — Yaakov — *was an oved Arami* — was something "lost" in the hands of the Aramean, Lavan.* That is, he was simply lost from the world, for twenty years. All those years, Lavan made Yaakov work for him, around the clock, un-

---

* The Hebrew root of *oved* can connote various meanings, one of which is "lost."

til in the end, the Aramean felt that everything was his — Yaakov's sheep, Yaakov's children, and even Yaakov himself! All had been lost and was now Lavan's!

However, Moshe *Rabbenu*'s words can be understood in another, happier, way. Lavan felt that he had defeated Yaakov. At the same time, he was willing to admit that whatever he had accomplished was only because he had used deceit, and had tricked Yaakov. Early in their relationship, Lavan had concluded that Yaakov was naive to the ways of trickery, and later, Lavan thought that he had succeeded in taking everything that Yaakov owned, precisely because Yaakov was naive.

The truth, however, was just the opposite: Yaakov knew full well how Lavan was trying to trick him. In fact, Yaakov was not defeated at all, because in the end he turned around and tricked Lavan! Thus, the meaning of the words can be understood as: "My father was lost to the Aramean!" That is, the tricks that Yaakov played on Lavan were "lost" on the Aramean! All those twenty years, while Lavan thought that he was tricking Yaakov, in truth Yaakov was tricking him! This became clear to Lavan in the end, when Yaakov left, taking a large family, two of Lavan's daughters, and practically all of Lavan's wealth.

Thus, Lavan had to admit that Avraham's dream remained alive. Not only that, but he realized that his own daughters had joined Yaakov in tricking him all those years. They had abandoned him in favor of Yaakov, and when Yaakov left, everything that he took with him came from Lavan himself! All those years, contrary to what he had thought, Lavan had not been destroying Avraham's dream — just the opposite! Thus, not only was Yaakov's trickery "lost on the Aramean." The whole turnaround was lost on the Aramean!

Yaakov left the house of Lavan without telling him. The Torah tells us (*Bereshis* 31:23) that when Lavan discovered that Yaakov had gone and had taken everything with him, Lavan "took his brothers in hand, and chased him." Lavan was burning with anger. The Torah tells us that Yaakov had a seven-day lead, but Lavan caught up in only one day. He was fuming, intent on killing not only Yaakov, but also his own grandsons! As long as Lavan had the strength to conquer Yaakov, he would do so and not leave any survivors, perhaps not even his own daughters!

So great is the jealousy that non-believers have of those who are faithful to God. Avraham served God with all his might, yet his door was always open, even to those who worshiped idols. Anyone who came to Avraham's tent hungry would go away satisfied, for Avraham fed all who were in need of food. Even if the guest was ungrateful, or his manner was disagreeable in some other way, Avraham would give him his blessing. He would say, "After all, God has given you life and provided you with food. If so, how can I deprive you?" Look now at the evil Lavan. Out of foolish jealousy, he had no mercy at all, not even on his own daughters and grandchildren! He sought to destroy them all!

At that time, Yaakov was able to remain steadfast, not because of his of wisdom, and not because of his strength or the strength of his sons. Lavan was afire with anger, and so were those who were accompanying him — the citizens of his town, his friends. Lavan's army was large, mighty, and well-armed. It was the mercy of God that saved Yaakov, just as God's mercy had saved him when he was forced to flee his parents' home.

God did not send angels to deal with Lavan, and to punish him for his intentions. Rather, God decided on something that would be even more difficult for this evil man. God Himself, in all His Glory, appeared to Lavan, as the Torah states (*Bereshis* 31:24): *And God came to Lavan the Aramean in a dream, saying, "Watch yourself..."* Why did God, so to speak, "trouble" Himself this way? He wanted to show the world how precious Yaakov was to Him — that in order to save Yaakov, He would even appear to someone who was not worthy of such a thing. Because Lavan heard God's warning, Yaakov was able to continue on his way, to the land where his father dwelled.

And as Yaakov came from Paddan Aram, God appeared to him again, and blessed him, saying, "Be fruitful and multiply; a nation and a company of nations shall be from you, and kings shall come from your loins. And the land which I gave to Avraham and Yitzchak, I shall give to you, and to your seed after you I shall give the land." And God went up from him, in the place where He spoke with him. (*Bereshis* 35:9-13)

This was the last time Yaakov had prophecy, until 33 years later, when he was about to descend into Egypt, and God told him (*Bereshis* 46:3): *Do not fear going down to Egypt.*

In the interim, troubles befell Yaakov, one after another. He temporarily was saved from the hands of Esav, but his brother's hatred for him would last forever. He had Esav coming at him from one side, Lavan coming at him from the other, the terrible pain he suffered from the incident with his daughter Dina and the following trouble with the city of Shechem, and then the death of his beloved Rachel.

In the land of Canaan, Yaakov had no peace, though God had promised him this land. Yaakov understood, however, that there was no contradiction, for the secret had been passed to him from his father Yitzchak, who had heard it from his father Avraham. God had made a covenant with Avraham, involving suffering to his descendants *in a land not theirs.* Before there would be peace, the future held in store purifying furnaces of a harsh servitude, at the hands of a foreign nation.

At the time of the Covenant between the Pieces, approximately four hundred years had passed since the world had been given a new start after the flood, in the days of No'ach. Sadly, however, the cleansing waters did not help, and the generations had again deteriorated into evil. Earlier, when the floodwaters subsided, God had promised that He would never cause water to cover the world again in order to destroy it. Four centuries later, when He made his covenant with Avraham, God said: "I give My world to you, Avraham, and I will make your descendants a kingdom of priests, to lead humanity to the proper way. I am keeping My world in existence only for your sake, and for the sake of your descendants — but you will do this thing: Just as I tolerated and suffered My world for these four hundred years, though the world did not deserve that I should suffer for it, so shall your descendants tolerate and suffer My world, also for four hundred years, though then, too, the world will not deserve that they suffer for it.

"In those four hundred years, your descendants shall be cleansed of all the impurities of the generations of the past. They shall learn to abhor the abominations committed by the nation that subjugates them and oppresses them. When they leave, they will not take any such abominations to their own land. And even if some of your descendants do contract some of the sicknesses of the nation that enslaves them, I will take them away from there, and cleanse them of their infection, for such is not their way. Once they are cleansed, they will see the difference between pure and impure, and they will always strive to preserve their elevated state, working also to elevate the rest of humanity, in order to remove the world's impurity! For this purpose I will liberate them, raise them high, and educate them. They will not be priests who will be withdrawn from My world. No, they shall be given to My world, and I shall sink them into it, they will be of it and they will become dirtied by it. But later, I will extract them from it, and they will be purified and clean!

"I am giving your descendants all these territories. Nevertheless, they will be *strangers in a land that is not theirs*. Behold! The earth and everything in it belongs to Me, yet I, so to speak, have been a stranger here for some four hundred years. So shall this covenant be, that you, so to speak, shall be as I have been! Estranged and put through suffering, purified, smelted and refined. If your sons will pass through this, I will make them Mine forever. I will redeem them, punish their oppressors, and give them a great treasure. My whole world, every prized thing in the entire creation — all will be theirs!"

Yitzchak spent his whole life dwelling in Canaan, as if he were a stranger in a land which was not his. The Torah refers to Yitzchak's "sojourning," for he never owned the land where he lived, and thus truly was a "stranger."

Yosef, the last son born to Yaakov, was closer to his father than were any of his brothers, and Yaakov taught more of his wisdom to Yosef than to his other sons. Only to Yosef did Yaakov reveal the secret condition of the Covenant between the Pieces, for Yitzchak did not command him to reveal it to the others. As a result, Yosef, too, behaved as a "stranger" in Canaan, while all the other brothers behaved as if they were already free men, living in a land that they thought was already theirs.

Esav still posed a threat, and Lavan's anger had not subsided either. The Canaanite and the Perizite nations had settled the land, and Nimrod, never having forgotten his rival Avraham, ruled all the nations of Cham, and was deeply jealous of Avraham's descendants. As Yaakov says, *And I am so few in number, what will be if they all gather together to attack me (Bereshis 34:30)*, for we are strangers here.

And Yisrael loved Yosef more than all his other sons (Bereshis 37:3). The events unfolded, and finally, our forefathers descended into Egypt. If they had not lived in the land of Canaan as strangers, they would live in the land of Egypt as strangers. And Yaakov went down to Egypt with them.

What was Egypt? The sickest and most immoral nation in the world. Filthy and impure, the blackest of the black, the most powerful commonwealth in the kingdom of Cham. Anyone who went to Egypt became trapped there, sinking deeper and deeper into the mire and never coming out again. To such a place Yaakov and his sons fled?! Four generations had spent all their energies trying to avoid the pitfalls of places like Egypt. Avraham, Yitzchak, Yaakov and his sons all abhorred such abominations, and now they descended into Egypt on their own accord? Willingly?

It is like a man who is running away from thieves. In his flight, he enters a hotel for the night, only to see that thieves are staying there, too, and there is no getting away. What does he do? While the thieves aren't looking, he hides all his valuables in their luggage. Later, the thieves sieze him, search his possessions the whole night long, but find nothing of any interest to them. They release him. In the morning, he goes to the town's authorities, and tells them, "I had this much jewelry, this amount of gold coins, this amount of silver, etc., and I know where it is. Thieves have it, and they slept in your hotel last night!" The authorities come to the hotel, search the suspect luggage, find the valuables where the owner had hidden them, return them to him, and send him on his way in peace.

So it was with Yaakov. When he began his flight from the house of Lavan, and came out into the open, he knew that the world's evil ones all would unite together to try to destroy him, for he was few in number. What did he do? He descended into Egypt, there hiding everything that he had! Those who chased him said: Now that Yaakov is in Egypt, he will never come out again, for "no slave ever escaped from Egypt." All through Yaakov's long, dark exile in Egypt, his enemies searched for him, and also for his sons. Yaakov and his family were nowhere to be found, however, for as the night of the exile wore on, they came to look no different from their taskmasters, and blended in with the Egyptians completely.

When the time of redemption arrived, it was as if the light of morning broke, and God came and took them out of there. As they were leaving, everyone recognized who they were. These were not slaves. These were not broken people. How different they appeared from how they looked previously! Kohanim, Levites, four different camps with flags and banners! Kings and ministers! Sages, judges, and elders! It was the army of God that was leaving Egypt!

The debt had been paid. The covenant had been fulfilled. God used His own calculation to determine when the end of the exile should come, for He wanted to fulfill His promise to Avraham.

📖

At first, our forefathers were idol-worshipers, but now the Everpresent One has brought us close, to serve Him — In between, how many rivers and oceans of tears did we shed! How many hundreds of years of prolonged suffering, and we still held out hope! How much of our blood was spilled, and how many thousands of Jewish infants were cast in the Nile! How many were slaughtered and strangled! How frightful was the exile in Egypt — day after day, year after year — pillaging us, enslaving us, and wielding the sword on us and our children!

But now God has drawn us close to Him, and we are serving Him. He has lifted us out of Egypt's terror and abominations, and has given us true freedom. What fool would suggest that we return to Egypt, or to its impurities? How could it enter our minds to distance ourselves from God and His commandments? Today, who can be so foolish, and so evil, as to ignore our suffering and our redemption and say, "*What is this service to you*, anyway?"

בָּרוּךְ שׁוֹמֵר הַבְטָחָתוֹ לְיִשְׂרָאֵל, בָּרוּךְ הוּא, שֶׁהַקָּדוֹשׁ בָּרוּךְ הוּא חִשַּׁב אֶת הַקֵּץ לַעֲשׂוֹת. כְּמָה שֶּׁאָמַר לְאַבְרָהָם אָבִינוּ בִּבְרִית בֵּין הַבְּתָרִים. שֶׁנֶּאֱמַר, וַיֹּאמֶר לְאַבְרָם יָדֹעַ תֵּדַע כִּי גֵר יִהְיֶה זַרְעֲךָ בְּאֶרֶץ לֹא לָהֶם וַעֲבָדוּם וְעִנּוּ אֹתָם אַרְבַּע מֵאוֹת שָׁנָה. וְגַם אֶת הַגּוֹי אֲשֶׁר יַעֲבֹדוּ דָּן אָנֹכִי וְאַחֲרֵי כֵן יֵצְאוּ בִּרְכֻשׁ גָּדוֹל:

Blessed is He Who keeps His promise to Israel — Only to Israel was this promise made, and not to Esav. Both the redemption and the enslavement were for the good, and if God had not excluded Esav, although he was a "stranger" and a slave, he would have had a share in liberation and "great wealth" at the end.

For the Holy One calculated when the end — He included, in the decree of four hundred years, one hundred and ninety from the birth of Yitzchak until the descent of Yaakov into Egypt. These years also spanned a time that the seed of Avraham were *strangers in a land not theirs*, for even though Yitzchak never left Canaan at all, Canaan was still in the hands of the sons of Cham. Yaakov also lived in exile — mostly in Canaan and the remainder of the time in Paddan Aram.

The end — The Hebrew for "end" is סוף, whose numerical value is 190 — the number of years from Yitzchak's birth until Yaakov's descent into Egypt!

In order to fulfill what He had said — For even when He first made the Covenant, God told Avraham that he would include those 190 years as years of exile. (*Rashi, Rashba* and others)

Your seed shall be strangers — The word "stranger" in Hebrew is גר

Blessed is He Who keeps His promise to Israel — Blessed is He. For the Holy One calculated when the end [of our oppression in Egypt] would be, in order to fulfill what He had said to Avraham Avinu at the Covenant between the Pieces, as it is written (Bereshis 15:13): "And He said to Avram, 'Know for certain that your seed shall be strangers in a land that is not theirs. And they [the native people] will work them as slaves, and will oppress them for four hundred years. But I also will execute judgments on the nation that enslaves them, and afterwards they [your seed] will leave there with great wealth.'"

(*ger*), similar to גרגיר (*gargir*), a seed of grain — something which became uprooted from the place where it had grown. In other words, you shall not be as a *leafy tree in its native soil* — an *ezrach ra'anan* (Tehillim 37:35) — staying fresh and green and enjoying stable conditions. (*Ibn Ezra*)

 🕮

Your seed shall be strangers — 190 years; *and they will work them as slaves* — 124 years; *and they will oppress them* — 86 years, from when Miriam died. From then on the Egyptians *embittered their lives with hard labor*, as the Torah says. This turned out to be the reason for her being called *Miriam* (מרים) — for מר in Hebrew connotes bitterness, and her people suffered the worst bitterness of their exile starting from the day that she died. Thus 190+124+86 = 400, the number of years of our oppression mentioned by God.

The Hebrew word for exile, גלות (*galus*), can suggest גלוי (*galui*), which means "revealed." By means of our being in exile, the inner meaning of God's concealing His "face" from us becomes revealed. (*Sefas Emes*)

 🕮

[And they] will oppress them — The exile of our people to Egypt was for the purpose of taking our impurities out of us, as a smelting furnace removes impurities from metals, leaving them totally free of unwanted material. This analogy was first used by Moshe *Rabbenu*

(*Devarim* 4:20), and is also found in the words of a later Prophet (*Zecharyah* 13:9): *And I will bring the third part [Israel] into fire, and will refine them as one refines silver, and test them as one tests gold. He shall call out My Name, and I shall answer him. I shall say, "My nation!" and he shall say, "My God!"* Similarly, some of the Jews in Egypt had become so evil, so corrupted, that they were not willing to change for the better, and died during the three days of darkness.

The Jews who remained alive were the ones to pass through the purifying furnace that was Egypt, and through suffering brutal oppression there they were cleansed of all the bad character traits associated with cruelty, haughtiness, and hatred. The Jews who were redeemed possessed the character traits of Avraham *Avinu*. They were merciful, modest, and did acts of kindness for others. The Jew who showed love and care for all who are in God's image — he is the Jew who survived the purification process in Egypt, and went on to receive the Torah at Mount Sinai. (*Alshich*)

Moshe *Rabbenu* told the people (*Devarim* 4:20): *And God took you to Him, and brought you out from Egypt, out of the iron furnace, to be His nation and inheritance.* Just as he who works at the smelting furnace must stretch his hand into the fire in order to take out the gold, so did God have to stretch out His Hand to take Israel out of Egypt. (*Yalkut Shimoni, Parashas vaEs'chanan*)

We have heard that the Torah calls Egypt *the iron furnace.* However, it cannot be that the term is used in reference to purification of the body alone, for our Sages teach us that as early as Rosh Hashanah, in that year, months before the actual Exodus, the Egyptians no longer oppressed the Jews at all. The enslavement was over! When the night of the redemption finally arrived, the Jews had long been at peace with the Egyptians, who had come to fear and respect them. The Jewish nation enjoyed a lofty place in the eyes of Pharaoh and his people, and because the Jews were so highly regarded, they could have whatever they wanted from Egypt, just so that their former taskmasters would not suffer any further injury and insult. Until then, "no slave ever escaped from Egypt," and in order to keep things that way, the Egyptians sought to keep the Jews happy. Thus, the question arises: When the Torah states that God took us out from the smelting furnace, what does it mean? It means as the Sages say: "Just as he who works at the smelting furnace must stretch his hand..."

Until gold has been purified of its foreign materials, such as iron and various sediments, much that is unwanted clings to it, inside and out. If there is salt or sulfur in the mixture, these materials can consume the precious gold so that only the iron and other unwanted materials remain. How then does one salvage the gold before it is eaten away? One places it in a furnace, in fire. The craftsman knows well the secrets of refining. He knows precisely at what state in the heating process he must reach in with his skilled hand and extract the gold, before it is consumed by the unwanted foreign substances.

In Egypt, too, much that was unwanted clung to the Jews, inside and out. There was so much impurity present, that there was danger that it would consume their holiness completely, down to their very foundations, so that there would be nothing precious left to extract and purify. The slavery and oppression had been like a fire refining them. The Exodus itself, when it came, in its proper time, but in haste — this was the last step in the refining process, the crucial step where the gold has to be taken from the unwanted materials in a hurry, before it is consumed by them. As a skilled Craftsman, God discerned that the Jews were already at the 49th level of impurity — Egyptian impurity — and He saw that if He did not take them out *with a strong hand*, at the last moment, quickly, there would be nothing left of Israel to redeem. No precious material would have remained out of which to build His nation of priests!

The departure from Egypt is mentioned in the Torah fifty times. We might ask: God promised Avraham that He would take the nation out of Egypt. Since God promised, and always keeps His promises, why does the Torah remind us over and over again that He kept this particular promise? What praise is there in this?

The answer is as follows: Really, the Torah is telling us that God performed fifty redemptions in Egypt, for it was from the forty-ninth level of impurity that He took us out, and if we had descended to the fiftieth level, there would have been nothing left of us and we would have stayed in Egypt forever. Happily, God took us out at the last minute, and then we were able to climb upwards, step by step, towards the fiftieth level of purity! Once we had entered the gates of purity, it was there that we would stay forever! (*Sefas Emes*)

Cover the matzos and pick up the cup. Then everyone says:

וְהִיא שֶׁעָמְדָה לַאֲבוֹתֵינוּ וְלָנוּ. שֶׁלֹּא אֶחָד בִּלְבָד עָמַד עָלֵינוּ לְכַלּוֹתֵנוּ, אֶלָּא שֶׁבְּכָל דּוֹר וָדוֹר עוֹמְדִים עָלֵינוּ לְכַלּוֹתֵנוּ, וְהַקָּדוֹשׁ בָּרוּךְ הוּא מַצִּילֵנוּ מִיָּדָם:

I also will execute judgments on the nation that enslaves them — For out of their evil hearts will the Egyptians oppress them, and not because of My decree; I will see that the treatment they will give them will not be that which is normally given to slaves — for is it normal that (*Shemos* 1:22): *Any son born to them shall be cast in the river?!* (*Rambam, Ramban*)

📖

And afterwards they [your seed] will leave — The Torah, to say "afterwards," just as well could have written אחר and not אחרי. However, the Torah adds the letter *yud*, whose numerical value is ten, to hint that "after ten they will leave" — after ten plagues. (*Da'as Zekenim* of the *Baalei Tosafos*)

📖

With great wealth — God promised Avraham that his descendants would take out of Egypt with them whatever sparks of holiness that were left there. Avraham was the first of all "converts," and he wanted to bring all of God's creations to the Holy One. Although the Jews who were freed from Egypt did not seek to make converts of any of the Egyptians, they did accept converts, for they saw in God's promise to Avraham that they should do so. After all, how could they allow it to be said that this part of God's promise to the righteous Avraham did not come true? (*Sefas Emes*)

📖

With great wealth — It is written (*Tehillim* 68:19): *And even those who were turned to the side obtained a place with Hashem.* These are the souls who were far away in the land of Egypt, but converted to our faith and joined us when we were liberated and left Egypt to accept the Torah. These souls were a *great wealth* in God's eyes, and it is for

Cover the matzos and pick up the cup. Then everyone says:

𝒜ND THIS IS WHAT HAS STOOD *for our fathers and for us — because not just one rose up against us to destroy us. Rather, in every generation they rise up against us to destroy us, but the Holy One, blessed is He, saves us from their hand.*

souls such as these that we are scattered among the nations today — to fill God's warehouses with grain. When God sends us out into exile, He does not send us for naught, for certainly, the good souls who are found among the nations will join us. (*Yavetz*)

This is what has stood — When this is said, everyone at the table raises his cup (the one he is using for the obligatory four cups of wine). This is the custom, because here we are speaking of salvations that we have had, and the verse says (*Tehillim* 116:13): *I shall lift up the cup of salvation*. (*Baal haRoke'ach,* in the name of his father)

The cup we are holding now, the second cup, corresponds to *I shall save*, the second expression of redemption used by God when He told Moshe *Rabbenu* to relay to the nation that they soon would be liberated. We raise the cup as a testimony that God continually has saved us, and stands ready to do so always. (*Maharal*)

And this is what has stood for our fathers and for us — That is, the promise that God gave to Avraham at the Covenant between the Pieces, that his seed would be redeemed from Egyptian bondage, and also from the four exiles that would follow. This promise has stood for us, that we would be redeemed from Egypt, Babylonia, Persia, Greece, and Edom, the current exile. (*Shibolei haLeket*)

Also, the Glory of the *Shechinah* has accompanied the Jewish People throughout all of its exiles, as is written regarding Yaakov's descent into Egypt (*Bereshis* 46:4): *And I will go down into Egypt with you* (*Iyun Tefillah*). Similarly, He has executed judgments upon all of our oppressors, as He did upon Egypt, and this causes the nations to fear us (*Eshel b'Rama*).

Put down the cup and uncover the matzos. Then continue:

צֵא וּלְמַד מַה בִּקֵּשׁ לָבָן הָאֲרַמִּי לַעֲשׂוֹת לְיַעֲקֹב אָבִינוּ. שֶׁפַּרְעֹה לֹא גָזַר אֶלָּא עַל הַזְּכָרִים וְלָבָן בִּקֵּשׁ לַעֲקֹר אֶת הַכֹּל. שֶׁנֶּאֱמַר: **אֲרַמִּי אֹבֵד אָבִי וַיֵּרֶד מִצְרַיְמָה וַיָּגָר שָׁם בִּמְתֵי מְעָט, וַיְהִי שָׁם לְגוֹי גָּדוֹל עָצוּם וָרָב:**

<u>וַיֵּרֶד מִצְרַיְמָה</u>, אָנוּס עַל פִּי הַדִּבּוּר:

<u>וַיָּגָר שָׁם</u>, מְלַמֵּד שֶׁלֹּא יָרַד יַעֲקֹב אָבִינוּ לְהִשְׁתַּקֵּעַ בְּמִצְרַיִם אֶלָּא לָגוּר שָׁם. שֶׁנֶּאֱמַר, וַיֹּאמְרוּ אֶל פַּרְעֹה לָגוּר בָּאָרֶץ בָּאנוּ כִּי אֵין מִרְעֶה לַצֹּאן אֲשֶׁר לַעֲבָדֶיךָ כִּי כָבֵד הָרָעָב בְּאֶרֶץ כְּנָעַן, וְעַתָּה יֵשְׁבוּ נָא עֲבָדֶיךָ בְּאֶרֶץ גֹּשֶׁן:

<u>בִּמְתֵי מְעָט</u>, כְּמָה שֶׁנֶּאֱמַר, בְּשִׁבְעִים נֶפֶשׁ יָרְדוּ אֲבוֹתֶיךָ מִצְרָיְמָה, וְעַתָּה שָׂמְךָ יְהֹוָה אֱלֹהֶיךָ כְּכוֹכְבֵי הַשָּׁמַיִם לָרֹב:

And this is what has stood — The calculations which God makes before He comes to save us, have stood for us in the past, and stand for us now during the present exile. Even though the time for the Ultimate Redemption has not yet arrived, we are content with the knowledge that He is always making calculations on our behalf, keeping us in mind at all times, helping us to survive, and protecting us from our enemies. (*Ma'asei Nissim*)

The Holy One, blessed is He, saves us from their hand — Even

Put down the cup and uncover the matzos. Then continue:

COME AND LEARN WHAT LAVAN *the Aramean sought to do to Yaakov Avinu.* For Pharaoh made his decree only against the male children, while Lavan sought to uproot everything, as it is written: *"My father was a wandering Aramean, who went down to Egypt and abode there as a small group. There he became a nation, great, populous, and numerous"* (Devarim 26:5).

Who went down to Egypt — compelled by the Divine word.

And abode there — [the choice of words] teaches us that Yaakov Avinu did not go down to Egypt with the idea of settling there, but only to abide there a while, as it is written: "They said to Pharaoh, 'We have come to abide in the land, for there is no pasturage for your servants' flocks, so severe is the famine in the land of Canaan; now let your servants dwell in the land of Goshen'" (Bereshis 47:4).

As a small group — as it is written: "Your fathers went down to Egypt with seventy souls, and now Hashem your God has made you as numerous as the stars in the sky" (Devarim 10:22).

though the nations always are plotting to destroy us, God frustrates their plans, for God told Avraham that *they shall work them...and oppress them*, but would not be able to destroy them. (*Or Yesharim*)

    God did not let our worst enemies live at the same time, during the same period of history, and this prevented them from being able to band together against us. By keeping our most evil enemies apart from one another, spreading them out throughout the whole span of history, God has saved us from their hands. Thus, Moshe *Rabbenu* said to the Jewish People (*Devarim 7:7*): *For you are the small among all the nations.* That is, against all the nations who hated you and will hate you, you are small; but compared to each one individually, you are greater! (*Sefas Emes*) (See also the commentary of the *Ramban* on *Devarim* 4:27: *And you will be few in number among the nations.*)

📖

Saves us from their hand — God causes salvation to come to us from the very hand of the ones who hate us! This we see, for example, in the story of Purim, where Achashverosh wanted to destroy the Jewish People, but in the end, it was his hand that saved us! (*Etz Chayim*)

📖

Come and learn — For *in every generation they rise up against us to destroy us...* beginning with Lavan, even though he and Yaakov were family to one another! But God in His Mercy saved Yaakov, and sent him out of Egypt *with great wealth. Come and learn* from this, for the experiences of our forefathers were a sign of what we, their descendants, would experience! (*Ritva, Maharal*)

📖

Come and learn — How great were the trials of our forefathers, yet they persevered and overcame them!

📖

What Lavan the Aramean sought to do — Although he had no valid reason to hate Yaakov. Neither did Pharaoh have a valid reason to issue his decree to kill infants. Esav, however, is not mentioned here, for he did have a reason to hate Yaakov. (*Maharal*)

📖

Lavan the Aramean — We have begun with Lavan, who was the first of the evil ones who sought our annihilation. The Haggadah has us do so, in order to lead into a declaration made in the days of the Temple, when Jews would bring the obligatory offering of first fruits (*Devarim* 26:5-8). Lavan's plotting is mentioned in the first of four verses which comprise that declaration, which briefly tells the story of our suffering and redemption, and expresses thanks for God's kindnesses. We want to elaborate, and thus we now expound upon the declaration's verses. (*Rashbatz*)

📖

My father was a wandering Aramean — The Hebrew words, *Arami oved avi*, can also mean: "The Aramean was [planning on] making my father lost to the world"; for what caused Yaakov to have to descend into Egypt, where he almost was destroyed? It all started because of the brothers' jealousy toward Yosef. And how did the jealousy begin? Because Lavan tricked Yaakov, and first gave him Leah to be his wife before Rachel. If Yaakov had married Rachel first, as he wanted, Yosef would have been the firstborn, and his brothers would not have envied him, for a firstborn is entitled to special treatment. (attributed to *Mahari Bei Rav*)

Lavan did not succeed [in making Yaakov lost to the world], but he did intend to destroy Yaakov. Regarding the nations, it is said that God considers evil thoughts as evil actions.

Lavan wanted to uproot everything, but measure for measure, he did not accomplish anything that he wanted. So, too, do we find regarding Haman, who also wanted nothing to remain of us. For this reason, nothing that he wanted was realized. (*Sefas Emes*)

Compelled — This teaches us that even though Yaakov lived a life of peace and tranquillity in Egypt, and while his sons lived, the Jews were not oppressed at all, nevertheless, Egypt remained in their minds a land of exile. They did not go there willingly, and if they'd had a choice in the matter, they would have gone back to Canaan immediately. (*Chida*)

Compelled — If Yaakov had been compelled to go down to Egypt simply because of the Covenant between the Pieces, which said that Avraham's seed would be enslaved and oppressed, one might think, as our Sages comment, that it would have been fitting that he enter Egypt "in chains made of iron." Actually, because of his righteousness, Yaakov was compelled to go down to Egypt because of a different Divine decree, which was made when God told him (*Bereshis* 46:3): *Do not fear going down to Egypt.* (*Vilna Gaon*)

Compelled by the Divine word [decree] — The Sefas Emes writes that the Haggadah might mean here that the "word" which compelled Yaakov to go down to Egypt was the word that Yosef sent him, after all the years that Yaakov had thought that Yosef was dead (*Bereshis* 45:9): *Come down to me here! Do not delay!*

וַיְהִי שָׁם לְגוֹי, מְלַמֵּד שֶׁהָיוּ יִשְׂרָאֵל מְצֻיָּנִים שָׁם:

גָּדוֹל עָצוּם, כְּמָה שֶׁנֶּאֱמַר, וּבְנֵי יִשְׂרָאֵל פָּרוּ וַיִּשְׁרְצוּ וַיִּרְבּוּ וַיַּעַצְמוּ בִּמְאֹד מְאֹד, וַתִּמָּלֵא הָאָרֶץ אֹתָם:

וָרָב, כְּמָה שֶׁנֶּאֱמַר, רְבָבָה כְּצֶמַח הַשָּׂדֶה נְתַתִּיךְ וַתִּרְבִּי

Israel was distinct there — The Haggadah says they became *great and mighty*, but beyond that, another positive trait was that they also were obviously different from the Egyptians. Some explain that this means they were tall and handsome. Others say it means that they did not change their manner of dress, or their language, or their names, in an effort to mix in with the native population. Others explain that they were "distinct" simply because they all lived together in one place, in Goshen, which was away from the main part of Egypt.

Some explain that in Egypt, it was the nature of the Jewish women that made them "distinct," in terms of their fertility. It is said that the Jewish women gave birth very frequently, and each time, they bore many infants at once, usually six at a time! This miraculous fertility greatly distinguished them from the Egyptians, and it also differed from the way the Jews had themselves been in Canaan. (*Rashi, Ramban,* and others)

📖

Great — In terms of their importance.
Great — They were tall, and their physical appearance was impressive.
Mighty — In number.
Mighty — In strength. Even though each Jewish mother gave birth to many children at once, each child would be healthy and strong. (*Abarbanel*)

There he became a nation — *[the fact that the Jews are called a nation] teaches us that Israel was distinct there.*

Great and mighty — *as it is written: "And the Children of Israel were fruitful and increased abundantly and multiplied, and became very mighty, and the land was filled with them" (Shemos 1:7).*

And populous — *as it is written: "I gave you to thrive, to be as the brush of the fields. You multiplied and grew, and you became*

Great and mighty...and populous — These three terms correspond to the three Patriarchs:
Great — corresponds to Avraham, for God promised him: *I will make you a great nation* (Bereshis 12:2).
Mighty — corresponds to Yitzchak, for Avimelech said to him: *You are mightier than we* (Bereshis 26:16).
Populous — corresponds to Yaakov, who had many children, in fulfillment of the blessing given to him by his father Yitzchak: *May God, the Almighty, bless you, and make you fruitful, and multiply you* (Bereshis 28:3). (Maharal)

As the brush of the fields — Which grows by itself. That is, the Jewish children grew up healthy and strong, without needing care or attention from their parents, who were busy with their slave labor.

Moreover, the more the brush is cut back, the hardier the bushes become. So, too, the more harshly the Egyptians treated us, the more we were fruitful and multiplied. (Ritva, Avudraham)

And you became too numerous to count — A Midrashic interpretation renders the Hebrew phrase as meaning "flock after flock" (see Bereshis 32:17). Thus, as mentioned above, the Jewish women would go out to the fields to give birth, where they would not be seen, for fear of the decree against all newborn Jewish males. If the child was a

וַתִּגְדְּלִי וַתָּבוֹאִי בַּעֲדִי עֲדָיִים, שָׁדַיִם נָכֹנוּ וּשְׂעָרֵךְ צִמֵּחַ וְאַתְּ עֵרֹם וְעֶרְיָה: וָאֶעֱבֹר עָלַיִךְ וָאֶרְאֵךְ מִתְבּוֹסֶסֶת בְּדָמָיִךְ וָאֹמַר לָךְ בְּדָמַיִךְ חֲיִי וָאֹמַר לָךְ בְּדָמַיִךְ חֲיִי:

boy, he would be miraculously swallowed into the ground for safekeeping. The unknowing Egyptians would plow their fields directly above where the children were concealed, as a verse in *Tehillim* alludes (129:3). Afterwards [our Sages tell us], the children would sprout up out of the earth as field brush, and go to their homes "flock after flock."

📖

Your breasts were prepared — Moshe and Aharon, who stood ready to provide sustenance to Israel.
Your hair had grown — For the time to redeem you had arrived, as a young maiden, reaching adolescence, could then be married.
But you were naked — Of mitzvos.
And bare — You had not been circumcised.
And I passed over you — To free you. For this purpose [God says] I gave you two commandments to perform: the Pesach offering and circumcision, and in the merit of these mitzvos you would merit the redemption. (*Rashbam* and others, based on *Mechilta, Parashas Bo*)

📖

And [I] saw you rolling in your blood... Through your blood you shall live! Through your blood you shall live! — You fulfilled these two mitzvos of Mine, causing you to be covered in the blood of the Pesach offering and the blood of the circumcision.

The blood of the Pesach offering is the blood mentioned first, because in that generation, as our Sages teach (*Midrash Rabbah, Shir haShirim*) there were Jews who did not want to have the circumcision. When Moshe *Rabbenu*, who of course was circumcised, slaughtered his Pesach offering, God brought sweet-smelling breezes from Gan Eden, which wafted over the offering. The pleasant fragrances *too numerous to count. Your breasts were prepared. Your hair had grown, but you were naked and bare. And I passed over you, and saw you rolling in your blood. And I said to you, 'Through your blood you shall live! Through your blood you shall live!'"* (Yechezkel 16:7)

mixed, and carried for great distances, until all of Israel arrived at the scene and said, "Give us to eat from the Pesach offering!" Moshe *Rabbenu* answered them, "All those who are uncircumcised shall not eat of it." They then circumcised themselves. Therefore, the blood of the Pesach offering is referred to first, and the blood of the circumcision afterwards.

Through your blood you shall live! Through your blood you shall live! — Rabbi Eliezer said, "What did the verse see that made it say the same thing twice?" God said, "I have redeemed you in the merit of the blood of the Pesach offering and also the blood of the circumcision, and in the merit of these two mitzvos I will bring about the Final Redemption, too!" (*Pirkei d'Rabi Eliezer; Yalkut Shimoni, Yechezkel 354*)

Through your blood — The Pesach offering and circumcision are the only two cases in the entire Torah where intentional failure to perform a positive mitzvah carries the punishment of *kares*, Divine excision or "cutting off." Regarding other positive mitzvos, the Torah does not even state a punishment for failure to do them. Being that the punishment in the case of these two mitzvos is so severe, all the more so is the reward for performing them unimaginably sublime! One gains life itself, in this world and in the Next, for Hashem wants to give reward more than He wants to punish! (*Chiddushei haRim*)

Why specifically is "cutting off" the punishment? Because it was in the merit of these two mitzvos that Israel was freed and became connected to God forever. Therefore, anyone who intentionally ignores these mitzvos is cut off, both from Life and from his Nation, as if he had never left Egypt at all. (*Bnei Yissachar*)

וַיָּרֵעוּ אֹתָנוּ הַמִּצְרִים וַיְעַנּוּנוּ וַיִּתְּנוּ עָלֵינוּ עֲבֹדָה קָשָׁה:

וַיָּרֵעוּ אֹתָנוּ הַמִּצְרִים, כְּמָה שֶׁנֶּאֱמַר, הָבָה נִתְחַכְּמָה לוֹ פֶּן יִרְבֶּה וְהָיָה כִּי תִקְרֶאנָה מִלְחָמָה וְנוֹסַף גַּם הוּא עַל שֹׂנְאֵינוּ וְנִלְחַם בָּנוּ וְעָלָה מִן הָאָרֶץ:

And the Egyptians invented evil for us — When the Egyptians saw our People growing so numerous in a supernatural way, immediately they *invented evil for us*. That is, they imagined us to be bad, ungrateful people, who were conspiring and spying against them for some other nation that actually was their enemy. This probably is what the verse means, for if it meant that the Egyptians did evil "to" us, the Hebrew wording would have been otherwise. (*Rashbatz, Abarbanel*)

📖

And the Egyptians invented evil for us — Others explain that Moshe *Rabbenu* meant to say that the Egyptians intentionally led us to sin, in order to make us evil in the eyes of God. With premeditation, they also caused us to suffer the pangs of poverty, hoping that this would cause us to rebel against God. (R. Shelomo Alkabetz, *Yavetz*)

📖

And the Egyptians invented evil for us — In this verse, the second one in the declaration that was made upon the bringing of the first fruits, there are three things mentioned that the Egyptians had done to harm us: *invented evil, oppressed us, and imposed hard labor upon us*. These correspond to three things mentioned about us in the previous verse: that we were *populous, great,* and *mighty*.

Thus: 1) The Egyptians invented evil thoughts about us, in order to justify murdering our male children — so that we would not become too populous; 2) the Egyptians oppressed us in order to humble us and destroy our self-esteem, so that we could not look at ourselves as being a great nation anymore; and 3) the Egyptians imposed hard labor on us, more than a person can endure, in order to break our

"And the Egyptians invented evil for us, they oppressed us, and imposed hard labor upon us" (Devarim 26:6).

And the Egyptians invented evil for us — as it is written: *"Come, let us be clever with him, lest he grow too numerous, and should a war come, he might ally himself to our enemies, and fight us and leave the country"* (Shemos 1:10).

strength and spirit. (*Maharal*)

Come, let us be clever with him — That is, they said, "Let us be more clever than our predecessor, Esav, who was foolish for not killing Yaakov immediately! Little did he know that Yaakov would have so many children!" (*Rashi* and others, based on the Sages)

Come, let us be clever with him — They said, "Let us be clever about how we destroy the infant who, when he grows up, is supposed to lead them to freedom! Let us cast all male infants into the water." The Egyptians knew that after the flood in the days of No'ach, God had sworn that He would never again judge the world with water. They thought that this assured them of safety, for if they fought against Him with water, He no longer could retaliate with water. They failed to note, however, that God had sworn only to not use water against the entire world. He could, however, use water to retaliate against only one land — and in the end, at the splitting of the sea, this is what He did.

And they put... over him — "Him," and not "them." It was said in the house of study of R. Elazar, son of R. Shimon, "This teaches us that Pharaoh had the taskmasters tie on him a mold for making bricks, hanging it on a string around his neck. Then, they brought before Pharaoh, one by one, each Jew who had protested that he was delicate, and the work was too hard for him. They said to him, "Are you more delicate than Pharaoh?" (*Sotah* 11a; *Shemos Rabbah* 1)

וַיְעַנּוּנוּ, כְּמָה שֶׁנֶּאֱמַר, וַיָּשִׂימוּ עָלָיו שָׂרֵי מִסִּים לְמַעַן עַנֹּתוֹ בְּסִבְלֹתָם וַיִּבֶן עָרֵי מִסְכְּנוֹת לְפַרְעֹה אֶת פִּתֹם וְאֶת רַעַמְסֵס:

וַיִּתְּנוּ עָלֵינוּ עֲבוֹדָה קָשָׁה, כְּמָה שֶׁנֶּאֱמַר, וַיַּעֲבִדוּ מִצְרַיִם אֶת בְּנֵי יִשְׂרָאֵל בְּפָרֶךְ:

And they put taskmasters over him — All of this was in order to crush them, and destroy them. It began with the Egyptians suggesting to the Jews that they help their host nation to build strong buildings, which was an important national project. They assured the Jews that even Pharaoh himself would assist in the work! Our Sages teach us that Pharaoh had a brick mold tied around his neck. This was to show the Jews that the job was so important that even Pharaoh was taking part! Only afterwards did it become tortuous slave labor. That is, the Egyptians brought us under their whip slowly and gradually, step by step. Thus we use *maror* to remember those experiences, for in the beginning *maror* is soft and sweet, just as our "national service" in Egypt, and only later does it harden and become bitter.

Our Sages teach us that at the outset, the Egyptians told the Jews that their help was needed only on an emergency basis, and the job would be completed in one day. They said that it would certainly be worthwhile, for by helping to complete such an important job, they would find favor in Pharaoh's eyes, and he would show gratitude towards them to the end of time. Therefore, the Jews agreed, working very hard that day, producing many bricks. This amount was made their quota for the many days to follow. Thus, by a play on the Hebrew, the Sages interpret *And they worked them strenuously — b'parech* — that they succeeded in getting them to work "with a soft mouth" — *b'peh rach*. (Ritva)

And they imposed hard labor upon us — From the very names of the cities that the Jews built, we see that their labor was not only strenu-

They oppressed us — as it is written: "And they put taskmasters over him [the people], in order to torture him with their burdens. And [the people] built storage cities for Pharaoh, Pitom and Raamses" (Shemos 1:11).

And they imposed hard labor upon us — as it is written: "And Egypt worked the Children of Israel strenuously" (Shemos 1:13).

ous, but also futile: Pitom is like the Hebrew *pi tehom*, which means "mouth of the abyss." That is, Pitom was built on ground that was sinking, so that as the Jews laid the bricks, each brick was swallowed into the earth, one after the other.

Raamses is like the Hebrew *mitroses*, which means "to be cracked or crushed." That is, this city's buildings crumbled, and fell apart.

Strenuously — As we mention above, R. Elazar explained: with a soft mouth. Pharaoh said, *Come, let us be clever...* Then he called all the Jews together and said to them, "Today, do a favor for me." Pharaoh himself took a rake and a sack (to collect straw for bricks), and all the Jews who saw this did the same, and Pharaoh and the Jews made bricks together. The Jews exerted themselves with enthusiasm, and worked with Pharaoh the entire day, to the limit of their strength. As soon as it became dark, Pharaoh placed taskmasters over them, ordering them to count all the bricks that the Jews had made. The taskmasters then told the Jews, "This will be the number of bricks that you will have to make every day!" (*Midrash Tanchuma, B'Ha'alos'cha*; *Sotah* 11a)

Strenuously — The verse continues: *And every kind of work* (Shemos 1:14). The Egyptians made the men do women's work, and the women do men's work. One would order a man, "Get up and bake something." A woman would be commanded, "Fill this barrel, chop this piece of wood, go to the garden and bring back vegetables." (*Midrash Tanchuma, Vayetze*)

וַנִּצְעַק אֶל יְהֹוָה אֱלֹהֵי אֲבֹתֵינוּ, וַיִּשְׁמַע יְהֹוָה אֶת קֹלֵנוּ וַיַּרְא אֶת עָנְיֵנוּ וְאֶת עֲמָלֵנוּ וְאֶת לַחֲצֵנוּ:

וַנִּצְעַק אֶל יְהֹוָה אֱלֹהֵי אֲבֹתֵינוּ, כְּמָה שֶׁנֶּאֱמַר, וַיְהִי בַיָּמִים הָרַבִּים הָהֵם וַיָּמָת מֶלֶךְ מִצְרַיִם וַיֵּאָנְחוּ בְנֵי יִשְׂרָאֵל מִן הָעֲבֹדָה וַיִּזְעָקוּ, וַתַּעַל שַׁוְעָתָם אֶל הָאֱלֹהִים מִן הָעֲבֹדָה:

And we cried out — This verse also is a part of the declaration made upon the bringing of the first fruits. The verses used by the Haggadah to explain it are from the beginning of *Sefer Shemos*.

📖

The king of Egypt died — Really, he only had contracted *tzara'as*, but someone with *tzara'as* is regarded as dead, as we see from the request made by Aharon to Moshe *Rabbenu*, that he pray for their sister Miriam, when she was stricken with this disease: *Please, let her not be as a dead person (Bemidbar 12:12)*. (*Shemos Rabbah 1*)

📖

The king of Egypt died — Whenever the Scriptures write "died," even where it was a king that died, the Scriptures never say, "King so-and-so died" or "The king died." Only the person's name is written. Why is this so? Our Sages explain: On the day that a king dies, his kingship dies with him. Here, then, where the Torah does state: *The king of Egypt died*, it must mean that he was still alive — and his "dying" connotes *tzara'as*. (*Vilna Gaon*)

📖

And the Children of Israel groaned from their servitude — Why did they groan? The magicians of Egypt told Pharaoh that he would not be cured unless 300 Jewish children were slaughtered daily — 150 in

"And we cried out to Hashem, the God of our fathers. And Hashem heard our voice and He saw our privation, our toil, and our distress" (Devarim 26:7).

And we cried out to Hashem, the God of our fathers — as it is written: "It happened, during that long time, that the king of Egypt died. And the Children of Israel groaned from their servitude and they cried out. And their pleadings rose to God from the work" *(Shemos 2:23).*

the morning and 150 in the evening, so that Pharaoh could bathe in their blood twice a day. Hearing the terrible decree, the Jews began to groan and lament their plight. (*Shemos Rabbah*, Chapter One)

The king of Egypt died. And the Children of Israel groaned from their servitude — Although their labors were tortuous, they were even afraid to groan, lest the Egyptians punish them for complaining. However, when the king of Egypt died (and one opinion says the verse should be read literally, that he actually did die), even the Egyptians were wailing and groaning, mourning for their king. Thus, the Jews were able to let their groans be heard *from their servitude*, and the Egyptians thought that the Jews were mourning the death of the king! Thus, the verses conclude (*Shemos 2:25*): *And God knew.* He knows the inner thoughts of all men, and He knew the real reason that the Jews were wailing. (*Sha'ar haShamayim*)

And the Children of Israel groaned from their servitude — The word "servitude" in Hebrew (*avodah*) can also be seen as referring to idol-worship. The Egyptians compelled the Jews to serve idols, and the Jews groaned from having to perform such service. (*Rashi*)

וַיִּשְׁמַע יְהֹוָה אֶת קֹלֵנוּ, כְּמָה שֶׁנֶּאֱמַר, וַיִּשְׁמַע אֱלֹהִים אֶת נַאֲקָתָם וַיִּזְכֹּר אֱלֹהִים אֶת בְּרִיתוֹ אֶת אַבְרָהָם אֶת יִצְחָק וְאֶת יַעֲקֹב:

וַיַּרְא אֶת עָנְיֵנוּ, זוֹ פְּרִישׁוּת דֶּרֶךְ אֶרֶץ. כְּמָה שֶׁנֶּאֱמַר, וַיַּרְא אֱלֹהִים אֶת בְּנֵי יִשְׂרָאֵל וַיֵּדַע אֱלֹהִים:

And Hashem heard our voice — He recognized in it the voice of each of the Patriarchs. The Torah writes the word "voice" regarding all three: for Avraham, *because Avraham listened to My voice* (Bereshis 26:5); for Yitzchak and Yaakov, when Yitzchak says, *The voice is the voice of Yaakov.* (Bereshis 27:22)

That is, the verse in *Shemos* 2:24 first says that God heard our cries. Then it says that because of our cries, He remembered His covenant. Finally, the verse concludes by saying that our cries made God remember not only His covenant, but also Avraham, Yitzchak and Yaakov, because in our crying voices, He recognized their voices!

📖

And God heard their cries — Pharaoh's emissaries would strangle Jews and use their bodies as filler for the bricks of the buildings the Jews were constructing. And the Jews would cry out from inside the buildings, and from inside the walls of the buildings, and Hashem heard their cries. (*Shemos Rabbah*)

📖

And He saw our privation — This refers to the breaking up of family life — This was a quiet, unpublicized brand of oppression, which only God was able to notice. Thus, the Torah says: *And God knew* — only God. (*Rashbatz*)

These verses are explained along the same lines as the earlier ones, where the Torah says (*Shemos* 1:10-11): *Come, let us be clever with him, lest he multiply... and they set taskmasters over him, in order to torture him.* That is, the Egyptians wanted their taskmasters to exhaust the Jews with hard labor, hoping that this would make it impossible for the Jews to multiply any further. Thus, in *Devarim* 26:6, where Moshe *Rabbenu* says the Egyptians made us out to be evil and

And Hashem heard our voice — *as it is written: "And God heard their cries, and God remembered His covenant with Avraham, with Yitzchak, and with Yaakov" (Shemos 2:24).*

And He saw our privation — *this refers to the breaking up of family life, as it is written: "God saw the Children of Israel, and God knew" (Shemos 2:25).*

afflicted us, and then he says *God saw our privation*, he was referring to everything that the Egyptians did in order to try to prevent us from having children — the open oppression and then the private, quiet kind.

This refers to the breaking up of family life — The Egyptians wanted to keep the Jewish husbands away from their wives, in order that no new children would be born to them. As a pretext, the Egyptians told them, "If we let you sleep at home, you won't get up early enough in the morning to make enough bricks to meet your quota." Thus, the Egyptians made the men sleep in the fields. The wives would bring their husbands bread and food, and be with them under the apple trees, where they conceived. When it was time to give birth, they would secretly go out into the fields again, under those apple trees, and God would send angels to be midwives, and to provide food for the mothers. If Egyptians appeared, the infants would miraculously be swallowed in the ground, where they would be protected, while above them the Egyptians sowed and plowed. (*Kol Bo*, based on *Sotah* 11a)

The breaking up of family life — Many Jewish husbands had decided on their own to separate from their wives because Pharaoh had decreed, *Every newborn son shall be cast into the river.* The Jewish men said, "Why should we bring children into the world, only to have them killed?" They changed their minds, however, because of what Miriam said to her father: "Your decision is more harsh than Pharaoh's, for he has decreed only against the boys — your decree, however, is against the girls, too!" (*Shemos Rabbah*, Chapter One)

וְאֶת עֲמָלֵנוּ, אֵלּוּ הַבָּנִים. כְּמָה שֶׁנֶּאֱמַר, כָּל הַבֵּן הַיִּלּוֹד הַיְאֹרָה תַּשְׁלִיכֻהוּ וְכָל הַבַּת תְּחַיּוּן:

וְאֶת לַחֲצֵנוּ, זֶה הַדְּחַק. כְּמָה שֶׁנֶּאֱמַר, וְגַם רָאִיתִי אֶת הַלַּחַץ אֲשֶׁר מִצְרַיִם לֹחֲצִים אֹתָם:

וַיּוֹצִיאֵנוּ יְהֹוָה מִמִּצְרַיִם בְּיָד חֲזָקָה וּבִזְרֹעַ נְטוּיָה וּבְמֹרָא גָּדֹל וּבְאֹתוֹת וּבְמֹפְתִים:

📖

Our toil — this refers to children — A father's toil is only for the sake of his children, and Pharaoh, by murdering our children, was making all our toil to be for nothing. (*Ritva*)

📖

This refers to children — Before commanding his people to cast newborn boys into the river, Pharaoh commanded the Jewish midwives to kill the infant boys discreetly, at the time of their birth. Rav Shmuel bar Nachmani said that the midwives were mother and daughter — Yocheved and Miriam. Miriam was then only five years old, but she helped her mother with enthusiasm.

Miriam was called "Puah," for, as her mother, she refused to obey Pharaoh, and had the courage to "stand before him" — the Hebrew of which includes the same letters as those in "Puah." She stood before him face to face, and raised her nose to him, saying with insolence, "Woe to the wicked one when God comes to pay him for his wickedness!" Pharaoh was furious, and wanted to kill her. Yocheved, however, was called "Shifrah," whose Hebrew root connotes "improvement," and she was able to calm Pharaoh down by "improving" or "fixing up" her daughter's words, saying, "Do not allow her words to bother you. What does she know, anyway? She's only five years old!"

Our toil — *this refers to children, as it is written: "Every newborn son shall be cast into the river, and every daughter you shall let live" (Shemos 1:22).*

And our distress — *this refers to the pressure, as it is written: "And I also have seen how the Egyptians have pressured you" (Shemos 3:9).*

"And God took us out of Egypt with a strong hand and with an outstretched arm, and with great awe, and with signs and with wonders" (Devarim 26:8).

The Torah praises the Jewish midwives, saying (*Shemos* 1:17): *They did not listen to Pharaoh's decree, and they let the children live.* Now, once the Torah says that they did not listen, one would infer that of course they let the children live! But what the Torah is teaching us is that not only did they not listen [and let the children live], but they did everything possible to *improve* the lives of the newborn babies. Some were born into poverty — for these, the midwives provided food, clothing, and water. Some were born sickly — for these, the midwives provided medicine and care. (*Shemos Rabbah*, Chapter One)

And our distress — this refers to the pressure — Of overcrowding. The Jews multiplied greatly, yet Pharaoh confined them to Goshen, the small amount of territory which had been allotted to Yaakov and his family, who at first numbered only seventy souls. (*Rabbenu Bachyeh*)

And God took us out of Egypt — As noted, this verse is a continuation of the declaration made upon the bringing of the first fruits to the Temple.

וַיּוֹצִיאֵנוּ יְהֹוָה מִמִּצְרַיִם, לֹא עַל יְדֵי מַלְאָךְ וְלֹא עַל יְדֵי שָׂרָף וְלֹא עַל יְדֵי שָׁלִיחַ. אֶלָּא הַקָּדוֹשׁ בָּרוּךְ הוּא בִּכְבוֹדוֹ וּבְעַצְמוֹ. שֶׁנֶּאֱמַר, וְעָבַרְתִּי בְאֶרֶץ מִצְרַיִם בַּלַּיְלָה הַזֶּה וְהִכֵּיתִי כָל בְּכוֹר בְּאֶרֶץ מִצְרַיִם מֵאָדָם וְעַד בְּהֵמָה וּבְכָל אֱלֹהֵי מִצְרַיִם אֶעֱשֶׂה שְׁפָטִים אֲנִי יְהֹוָה:

וְעָבַרְתִּי בְאֶרֶץ מִצְרַיִם בַּלַּיְלָה הַזֶּה, אֲנִי וְלֹא מַלְאָךְ.

וְהִכֵּיתִי כָל בְּכוֹר בְּאֶרֶץ מִצְרַיִם אֲנִי וְלֹא שָׂרָף.

וּבְכָל אֱלֹהֵי מִצְרַיִם אֶעֱשֶׂה שְׁפָטִים, אֲנִי וְלֹא הַשָּׁלִיחַ.

אֲנִי יְהֹוָה, אֲנִי הוּא וְלֹא אַחֵר:

And God took us out of Egypt — not by means of an angel — In Egypt, Moshe told the people that when the tenth plague would come, *God will pass through and smite the Egyptians... He will not allow the destroyer to come into your homes* (Shemos 12:23). The "destroyer" to which Moshe referred must be the plague itself, for the Haggadah tells us that God took us out of Egypt that night "Himself." (*Shibolei haLeket, Avudraham*)

📖

Not by means of an angel — Possibly, Moshe was referring to the angel of death, and he was telling the people that when the night of the tenth plague would come, God would not permit the angel of death to enter their homes to take the life of any of them, even those who were very old, and whose time to die had actually arrived. In Egypt at that time, there were over three million Jews, but that night, not even one of them passed away, in order that the Egyptians should not hear of the death, and say that the plague had struck Israel, too. (*Likkutei Ritzba*)

And God took us out of Egypt — *not by means of an angel, and not by means of a seraph, and not by means of a messenger. Rather it was the Holy One in His Glory, by Himself! As it is written: "For I will pass through the land of Egypt this night, and I will smite every firstborn in the land of Egypt, both man and beast; and I will execute judgment against all the gods of Egypt; I am God" (Shemos 12:12).*

I will pass through the land of Egypt — *I, and not an angel.*

And strike every firstborn — *I, and not a seraph.*

And I will execute judgment against all the gods of Egypt — *I, and not the messenger.*

I am the Lord — *I will do it and no one else.*

Not by means of an angel — For even an angel cannot distinguish between the seed that conceived the firstborn and the seed that conceived his twin brother. (*Bava Metzia* 61)

Not by means of an angel — For every nation on earth has an angel in heaven appointed over it, and in those days, Egypt was the most powerful nation on earth. As a result, Egypt's angel in heaven was so powerful that no angel of any other nation could defeat it. Moreover, Egypt was so full of abomination and defilement, that no angel could enter there and survive. Thus, only God Himself could take us out. (*Yad Chazakah*)

Not by means of an angel — Not by means of Micha'el, who is the angel appointed over Israel (as is written about the Jews entering the Land of Israel [*Shemos* 23:23]: *For My angel shall go before you* — the Hebrew letters of "my angel" are those which spell *Micha'el*).

Not by means of a seraph — Not by means of Gavriel, who is the angel appointed over fire (the letters of *"seraph"* in Hebrew also connote "fire").

📖

Not by means of a messenger — Not by means of Mattatron, who is the angel appointed over the world (and regarding him does the verse say: *Behold I send an angel before you, to guard you... Take heed of him...for My Name is within him* (Shemos 23:20-21). The numerical equivilent of *Mattatron* is 314, the same as *Shaddai*, one of God's Names.) (*Maharal*)

📖

And not by means of a messenger — In Egypt, therefore, Moshe *Rabbenu* was God's messenger only with respect to relaying God's Word to Pharaoh and to the Jews. Forty years later, when the Jews were nearing the Land of Israel, Moshe *Rabbenu* sent a request to Edom, asking Edom to let the nation pass through their territory, and in his request, he briefly recounted the story of the Exodus, saying (*Bemidbar* 20:16): *And we cried out to God and He heard our voice, and sent an angel, and brought us out of Egypt.* The "angel" was Moshe *Rabbenu*, who was sent to relay God's Word, but it was God Himself Who *brought us out of Egypt.* (*Avudraham* based on *Rashi*)

Since on the night of the Seder — the night of the tenth plague — it was God Himself Who took us out of Egypt, the Haggadah is careful not to mention Moshe *Rabbenu*'s role at all, save for once, later on, when R. Yosei the Galilean expounds a verse about the splitting of the sea, which was a week after the tenth plague! Even there (*Shemos* 14:31), Moshe *Rabbenu* is mentioned only as being a "servant" of God. (*Vilna Gaon*)

As to the role of Moshe *Rabbenu* in taking the Jews out of Egypt, the *Midrash* interprets a verse as saying that Moshe *Rabbenu* himself wondered why he should have any role at all. At the burning bush, when God appeared to him, and commanded him to take the Jews out, Moshe *Rabbenu* responded (*Shemos* 3:11): *Who am I that I should go to Pharaoh? That I should bring out the children of Israel from Egypt?!*

The word *Anochi* ("I") is a term that generally connotes God's immediate Presence, and the *Midrash* points out that Moshe knew this, for he knew that God had used the term when He told Yaakov not to fear going down to Egypt: *I (Anochi) will go down with you to Egypt, and I (Anochi) will bring you out, and surely you will leave (Bereshis 46:4).*

Thus, at the burning bush, Moshe *Rabbenu* wondered, "How can You tell me, *And now, come, and I will send you to Pharaoh (Shemos 3:10).* What about when you said to Yaakov *Avinu* that the *Shechinah* [You] would take them out!" It was Moshe *Rabbenu's* desire that the redemption from Egypt be a complete redemption, and he knew that such could come about only if God performed the redemption Himself, without any human hand mixing in at all.

In truth, Moshe *Rabbenu* had so perfected the trait of humility, that it *was* as if no human hand had mixed in at all, and God, in fact, did do everything by Himself! What is more, it is a principle of Torah law that "a messenger is considered as the sender himself," and the verse says *(Yeshayahu* 57:15): *God dwells on high, yet on earth He rests His Spirit upon the humble and contrite.* It was fitting that Moshe *Rabbenu* be God's messenger, for the Spirit of God was always upon him, and thus, in whatever he did, he was "as the sender Himself"! Moshe *Rabbenu* asked God: *Who am I, that I should go to Pharaoh...* but God answered him: *Certainly I will be with you ...for I am sending you [the most humble of men] (Shemos* 3:12). Moshe *Rabbenu,* however, did not realize that he had so perfected the trait of humility, and he therefore wondered, *Who am I? (Sefas Emes)*

📖

For I will pass through the land of Egypt — God would, so to speak, travel from place to place within Egypt. This expression is used because elsewhere *(Shemos* 12:29), the Torah says that He smote the firstborn at "midnight." Since Egypt was a very large country, the exact moment that midnight fell varied from place to place. *(R. Yehoshua Leib Diskin)*

📖

And I will execute judgment against all the gods of Egypt — The *Mechilta* says *(Parashas Bo,* Chapter Five) that at midnight, wooden idols rotted, and those made of metal melted, for God at that moment crushed the higher powers that had stood behind the idols and had helped them to stand. Thus it was clear that the tenth plague was by the Hand of God. *(Ritva)*

בְּיָד חֲזָקָה, זוֹ הַדֶּבֶר. כְּמָה שֶׁנֶּאֱמַר, הִנֵּה יַד יְהֹוָה הוֹיָה בְּמִקְנְךָ אֲשֶׁר בַּשָּׂדֶה בַּסּוּסִים בַּחֲמֹרִים בַּגְּמַלִּים בַּבָּקָר וּבַצֹּאן דֶּבֶר כָּבֵד מְאֹד:

וּבִזְרֹעַ נְטוּיָה, זוֹ הַחֶרֶב. כְּמָה שֶׁנֶּאֱמַר, וְחַרְבּוֹ שְׁלוּפָה בְּיָדוֹ נְטוּיָה עַל יְרוּשָׁלָיִם:

With a strong hand — this refers to the pestilence — Every plague that was brought upon Egypt was accompanied by pestilence. (*Midrash Tehillim, Tehillim 78*)

📖

With a strong hand — Perhaps one should understand this expression along the same lines as a verse in the Prophetic writings (*Yechezkel 20:23*): *As I live, says the Lord God, surely with a strong hand...I will be King over you.* At first, that is, the Jews might not have wanted to leave the lush land of Egypt at all. Therefore, God caused the Egyptians to embitter their lives, as it says in *Tehillim 105:25*: *And God reversed the hearts of the Egyptians to hate His Nation.* By sending Egypt upon them, with *a strong hand*, God made the Jews want the redemption. (*Sefas Emes*)

📖

With a strong hand...as it is written: *See, the hand of Hashem is on your herds* — the Hebrew "is on" is spelled with the same letters of God's four-letter Name, not in sequence. As is known, the four-letter Name connotes the Divine attribute of Mercy. Here, we learn, the letters are not in order because God is exercising His attribute of Justice. (*Alshich*)

📖

With a strong hand — this refers to the pestilence... Outstretched arm — this refers to the sword — The declaration in *Devarim* mentions these two plagues because pestilence was the fifth plague, and the sword was the tenth. It is said that each one was so intense, it also

With a strong hand — *this refers to the pestilence, as it is written: "See, the hand of Hashem is on your herds in the fields — on your horses and donkeys, on your camels, oxen and sheep — causing a very virulent pestilence" (Shemos 9:3).*

And with an outstretched arm — *this refers to the sword, as it is written: "His drawn sword in His hand, outstretched over Jerusalem" (Divrei Hayamim I 21:16).*

included the four plagues which preceded it. (*Vilna Gaon; Ma'asei Nissim*)

And with an outstretched arm — this refers to the sword — The sword that the firstborn of Egypt used on their fellow Egyptians (see *Tehillim* 136:10: *To He Who slays the Egyptians through their firstborn*). The Midrash says that when the firstborn heard of their impending fate, they took up arms against their own government, to force the Egyptian authorities to free the Jews, so that the tenth plague would not take place at all, and they, the firstborn, would live. (*Kol Bo*)

This refers to the sword — Or, "the sword" refers to the tenth plague itself, and that night, even the Egyptians who were not firstborn were wounded, though not fatally. They would perish later, when God would drown them in the sea, but even on the night of the tenth plague, they felt God's Arm stretched out against them. This would explain why, on the night of the tenth plague, even though only the firstborn Egyptians were found dead, the Torah tells us that the surviving Egyptians cried out in fear (*Shemos* 12:33): *We are all dead!* for it appeared to them that the attack was being carried out against all of them. (*Akedas Yitzchak*)

The sword — As a result of the tenth plague, three groups of Egyptians perished: those who were slain by the firstborn of Egypt; the

וּבְמֹרָא גָּדֹל, זֶה גִּלּוּי שְׁכִינָה. כְּמָה שֶׁנֶּאֱמַר, אוֹ הֲנִסָּה אֱלֹהִים לָבוֹא לָקַחַת לוֹ גוֹי מִקֶּרֶב גּוֹי בְּמַסֹּת בְּאֹתֹת וּבְמוֹפְתִים וּבְמִלְחָמָה וּבְיָד חֲזָקָה וּבִזְרוֹעַ נְטוּיָה וּבְמוֹרָאִים גְּדֹלִים, כְּכֹל אֲשֶׁר עָשָׂה לָכֶם יְהֹוָה אֱלֹהֵיכֶם בְּמִצְרַיִם לְעֵינֶיךָ:

וּבְאֹתוֹת, זֶה הַמַּטֶּה. כְּמָה שֶׁנֶּאֱמַר, וְאֶת הַמַּטֶּה הַזֶּה תִּקַּח בְּיָדֶךָ אֲשֶׁר תַּעֲשֶׂה בּוֹ אֶת הָאֹתֹת:

firstborn themselves; and Egyptians killed by Pharaoh, for having advised him not to free the Jews. (*Yavetz*)

📖

The sword — This refers to the seventy-two-letter Name of God, which was written in the "Book of Secrets." Moshe *Rabbenu* had used the Name as a sword, to kill an Egyptian taskmaster (see *Rashi, Shemos* 2:14), and he also used the Name for the sake of all the signs and wonders he performed in Egypt. (*Shibolei haLeket*)

📖

And with great awe — this refers to the revelation of the Shechinah — The word *mora*, which connotes "awe," resembles the word *mareh*, which means an "appearance" or a "vision." Similarly, the Targum renders the phrase: "a magnificent sight." (*Rashi* and others)

📖

The Shechinah — Although the land of Egypt was filled with graven images that the native population used for idolatry, God allowed His Presence to be revealed there, to fulfill His promise to Yaakov *Avinu*: *I will go down into Egypt with you, and I will take you out, and you will leave there* (*Bereshis* 46:4). The *Shechinah* also appeared on Mount Sinai for the giving of the Torah.

It is called *mora*, which connotes "awe," because when the *Shechi-*

And with great awe — *this refers to revelation of the Shechinah [Divine Presence], as it is written: "Or has God ever before come to take for Himself a nation from amidst another nation, with miracles, signs and wonders, with war, and a strong hand, with an outstretched arm, and great awesomeness, as Hashem your God did for you in Egypt?" (Devarim 4:34).*

And with signs — *this refers to the staff, as it is written: "And take this staff in your hand, with which you will perform the signs" (Shemos 4:17).*

nah appears, anyone who is not accustomed to seeing It is struck with awe and fear, and falls on his face immediately. The *Sifri* interprets "with great awe" as referring to the splitting of the sea, for there, the Jews saw "the Face of the *Shechinah*" and pointed at It, saying (*Shemos* 15:2): *This is my God, and I shall glorify Him!* (*Ritva*)

📖

And with signs — this refers to the staff — Inscribed on the staff of Moshe and Aharon were the letters דצ"ך עד"ש באח"ב, representing the ten plagues that God brought upon Egypt, in their proper order. (*Kol Bo*)

📖

The staff — The initials of the plagues inscribed on the staff have the numerical equivalent of 501. As the Jewish People entered the desert, after God drowned the Egyptians in the sea, God told the Nation that if they would abide by His statutes, then: *All the diseases that I put upon Egypt I will not put upon you* (*Shemos* 15:26).

The numerical equivalent of the word "that" (*asher*) is also 501 — thus God was saying that if the Nation followed His statutes, they would not be struck by plagues like those which had hit Egypt. (*Hagahos Maimonides*)

וּבְמוֹפְתִים זֶה הַדָּם. כְּמָה שֶׁנֶּאֱמַר. וְנָתַתִּי מוֹפְתִים בַּשָּׁמַיִם וּבָאָרֶץ:

While saying the following three words, one dips one's finger into his cup of wine three times, and removes a bit of wine each time.

דָּם. וָאֵשׁ. וְתִימְרוֹת עָשָׁן:

This is the blood — The clearest waters of the world were Egypt's, yet they turned into blood, even as the Egyptians held the water in their hands! Moreover, if a Jew and an Egyptian were drinking water from the same glass, the side from which the Jew was drinking would remain water, and the other side — blood! (*Ritva*, based on *Midrash*)

This is the blood — Here, the verses quoted by the Haggadah do not refer not to the miracle in which the Nile's waters turned to blood, but rather to the water in puddles and in other places on dry land, that Moshe *Rabbenu* turned to blood before the eyes of the Jewish elders. It was through this that they believed him, that he had been sent by God. (*Kol Bo*)

And with wonders — this is the blood — The Malbim notes that the plural form is used: "wonders." Thus the reference is probably to both the Nile and to the water on dry land, turning to blood.

I will place wonders — When God desires to perform miracles, for the congregation or for individuals, and He therefore does things which are against the natural order, it becomes clear to all how false these heretical ideologies are, for the miracle demonstrates that the creation is ruled by God, Who renews it, sustains it, knows what is hap-

And with wonders** — this the blood, as it is written:* ***I will place wonders in Heaven and on earth,

While saying the following three words, one dips one's finger into his cup of wine three times, and removes a bit of wine each time.

blood, and fire, and columns of smoke *(Yoel 3:3).*

pening in it, and is able to do whatever He wishes with it.

And when the miracle is announced beforehand by a Prophet, the miracle also demonstrates that there is such a thing as Prophecy — that God speaks to human beings, revealing His secrets to those who truly are servants to Him. This is the basis of the entire Torah. Thus, regarding the plagues, which were "signs" to all of mankind, the verses often say (e.g., *Shemos* 8:18) that God brought it *in order that you may know that I am God, in the midst of the world.*

However, the Holy One is not willing to do miracles in every generation, before the eyes of heretics and other wicked people. For this reason, He commanded us that we should keep daily remembrances of the miracles that we experienced, and relay the matter to our children and our children's children, to the very end of time. (*Ramban* on *Shemos* 13:1)

I will place wonders...blood, and fire, and columns of smoke — Though this prophecy, from the Book of Yoel, is about the future redemption, it nevertheless shows that the word "wonders" is connected to blood. In addition, it is said that the miracles in Egypt served as the roots and examples for the miracles of the future. The Ritva cites the *Mechilta* of Rabbi Shimon bar Yochai, which says that in Egypt, when the waters turned to blood, the blood was as hot as fire, and gave off smoke which covered the city of Pharaoh.

דָּבָר אַחֵר, בְּיָד חֲזָקָה – שְׁתַּיִם. וּבִזְרֹעַ נְטוּיָה – שְׁתַּיִם. וּבְמֹרָא גָּדֹל – שְׁתַּיִם. וּבְאֹתוֹת – שְׁתַּיִם. וּבְמֹפְתִים – שְׁתַּיִם. אֵלּוּ עֶשֶׂר מַכּוֹת שֶׁהֵבִיא הַקָּדוֹשׁ בָּרוּךְ הוּא עַל הַמִּצְרִים בְּמִצְרַיִם וְאֵלּוּ הֵן:

While reading the names of the ten plagues, one dips one's finger into his cup of wine, once for each plague, and removes a bit of wine each time:

דָּם. צְפַרְדֵּעַ. כִּנִּים. עָרוֹב.
דֶּבֶר. שְׁחִין. בָּרָד. אַרְבֶּה.
חֹשֶׁךְ. מַכַּת בְּכוֹרוֹת:

רַבִּי יְהוּדָה הָיָה נוֹתֵן בָּהֶם סִמָּנִים:

As each word is said, a little wine is removed from the cup, as above.

דְּצַ"ךְ עֲדַ"שׁ בְּאַחַ"ב:

With a strong hand — two; and with an outstretched arm — two; etc. — The verse uses five different expressions to describe how God took us out of Egypt, and since some are stated in the plural, each different expression is said to hint at two plagues, for the total was ten. (*Kol Bo*)

The Ten Plagues

God brought the plagues upon Egypt in the way that a king makes war. That is, when a king of flesh of blood sees that one of the nations of his kingdom is rebelling against him, what does he do? First, he

ANOTHER INTERPRETATION: *With a strong hand — two; and with an outstretched arm — two; and with great awe — two; and with signs — two; and with wonders — two. These are the ten plagues that the Holy One brought upon the Egyptians in Egypt. And these are they:*

While reading the names of the ten plagues, one dips one's finger into his cup of wine, once for each plague, and removes a bit of wine each time:

Blood, Frogs, Lice, Wild Beasts, Pestilence, Boils, Hail, Locusts, Darkness, the Slaying of the Firstborn.

RABBI YEHUDAH GAVE memory aids for them [comprised of each plague's first initial].

As each word is said, a little wine is removed from the cup, as above.

DETZACH ADASH B'ACHAV

sends his legions to surround them and commands them to cut off the rebelling nation's water supply. If they surrender, fine; but if not, he has his legions make fearful battle noises. If this works, fine; but if not, he has his legions shoot arrows at them. If that works, fine; but if not, he dispatches barbarians to attack them. If that doesn't work, he sends troops of retribution, who do not distinguish between the guilty and the innocent. If that stops the rebellion, fine; but if not, he throws burning oil on them. If that doesn't work, he catapults boulders upon them. If that doesn't work, he sends masses of infantry against them. If that doesn't work, he puts them in prison. If that stops the rebellion, fine; but if not, he kills their leaders.

So, too, were the strategies of the Holy One against the Egyptians. First, He cut off their water supply, turning all of their rivers to blood. That did not stop them, so He filled their ears with loud, fearful noises — the croaking frogs, who caused the Egyptians great discomfort. When that did not cause them to relent, He shot arrows at them — the lice, which pierced their skin like arrows. That did not work either, so He brought barbarians upon them — the wild beasts. When that did not stop them, He dispatched troops of retribution — the pestilence, which destroyed Egypt's herds. That did not stop them, so He threw burning oil on them — boils. That did not work, so He catapulted stones upon them — the hail. That didn't work, so He sent masses of infantry against them— the locusts. That didn't work, so He imprisoned them — shutting them in darkness for three days. That didn't work, so He killed their leaders — *And God struck every firstborn of Egypt*. (*Midrash Tanchuma, Parashas Bo*)

Why was blood the first plague?

Pharaoh and the Egyptians worshiped the Nile. God said, "I will strike their god first, and I will strike at them afterwards." A common expression states: Strike their god and the priests will be terrified.

The Egyptians thought that the Jews were drinking Egypt's water. Therefore, *He turned their waters to blood*. (*Tehillim* 78:44; *Shemos Rabbah*, Chapter Nine; *Tanchuma, Parashas Bo*)

The Egyptians had cast untold numbers of Jewish children into the river. Therefore, the first plague was a message: "Come, look now at your whole land, at its rivers that are flowing with the Jewish blood that you spilled." (*Abarbanel*)

Why did God use frogs to afflict the Egyptians?

The Egyptians would taunt the Jews, and cause them revulsion, saying, "Bring us unkosher animals so that we may play with them and take pleasure in them." To repay them, God caused the Egyptians a similar revulsion. (*Shemos Rabbah; Tanchuma, Parashas Va'era*)

The Egyptian taskmasters would noisily awaken the Jews to go to work in the morning, banging on doors and windows. God paid them back with frogs, who croaked loudly and swarmed everywhere. (*Midrash Torah Shelemah*)

The Egyptian taskmasters shouted at the Jews all day and all night, to strike fear into them. (*Toldos Adam*)

The Egyptians forced the Jews to load their freight; therefore God sent the frogs to dirty and spoil that freight. (*Tanchuma, Parashas Bo*)

The Egyptians would steal Jewish children from their homes, take them away and murder them, and the parents would cry and scream for mercy, but the Egyptians would not listen. As punishment, God brought the frogs, who croaked loudly — and the Egyptians had to listen. (*Abarbanel*)

Why did God use lice to afflict the Egyptians?

The Egyptians gave the Jews brooms, and forced them to sweep the houses, courtyards, and streets of Egypt. Therefore, God turned all the dust of Egypt into lice, which clung to the Egyptians, and as a result, there was no more dust that needed to be swept. (*Yalkut Shimoni, Parashas Va'era*)

The Egyptians prevented the Jews from bathing, causing them to suffer from lice. Therefore God afflicted the Egyptians with lice. (*Midrash Torah Shelemah*)

Why did God bring wild beasts upon them?

Once Egypt had suffered the first three plagues, the Jews were no longer forced to work in the fields with straw and bricks. The Egyptians then tried a new way to harm them, and ordered them, "Go into the wilderness and bring us back lions and bears, so that we can make a circus and enjoy ourselves." Therefore, God brought the wild beasts into the very streets of Egypt.

Pharaoh wanted to kill all the Jewish male children and keep the females alive, so that the Egyptians could intermarry with them. Therefore God said, "You sought to mix with the daughters of Israel?! Mix with these wild animals instead!" And because the Egyptians exchanged wives with one another, and mixed their lineage lines, it was fitting that they be attacked by a mixture of wild beasts.

The Egyptians made peace with all their enemies, in order that they all join together against Israel. Therefore God caused the beasts to make peace with one another, too, so that they would join together against Egypt. (*Midrash haGadol; Shemos Rabbah,* Chapter 10; *Midrashim* from *Torah Shelemah; Midrash Tehillim,* Psalm 75)

The Egyptians would break into Jewish homes, snatch the children, and make them toil as slaves. Therefore wild beasts now would enter Egyptian homes, snatch their children, and tear them to pieces. (*Abarbanel*)

The plague of the wild beasts could be brought about only by God. The nature of beasts is to stay in the wilds because God made them that way, and only He can cause them to go against their nature.

Why did God bring pestilence upon them?

The Egyptians made the Jews tend their flocks and herds. Therefore God caused the flocks and herds of the Egyptians to die. Also, the Egyptians wanted to steal whatever animals the Jews had. Therefore they lost theirs. Moreover, once the previous plagues had struck and Pharaoh had freed the Jews from hard labor, many Egyptians nevertheless refused to allow their Jewish slaves to rest. It was then that they made the Jews tend their herds and flocks, saying, "Our children used to do this for us, but they were killed by the wild beasts." Therefore the pestilence came, to free the Jews from this work as well. (*Shemos Rabbah,* Chapter 11; *Mishnas Rebbe Aharon,* Chapter 19)

Why did God give them boils?

The Egyptians made the Jews prepare their baths for them. Their animals had died in the pestilence, but they still sought to pamper themselves in the bath houses. They said to the Jews, "You have nothing better to do — come, heat our water!" God said, "You seek to pamper yourselves?! I will give you just the opposite, and it will be impossible for you to wash!" (*Shemos Rabbah,* Chapter 11; *Mishnas Rebbe Aharon,* Chapter 19)

They beat the Jews until their bodies were covered with cuts and boils... (*Toldos Adam*)

The Egyptians caused to Jews to feel dirty and disgusting. Therefore

God made the Egyptians feel even worse. (*Abarbanel*)

Why did God bring hail upon them?

The Egyptians made the Jews plant orchards and vineyards for them, and never paid them a salary. They also planned that if the Jews ever tried to escape their bondage, they would hurl stones upon them and beat them. Therefore, God sent hailstones upon the Egyptians, and also upon their orchards and vineyards, to destroy everything that the Jews had planted for them. (*Midrash ha-Gadol; Shemos Rabbah*, Chapter 12)

Why did God send locusts upon them?

The Egyptians had made the Jews sow wheat and barley in their fields, and never paid them for their work. Therefore, God sent the locusts to devour everything that the Jews had planted for them. (*Shemos Rabbah*, Chapter 13; *Midrash Tanchuma*)

The Egyptians stole whatever grains the Jews were able to grow for themselves. Therefore God sent locusts upon them. (*Abarbanel*)

Why did God bring darkness upon them?

There were evil Jews in Egypt who patronized the Egyptians, acquiring so much wealth and status that they wanted to remain in Egypt. Therefore, God said, "If I kill them openly, the Egyptians will say, 'Just as He smites us, He smites the Jews, too'!" Therefore, God enveloped the Egyptians in darkness for three days, during which time the Jews were able to bury their dead, without their enemies seeing. (*Shemos Rabbah*, Chapter 13)

The Egyptians wanted to keep the Jews in captivity and hold them in prisons. To repay them, God held the Egyptians in a thick darkness, about which it is written (*Shemos* 10:23), *One man could not see his fellow, and no man could rise from his place.* (*Tanchuma*)

The Egyptians had darkened the lives of the Jews. Therefore their own lives had to be darkened. (*Abarbanel*)

The Slaying of the Firstborn — why this plague?

The Egyptians wanted to kill us (*Tanchuma*), and God calls Israel: *My firstborn son* (*Shemos* 4:22). Therefore, God slayed their firstborn. (*Abarbanel*)

The Ten Plagues — Three plagues were initiated by Aharon — the first three; another three were initiated by Moshe *Rabbenu* — hail, locusts, and darkness; another three were by God alone — wild beasts, pestilence, and the slaying of the firstborn. The plague of boils was brought on by all three together. Whatever Moshe and Aharon did, however, was only with explicit instructions from the Holy One. (*Shibolei Leket, Rashbatz*, and others)

📖

The ten plagues were sent in groups of three. For the first two of each group, Pharaoh was given a warning; this was not the case regarding the third and last plague in each group. Inscribed on the staff used by Moshe and Aharon to initiate the plagues, was the first initial of each plague, and these initials also were arranged in groups of three. The tenth plague did not belong to any group, and its initial was inscribed on the staff along with the initials of the last group of three. (*Rashi*, in the name of *Midrash Shochar Tov; Ritva, Malbim* and others)

📖

We find that God strengthened Moshe *Rabbenu* to help him continue to carry out His commands. Pharaoh was obstinate, even after being struck by plague after plague, but Moshe *Rabbenu* persisted in his efforts to try to bring Pharaoh to his senses, so that he would agree to allow the Jews to leave. Also, God did not even start sending plagues against Pharaoh without first having Moshe *Rabbenu* warn him, for He wanted to give Pharaoh the opportunity to repent his ways. (*Shibolei Leket*, based on *Shemos Rabbah*, Chapter 12)

📖

When Moshe *Rabbenu* was an infant but his parents could no longer keep him in the house [without being discovered], they made a basket for him, and his mother and sister hid the basket in the reeds of the Nile, with Moshe inside it. As is known, Moshe *Rabbenu* was retrieved from the river by Pharaoh's daughter, who took him and raised him, and thus the river had served to protect him. Later, after Moshe killed an Egyptian taskmaster, he used dirt to hide the body, and thus the dirt, as well, had served to protect Moshe. Accordingly, the Nile was turned to blood not by Moshe, but by Aharon. The plague of frogs was like the plague of blood, for it, too, was initiated by striking the river. Therefore Aharon, and not Moshe, was chosen to do so. Similarly, it was not Moshe, but Aharon who struck the dirt of Egypt to initiate the plague of lice, for just as Moshe had been protected by the water of Egypt, he also had been protected by the dirt of Egypt. (*Rashi, Shemos* 7:19; 8:12, based on *Shemos Rabbah*)

The ten plagues had a positive effect on the ten "sayings" through which God created the world (*Pirkei Avos* 5:1). The plagues served to make these ten "sayings" more revealed, and this paved the way for the giving of the Ten Commandments.

And why are the Ten Commandments called *dibros* while the ten sayings are called *ma'amaros*? We see from Scripture that the concepts connoted by the Hebrew root of *dibros* (דבר) are associated not only with "words" and "speech" and "commandments," but with "direction" or "management" by a higher power. Thus the Ten Commandments are called the *dibros* because from the moment that they were given, God's direction and management of the world became clearly recognized. Everyone saw that He is the Authority Who runs the world. The inner power which gives everything its existence stems from the "sayings" that He uttered at the very beginning, when no man existed to hear! Through the Ten Commandments, which were given in public to the entire Jewish Nation, the many layers and coverings of nature no longer concealed the fact that God's powers are at the root of the Creation, and Pharaoh could no longer say, "*I* made the river." (*Sefas Emes* in the name of the *Chiddushei haRim*)

Detzach, etc. — Memory aids must be brief — as our Sages say, "One should always take the shortest way to explain things." We find that Rabbi Yehudah made memory aids in order to recall details of his learning, as well (*Mishnah, Menachos*, Chapter 11, *fourth mishnah*). (*Ritva*)

In Rabbi Yehudah's opinion, this arrangement of the initials was engraved on the staff which was used by Moshe and Aharon to initiate the plagues. The numerical equivalent of the initials totals 501 (see above). The first time that Moshe and Aharon appeared before Pharaoh and told him that God had sent them to say, *Let My people go*, Pharaoh replied: *Who is the Lord that [asher] I shall hearken to His voice?*

(*Shemos* 5:2). Without realizing it, Pharaoh had prophesied, that after 501 — the ten plagues as inscribed on the staff — *I shall hearken to His voice.* (haAri, z"l)

The third plague in each set (lice, boils, darkness) came without warning, and these are the plagues that the Egyptian sorcerers were not able to imitate. From the letters which compose the names of these three plagues, there is a clear indication that these particular plagues are intimately related to one another, for if we write their names one atop the other, we can read the names of the plagues not only from right to left, but also from top to bottom (*Hagahos Maimonides*):

ח ש כ

ש ח נ

כ נ ם

Removing drops of wine when mentioning the plagues

It has become a universally accepted custom to remove a bit of wine from one's cup as one reads the verse from *Yoel*. One first removes some when he says, "blood"; again, when he says, "fire"; and a third time when he says, "columns of smoke." Afterwards, as well, when he mentions the plagues explicitly, one by one, each time he says the name of a plague, he removes some wine from his cup. He removes a little wine three more times as he says the three memory aids of Rabbi Yehudah. Many use a finger for this purpose, as a reminder of what the Egyptian sorcerers said about the plague of lice, when they could not duplicate it: that it was *the Finger of God* (*Shemos* 8:15). Others remove the wine by simply tipping the cup, which was the custom of the *Ari, z"l*.

The commentators explain that by removing drops of wine, we present testimony that our happiness on the Seder night is tempered by sadness. Our cup of salvation is "not completely full," for our freedom had to come about through punishments that were meted out to other human beings. True, the Egyptians deserved to suffer the ten plagues, but the verse teaches (*Mishlei* 24:17): *When your enemy falls, do not rejoice.* (Abarbanel)

Accordingly, in the Torah's verses about the holiday of Pesach, there is no explicit command to be "happy," and neither does the Torah say that Pesach is in remembrance of any of the plagues. Rather, Pesach is in remembrance only of our "leaving" Egypt. Only the positive aspect is mentioned, for this is what we are to celebrate, not our enemy's downfall.

This principle helps explain something which, on the surface, seems very bizarre. Regarding the Jews of that generation, the prohibition on the possession of *chametz* was for one day only — the actual day of the Exodus. For them, Pesach was not seven days long! Nevertheless, it says in the Torah that while the plagues still were in process, Moshe *Rabbenu* commanded the Jews (*Shemos* 12:15-16): *Seven days you shall eat matzos...for anyone who eats chametz from the first day to the seventh day, his soul shall be cut off. And the first day shall be a holy convocation, and the seventh day shall be a holy convocation.* Why did God have Moshe *Rabbenu* speak about what would apply only in the future? The seventh day of Pesach coincides with the day that the Egyptians drowned in the sea. Why not wait for then to tell the Jews that Pesach was to be seven days long?

According to the above, however, everything is understood. If the law that Pesach is seven days long had been told to them after the Egyptians had been drowned, the Jews might have thought that the purpose of the seventh day of Pesach was to celebrate the drowning! However, now that we see that the mitzvah of keeping the seventh day as a holiday was given even beforehand, all realize that the seventh day is a holiday simply because this is God's Will, and the seventh day's purpose is not to celebrate the downfall of the Egyptians. It is not the way of the Holy One to be glad when His creations are killed, for *when your enemy falls, do not rejoice.* (*Meshech Chochmah, Parashas Bo*; see also *Yalkut Shimoni*)

And why does it come out that we remove wine from our cup sixteen times? Because each week, in the days of Temple, sixteen lambs were brought on the altar as community offerings — two lambs on each of the seven days, and an additional two lambs on Shabbos for the *Musaf* offering. Nowadays, over the course of the week, sixteen people (not including *Maftir*) are called up in the synagogue for the community Torah readings. (*Amarcal* in the name of the *Roke'ach*)

Afterwards, refill the cups, and continue:

רַבִּי יוֹסֵי הַגְּלִילִי אוֹמֵר, מִנַּיִן אַתָּה אוֹמֵר שֶׁלָּקוּ הַמִּצְרִים בְּמִצְרַיִם עֶשֶׂר מַכּוֹת וְעַל הַיָּם לָקוּ חֲמִשִּׁים מַכּוֹת. בְּמִצְרַיִם מַה הוּא אוֹמֵר, וַיֹּאמְרוּ הַחַרְטֻמִּם אֶל פַּרְעֹה אֶצְבַּע אֱלֹהִים הִיא. וְעַל הַיָּם מַה הוּא אוֹמֵר, וַיַּרְא יִשְׂרָאֵל אֶת הַיָּד הַגְּדֹלָה אֲשֶׁר עָשָׂה יְהֹוָה בְּמִצְרַיִם וַיִּירְאוּ הָעָם אֶת יְהֹוָה וַיַּאֲמִינוּ בַּיהֹוָה וּבְמֹשֶׁה עַבְדּוֹ. כַּמָּה לָקוּ בְאֶצְבַּע עֶשֶׂר מַכּוֹת. אֱמֹר מֵעַתָּה, בְּמִצְרַיִם לָקוּ עֶשֶׂר מַכּוֹת וְעַל הַיָּם לָקוּ חֲמִשִּׁים מַכּוֹת:

R. Yosei the Galilean — Regarding the plagues that God put on the Egyptians in Egypt, the Torah says that the plagues were sent by God's "finger," while the plagues at the sea were sent by God's "hand." It is worthwhile to add that in the Prophetic Writings about the Redemption to Come, we find, so to speak, even greater "involvement" of the Holy One, for it is written (Yeshayahu 25:9): *And they shall say on that day, "This is our God. We have hoped for Him. Let us rejoice in His salvation."* In a manner of speaking, "all" of God will be taking part!

    This way of thinking raises a question, however, for when speaking about the redemption from Egypt, the verse in *Devarim* (26:8) states that God took us out not only *with a strong hand*, but also *with an outstretched arm*. Is not the "arm" greater than the "hand"? Why, then, did Rabbi Yosei the Galilean compute the number of plagues at the sea by taking the number of plagues in Egypt (10) and multiplying it only by five (because of the word "hand") — to arrive at fifty?

Afterwards, refill the cups, and continue:

RABBI YOSEI THE GALILEAN SAYS: *Where is there proof that the Egyptians were struck ten times in Egypt, but fifty times at the sea? For about the events in Egypt, what does the Torah write? — "The sorcerers said to Pharaoh, 'It is the Finger of God!'" (Shemos 8:15). About what happened at the sea, however, it writes, "And when Israel saw the Great Hand that God had used on the Egyptians, the Nation feared God and believed in God and in Moshe His servant" (Shemos 14:31). How many blows did one finger bring upon them in Egypt? Ten! Thus, you say, if in Egypt they received ten blows (from just one "finger"), then at the sea (where it was a whole "hand"), they must have received fifty!*

Why not multiply it by ten (because of the word "arm") and arrive at one hundred!?

We can explain, however, that the verse says the "arm" is "outstretched," implying that all the blows to come from the entire arm have not yet been delivered, but will bedelivered in the future. In Egypt, God hit only with the "hand" of His outstretched arm. In fact, a verse in Prophecy about the Final Redemption (*Yeshayahu* 53:1) can be interpreted to be saying that the redemption from Egypt was only a partial redemption: *And the arm of God until fifty was revealed.*

That is, as Rabbi Yosei the Galilean said, *only up to the hand of His arm* was revealed at the sea, so the number of plagues that took place there was only five times the number of plagues that took place in Egypt, and the rest of God's "arm" will be revealed only during the Redemption to Come! This is yet another way of seeing that the redemption from Egypt was actually the beginning of the Final Redemption! (*Sefas Emes*)

רַבִּי אֱלִיעֶזֶר אוֹמֵר, מִנַּיִן שֶׁכָּל מַכָּה וּמַכָּה שֶׁהֵבִיא הַקָּדוֹשׁ בָּרוּךְ הוּא עַל הַמִּצְרִים בְּמִצְרַיִם הָיְתָה שֶׁל אַרְבַּע מַכּוֹת. שֶׁנֶּאֱמַר, יְשַׁלַּח בָּם חֲרוֹן אַפּוֹ עֶבְרָה וָזַעַם וְצָרָה מִשְׁלַחַת מַלְאֲכֵי רָעִים.

עֶבְרָה   אַחַת.
וָזַעַם   שְׁתַּיִם.
וְצָרָה   שָׁלוֹשׁ.
מִשְׁלַחַת מַלְאֲכֵי רָעִים   אַרְבַּע.

אֱמֹר מֵעַתָּה, בְּמִצְרַיִם לָקוּ אַרְבָּעִים מַכּוֹת וְעַל הַיָּם לָקוּ מָאתַיִם מַכּוֹת:

רַבִּי עֲקִיבָא אוֹמֵר, מִנַּיִן שֶׁכָּל מַכָּה וּמַכָּה שֶׁהֵבִיא הַקָּדוֹשׁ בָּרוּךְ הוּא עַל הַמִּצְרִים בְּמִצְרַיִם הָיְתָה שֶׁל חָמֵשׁ מַכּוֹת. שֶׁנֶּאֱמַר, יְשַׁלַּח בָּם חֲרוֹן אַפּוֹ עֶבְרָה וָזַעַם וְצָרָה מִשְׁלַחַת מַלְאֲכֵי רָעִים.

חֲרוֹן אַפּוֹ   אַחַת.
עֶבְרָה   שְׁתַּיִם.
וָזַעַם   שָׁלוֹשׁ.
וְצָרָה   אַרְבַּע.
מִשְׁלַחַת מַלְאֲכֵי רָעִים   חָמֵשׁ.

אֱמֹר מֵעַתָּה בְּמִצְרַיִם לָקוּ חֲמִשִּׁים מַכּוֹת וְעַל הַיָּם לָקוּ חֲמִשִּׁים וּמָאתַיִם מַכּוֹת:

RABBI ELIEZER SAID: How do we know that each plague that the Holy One, blessed is He, brought upon the Egyptians in Egypt was divided into four plagues? For it is stated, "And He sent the fury of His anger upon them: wrath, indignation, and trouble, a contingent of harming angels" (Tehillim 78:49).

"Wrath" is	one;
"indignation,"	two;
"trouble,"	three;
"a contingent of harming angels,"	four.

As a result, the Egyptians were struck by forty blows in Egypt [not just ten] and by two hundred blows at the sea [not just fifty].

RABBI AKIVA SAID: How do we know that each plague that the Holy One, blessed is He, brought upon the Egyptians in Egypt, was divided into five plagues? For it is stated, "And He sent the fury of His anger upon them, wrath, indignation and trouble, and a contingent of harming angels."

"Fury of His anger" is	one;
"wrath" is	two;
"indignation,"	three;
"trouble,"	four;
"a contingent of harming angels,"	five.

As a result, the Egyptians were struck by fifty blows in Egypt [not by just forty], and by two hundred and fifty at the sea [not by just two hundred].

Fifty...two hundred — One Sage says there were fifty plagues at the sea; another Sage says no, there were two hundred plagues at the sea; a third Sage says no, the number was two hundred and fifty! But what does it really matter? The answer lies in a novel understanding of one of the promises made by God to the entire Jewish People (*Shemos* 15:26): *All the diseases that I put upon the Egyptians I will not put upon you.*

That is, the more diseases and plagues that we say God *put upon the Egyptians*, the more praiseworthy we are — for greater is the number of the diseases and plagues that God will not put upon us! (*Vilna Gaon*)

The number of plagues

After hearing what his colleagues had said, Rabbi Akiva stood up and said that, in fact, there were fifty plagues in Egypt — not ten, as Rabbi Yosei the Galilean had said, and not forty, as Rabbi Eliezer had said. So, too, said Rabbi Akiva, there were two-hundred-and-fifty plagues at the sea — not two hundred, and not fifty! Each opinion, of course, is correct, each in its place, for the law is, *Whoever elaborates on the story [of the Exodus] is to be praised.* We are permitted to divide each plague into many plagues, for this makes it more vivid and clear that God repaid Egypt in full for its evil deeds.

If we take the times that we remove wine from the cup — ten times while we are saying the names of the plagues, plus three more times while we are saying the three memory aids of Rabbi Yehudah — and then we add sixty (the total number of plagues, according to Rabbi Yosei the Galilean), plus two hundred and forty (Rabbi Eliezer's total), plus three hundred (Rabbi Akiva's total), we arrive at the number 613, the total number of mitzvos in the Torah!

Because we find in the *Zohar* that the 613 mitzvos are called "pieces of advice" that God has given us in order to fulfill the Torah, we can assume that, within each of us, there are 613 different types of resistance, serving as obstacles which can block us from fulfilling the Torah. By performing the thirteen dippings, and then reading the words of the three different Sages, we "spread" the plagues of our redemption to 613, precisely in order to counteract and break the 613 types of resistance!

Just as the ten plagues "spread" to 613 mitzvos, so, too, it is written that the Ten Commandments do the same, "spreading" out to include all of them! And just as regarding the plagues, the Torah first writes "finger," and later it writes "hand," so, too, regarding the Ten Commandments — the Torah first says that they were written on stone with the "finger" of God (*Shemos* 31:18), and later (in its very last verse) the Torah uses the word "hand" regarding the Ten Commandments! (*Sefas Emes*)

Up to this point in the Seder, the Haggadah has recounted the fulfillment of only part of the Covenant between the Pieces — the part about Avraham's seed being enslaved and oppressed, and the part where God promised Avraham that He would "execute judgments" on the oppressor nation. Now we turn to the other part of the Covenant between the Pieces — the promise that God made to Avraham that his seed would leave the land of their oppressors, and would *go out with great wealth.*

כַּמָּה מַעֲלוֹת טוֹבוֹת לַמָּקוֹם עָלֵינוּ:

אִלּוּ הוֹצִיאָנוּ מִמִּצְרַיִם, וְלֹא עָשָׂה בָהֶם שְׁפָטִים דַּיֵּנוּ:

אִלּוּ עָשָׂה בָהֶם שְׁפָטִים, וְלֹא עָשָׂה בֵאלֹהֵיהֶם דַּיֵּנוּ:

אִלּוּ עָשָׂה בֵאלֹהֵיהֶם, וְלֹא הָרַג אֶת בְּכוֹרֵיהֶם דַּיֵּנוּ:

אִלּוּ הָרַג אֶת בְּכוֹרֵיהֶם, וְלֹא נָתַן לָנוּ אֶת מָמוֹנָם דַּיֵּנוּ:

How many favors — These "favors," which gradually brought us to greater spiritual heights, are specifically fifteen in number, for they correspond to fifteen steps or "levels" which exist in the Creation itself. That is, the lowest level (1) is the physical world, which has above it seven "heavens"(1+7=8). Between the physical world and the lowest heaven, there is a level of "space" (+1)(8+1=9) and there also exists a level of "space" between each of the seven heavens (+6)(9+6=15). Thus, the verse in *Tehillim 68:5* says: *Soar up to Him, He Who rides upon the heavens, with yud (10) + heh (5), His Name.*

In the Temple, corresponding to fifteen levels in Creation, there were fifteen steps between the outer and inner courtyards, and David *haMelech* composed fifteen songs of "ascent" to be sung on the steps, by the Levites, when water offerings were brought on the holiday of Sukkos. When they went to get the water, they would sing the two-letter Name of God, whose numerical value is fifteen: *We belong to God [yud-heh] and our eyes look to God [yud heh]* Thus, there were fifteen generations between Avraham *Avinu* and Shelomo *haMelech*, who built the Temple. The Temple, as the Haggadah states, was our highest spiritual height, and the descendents of Avraham arrived at this pinnacle specifically after fifteen generations, as the moon reaches its fullness only after fifteen days have

*H*OW MANY FAVORS God bestowed on us, each one greater than the one previous to it!

If He had taken us out of Egypt and not wrought judgments upon them,   it would have sufficed for us!

If He had wrought judgments upon them and not upon their gods,   it would have sufficed for us!

If He had wrought judgments upon their gods, and not slain their firstborn,   it would have sufficed for us!

If He had slain their firstborn, and had not given us their wealth,   it would have sufficed for us!

passed of the month. (*Vilna Gaon*)

How many favors — Once the Haggadah has quoted the words of our Sages, who spoke of greater and greater numbers of plagues in Egypt and on the sea, it now wants to point out that so, too, the reasons that we have to praise God grow and grow. We must simply take time to think of what God has done for us, one great thing after another, out of His great love for us. (*Shibolei haLeket*)

If He had taken us out of Egypt, and had not wrought judgments upon them, it would have sufficed — That is, it would have given us sufficient reason to praise Him and thank Him. (*Malbim*)

If He had wrought judgments on their gods and had not slain their firstborn — These two "favors" were bestowed upon us simultaneously, as the verse says (Shemos 12:12): And I will smite all the firstborn in the land of Egypt...and against all the gods of Egypt I will execute judgments. Egypt had great esteem for their deities and their firstborn, and God thus saw fit to destroy both at once. (*Shibolei HaLeket*)

And had not given us their wealth — The wealth of the Egyptians who

אִלּוּ נָתַן לָנוּ אֶת מָמוֹנָם, וְלֹא קָרַע לָנוּ אֶת הַיָּם דַּיֵּנוּ:

אִלּוּ קָרַע לָנוּ אֶת הַיָּם, וְלֹא הֶעֱבִירָנוּ בְּתוֹכוֹ בֶּחָרָבָה דַּיֵּנוּ:

אִלּוּ הֶעֱבִירָנוּ בְּתוֹכוֹ בֶּחָרָבָה, וְלֹא שִׁקַּע צָרֵינוּ בְּתוֹכוֹ דַּיֵּנוּ:

אִלּוּ שִׁקַּע צָרֵינוּ בְּתוֹכוֹ, וְלֹא סִפֵּק צָרְכֵּנוּ בַּמִּדְבָּר אַרְבָּעִים שָׁנָה דַּיֵּנוּ:

were drowned in the sea. Prior to the tenth plague, God had told Moshe to tell the people to ask the Egyptians to lend them *vessels of silver and gold (Shemos 11:2)*, which they would take with them when they left Egypt. As God had promised *(Shemos 3:22)*, the Egyptians complied with the request, and the Jews not only were given the silver and gold, they were allowed to keep what they had "borrowed." This fulfilled the promise that God had made to Avraham in the Covenant between the Pieces, when God said Avraham's descendants would leave their bondage *with great wealth*. However, if this silver and gold is the "wealth" to which the Haggadah refers, why is it mentioned only after the tenth plague? The Jews acquired the silver and gold beforehand! Rather, the Haggadah here is referring to the wealth that washed up on the seashore afterwards, which was above and beyond what the Jews had "borrowed," and thus it was more than what God had promised to Avraham. *(Rashbam)*

📖

And had not given us their wealth — Some explain that this does refer to the silver and gold that the Jews "borrowed" and took out of Egypt. Its mention, in fact, does belong after the tenth plague, for only then did the Jews actually leave with the "borrowed" wealth, and though this silver and gold was the wealth that had been promised in the

If He had given us their wealth, and had not split the sea for us,   it would have sufficed for us!

If He had split the sea for us, and had not taken us through it on dry ground,   it would have sufficed for us!

If He had taken us through it on dry ground, and had not drowned our enemies in it,   it would have sufficed for us!

If He had drowned our enemies in it, and had not given us our needs in the desert for forty years,
                                        it would have sufficed for us!

Covenant between the Pieces, the promise did not imply that Avraham's descendants would gain the wealth by taking advantage of the Egyptians, and empty Egypt completely. (*Chukkas haPesach*)

And had not split the sea for us — For really, God could have led us out of Egypt not by way of the sea. (*Rashbam* and others)

And had not taken us through it on dry ground — God did not have to make the sea floor completely dry. He could have left it slightly wet and muddy. (*Rashbam*)

And had not drowned our enemies in it — God could have closed the sea behind us after we had entered, if all He wanted to do was to stop the Egyptians from attacking us. (*Sefer haShelah* and others)

And had not given us our needs in the desert — God did not have to perform miracles, such as providing quail for the entire Nation, when there was plenty of meat available from our sheep and cattle, and we had silver and gold, as well, and we could have purchased our food from others. (*Rashbam*)

אִלּוּ סִפֵּק צָרְכֵּנוּ בַּמִּדְבָּר אַרְבָּעִים שָׁנָה, וְלֹא הֶאֱכִילָנוּ אֶת הַמָּן דַּיֵּנוּ:

אִלּוּ הֶאֱכִילָנוּ אֶת הַמָּן, וְלֹא נָתַן לָנוּ אֶת הַשַּׁבָּת דַּיֵּנוּ:

אִלּוּ נָתַן לָנוּ אֶת הַשַּׁבָּת, וְלֹא קֵרְבָנוּ לִפְנֵי הַר סִינַי דַּיֵּנוּ:

אִלּוּ קֵרְבָנוּ לִפְנֵי הַר סִינַי, וְלֹא נָתַן לָנוּ אֶת הַתּוֹרָה דַּיֵּנוּ:

אִלּוּ נָתַן לָנוּ אֶת הַתּוֹרָה, וְלֹא הִכְנִיסָנוּ לְאֶרֶץ יִשְׂרָאֵל דַּיֵּנוּ:

And had not given us manna to eat — Manna was "bread from heaven," and God could have supplied us with normal food (*Rashbatz*). He also could have told us to take cakes with us when we left Egypt, for just as God performed a miracle and did not let our clothes wear out, even after 40 years in the desert, He also could have kept our cakes soft and fresh by means of a miracle. (*Kol Bo*)

If He had given us the Shabbos — Which was given when the Jews were camped at Marra, before they came to Mount Sinai to receive the Torah. (*Machzor Vitry*)

If He had brought us to Mount Sinai, and had not given us the Torah — Simply being brought to Mount Sinai was a great benefit, for there, the entire nation was cured of all illnesses, and the "venom of the snake" left them, as well. What is more, there they received "crowns" for having said "We shall do," before saying "We shall hear." They also learned many mystical secrets at Mount Sinai, during the three days that preceded the giving of the Torah. (*Machzor Vitry, Avudraham, Kol Bo, Sefer haMichtam*)

If He had given us our needs in the desert for forty years, and had not given us manna to eat, it would have sufficed for us!

If He had given us manna to eat, and had not given us the Shabbos, it would have sufficed for us!

If He had given us the Shabbos, and had not brought us to Mount Sinai, it would have sufficed for us!

If He had brought us to Mount Sinai, and had not given us the Torah, it would have sufficed for us!

If He had given us the Torah, and had not brought us into the Land of Israel, it would have sufficed for us!

If He had brought us to Mount Sinai, and had not given us the Torah — You might ask: What good would it have done us to simply be at Mount Sinai if we had not been given the Torah there? The answer is that our mere being there was like the giving of the Torah! How so?

The story is told of a convert who asked Hillel the Elder to teach him the whole Torah "standing on one leg." What was the Sage's response? He said, "Do not do unto others what you would not want them to do unto you. This is the entire Torah. The rest is commentary. Now go and learn!" Similarly, Rabbi Akiva said, "Love your neighbor as you love yourself — this is the guiding principle of all the Torah!"

Our Sages teach us that the Jews who left Egypt actually achieved this feeling for one another as soon as they came to the foot of Mount Sinai, and set up camp there, even before they received the Torah! Describing their progress, the Torah says "they": *And they traveled from Refidim...and they came to the Sinai desert...and they camped in the desert.* But now we are told (Shemos 19:2): *And there Israel encamped before the mount.*

Suddenly, the Torah speaks in the singular! Our Sages teach us that all the Jews had become "as one man, with one heart!" As soon as

אִלּוּ הִכְנִיסָנוּ לְאֶרֶץ יִשְׂרָאֵל, וְלֹא בָנָה לָנוּ אֶת בֵּית הַבְּחִירָה דַּיֵּנוּ:

עַל אַחַת כַּמָּה וְכַמָּה טוֹבָה כְפוּלָה וּמְכֻפֶּלֶת לַמָּקוֹם עָלֵינוּ. שֶׁהוֹצִיאָנוּ מִמִּצְרַיִם. וְעָשָׂה בָהֶם שְׁפָטִים. וְעָשָׂה בֵאלֹהֵיהֶם. וְהָרַג אֶת בְּכוֹרֵיהֶם. וְנָתַן לָנוּ אֶת מָמוֹנָם. וְקָרַע לָנוּ אֶת הַיָּם. וְהֶעֱבִירָנוּ בְתוֹכוֹ בֶּחָרָבָה. וְשִׁקַּע

one's heart is full of love and concern for one's fellow, and for the world at large, the heart itself becomes a source of Torah! It is an overflowing spring of Torah, and it teaches the person the Ten Commandments, and from these he arrives at the entire Torah — all 613 mitzvos and everything that the Rabbis taught, for everything is based on the same principle! Thus it would have been enough simply if God had brought us to Mount Sinai!

📖

And had not given us the Torah — That is, the Ten Commandments. God did not have to give us stone tablets with the Ten Commandments inscribed on them by His "finger." Rather, He could have given us the Ten Commandments in the same way that He gave us the remainder of the Torah-by telling them to Moshe *Rabbenu*, who would serve as intermediary and tell us what God had said. (*Kol Bo, Avudraham* and others)

📖

And had not given us the Torah — God wanted to give His Torah from atop a desert mountain, and in the desert adjacent to Egypt, there were many high and majestic peaks that seemed suitable for this purpose. However, He specifically chose Mount Sinai — the lowest mountain of all. Our Sages taught us that from God's preference for Mount Sinai, we see how tremendously important it is to develop the character trait of "lowliness," i.e., humility — that the more one succeeds in this, the more he will be a "place" for receiving the Torah. As

If He had brought us into the Land of Israel, and had not built the Holy Temple for us,   it would have sufficed for us!

All the more so, for the multiplicity of His favors! That He took us out of Egypt AND wrought judgments upon them AND their gods, AND slew their firstborn, AND gave us their wealth, AND split the sea for us, AND took us through it on dry land, AND

haughtiness disappears from one's thoughts, speech, and actions, he will merit to understand the Torah, and will see its light in perfect clarity. Our Sages taught, in fact, that no character trait is more important than humility, and *What wisdom used as a crown for its head, humility used as a sole for its shoe.* (*Talmud Yerushalmi, Shabbos*, Chapter One, *mishnah* 3)

All the more so, for the multiplicity of His favors — That is, God has in store for us many, many more favors, which He will bestow upon us in the Redemption to Come, when He again will do miracles for us as the ones He wrought in Egypt. Everything which occurred in Egypt is a sign for the future, as our Sages teach, "What happened to our forefathers is a sign for what will happen to us." The wonders in Egypt serve as examples of what the future miracles will be. (based upon *Ma'asei Nissim*)

And split the sea for us — Our Sages teach us, "Everything about dry land is also true about the sea," although the sea and the land are each creations in their own right. God wanted to change the laws of nature for the sake of His nation. After having done so on the dry land — by means of the ten plagues in Egypt — He also wanted to do so at the sea, by means of ten additional miracles. Afterwards, He performed ten miracles in the heavens, too, by bringing down the Ten Commandments through them, onto Mount Sinai. (*Sefas Emes*)

צָרֵינוּ בְּתוֹכוֹ. וְסִפֵּק צָרְכֵּנוּ בַּמִּדְבָּר אַרְבָּעִים שָׁנָה. וְהֶאֱכִילָנוּ אֶת הַמָּן. וְנָתַן לָנוּ אֶת הַשַּׁבָּת. וְקֵרְבָנוּ לִפְנֵי הַר סִינַי. וְנָתַן לָנוּ אֶת הַתּוֹרָה. וְהִכְנִיסָנוּ לְאֶרֶץ יִשְׂרָאֵל. וּבָנָה לָנוּ אֶת בֵּית הַבְּחִירָה לְכַפֵּר עַל כָּל עֲוֹנוֹתֵינוּ:

רַבָּן גַּמְלִיאֵל הָיָה אוֹמֵר, כָּל שֶׁלֹּא אָמַר שְׁלוֹשָׁה דְּבָרִים אֵלּוּ בַּפֶּסַח לֹא יָצָא יְדֵי חוֹבָתוֹ, וְאֵלּוּ הֵן:

פֶּסַח. מַצָּה. וּמָרוֹר:

And built us the Temple — The last step in our spiritual ascent is the Temple. The Haggadah immediately afterwards begins to speak about the Pesach offering that was brought there. (*Shibolei haLeket*)

To bring us atonement for all of our sins — By saying "all," the Haggadah is reminiscent of a teaching of the Sages (*Pesikta Rabbah*, Chapter 16): In Jerusalem, never did anyone go to sleep with a sin on his hands, as the verse says (Yeshayahu 1:21): "Righteousness rests there." How did this come to be? The community offering that was brought in the morning atoned for sins that were committed during the previous night, and the community offering that was brought in the evening atoned for those committed the previous day. (*Shibolei haLeket*)

To bring us atonement for all of our sins — The Temple still provides this benefit to us, even though we no longer have it. We sinned, and instead of pouring out His anger upon us, He poured it out upon the wood and stone of the Temple. Thus, even to this day, the Temple atones for us. (based on *Yavetz*)

Has not fulfilled his obligation — As discussed above, one fulfills his obligation to tell his son about the Exodus from Egypt by beginning with the shameful part of Jewish history, and by ending with the glo-

drowned our enemies in it, AND gave us our needs in the desert for forty years, AND gave us manna to eat, AND gave us the Shabbos, AND brought us to Mount Sinai, AND gave us the Torah, AND brought us to the Land of Israel, AND built us the Temple, to bring us atonement for our all of our sins!

R̶ABBAN GAMLIEL USED TO SAY: On Pesach night, whoever does not speak about three things has not fulfilled his obligation, namely:

the Pesach offering, matzah, and maror.

rious part. This already has been done for the wise son, and the father also has already answered the question that was posed by the wise son. The wicked son also has been told about the history of our people — that *at first, our forefathers were idol-worshipers, but now, the Everpresent One has brought us close, to serve Him.*

These words are said to the wicked son with the hope that they will reach to his heart, so that he, too, will be drawn to the pleasant and correct way [for as noted above, one of the nuances of the Hebrew root of "and you shall tell" is "persuade" or "pull"]. On the other hand, the wicked son also asked a question, namely, *What is this service to you?* As yet, the father has not answered his question, and until he does, how can he have fulfilled the Torah's command, *And you shall tell your son*? This command applies regarding all of one's sons, but the verse where it is written is one about the son who is closely associated with the wicked son — the one who is so disinterested, he *does not know to ask*!

To both the wicked son and to the one who does not know to ask, the father replies (Shemos 13:8): *Because of this did God do wonders for me*.... and when he says these words, the meat of the Pesach sacrifice is on the table in front of him, along with the matzah and the *maror*. Rabban Gamliel teaches us that it is at this point that the father fulfills his obligation, and in order to do so, the father must show

Do not pick up the roasted bone from the Seder plate nor point at it while saying this:

פֶּסַח שֶׁהָיוּ אֲבוֹתֵינוּ אוֹכְלִים בִּזְמַן שֶׁבֵּית הַמִּקְדָּשׁ הָיָה קַיָּם עַל שׁוּם מָה. עַל שׁוּם שֶׁפָּסַח הַקָּדוֹשׁ בָּרוּךְ הוּא עַל בָּתֵּי אֲבוֹתֵינוּ בְּמִצְרַיִם. שֶׁנֶּאֱמַר, וַאֲמַרְתֶּם זֶבַח פֶּסַח הוּא לַיהוָה אֲשֶׁר פָּסַח עַל בָּתֵּי בְנֵי יִשְׂרָאֵל בְּמִצְרַיִם בְּנָגְפּוֹ אֶת מִצְרַיִם וְאֶת בָּתֵּינוּ הִצִּיל וַיִּקֹּד הָעָם וַיִּשְׁתַּחֲווּ:

these two sons the three different mitzvos of this night, around which the whole Seder revolves. The father fulfills his obligation towards these two sons by answering, "Precisely because of this service, and because of what these three mitzvos represent, God did wonders for me and took me out of slavery. It is a service for me and also for you!"

The Pesach offering...what did it recall? — This miracle was necessary only because in Egypt there were wicked Jews who did not actually deserve to be spared, as the accuser asked, "What difference is there between these and these?" It was for these Jews that the miracle occurred, but only on condition that they take upon themselves to do the mitzvos in the future. Thus, in effect, the father answers his wicked son: "You are correct! In fact, the service of this night is not really that pertinent to me. It is more pertinent to you!"

The Pesach offering — In the days of the Temple, they would say at the Seder table, "This Pesach offering that we are eating, what does it recall?" Today, we are able to say only: *The Pesach offering that our forefathers used to eat...* Even today, however, we say *This matzah* and *This maror* in order to tell the story of the Exodus the way that

Do not pick up the roasted bone from the Seder plate nor point at it while saying this:

*T*HE PESACH OFFERING *that our forefathers used to eat [on the Seder night] during the time that the Temple stood — what did it recall? That the Holy One, blessed is He, passed over the houses of our forefathers in Egypt, as it is written: "And you shall say, 'It is a Pesach offering to Hashem, Who passed over the houses of the Children of Israel in Egypt, when He struck the Egyptians but spared us.' And the people bowed down and prostrated themselves" (Shemos 12:27).*

the Torah commands us to perform this mitzvah — by saying (*Shemos* 13:8): *Because of this,* while the matzah and *maror* are on the table in front of us.

📖

That the Holy One...passed over — God told Moshe *Rabbenu* to tell the people to put blood from the Pesach offering on their "doorposts and lintel," so that God would "pass over" their "houses" (*Shemos 12:7*). When Moshe *Rabbenu* relayed this command, he told them that God would pass over the door. Now, the Hebrew word *petach* means not only "door," but also any "opening," even a small one. Our Sages taught, "God says: Open for me a hole the size of the head of a needle, and I will open for you an opening the size of a palace door." That is, before a person can really become close to God, he first must make an effort on his own to draw closer. Once he makes that effort, from "below," even if it is only a small effort, what he does is so precious in the eyes of God, that God is moved to do His part from "above," and God does a lot more to bring the person close to Him.

In Egypt, however, the Jews had already sunk to the forty-ninth level of impurity, and God could not wait for any efforts from "below." He saw that He had to forego that "opening," and start right

Pick up the middle matzah so that everyone can see it, and continue:

מַצָּה זוֹ שֶׁאָנוּ אוֹכְלִים עַל שׁוּם מָה. עַל שׁוּם שֶׁלֹּא הִסְפִּיק בְּצֵקָם שֶׁל אֲבוֹתֵינוּ לְהַחֲמִיץ עַד שֶׁנִּגְלָה עֲלֵיהֶם מֶלֶךְ מַלְכֵי הַמְּלָכִים הַקָּדוֹשׁ בָּרוּךְ הוּא וּגְאָלָם. שֶׁנֶּאֱמַר, וַיֹּאפוּ אֶת הַבָּצֵק אֲשֶׁר הוֹצִיאוּ מִמִּצְרַיִם עֻגֹת מַצּוֹת כִּי לֹא חָמֵץ כִּי גֹרְשׁוּ מִמִּצְרַיִם וְלֹא יָכְלוּ לְהִתְמַהְמֵהַּ וְגַם צֵדָה לֹא עָשׂוּ לָהֶם:

away from "above" to take them out of the impurity towards Him. Thus, we can understand in a deeper sense that Moshe *Rabbenu* told our forefathers that God would "pass over the opening." (*Chessed l'Avraham*)

📖

This matzah...what does it recall? That our forefathers' dough did not have time to rise — Again, the problem was the evil Jews of that generation, for if the Holy One had let them tarry in Egypt even one moment longer, they would have sunk so deeply into the impurity there, that they would never have been able to leave. Thus, my wicked son, this service — the mitzvah of eating matzah — is also especially for you, because the Holy One cares about Jews such as you, and wants to bring them close to Him! Only because of the Jews who acted like you do now did the entire Nation have to rush out of Egypt so quickly!

📖

This matzah...what does it recall? That our forefathers' dough did not have time to rise — Long before the night of the Exodus, they had been commanded about the prohibition on eating and even possessing *chametz* during the seven days of Pesach. However, these prohibitions were to apply only from the next year and onwards, only after they already had left Egypt, as Moshe *Rabbenu* later said (*Devarim* 16:3): *You shall not eat chametz...seven days you shall eat matzos...because you went out of Egypt in haste*. (*R. Yeshaya Ditrani*)

Pick up the middle matzah so that everyone can see it, and continue:

*T*HIS MATZAH *that we eat — what does it recall? That our forefathers' dough did not have time to rise before the King of kings, the Holy One, blessed is He, appeared to them and redeemed them, as it is written: "And they baked unleavened cakes from the dough they were taking from Egypt, cakes which had not risen, because the Egyptians drove out our forefathers, and they could not tarry, and they could not even prepare provisions for the way" (Shemos 12:29).*

This matzah that we eat — Regarding the meal offering brought in the Temple throughout the year, the Torah states (Vayikra 6:9): Matzos shall be eaten in a holy place. In the court of the tent of meeting they shall eat it. They expounded upon this verse, and found in it a hint about the mitzvah of eating matzah on the Seder night. Before Pesach, a person must prepare himself for this mitzvah, sanctifying and purifying himself, so that when the matzah enters him, it enters a "holy place." If he has prepared himself this way, then wherever he is, it will be just as if he is eating the matzah on the Temple grounds, *in the court of the tent of meeting*!

This matzah — This is what *Targum Yonatan* writes on the verse (Shemos 19:4): And I will raise you on eagles' wings and bring you to Me — that when the Jews in Egypt were about to slaughter the Pesach offering, God's clouds of glory lifted them aloft and brought them to the Temple grounds in Jerusalem, and there they brought the offering! Afterwards, the clouds returned them to Egypt, and the next morning they left Egypt as free men. So, too, today, if one performs the mitzvah of matzah with the proper intent and preparation, in purity and in holiness, it will be as if the earth folds beneath him, until he finds himself in Jerusalem on the holy ground of the Temple itself! (*Tiferes Shelomo*)

This matzah — Matzah teaches us about all the mitzvos. The Torah says (Shemos 12:17): And you shall guard the matzos. The Sages expound upon this, for the Hebrew letters of *matzos* are the same as those for *mitzvos*. Mitzvos are like matzos. Regarding the dough of the matzah, if you knead it constantly, and get it into the oven in the allotted time, it is called *matzah*, but if you let it sit too long, or get it into the oven just a moment too late, it is called *chametz*. So, too, regarding mitzvos. If you perform a mitzvah in its proper time, immediately, as soon as the time to do it comes, then it is called a *mitzvah*. If you delay, however, it is as if the mitzvah became *chametz*, and it loses its power. (*Vilna Gaon*)

And they baked unleavened cakes...which had not risen, because...they could not tarry — One might ask, "Even if there had been time, would it not have been forbidden for them to take *chametz* with them? After all, one is not allowed to even possess *chametz* all seven days of Pesach!" In Egypt, however, *chametz* was prohibited for only one day, and it was prohibited only to eat it. Therefore, they could have baked normal bread in Egypt, for the sake of meals they would eat on the following days, after the day they left Egypt. Because they were hurried, however, the dough that they prepared even for those days had no time to rise. (*Rabbenu Nissim, R. Yeshaya Ditrani*)

Because the Egyptians drove out our forefathers — The Torah says (Shemos 12:30-31): *And he (Pharaoh) called to Moshe and Aharon that night* — Pharaoh went to the homes of his servants, and ordered each one of them to come out with him, to the marketplaces, to ask whomever was there, "Where is Moshe? Where does he live?"

Among those Jews he encountered, there were those who made fun of him, asking, "Pharaoh, where are you going at this time of night?" He answered, "I am looking for Moshe!" They said, "Oh, Moshe lives there. No, there, there!" and Pharaoh had to go from house to house until he finally found him.

Pharaoh said to Moshe, "Get up, all of you, and leave my land!" Moshe answered, "What, are we thieves, that we should go out in the middle of the night?! The Holy One has commanded us, 'And you shall not walk out the door of your house, not one of you, until the morning comes.' No, Pharaoh, we are not leaving until it is day. We will leave victoriously, in full view of your entire nation." (*Midrash Tanchuma, Parashas Bo*)

When Moshe *Rabbenu* first came back to Egypt, having taken upon himself to be God's intermediary to free the Jews, things at first got worse. At that point, the Torah records that God told Moshe not to worry, saying (Shemos 6:1): Now you will see what I shall do to Pharaoh, for with a strong hand he shall send them [the Jews] away, and with a strong hand he will drive them out of his land. It appears that God was promising something that would provide comfort to Moshe, and ease his worries, but what comfort is there in Pharaoh's "driving the Jews out" with "a strong hand"? Later, after striking Egypt with nine plagues, God again "assured" Moshe (Shemos 11:1): One more plague I will bring upon Pharaoh and Egypt. Afterwards he will send you away from here, and when he does so, he will send you out forcibly, and drive you out completely. Is it good to be driven away forcibly?

Moshe, however, had a worry in his heart: Maybe Pharaoh is going to be clever. Maybe he will ease up on the slavery, and promise the Jews a life of comfort and prosperity in Egypt. Maybe he will make things sound so attractive, that many Jews will be persuaded to remain in Egypt, saying, "Everything we could ever need is here! Why should we subject ourselves to a difficult trip through a barren desert, followed by full-scale warfare in order to conquer a land that is possessed by so many powerful nations? The finest things of Egypt are right here at our disposal!" Moshe feared this, for it would be a desecration of the Name of God. Moreover, how can there be a redemption if the ones being redeemed actually want to stay where they are?!

For this reason, God promised Moshe that Pharaoh personally would drive them out, completely — all of them! Even if some Jews would want to stay, Pharaoh would refuse to permit it. Just as God would harden Pharaoh's heart to the plagues and make him refuse to send the Jews out, no matter how badly Egypt was suffering, so, too, when the time to leave finally came, God also would harden Pharaoh's heart regarding any Jews who wanted to stay! God assured Moshe that Pharaoh was totally in His Hands, and his free will would be taken away, so there was no need to worry. On the other hand, God did not want to take the power of free will away from the Jews, for God wanted them to accept the yoke of Torah and mitzvos willingly.

Now pick up the maror so that everyone can see it, and continue:

מָרוֹר זֶה שֶׁאָנוּ אוֹכְלִים עַל שׁוּם מָה. עַל שׁוּם שֶׁמֵּרְרוּ הַמִּצְרִים אֶת חַיֵּי אֲבוֹתֵינוּ בְּמִצְרָיִם. שֶׁנֶּאֱמַר, וַיְמָרְרוּ אֶת חַיֵּיהֶם בַּעֲבֹדָה קָשָׁה בְּחֹמֶר וּבִלְבֵנִים וּבְכָל עֲבֹדָה בַּשָּׂדֶה אֵת כָּל עֲבֹדָתָם אֲשֶׁר עָבְדוּ בָהֶם בְּפָרֶךְ:

God would strike Egypt with plague after plague, and each time, soon after a plague hit, Pharaoh would agree to allow the Jews to leave, and the plague would be lifted. After the terror of the plague had passed, however, Pharaoh would change his mind and say the Jews could not leave. After this had happened several times, Pharaoh's servants began trying to coax and prod him to free the Jews for good, but to no avail, because God had hardened his heart. Now, after the tenth plague, Pharaoh once more conceded to let the Jews go, but his servants were still worried — maybe he will change his mind again! Therefore, they hurried to drive the Jews away, every one of them, as quickly as possible, so that in the meantime, even if Pharaoh did change his mind, it would be too late. (*Chessed L'Avraham*)

They could not even prepare provisions for the way — Not for nothing did our Sages call those Jews "the generation of wisdom." How great they were, for only yesterday they were slaves — slaves of slaves — sunken so deeply into Egypt's abominations that they had reached the forty-ninth level of impurity. When they were redeemed, however, despite the haste of the Exodus, not only did they achieve belief in God, but they reached such a high level of trust in Him that they felt no need even to prepare provisions for the way, though they knew that it was a barren, hostile desert that lay ahead of them! This is what the Prophet said (Yirmeyahu 2:2): I remember to your favor, the devotion of your youth, how you loved Me as a bride, and

Now pick up the maror so that everyone can see it, and continue:

THIS MAROR that we eat — what does it recall? That the Egyptians embittered the lives of our forefathers in Egypt, as it is written: "And they embittered their lives with hard labor, mortar and bricks, and every kind of work in the fields; all the work that they forced them to do was strenuous" (Shemos 1:14).

followed Me into the desert, into a land that was not sown. Only someone who serves God out of love can achieve such strong and complete trust in Him. *(Sefas Emes)*

📖

This maror...what does it recall? That the Egyptians embittered their lives — The Egyptians never would have treated our People so cruelly, had it not been for the many wicked Jews among us who started to behave exactly as Egyptians, and even went so far as to not observe the mitzvah of circumcision. On the verse that says that the evil decrees against the Jews in Egypt were made when *a new king arose in Egypt*, our Sages teach that really, it was not a "new" king who did not "know" Yosef. Rather, it was the same Pharaoh of old who instituted these decrees, because it had come to a point where he no longer recognized Yosef in the Jews! Thus, all three of these mitzvos in front of you are pertinent to you, my son. Tonight's entire service is to rectify the sins of Jews who acted in Egypt as you act now. God cared for all of the Jews in Egypt, and He wanted to bring them all close to Him, by giving them the Torah and its commandments. This is what He wants for you, as well!

Therefore, it is our duty — All of us are obligated, even those who are far from Torah and mitzvos.

📖

Matzah and maror — Dough becomes *chametz* by means of fermenta-

tion, which changes the dough; matzah results when dough is baked before there is any fermentation or change. There is a parallel here to the Children of Israel, who were as matzah, because during all their years in Egypt, they did not change. As our Sages teach us (on *Devarim 26:5*): They retained their language, their Jewish names, and their Jewish clothing. The Children of Israel went down into Egypt, and the same Children of Israel left Egypt. In fact, it was a kindness from God that the "dough" of our forefathers did not have time to become *chametz* in Egypt, for God stepped in just at the right time to stop that from happening.

But why hadn't it happened before then? The explanation lies in the *maror*. Due to the fact that the Egyptians embittered our lives, we kept away from them as much as we could, and this helped us stay clean of all of their impurities. (*Zohar, Parashas Shemos*)

Thus, Hillel would eat the matzah and the *maror* together, to tell us that our salvation was only by means of both these elements together, as God had promised Yaakov (*Bereshis 46:4*): *I will go down with you...and I will bring you out* — it was the bitterness that led to the good. (*Sefas Emes*)

📖

The Pesach offering, matzah, and maror — The Pesach offering signifies the rising of the *Shechinah* out of exile, as our Sages teach us (*Pirkei d'Rabi Eliezer, Pesikta*) in expounding upon the continuation of the above verse containing God's promise to Yaakov, which on the surface seems redundant: *And I will bring you out, and also [you, I] will go out*. This teaches that when the descendants of Yaakov left Egypt, the *Shechinah* Itself left with them. The same idea is expressed in Rabbinic exposition on the verse (*Shemos 12:11*): *And you shall eat it in haste*, for the word *oto* literally means "it," but can also be read *eeto*, which means "with Him," as if God Himself were in a hurry to leave Egypt that night. (*Mechilta, Parashas Bo*)

Matzah signifies the redemption of the Jewish People, who earned salvation by not "changing" — by retaining their identity — and by refusing to let their dough "ferment" even though they lived under the rulership of an immoral and corrupt people, the Egyptians.

Maror signifies the downfall of the wicked Egyptians, who embittered our lives. In a verse about the Pesach offering (*Bemidbar 9:11*), we read: *With matzos and maror you shall eat it.* There is a slight quirk in the text, for in order to say "with," the Torah uses the word *al*, which usually means "on" or "above." This is to teach us that the Pesach offering is to be "on" and "above" matzah and *maror*. That is, when the night of the Seder arrives, our primary source of joy should not be matzah — our own redemption, and neither should it be *maror* — the downfall of the Egyptians. Rather we should be happiest about the fact that when the Exodus occurred, the *Shechinah* was finally able to leave the terrible impurity of Egypt. This is what the verse (*Shemos 12:27*) says, that the Pesach offering is *a Pesach for God* — it is offered for the sake of Heaven.

The Seder night's four mitzvos: The Pesach offering, matzah, *maror*, and *Haggadah*, telling the story of the Exodus, correspond to the four kingdoms that subjugated Israel after the redemption from Egypt: Babylonia, Persia, Greece, and Rome. The four mitzvos also serve as rectification for four major sins: idolatry, immorality, murder, and slander.

The Pesach offering rectifies idolatry, for Egypt worshiped the lamb, and the Jews slaughtered lambs as their offering to God. Matzah rectifies immorality, for *chametz* in dough symbolizes the evil inclination in a person (see *Tikkunim*), but matzah is free of *chametz*. *Maror* rectifies murder, for the *gematria* (numerical equivalent) of *maror* in Hebrew is 444, which is also the *gematria* of the word *mavess*, "death." *Haggadah* rectifies slander, which arises from baseless hatred, the primary sin that led to our present exile. Thus, *he who elaborates on the story of the Exodus is to be praised.* (*Sefas Emes*)

💭

And they embittered their lives with hard labor...and every kind of work in the fields — That is, after a whole day's work with mortar and bricks, the Jews would return to their homes to rest, only to find Egyptians waiting for them, who would say, "Go to the gardens to pick me some vegetables. Cut this piece of wood for me. Take this barrel to the river, fill it with water and bring it back." This is the meaning of: *and every kind of work in the fields.* (*Midrash Tanchuma, Parashas Vayetze*)

בְּכָל דּוֹר וָדוֹר חַיָּב אָדָם לִרְאוֹת אֶת עַצְמוֹ כְּאִלּוּ הוּא יָצָא מִמִּצְרַיִם. שֶׁנֶּאֱמַר, וְהִגַּדְתָּ לְבִנְךָ בַּיּוֹם הַהוּא לֵאמֹר בַּעֲבוּר זֶה עָשָׂה יְהֹוָה לִי בְּצֵאתִי מִמִּצְרָיִם. לֹא אֶת אֲבוֹתֵינוּ בִּלְבָד גָּאַל הַקָּדוֹשׁ בָּרוּךְ הוּא, אֶלָּא אַף אוֹתָנוּ גָּאַל עִמָּהֶם. שֶׁנֶּאֱמַר, וְאוֹתָנוּ הוֹצִיא מִשָּׁם לְמַעַן הָבִיא אֹתָנוּ לָתֶת לָנוּ אֶת הָאָרֶץ אֲשֶׁר נִשְׁבַּע לַאֲבֹתֵינוּ:

Cover the matzos. Everyone lifts his cup of wine and says aloud with joy:

לְפִיכָךְ אֲנַחְנוּ חַיָּבִים לְהוֹדוֹת לְהַלֵּל לְשַׁבֵּחַ לְפָאֵר לְרוֹמֵם לְהַדֵּר לְבָרֵךְ לְעַלֵּה וּלְקַלֵּס לְמִי שֶׁעָשָׂה לַאֲבוֹתֵינוּ וְלָנוּ אֶת כָּל הַנִּסִּים הָאֵלֶּה. הוֹצִיאָנוּ

מֵעַבְדוּת	לְחֵרוּת,
מִיָּגוֹן	לְשִׂמְחָה,
מֵאֵבֶל	לְיוֹם־טוֹב,
וּמֵאֲפֵלָה	לְאוֹר גָּדוֹל,
וּמִשִּׁעְבּוּד	לִגְאֻלָּה,

וְנֹאמַר לְפָנָיו שִׁירָה חֲדָשָׁה הַלְלוּיָהּ:

In every generation — The word for "Egypt" in Hebrew is *Mitzrayim*, from the root which connotes distress and oppression. Thus, every exile of the Jewish people can be called "*Mitzrayim*," and all the different world leaders who have tried to destroy us can be called "Pharaoh." When God freed us from Egypt, He implanted in us eternal freedom, so that from then on, we would never be enslaved to any "Pharaoh" again. Even today, in the midst of the darkness of the

IN EVERY GENERATION, each individual is obligated to see himself as if he actually went out of Egypt, as it is written: "And you shall tell your son on that day, 'Because of this did God do wonders for me when I went out of Egypt'" (Shemos 13:8). The Holy One, Blessed is He, redeemed not only our forefathers. He redeemed us with them, as it is written: "And He took us out from there, in order to bring us to the land that He swore to our forefathers, and give it to us" (Devarim 23:6).

Cover the matzos. Everyone lifts his cup of wine and says aloud with joy:

THEREFORE IT IS OUR DUTY to thank, praise, laud, glorify, exalt, honor, bless, extol, and celebrate the One Who did all these miracles for our forefathers and for us, Who took us

from slavery	into freedom,
from grief	to joy,
from mourning	to festivity,
from darkness	to bright light,
and from subjugation	to redemption.

Therefore, let us sing a new song before Him: Halleluyah!

longest exile in our history, we are completely free men, for in our hearts that is what we feel. Although we may appear to be slaves again, inside we are totally free. Our bodies might be subjugated, but our souls are a different matter entirely. (*Maharal*)

Therefore — We take the cup of wine in hand because we are about to say *Hallel*, songs of praise to God, and songs of praise to God are always sung over wine. *(Sefer haPardes of Rashi, Shulchan Aruch, Orach Chayim 473:7)*

To thank, praise, laud...and celebrate — These nine expressions plus *Halleluyah* at the end make ten, corresponding to the ten different ways that *Tehillim* (the Psalms) begin. The greatest praise of all, however, is *Halleluyah*, for this term connotes praise and also the two-letter Name of God — thus indicating Who is being praised! *(Maharal)*

Who took us — Five different kindnesses are mentioned here, beginning with *from slavery into freedom*. These correspond to five great merits that the Jews had in Egypt: They did not change their language, or their clothes; there were no informers among them; not one of them engaged in illicit relations; and they all were to receive the Torah. *(R. Shelomo Kluger)*

In fact, the *Halleluyah* said at the end contains a hint to both the five kindnesses and the ten expressions of praise: The word *Hallelu* means "Let us praise," the numerical value of the letter *yud* is ten, and the numerical value of the letter *heh* is five. Therefore, we can understand the Hebrew word *Halleluyah* as: "Let us praise ten [times] to God for His five [favors]!"

The five different kindnesses can be explained as follows:
FROM SLAVERY INTO FREEDOM — When we left Egypt.
FROM GRIEF TO JOY — At the sea, for until the waters split there was worry about what would be, for Pharaoh and his army were bearing down on them, with swords drawn.
FROM MOURNING TO FESTIVITY — Mourning over our sin of the golden calf (for the Torah states that we "mourned" then); festivity on Yom Kippur, when Moshe *Rabbenu* came down from Mount Sinai with the second set of Tablets, and we were forgiven for that sin. Our Sages call Yom Kippur a festival (*Yom Tov*): "The greatest *Yamim Tovim* for Israel were the Fifteenth of Av and Yom Kippur."
FROM DARKNESS TO BRIGHT LIGHT — The darkness of the forty years of wandering in the desert; the bright light upon entering the Land of Israel.

FROM SUBJUGATION TO REDEMPTION — Subjugation in the days of the Judges, when Israel's neighbors waged war against them; redemption in the days of David *haMelech* and Shelomo *haMelech*, when Israel dwelled securely on its land. (*Vilna Gaon*)

📖

These five can also be seen as kindnesses which cover an even longer span of history:

FROM SLAVERY — Egypt — TO FREEDOM.
FROM GRIEF — Babylonia — TO JOY, the rebuilding of the Temple.
FROM MOURNING — in Persia (over the decree of Haman).
TO FESTIVITY — Purim (see *Megillas Esther*, Chapter Nine).
FROM DARKNESS — Greece (as our Sages expound, for the Greeks "darkened Israel's eyes with their evil decrees") — TO BRIGHT LIGHT, Chanukah, the miracle of the oil, after the Maccabees defeated the Greeks.
FROM SUBJUGATION — The current exile, which seems to have no end to it, and we are downtrodden — TO REDEMPTION, the Ultimate Redemption, may it come speedily in our days. (based on *Maasei Nissim*)

📖

R. Yitzchak Abarbanel explains according to the Sephardic text of the Haggadah:

FROM SLAVERY — Egypt — TO FREEDOM.
FROM SUBJUGATION — Babylonia — TO REDEMPTION, in the days of Ezra.
FROM GRIEF — Persia — TO JOY, Purim.
FROM MOURNING — Greece — TO FESTIVITY, Chanukah.
FROM DARKNESS — our current exile, under Edom — TO BRIGHT LIGHT, to the Ultimate Redemption, which we anticipate every day!

Put down the cup and uncover the matzos, and continue:

הַלְלוּיָהּ הַלְלוּ עַבְדֵי יְהֹוָה הַלְלוּ אֶת שֵׁם יְהֹוָה: יְהִי שֵׁם יְהֹוָה מְבֹרָךְ מֵעַתָּה וְעַד עוֹלָם: מִמִּזְרַח שֶׁמֶשׁ עַד מְבוֹאוֹ מְהֻלָּל שֵׁם יְהֹוָה: רָם עַל כָּל גּוֹיִם יְהֹוָה עַל הַשָּׁמַיִם כְּבוֹדוֹ: מִי כַּיהֹוָה אֱלֹהֵינוּ הַמַּגְבִּיהִי לָשָׁבֶת: הַמַּשְׁפִּילִי לִרְאוֹת בַּשָּׁמַיִם וּבָאָרֶץ: מְקִימִי מֵעָפָר דָּל מֵאַשְׁפֹּת יָרִים אֶבְיוֹן: לְהוֹשִׁיבִי עִם נְדִיבִים עִם נְדִיבֵי עַמּוֹ: מוֹשִׁיבִי עֲקֶרֶת הַבַּיִת אֵם הַבָּנִים שְׂמֵחָה הַלְלוּיָהּ:

Servants of God — And no longer servants of Pharaoh! Whenever a human being is forced to be a servant to another human being, the slave's soul is brought to grief, and he will never stop trying to find ways to free himself of his obligations to his master. Serving the Holy One, however, brings joy, causing the servant of God to want to do more and more for his Master, so that he can come closer to Him. The Prophet praised Israel for accepting servitude to God joyfully, for the Nation actually ran into the desert in order to "follow after" God (*Yirmeyahu 2:2*)! This was clear proof of what God had Moshe write in the Torah (*Vayikra 25:25*): They are My servants!

Every good Jew is constantly looking for ways to make God even more of a Master and King over him, which is the opposite of what those who serve masters of flesh and blood try to do. This way, the Nation of Israel testifies that the Creator of the World is Unique, and only He deserves to be Master and King. Thus, on Pesach, the joy that we feel arises primarily from the fact that our Nation accepted God as Master and King, and thereby we, too, gained the privilege of serving Him and being close to Him. (*Sefas Emes*)

Put down the cup and uncover the matzos, and continue:

𝓗ALLELUYAH! *Give praise, servants of God. Praise God's Name. Blessed be the Name of God, from now and forever! From the rising of the sun until its setting, God's Name is praised. He is exalted over all nations. His glory is above the Heavens. Who is like the Lord our God, Who is elevated on His throne, yet drops down to look upon the heavens and the earth? He raises the poverty-stricken out of the dust, and lifts up the needy from the trash heaps, to seat them with the distinguished, with the notables of His nation. He transforms a barren housewife to a happy mother of children. Halleluyah!*

Give praise, servants of God — Who said these words? It was Pharaoh, for the verse tells us that on the night of the tenth plague, Pharaoh commanded the Jews, "Get up, leave!" In the middle of the night, he went knocking on the doors of Moshe and Aharon, who said to him, "Fool! You think we're going to leave Egypt at this hour?!" Pharaoh repeated, "Get up, leave!" They answered him, "What, are we thieves? We are not going to leave until the morning." Pharaoh cried, "But everyone in Egypt is dying!" They said, "Ah, and you want the plague not to strike you? If so, say the following: 'Behold, you are all free to do as you wish. Behold, you are now servants of the Holy One.'" Pharaoh immediately began to shout, "In the past, you were my slaves, but now you are free! Do what you wish! Go say praises to the Holy One, that you are now His servants! *Give praise, servants of God!*" (Yalkut Shimoni, Shemos, 208)

📖

He is exalted over all nations. His glory is above the Heavens — The nations of the world say that God is too exalted, too far away to see or care what transpires on earth. God is so high, they say, that He is detached from the world, and His glory is only above the Heavens. We say differently, that:

> WHO IS LIKE THE LORD OUR GOD, WHO IS ELEVATED ON HIS THRONE, YET DROPS DOWN — His "throne," so to speak, is not simply "on high." It is everywhere. That is, His Influence is ever-present — in the lowest world, our physical world and all the way up through the higher spiritual worlds. The whole Creation is filled with His glory!

📖

Yet drops down to look upon the heavens and the earth — For due to His Sublime Majesty, even the heavens are not really suitable to serve as a place for His throne. From His perspective, there really is no great difference between the heavens and the earth. Yet this is one of the kindnesses that God shows to His creations, that He lets His *Shechinah* descend to "look upon them" and be with them. (*Vilna Gaon*)

📖

Elevated...He drops down...He raises...to seat...He transforms — In the Hebrew, each of these five words ends with the letter *yud* and each time, the *yud* seems "extra." In fact, these five oddities correspond to the five "fingers" on God's "Hand" which hit the Egyptians when He split the sea. Five times *yud*, whose numerical equivalent is ten, equals fifty, and as Rabbi Yosei the Galilean said, there at the sea God struck the Egyptians with fifty plagues. (*Rashbam*)

📖

Elevated, etc. — With these five phrases, Moshe *Rabbenu*, who authored this psalm, may well have been referring to five different things that God did for the Nation of Israel:

> ELEVATED — When the Jews first descended into Egypt, God elevated them, by having them settled in Goshen, which Pharaoh called Egypt's "choicest land" (*Bereshis 47:6*). There they dwelled as princes, and were highly honored.
>
> DROPS DOWN — Afterwards, He dropped us down into slavery and oppression, so that out of the darkness, we would see the miracles that He would perform for our benefit, "in the heavens and on the earth." (*Yoel 3:3*)

RAISES...TO SEAT — Next, he raised us up out of the dust, and: lifted us from the trash heaps, not simply to save us, but rather to establish us as being even better off than when we were in Goshen, for then, we were nobly seated with Pharaoh among the princes of Egypt. Now, God had us seated with Moshe, Aharon, the seventy Elders-the princes of His Nation! But God had even more good things in store for us:

TRANSFORMS — He settled us in our land, our inheritance, for as long as we were living elsewhere, we were as a housewife uprooted from her home. The seven nations that had been dwelling there until now were as a maidservant who took what belonged to her mistress, but now that God "is returning me my home," I am as *a happy mother of children*! As the verse says *(Yeshayahu 49:21): And you shall say in your heart: Who has begotten me these!* And (Tehillim 147:12): Praise the Lord, O Jerusalem. Praise God, O Zion. For He has strengthened the bars of your gates, and has blessed you with children. *Halleluyah!*

He lifts up the needy from the trash heaps — An *evyon* is someone "needy," to the extent that his heart yearns for everything that looks good to him, even things that are not essential or important at all. When he has fallen into need, he feels good even when something worthless comes into his possession — something that he finds in the trash! Clearly, though, when God starts to make things better for him, and He begins to lift him out of his sad situation, God raises this person's desires and aspirations as well. In the end, instead of desiring things that are found in trash heaps, he is so grateful that he wants only to serve his Creator, and his heart loathes all his former desires. Once he is a man of wealth, he realizes that the many things that he so fancied in the past are actually worthless and totally unimportant. It becomes clear to him that it was foolish and absurd to desire these things in the first place!

So it was with the Jews once they had been freed from Egypt. As God revealed Himself to them, saving them from their plight and drawing them close to Him, they began to become so afire with gratitude and love for Him, that their only desire was to perform His commandments and serve Him, in every way possible. The things they

בְּצֵאת יִשְׂרָאֵל מִמִּצְרָיִם בֵּית יַעֲקֹב מֵעַם לֹעֵז: הָיְתָה יְהוּדָה לְקָדְשׁוֹ יִשְׂרָאֵל מַמְשְׁלוֹתָיו: הַיָּם רָאָה וַיָּנֹס, הַיַּרְדֵּן יִסֹּב לְאָחוֹר: הֶהָרִים רָקְדוּ כְאֵילִים, גְּבָעוֹת כִּבְנֵי צֹאן: מַה לְּךָ הַיָּם כִּי תָנוּס, הַיַּרְדֵּן תִּסֹּב לְאָחוֹר: הֶהָרִים תִּרְקְדוּ כְאֵילִים, גְּבָעוֹת כִּבְנֵי צֹאן: מִלִּפְנֵי אָדוֹן חוּלִי אָרֶץ, מִלִּפְנֵי אֱלוֹהַּ יַעֲקֹב: הַהֹפְכִי הַצּוּר אֲגַם מָיִם, חַלָּמִישׁ לְמַעְיְנוֹ מָיִם:

had wanted in the past while they were lowly slaves became totally insignificant to them. They now were truly free, for they had been liberated from the mundane desires that had gripped their hearts in the past. In Egypt, while they were slaves, the evil inclination had caused all sorts of yearnings to well up in them, but now it was clear to them that all those old yearnings were pure foolishness. (*Sefas Emes*)

📖

The first four phrases of this psalm are tributes to the laudable ways that the Jews conducted themselves throughout the Egyptian enslavement:

WHEN ISRAEL WENT OUT OF EGYPT — The same "Israel" that entered Egypt went out of Egypt later, that is, they had not changed their names.

THE FAMILY OF YAAKOV FROM A FOREIGN PEOPLE — Even regarding the least distinguished members of the family — when they left, it was a "foreign" people that they left. Egypt spoke a completely different language, for the family of Yaakov did not change their native tongue, either.

IT WAS FOR YEHUDAH TO SANCTIFY HIM — Even in their poverty, during the worst days of the enslavement, they retained their sanctity, and did not engage in illicit relations.

WHEN ISRAEL WENT OUT OF EGYPT — the family of Yaakov from a foreign people — it was for Yehudah to sanctify Him. Israel would be His dominion. The sea saw, and fled. The Jordan turned back. The mountains stepped as gingerly as rams, the hills as young sheep. What is the problem, O sea, that you flee, O Jordan that you turn back, O mountains that you dance as rams, O hills as young sheep? The earth trembles before its Master — before the God of Yaakov, Who turns rock into a pool of water, and flint into a spring of water!

ISRAEL WOULD BE HIS DOMINION — For although the Children of Israel were ruthlessly dominated by their Egyptian oppressors, never were there informers among them trying to win the Egyptians' favor and escape the oppression. Rather, they stood stalwartly together — a unified and independent nation. (*Chasam Sofer*)

The Vilna Gaon interprets the Hebrew word *lo'ez* in *am lo'ez* not as "foreign," but rather, as connoting "slander" or "malignment," so that Egypt here is being portrayed not as a "foreign" people in reference to the family of Yaakov, but rather as a "slandering" people. Thus we understand:

WHEN ISRAEL WENT OUT — The men and boys.

THE FAMILY OF YAAKOV — The women and girls.

FROM THE SLANDERING NATION — The family of Yaakov would have been slandered by the Egyptians, saying that the lineage lines to the Patriarchs had been broken. But God saved them from this. God made it clear that despite the slavery and the heavy-handedness of the Egyptians, the oppressors did not succeed with the Jewish women. Rather, the wives remained true to their husbands and their lineage remained pure. In the Torah, God publicizes this fact, for the verse says (*Vayikra 24:10*) that only one child was born of an Egyptian father while the Jews were slaves in Egypt. Yehudah — the family — remained "one" and this sanctified the Name of God. (*Vilna Gaon*)

It was for Yehudah to sanctify Him. Israel would be His dominion — Only because Yehudah had sanctified Him would Israel become His dominion. That is, the nations of the world had been casting aspersions on Israel's integrity, saying, "If Egypt subjugated your bodies, all the more so did they take your souls!" Now, however, Israel was seen under God's dominion, organized into a grand and holy army comprised of several divisions — *Kohanim, Leviyim,* princes and vice-princes, all in the service of the Holy One. As a result, it became obvious that actually, our souls had remained pure in Egypt! Yehudah had sanctified Him, by being careful about prohibited relations. Nothing untoward could be found at all in the nation's family life. If, God forbid, there had been anything irregular in this area, the Holy One, blessed is He, would not have taken us to be His people. (*Chida*)

It was for Yehudah to sanctify Him. Israel would be his dominion — In the Talmud it says that Yehudah sanctified God; Nachshon, from the tribe of Yehudah, was the first to enter the sea, even before it split, and he urged all the other Jews to follow him. Thus, in the future, *Israel would be his dominion* — Yehudah's. All the kings of Israel would be from the tribe of Yehudah, in the merit of Nachshon, who made it clear that his was the tribe which possessed the nation's leaders. (*Rashi*)

The sea saw, and fled — What did it see? It saw the coffin of Yosef approaching. Said the Holy One to the sea, "Flee from the one who fled!" for the Torah tells us (*Bereshis 39:13*) that when Potiphar's wife tried to entice Yosef, he fled from her. (*Yalkut Shimoni, Tehillim 873*)

The sea saw — It is difficult and takes great strength to change the natural order that God created for the world. From the day that God made it, the sea had not changed its way even once. Therefore, as the Children of Israel stood at the edge of the sea, the sea at first was unwilling to make its waters part for them. However, when the sea saw the coffin of Yosef approaching, it recognized a power that was even stronger than the natural order. That is, Potiphar's wife had made every effort to entice Yosef to immorality, and Yosef's evil inclination was hard at work trying to make him agree to her desire. It took extraordinary strength to resist all this, and the sea recognized that Yosef's strength was greater than the strength of the natural order — and thus it split for him! (based on *Tiferes Shelomo*)

📖

The sea saw, and fled — When the sea saw that the entire Nation followed Nachshon into the water, and waded in up to their noses, it parted for them. (*Yalkut Shimoni, Tehillim 873*)

📖

The Jordan turned back — What does the Jordan turning back have to do with the Exodus from Egypt? That miracle took place years later! This can be understood as an example of a famous saying: "If the most skilled workers flee, the ones who are less skilled will flee, too." Since the Jordan, a mere river, had seen the mighty sea split, it was willing to do the same. (*Ibid*)

📖

Who turns rock into a pool of water — These are actually the words of the sea, which said to the Children of Israel, "I am not fleeing because of you. I am fleeing for the One Who can easily make me as dry as a rock! In the future, in fact, when you will be in the desert, He will do the opposite for you: *He turns flint into a spring of water!* (*Malbim*)

בָּרוּךְ אַתָּה יְהֹוָה אֱלֹהֵינוּ מֶלֶךְ הָעוֹלָם, אֲשֶׁר גְּאָלָנוּ וְגָאַל אֶת אֲבוֹתֵינוּ מִמִּצְרַיִם, וְהִגִּיעָנוּ הַלַּיְלָה הַזֶּה לֶאֱכָל־בּוֹ מַצָּה וּמָרוֹר. כֵּן יְהֹוָה אֱלֹהֵינוּ וֵאלֹהֵי אֲבוֹתֵינוּ יַגִּיעֵנוּ לְמוֹעֲדִים וְלִרְגָלִים אֲחֵרִים הַבָּאִים לִקְרָאתֵנוּ לְשָׁלוֹם, שְׂמֵחִים בְּבִנְיַן עִירֶךָ, וְשָׂשִׂים בַּעֲבוֹדָתֶךָ, וְנֹאכַל שָׁם מִן הַזְּבָחִים וּמִן הַפְּסָחִים (במוצ"ש אומרים: מִן הַפְּסָחִים וּמִן הַזְּבָחִים) אֲשֶׁר יַגִּיעַ דָּמָם עַל קִיר מִזְבַּחֲךָ לְרָצוֹן וְנוֹדֶה לְךָ שִׁיר חָדָשׁ עַל גְּאֻלָּתֵנוּ וְעַל פְּדוּת נַפְשֵׁנוּ: בָּרוּךְ אַתָּה יְהֹוָה גָּאַל יִשְׂרָאֵל:

Before making the berachah over the second cup, some say:

הִנְנִי מוּכָן וּמְזֻמָּן לְקַיֵּם מִצְוַת כּוֹס שֵׁנִי שֶׁל אַרְבַּע כּוֹסוֹת.

Everyone drinks the second cup. The whole cup, or at least most of it, should be drunk without pause while reclining on the left side. Before reclining make the berachah:

בָּרוּךְ אַתָּה יְהֹוָה אֱלֹהֵינוּ מֶלֶךְ הָעוֹלָם בּוֹרֵא פְּרִי הַגָּפֶן:

Have in mind that this is the mitzvah of drinking the second of the Four Cups.

Who redeemed us... and brought us... So, too... bring us — We say the first half of *Hallel* before the meal, to give thanks for the redemption from Egypt. This is called *Hallel Mitzri* — the "Egyptian *Hallel*," about the redemption of the past. These words are in the past tense (*Who redeemed us*), about the redemption from Egypt, but also in the future tense (*bring us*), about the Redemption to Come. The second

BLESSED ARE YOU, Hashem our God, King of the Universe, Who redeemed us and our forefathers from Egypt, and brought us to this night, to eat matzah and maror. So, too, Hashem our God, and God of our forefathers, bring us to other future holidays and festivals, in peace, and may we happily witness the rebuilding of Your City, and rejoice in serving You. And there we shall eat of the offerings, and of the Pesach lamb [Motzaei Shabbos: of the Pesach lamb and of the offerings], their blood reaching the wall of Your altar and being pleasing to You. And we shall thank You with a new song, for our redemption, and for the deliverance of our souls. Blessed are You, Hashem, Who redeemed Israel.

Before making the berachah over the second cup, some say:

Here I am, ready and willing to fulfill the mitzvah of drinking the second cup of the Four Cups.

Everyone drinks the second cup. The whole cup, or at least most of it, should be drunk without pause while reclining on the left side. Before reclining make the berachah:

*B*LESSED ARE YOU, Hashem our God, King of the Universe, Creator of the fruit of the vine.

Have in mind that this is the mitzvah of drinking the second of the Four Cups.

half of *Hallel*, said after the meal, begins with the words *Not to us*, which refer to the Redemption to Come. (*Abarbanel*)

So, too...bring us to other future holidays and festivals — The future "holidays" are Rosh Hashanah and Yom Kippur, while the other "festivals" are Shavuos and Sukkos. Just as He has brought us to the Se-

רָחְצָה

Wash the hands for the meal, which begins with the mitzvah of eating matzah. After washing the hands, before drying them, say the following blessing.

בָּרוּךְ אַתָּה יְהֹוָה אֱלֹהֵינוּ מֶלֶךְ הָעוֹלָם אֲשֶׁר קִדְּשָׁנוּ בְּמִצְוֹתָיו וְצִוָּנוּ עַל נְטִילַת יָדָיִם:

der night, to rejoice in Him and to fulfill His commandments in peace, safe from our enemies, we pray that He also will bring us to future holidays and festivals in the same way, until finally we will celebrate this festival during the year of the Ultimate Redemption. Then, we are destined to rejoice in the rebuilding of Jerusalem and the Holy Temple, and in the reinstitution of the offerings and all the other services in the Temple. (*Shibolei haLeket*)

Other future holidays and festivals — New ones that we do not have now, that will come to be celebrated because of the Final Redemption. (based on *Maharal*)

Of the offerings, and of the Pesach lamb — This refers to the *Chagigah* or "holiday offering" that was brought the afternoon before the Seder, with the Pesach offering, and was eaten at night beforehand, so that the *Pesach*, as required, would be eaten when no one was hungry anymore. (*Tosafos, Pesachim 116a; Mordechai there; Avudraham* and others)

And we shall thank You with a new song — The "new song" will be about the Ultimate Redemption, and this explains the fact that the word appears in its masculine form — *shir chadash*. Usually, when the Scriptures refer to a "song" about a redemption of the past, such as the one from Egypt (See *Shemos 15:1, Bemidbar 21:17* and others) the word "song" appears in its feminine form — *shirah*. Thus the past redemptions can be compared to women, who give birth, become

Rachtzah — Washing for the Meal

Wash the hands for the meal, which begins with the mitzvah of eating matzah. After washing the hands, before drying them, say the following blessing.

***B**LESSED ARE YOU, Hashem our God, King of the Universe, Who has sanctified us with His mitzvos, and has commanded us regarding the washing of hands.*

pregnant, give birth, etc. Such were the past redemptions — each one was followed by another exile, then a redemption, then another exile, etc., over and over again. The "song" of the Ultimate Redemption, however, is different, because after that Redemption, there will not be any more exiles, just as males do not bear children. (based on *Shemos Rabbah*, Chapter 23)

Our Sages had yet another explanation for the change in gender. When our forefathers left Egypt and came to the Land of Israel, they inherited it from seven nations. Then, as now, there were seventy nations in the entire world, so that it was as if our people's inheritance was one-tenth of the total. Thus we can understand why the "song" about the redemption from Egypt is stated in the feminine: According to the Sages, when a father dies, the share in the inheritance that a daughter receives is usually one-tenth. Regarding a son, however, he can inherit the entire estate. Therefore, regarding the Final Redemption, the "song" is stated in the masculine (*Tehillim 96:1*) — for when that redemption comes, Israel will inherit all the nations. (based on *Shir haShirim Rabbah 1:23*)

📖

And we shall thank you with a new song, for our redemption — The Redemption to Come.
And for the deliverance of our souls — The redemption from Egypt. This is a fitting way to end the blessing, for a blessing's "signature" should resemble its body, and both redemptions were acknowledged in the blessing's body. What is more, we also will mention both redemptions in the days of the *Mashiach*. (*Kol Bo Avudraham*)

מוֹצִיא

No one speaks. The leader then takes the three matzos in his two hands, and says:

הִנְנִי מוּכָן וּמְזוּמָן לְקַיֵּם מִצְוַת אֲכִילַת מַצָּה.

Next, he says the blessing that normally is said over bread, having in mind to include everyone in his blessing, and the other participants answer, Amen.

בָּרוּךְ אַתָּה יְהֹוָה אֱלֹהֵינוּ מֶלֶךְ הָעוֹלָם הַמּוֹצִיא לֶחֶם מִן הָאָרֶץ:

מַצָּה

The leader lets go of the lowest matzah (Yisrael), and while holding only the top matzah (Kohen), which is whole, and the middle matzah (Levi), which is now only a piece, he says the following blessing, again having everyone else in mind, and everyone answers, Amen.

בָּרוּךְ אַתָּה יְהֹוָה אֱלֹהֵינוּ מֶלֶךְ הָעוֹלָם אֲשֶׁר קִדְּשָׁנוּ בְּמִצְוֹתָיו וְצִוָּנוּ עַל אֲכִילַת מַצָּה:

He takes for himself one k'zayis from the Kohen matzah and another k'zayis from the Levi matzah, and gives the other participants the same (or they eat the required amount from their own matzos). The matzah must be eaten while leaning on one's left side, and without interruption. (One must take care not to speak, from the washing of the hands until after eating of the Korech.)

Motzi

No one speaks. The leader then takes the three matzos in his two hands, and says:

Here I am, ready and willing to fulfill the mitzvah of eating matzah.

Next, he says the blessing that normally is said over bread, having in mind to include everyone in his blessing, and the other participants answer, Amen.

BLESSED ARE YOU, Hashem our God, King of the Universe, Who brings forth bread from the earth.

Matzah

The leader lets go of the lowest matzah (Yisrael), and while holding only the top matzah (Kohen), which is whole, and the middle matzah (Levi), which is now only a piece, he says the following blessing, again having everyone else in mind, and everyone answers, Amen.

BLESSED ARE YOU, Hashem our God, King of the Universe, Who has sanctified us with His mitzvos, and has commanded us regarding the eating of matzah.

He takes for himself one k'zayis from the Kohen matzah and another k'zayis from the Levi matzah, and gives the other participants the same (or they eat the required amount from their own matzos). The matzah must be eaten while leaning on one's left side, and without interruption. (One must take care not to speak, from the washing of the hands until after eating of the Korech.)

מָרוֹר

Now the leader takes a k'zayis of maror, first for himself, and then he distributes a similar amount to all the others at the table. Each portion is dipped into charoses, which is then shaken off. Before eating, some say:

הִנְנִי מוּכָן וּמְזוּמָן לְקַיֵּם מִצְוַת אֲכִילַת מָרוֹר.

The leader says the following blessing, and eats the k'zayis of maror, without interruption, and without having to lean.

בָּרוּךְ אַתָּה יְהֹוָה אֱלֹהֵינוּ מֶלֶךְ הָעוֹלָם אֲשֶׁר קִדְּשָׁנוּ בְּמִצְוֹתָיו וְצִוָּנוּ עַל אֲכִילַת מָרוֹר:

Have in mind that this berachah also covers the maror eaten at Korech.

כּוֹרֵךְ

Break the third matzah (Yisrael), and from two pieces of it, totaling a k'zayis, make a sandwich, placing maror in between. Whether the sandwich is dipped in charoses is dependent upon custom. The others at the table also make such a sandwich (using their own matzah if necessary), which is eaten while reclining, without interruption. Before starting to eat the sandwich, one does not say any blessing. Rather, he says:

זֵכֶר לְמִקְדָּשׁ כְּהִלֵּל. כֵּן עָשָׂה הִלֵּל. בִּזְמַן שֶׁבֵּית הַמִּקְדָּשׁ הָיָה קַיָּם, הָיָה כּוֹרֵךְ פֶּסַח מַצָּה וּמָרוֹר וְאוֹכֵל בְּיַחַד, לְקַיֵּם מַה שֶּׁנֶּאֱמַר עַל מַצּוֹת וּמְרוֹרִים יֹאכְלֻהוּ:

Maror

Now the leader takes a k'zayis of maror, first for himself, and then he distributes a similar amount to all the others at the table. Each portion is dipped into charoses, which is then shaken off. Before eating, some say:

Here I am, ready and willing to fulfill the mitzvah of eating maror.

The leader says the following blessing, and eats the k'zayis of maror, without interruption, and without having to lean.

*B*LESSED ARE YOU, Hashem our God, King of the Universe, Who has sanctified us with His mitzvos, and has commanded us regarding the eating of maror.

Have in mind that this berachah also covers the maror eaten at Korech.

Korech — Matzah & Maror Together

Break the third matzah (Yisrael), and from two pieces of it, totaling a k'zayis, make a sandwich, placing maror in between. Whether the sandwich is dipped in charoses is dependent upon custom. The others at the table also make such a sandwich (using their own matzah if necessary), which is eaten while reclining, without interruption. Before starting to eat the sandwich, one does not say any blessing. Rather, he says:

*T*HIS IS IN REMEMBRANCE of the Temple days, according to the opinion of Hillel, for when the Temple stood, Hillel would put the Pesach offering, matzah, and maror together and eat them at once, to fulfill what is written: "They shall eat it [the Pesach offering] with matzos and maror" (Bemidbar 9:11).

שֻׁלְחָן עוֹרֵךְ

Shulchan Orech — The Seder Meal

Eat the meal. Some have the custom to begin the meal with hard-boiled eggs. The food of the main meal should be festive, and should be eaten with joy, but one must take care not to become full, so he can properly perform the mitzvah of Afikoman. One should speak words of Torah at the table, preferably about the story of Pesach.

צָפוּן

Tzafun — Eating the Afikoman

At the meal's end, one takes out the larger half of the Levi matzah, the half which had been hidden away since the start of the Seder. The leader takes for himself two k'zaysim from this matzah, and gives to the others at the table a like portion from it (and/or from other matzos). This matzah, called the Afikoman, must be eaten while reclining, and without interruption, before half the night has passed.

Some say:

In remembrance of the Pesach offering, which had to be eaten after one was no longer hungry.

Some say the following:

הִנְנִי מוּכָן וּמְזוּמָן לְקַיֵּם מִצְוַת אֲכִילַת אֲפִיקוֹמָן.

Here I am, ready and willing to fulfill the mitzvah of eating the Afikoman.

Barech — Grace after Meals

Everyone pours the third cup.
After the meal, as on Shabbos and other festivals, one sings
Shir haMaalos — "The Song of Ascents" — before the
Grace after Meals.

שִׁיר הַמַּעֲלוֹת, בְּשׁוּב יְהֹוָה אֶת שִׁיבַת צִיּוֹן הָיִינוּ כְּחֹלְמִים. אָז
יִמָּלֵא שְׂחוֹק פִּינוּ וּלְשׁוֹנֵנוּ רִנָּה, אָז יֹאמְרוּ בַגּוֹיִם הִגְדִּיל יְהֹוָה
לַעֲשׂוֹת עִם אֵלֶּה. הִגְדִּיל יְהֹוָה לַעֲשׂוֹת עִמָּנוּ, הָיִינוּ שְׂמֵחִים. שׁוּבָה
יְהֹוָה אֶת שְׁבִיתֵנוּ כַּאֲפִיקִים בַּנֶּגֶב. הַזֹּרְעִים בְּדִמְעָה בְּרִנָּה יִקְצֹרוּ.
הָלוֹךְ יֵלֵךְ וּבָכֹה נֹשֵׂא מֶשֶׁךְ הַזָּרַע. בֹּא יָבֹא בְרִנָּה. נֹשֵׂא אֲלֻמֹּתָיו:

A Song of Ascents. When Hashem brought back those returning to Zion, we were as if we had been dreaming. Then our mouths will be filled with laughter, and our tongues will be filled with song. Then the nations will say, "Hashem has done great things for them." Hashem, indeed, has done great things for us, and we have been happy. Bring us back, Hashem, from our captivity again, like flooded streams in the Negev. They who sow in tears shall reap in song. He who weeps as he goes, shall carry in what his seed shall yield. He will return with joy, carrying his sheaves.

Then our mouths will be filled with laughter — This is the usual understanding of this verse. On the other hand, we can also understand it as: "Then our mouths' laughter will be full."

That is, only at the time of the Ultimate Redemption will we be completely happy, and only then will our laughter be true. At present, it is as if we are dreaming. When a person dreams, he may see himself eating the finest of foods, but never is he actually satiated from them. He sees himself drinking the most exotic mixtures, but still he remains thirsty. Why? Because the food is not really food, and

Pour the third cup of wine. Some say:

הִנְנִי מוּכָן וּמְזוּמָן לְקַיֵּם מִצְוַת עֲשֵׂה שֶׁל בִּרְכַּת הַמָּזוֹן.

While saying the Grace after Meals, one should hold the cup of wine in one's right hand. If three males, at least of bar mitzvah age, have eaten together, they begin here (if there were ten, they say what is in parentheses):

The leader says: רַבּוֹתַי נְבָרֵךְ.

Everyone says: יְהִי שֵׁם יְהֹוָה מְבֹרָךְ מֵעַתָּה וְעַד עוֹלָם.

The leader repeats what they said, and then adds: בִּרְשׁוּת מָרָנָן וְרַבָּנָן וְרַבּוֹתַי נְבָרֵךְ (בעשרה: אֱלֹהֵינוּ) שֶׁאָכַלְנוּ מִשֶּׁלּוֹ.

Everyone says: בָּרוּךְ (בעשרה: אֱלֹהֵינוּ) שֶׁאָכַלְנוּ מִשֶּׁלּוֹ וּבְטוּבוֹ חָיִינוּ:

The leader repeats the last thing they said, and then adds: בָּרוּךְ הוּא וּבָרוּךְ שְׁמוֹ.

בָּרוּךְ אַתָּה יְהֹוָה אֱלֹהֵינוּ מֶלֶךְ הָעוֹלָם. הַזָּן אֶת הָעוֹלָם כֻּלּוֹ בְּטוּבוֹ, בְּחֵן בְּחֶסֶד וּבְרַחֲמִים. הוּא נוֹתֵן לֶחֶם לְכָל בָּשָׂר כִּי לְעוֹלָם חַסְדּוֹ. וּבְטוּבוֹ הַגָּדוֹל תָּמִיד לֹא חָסַר לָנוּ, וְאַל יֶחְסַר לָנוּ מָזוֹן לְעוֹלָם וָעֶד. בַּעֲבוּר שְׁמוֹ הַגָּדוֹל. כִּי הוּא אֵל זָן וּמְפַרְנֵס לַכֹּל וּמֵטִיב לַכֹּל

the drink is not really drink. Both are empty, lacking substance, for they all are part of his dream!

In the future, however, when we finally will be "awake," every happiness that we merit will be full and complete, of real substance. We will be happy, not because we will enjoy a multitude of pleasures,

Pour the third cup of wine. Some say:

Here I am, ready and willing to fulfill the positive mitzvah of saying the Grace after Meals.

While saying the Grace after Meals, one should hold the cup of wine in one's right hand. If three males, at least of bar mitzvah age, have eaten together, they begin here (if there were ten, they say what is in parentheses):

The leader says:	My friends, let us bless together!
Everyone says:	May Hashem's Name be blessed for now and forever!
The leader repeats what they said, and then adds:	With your permission, let us bless (our God) of Whose bounty we have eaten.
Everyone says:	Blessed be (our God) of Whose bounty we have eaten, and by Whose goodness we live.
The leader repeats the last thing they said, and then adds:	Blessed is He and blessed is His Name.

*B*LESSED ARE YOU, *Hashem our God, King of the Universe, Who in His goodness nourishes the whole world with boundless love, with kindness and mercy. He gives food to all flesh, for His kindness is eternal. Because of His great goodness, we have never lacked, and may we never lack nourishment ever, for the sake of His great Name. For He is the Power that nourishes and supports everything. He bestows good upon all, and prepares*

but because the pleasures that we will merit will be enjoyed in full. They will not be pleasures that we are dreaming! Each pleasure will truly be satisfying, as actual food!

We anticipate the days of the *Mashiach* not because they will bring us riches and a great many other pleasures. Rather, we look for-

וּמֵכִין מָזוֹן לְכָל בְּרִיּוֹתָיו אֲשֶׁר בָּרָא (כָּאָמוּר פּוֹתֵחַ אֶת יָדֶךָ וּמַשְׂבִּיעַ לְכָל חַי רָצוֹן). בָּרוּךְ אַתָּה יְהֹוָה הַזָּן אֶת הַכֹּל:

נוֹדֶה לְךָ יְהֹוָה אֱלֹהֵינוּ עַל שֶׁהִנְחַלְתָּ לַאֲבוֹתֵינוּ, אֶרֶץ חֶמְדָּה טוֹבָה וּרְחָבָה, וְעַל שֶׁהוֹצֵאתָנוּ יְהֹוָה אֱלֹהֵינוּ מֵאֶרֶץ מִצְרַיִם, וּפְדִיתָנוּ מִבֵּית עֲבָדִים, וְעַל בְּרִיתְךָ שֶׁחָתַמְתָּ בִּבְשָׂרֵנוּ, וְעַל תּוֹרָתְךָ שֶׁלִּמַּדְתָּנוּ, וְעַל חֻקֶּיךָ שֶׁהוֹדַעְתָּנוּ, וְעַל חַיִּים חֵן וָחֶסֶד שֶׁחוֹנַנְתָּנוּ, וְעַל אֲכִילַת מָזוֹן שָׁאַתָּה זָן וּמְפַרְנֵס אוֹתָנוּ תָּמִיד, בְּכָל יוֹם וּבְכָל עֵת וּבְכָל שָׁעָה:

וְעַל הַכֹּל יְהֹוָה אֱלֹהֵינוּ אֲנַחְנוּ מוֹדִים לָךְ, וּמְבָרְכִים אוֹתָךְ, יִתְבָּרַךְ שִׁמְךָ בְּפִי כָּל חַי תָּמִיד לְעוֹלָם וָעֶד. כַּכָּתוּב, וְאָכַלְתָּ וְשָׂבָעְתָּ, וּבֵרַכְתָּ אֶת יְהֹוָה אֱלֹהֶיךָ עַל הָאָרֶץ הַטֹּבָה אֲשֶׁר נָתַן לָךְ. בָּרוּךְ אַתָּה יְהֹוָה עַל הָאָרֶץ וְעַל הַמָּזוֹן:

רַחֶם נָא יְהֹוָה אֱלֹהֵינוּ, עַל יִשְׂרָאֵל עַמֶּךָ, וְעַל יְרוּשָׁלַיִם עִירֶךָ, וְעַל צִיּוֹן מִשְׁכַּן כְּבוֹדֶךָ, וְעַל מַלְכוּת בֵּית דָּוִד מְשִׁיחֶךָ, וְעַל הַבַּיִת הַגָּדוֹל וְהַקָּדוֹשׁ שֶׁנִּקְרָא שִׁמְךָ עָלָיו. אֱלֹהֵינוּ, אָבִינוּ, רְעֵנוּ, זוּנֵנוּ, פַּרְנְסֵנוּ, וְכַלְכְּלֵנוּ, וְהַרְוִיחֵנוּ, וְהַרְוַח לָנוּ יְהֹוָה אֱלֹהֵינוּ מְהֵרָה מִכָּל צָרוֹתֵינוּ. וְנָא, אַל תַּצְרִיכֵנוּ יְהֹוָה אֱלֹהֵינוּ לֹא לִידֵי מַתְּנַת בָּשָׂר וָדָם, וְלֹא לִידֵי הַלְוָאָתָם, כִּי אִם לְיָדְךָ הַמְּלֵאָה, הַפְּתוּחָה, הַקְּדוֹשָׁה וְהָרְחָבָה, שֶׁלֹּא נֵבוֹשׁ וְלֹא נִכָּלֵם לְעוֹלָם וָעֶד:

ward to a different brand of happiness — peace of mind, which will stem from the fact that even small things will give us great pleasure! Every Jew will have a sense of being complete, and he will not even *food for every creation which He formed. Blessed are you, Hashem, Who nourishes all.*

WE THANK YOU, Hashem our God, for having given our forefathers a desirable land, good and spacious; for having brought us, Hashem our God, out of the land of Egypt, and for having redeemed us from the house of bondage; for the covenant that You have signed in our flesh; for Your Torah that You have taught us, and for having informed us of Your laws; for having given us life, Your grace and Your kindness; and for the sustenance that You provide us steadily, every day, at all times.

AND FOR EVERYTHING, Hashem our God, we thank You and bless You. May Your Name blessed at all times and forever, by the mouth of every creature that lives, as is written in Your Torah: "You shall eat and be satisfied, and bless Hashem your God, for the good land that He gave you." Blessed are You, Hashem, for the Land and the sustenance.

HAVE MERCY, Hashem our God, on Israel, Your nation, on Jerusalem, Your city, and on Zion, where Your Glory dwells; on the kingship of the House of David, Your anointed one; and on the great and holy House that is associated with Your Name. Our God and Father, guide us, nourish, support and sustain us, and bring us relief. Relieve us of all of our grief, Hashem, our God, and please do not cause us to need charity or loans from flesh and blood. Let us be supplied our needs only from Your Hand, which is open, holy, and generously extended to us; so that we never are ashamed or humiliated.

think of what he does not possess. He will not experience any desires for these things, and what he does possess he will enjoy in full. Will our mouths be full? No, our laughter will be full! (*Michzeh Avraham*)

(On Shabbos add this:)

רְצֵה וְהַחֲלִיצֵנוּ יְהֹוָה אֱלֹהֵינוּ בְּמִצְוֹתֶיךָ וּבְמִצְוַת יוֹם הַשְּׁבִיעִי, הַשַּׁבָּת הַגָּדוֹל וְהַקָּדוֹשׁ הַזֶּה, כִּי יוֹם זֶה גָּדוֹל וְקָדוֹשׁ הוּא לְפָנֶיךָ, לִשְׁבָּת בּוֹ וְלָנוּחַ בּוֹ בְּאַהֲבָה כְּמִצְוַת רְצוֹנֶךָ, וּבִרְצוֹנְךָ הָנִיחַ לָנוּ יְהֹוָה אֱלֹהֵינוּ, שֶׁלֹּא תְהֵא צָרָה וְיָגוֹן וַאֲנָחָה בְּיוֹם מְנוּחָתֵנוּ, וְהַרְאֵנוּ יְהֹוָה אֱלֹהֵינוּ בְּנֶחָמַת צִיּוֹן עִירֶךָ, וּבְבִנְיַן יְרוּשָׁלַיִם עִיר קָדְשֶׁךָ, כִּי אַתָּה הוּא בַּעַל הַיְשׁוּעוֹת וּבַעַל הַנֶּחָמוֹת:

אֱלֹהֵינוּ וֵאלֹהֵי אֲבוֹתֵינוּ, יַעֲלֶה וְיָבֹא וְיַגִּיעַ, וְיֵרָאֶה וְיֵרָצֶה וְיִשָּׁמַע, וְיִפָּקֵד וְיִזָּכֵר זִכְרוֹנֵנוּ וּפִקְדוֹנֵנוּ, וְזִכְרוֹן אֲבוֹתֵינוּ, וְזִכְרוֹן מָשִׁיחַ בֶּן דָּוִד עַבְדֶּךָ, וְזִכְרוֹן יְרוּשָׁלַיִם עִיר קָדְשֶׁךָ, וְזִכְרוֹן כָּל עַמְּךָ בֵּית יִשְׂרָאֵל לְפָנֶיךָ, לִפְלֵיטָה, לְטוֹבָה, לְחֵן וּלְחֶסֶד וּלְרַחֲמִים, לְחַיִּים טוֹבִים וּלְשָׁלוֹם, בְּיוֹם חַג הַמַּצּוֹת הַזֶּה: זָכְרֵנוּ יְהֹוָה אֱלֹהֵינוּ בּוֹ לְטוֹבָה, וּפָקְדֵנוּ בוֹ לִבְרָכָה, וְהוֹשִׁיעֵנוּ בוֹ לְחַיִּים טוֹבִים. וּבִדְבַר יְשׁוּעָה וְרַחֲמִים, חוּס וְחָנֵּנוּ וְרַחֵם עָלֵינוּ וְהוֹשִׁיעֵנוּ, כִּי אֵלֶיךָ עֵינֵינוּ כִּי אֵל (מֶלֶךְ) חַנּוּן וְרַחוּם אָתָּה:

וּבְנֵה יְרוּשָׁלַיִם עִיר הַקֹּדֶשׁ בִּמְהֵרָה בְיָמֵינוּ. בָּרוּךְ אַתָּה יְהֹוָה. בּוֹנֵה בְרַחֲמָיו יְרוּשָׁלָיִם, אָמֵן:

בָּרוּךְ אַתָּה יְהֹוָה אֱלֹהֵינוּ מֶלֶךְ הָעוֹלָם. הָאֵל, אָבִינוּ, מַלְכֵּנוּ, אַדִּירֵנוּ, בּוֹרְאֵנוּ, גּוֹאֲלֵנוּ, יוֹצְרֵנוּ, קְדוֹשֵׁנוּ קְדוֹשׁ יַעֲקֹב, רוֹעֵנוּ רוֹעֵה יִשְׂרָאֵל, הַמֶּלֶךְ הַטּוֹב וְהַמֵּטִיב לַכֹּל. שֶׁבְּכָל יוֹם וָיוֹם הוּא הֵטִיב הוּא מֵטִיב הוּא יֵיטִיב לָנוּ. הוּא גְמָלָנוּ הוּא גוֹמְלֵנוּ הוּא יִגְמְלֵנוּ לָעַד, לְחֵן וּלְחֶסֶד

(On Shabbos add this:)

May it be Your will to strengthen us with Your mitzvos, Hashem, our God, also with the mitzvah of this seventh day, the great and holy Shabbos. For this day is great and holy to You, so that we may desist from work on it, and rest, with love for You, as it was Your Will to command. And may it be Your Will, Hashem our God, to allow us peace, so that on our day of rest we have no pain, grief or sighs. And show us, Hashem our God, Your city Zion finally consoled, Jerusalem Your holy city rebuilt, for from You come salvation and consolation.

OUR GOD and God of our forefathers, may our case and remembrance, and that of our forefathers, rise up to You, and come and arrive and be seen and heard with favor; and that of Mashiach, son of David, Your servant; and that of Jerusalem Your holy city, and that of all of Israel Your nation, before You, for deliverance and well-being, with favor, kindness and mercy; for life and peace on this day, the Festival of Matzos. Hashem, our God, remember us today for the good, and decide blessing for us upon it, save us today so that we may live, and pronounce salvation and mercy. Have pity. Spare us and have mercy on us and save us, for our eyes are upon You, for You are God and King, and You are loving and merciful.

AND MAY YOU BUILD the holy city of Jerusalem soon, in our days. Blessed are You, Hashem our God, Who builds Jerusalem with His mercy, Amen.

BLESSED ARE YOU, Hashem our God, King of the Universe, the Almighty, our Father, King, Master, Creator, Redeemer, Maker, and Holy One — the Holy One of Yaakov, Who guides us, Shepherd of Israel — the goodly King Who bestows good to all. For every day He did bestow favors, does bestow favors, and in the future will bestow favors upon us. He gave to us, gives and will give forever, with grace, kindness and mercy, to relieve and

וּלְרַחֲמִים וּלְרֶוַח הַצָּלָה וְהַצְלָחָה, בְּרָכָה וִישׁוּעָה, נֶחָמָה, פַּרְנָסָה וְכַלְכָּלָה, וְרַחֲמִים וְחַיִּים וְשָׁלוֹם וְכָל טוֹב. וּמִכָּל טוּב לְעוֹלָם אַל יְחַסְּרֵנוּ:

הָרַחֲמָן הוּא יִמְלֹךְ עָלֵינוּ לְעוֹלָם וָעֶד:

הָרַחֲמָן הוּא יִתְבָּרַךְ בַּשָּׁמַיִם וּבָאָרֶץ:

הָרַחֲמָן הוּא יִשְׁתַּבַּח לְדוֹר דּוֹרִים. וְיִתְפָּאַר בָּנוּ לָעַד וּלְנֵצַח נְצָחִים. וְיִתְהַדַּר בָּנוּ לָעַד וּלְעוֹלְמֵי עוֹלָמִים:

הָרַחֲמָן הוּא יְפַרְנְסֵנוּ בְּכָבוֹד:

הָרַחֲמָן הוּא יִשְׁבֹּר עֻלֵּנוּ מֵעַל צַוָּארֵנוּ וְהוּא יוֹלִיכֵנוּ קוֹמְמִיּוּת לְאַרְצֵנוּ:

הָרַחֲמָן הוּא יִשְׁלַח לָנוּ בְּרָכָה מְרֻבָּה בַּבַּיִת הַזֶּה וְעַל שֻׁלְחָן זֶה שֶׁאָכַלְנוּ עָלָיו:

הָרַחֲמָן הוּא יִשְׁלַח לָנוּ אֶת אֵלִיָּהוּ הַנָּבִיא זָכוּר לַטּוֹב וִיבַשֵּׂר לָנוּ בְּשׂוֹרוֹת טוֹבוֹת יְשׁוּעוֹת וְנֶחָמוֹת:

הָרַחֲמָן הוּא יְבָרֵךְ אֶת (אָבִי מוֹרִי) בַּעַל הַבַּיִת הַזֶּה, וְאֶת (אִמִּי מוֹרָתִי) בַּעֲלַת הַבַּיִת הַזֶּה, (אוֹתִי וְאֶת אִשְׁתִּי [בַּעֲלִי] וְאֶת זַרְעִי וְאֶת כָּל אֲשֶׁר לִי וְאֶת כָּל הַמְסֻבִּין כָּאן) אוֹתָם וְאֶת בֵּיתָם וְאֶת זַרְעָם וְאֶת כָּל אֲשֶׁר לָהֶם. אוֹתָנוּ וְאֶת כָּל אֲשֶׁר לָנוּ. כְּמוֹ שֶׁנִּתְבָּרְכוּ אֲבוֹתֵינוּ אַבְרָהָם יִצְחָק וְיַעֲקֹב בַּכֹּל, מִכֹּל, כֹּל. כֵּן יְבָרֵךְ אוֹתָנוּ כֻּלָּנוּ יַחַד בִּבְרָכָה שְׁלֵמָה. וְנֹאמַר אָמֵן:

spare us, to grant us success and blessing, salvation and consolation, livelihood, sustenance, mercy, life and peace, and all that is good, from all that is good. May He never leave us in want.

MAY the Merciful One be King over us forever.

MAY the Merciful One be blessed in the heavens and on earth.

MAY the Merciful One be praised in every generation, and may He be glorified through us forever, and be revered through us for all time.

MAY the Merciful One provide us with honorable livelihoods.

MAY the Merciful One break off the yoke from our necks, and lead us to our Land, standing erect.

MAY the Merciful One send bountiful blessings upon this house, and upon this table where we have eaten.

MAY the Merciful One send us Eliyahu the Prophet, of blessed memory, who will bring good tidings to us, salvation and consolation.

MAY the Merciful One bless [my father, my teacher] the master of this house and [my mother, my teacher] the mistress of this house, [me, my wife/husband and my children] and all that is mine, and all that sit here, both them, their household, their children and all that belongs to them, also us and all that is ours, even as our fathers, Avraham, Yitzchak, and Yaakov were blessed in everything, from everything, and with everything, so may He bless all of us together with a perfect blessing. And let us say, Amen.

בַּמָּרוֹם יְלַמְּדוּ עֲלֵיהֶם וְעָלֵינוּ זְכוּת שֶׁתְּהֵא לְמִשְׁמֶרֶת שָׁלוֹם. וְנִשָּׂא בְרָכָה מֵאֵת יְהוָה. וּצְדָקָה מֵאֱלֹהֵי יִשְׁעֵנוּ. וְנִמְצָא חֵן וְשֵׂכֶל טוֹב בְּעֵינֵי אֱלֹהִים וְאָדָם:

(On Shabbos:)

הָרַחֲמָן הוּא יַנְחִילֵנוּ לְיוֹם שֶׁכֻּלוֹ שַׁבָּת וּמְנוּחָה לְחַיֵּי הָעוֹלָמִים:

הָרַחֲמָן הוּא יַנְחִילֵנוּ לְיוֹם שֶׁכֻּלוֹ טוֹב. לְיוֹם שֶׁכֻּלוֹ אָרוּךְ, יוֹם שֶׁצַּדִּיקִים יוֹשְׁבִים וְעַטְרוֹתֵיהֶם בְּרָאשֵׁיהֶם וְנֶהֱנִים מִזִּיו הַשְּׁכִינָה וִיהִי חֶלְקֵנוּ עִמָּהֶם:

הָרַחֲמָן הוּא יְזַכֵּנוּ לִימוֹת הַמָּשִׁיחַ וּלְחַיֵּי הָעוֹלָם הַבָּא: מִגְדּוֹל יְשׁוּעוֹת מַלְכּוֹ וְעֹשֶׂה חֶסֶד לִמְשִׁיחוֹ לְדָוִד וּלְזַרְעוֹ עַד עוֹלָם: עֹשֶׂה שָׁלוֹם בִּמְרוֹמָיו הוּא יַעֲשֶׂה שָׁלוֹם עָלֵינוּ וְעַל כָּל יִשְׂרָאֵל וְאִמְרוּ אָמֵן:

יְראוּ אֶת יְהוָה קְדֹשָׁיו כִּי אֵין מַחְסוֹר לִירֵאָיו: כְּפִירִים רָשׁוּ וְרָעֵבוּ וְדֹרְשֵׁי יְהוָה לֹא יַחְסְרוּ כָל טוֹב: הוֹדוּ לַיהוָה כִּי טוֹב כִּי לְעוֹלָם חַסְדּוֹ: פּוֹתֵחַ אֶת יָדֶךָ וּמַשְׂבִּיעַ לְכָל חַי רָצוֹן: בָּרוּךְ הַגֶּבֶר אֲשֶׁר יִבְטַח בַּיהוָה וְהָיָה יְהוָה מִבְטַחוֹ: נַעַר הָיִיתִי גַם זָקַנְתִּי וְלֹא רָאִיתִי צַדִּיק נֶעֱזָב וְזַרְעוֹ מְבַקֶּשׁ לָחֶם: יְהוָה עֹז לְעַמּוֹ יִתֵּן יְהוָה יְבָרֵךְ אֶת עַמּוֹ בַשָּׁלוֹם:

Young lions suffer lack and are hungry, but those who seek Hashem will not lack any good (*Tehillim* 34:11) — On the surface, things seem to be the opposite from what this verse says. That is, we see with our

LET THEIR MERITS and ours be pleaded on high, to give us lasting peace. May we bear blessings from Hashem, kindness from the God of our salvation. May we find favor and good consideration in the eyes of both God and mankind.

(On Shabbos:)

MAY the Merciful One cause us to inherit the day which will be wholly Shabbos and rest, for eternal life!

MAY the Merciful One cause us to inherit the day which will be totally good, the everlasting day, the day when the righteous sit with crowns on their heads and bask in the glow of the Shechinah — May our portion be with theirs.

MAY the Merciful One grant us the days of Mashiach, and life in the World to Come. He Who is a tower of salvation to his king, Who does kindness to His annointed one — to David and his seed — Who makes peace in Heaven... May He bring peace to us and to all of Israel, and let us say, Amen.

Keep fear for Hashem, His holy ones, for those who fear Him are never in want. Young lions suffer lack and are hungry, but those who seek Hashem will not lack any good. Thank Hashem, for He is Good, and His kindness endures forever. You open Your hand and satisfy the desires of every living thing. Blessed is the man whose trust is in Hashem, for Hashem will protect him. I was young and now I have grown old, and never did I see a righteous man abandoned, or his children begging for bread. Hashem will give strength to His People, and bless them with peace.

very own eyes that often people who fear God live in dire poverty, while it is the evil-doers that have the wealth and enjoyment in this world. King David himself wrote elsewhere (*Tehillim* 73:12): *Behold* these evil-doers, who are at ease in the world, attaining wealth and power. Don't these two verses contradict each other?

A third verse from *Tehillim* clarifies the matter: *I have placed Hashem before my eyes always. Because He is my right hand, I will not fall* (*Tehillim* 16:8). That is, when a person is truly serving God, and is aware of Him always, and trusts in Him, then he is able to happily accept anything that happens to him, whether it makes life easy and pleasant for him, or not. Whether joy or sorrow, it is all the same to him, because he knows that it all comes from God — his "right hand"! God is his Helper, so that in his eyes, whatever God sends him is a kindness and a benefit!

There is a *baraysa* called *Perek haShirah* which teaches that a person can learn to be happy simply by thinking about all the different things that God created, including the animals. *Perek haShirah* provides an appropriate Scriptural verse that each creature "sings," in a manner of speaking, as a praise of God. Our Sages taught: *All who learn Perek haShirah in this world will merit the World to Come.* In other words, even the least of God's creations are able to provide us with ways to thank and praise Him — even ants, which live but a brief time, and even [stray] dogs, who always are lacking food. All creatures are grateful, for simply being alive!

The word *neshamah* ("soul") in Hebrew is very much like the word *neshimah* ("breath"). Thus, on the verse *Tehillim* 150:6: *Every soul shall praise God*, our Sages teach: *For every breath you shall praise God!* (*Bereshis Rabbah*, Chapter 14). It is enough that we have life!

All who have been given life sing a praise of thanks to God, no matter what type of life they may have. Thus, if someone is having a difficult time, so much so that he is poverty-stricken and has no food to eat, is he in a worse position than a dog? Even a dog "sings praises" for the life that God gave him, and a person who is hungry and poverty-stricken can sing that song, too, as the verse says (*Tehillim* 95:6): *Let us prostrate ourselves, bow and bend our knees in thanks, before God, our Creator*. If a person accepts his suffering happily, knowing that it is Heaven-sent, he will merit the World to Come. When? He even gains a taste of the World to Come in this world!

The evil-doers are quite the opposite from this, for they are never satisfied with their lot. No matter how much they have, they always want more. Therefore, King David says here, *Keep fear for Hashem,*

His holy ones, for those who fear Him are never in want. If a person truly is one of God's "holy ones," his first desire is to serve the One Who helps him, and all other "good things in life" are secondary to him. He accepts this, even if materially he has very little, so that he is *never in want* — he never feels that he is lacking anything.

By contrast, *Young lions suffer lack and are hungry* — even if their cupboards are overflowing. They are the ones who are actually in want. They have one hundred, but what is it that they seek? Two hundred! Thus, King David observes, *But those who seek Hashem will not lack any good [kol tov].*

They *will not lack* — because [another rendering of *kol tov*]: "everything is good!" They are not in want of anything, because they accept that it is God Who arranges their lives, and thus they are happy with their lot. (*Michzeh Avraham*)

📖

How exalted is this meal that we eat on this night, in honor of the festival, for we say *Hallel* before it, and also after it! It is placed between two redemptions, too, for prior to the meal we spoke at length about the redemption from Egypt, and then we said the part of *Hallel* that gives thanks for that redemption. The meal over, we are glad at heart both from the wine of the mitzvah and from the matzah of the mitzvah, yet our yearning for the Future Redemption is not diminished in the least. On the contrary, it is precisely now, at this moment, that our mouths are filled with praise and with song, and our hearts are afire anticipating the Redemption, may it come soon, speedily in our days!

*Before the blessing over the third cup,
some say:*

הִנְנִי מוּכָן וּמְזוּמָן לְקַיֵּם מִצְוַת כּוֹס שְׁלִישִׁי מֵאַרְבַּע כּוֹסוֹת.

בָּרוּךְ אַתָּה יְהֹוָה אֱלֹהֵינוּ מֶלֶךְ הָעוֹלָם בּוֹרֵא פְּרִי הַגָּפֶן:

Everyone drinks the cup. One should drink the whole cup, or at least most of it, without pausing in the middle, while reclining on the left side. Have in mind that this is the mitzvah of the third of the four cups.

Some now pour the fourth cup of wine, before saying "Pour out Your wrath." Others wait, and pour the fourth cup only after "Pour out Your wrath." and immediately before reciting the second half of Hallel. An extra cup — that of Eliyahu — is poured now, although some pour the Cup of Eliyahu at the beginning of the Seder.

One of the Seder participants now opens the front door of the house, and everyone says, "Pour out Your wrath." (Some stand to say this.)

שְׁפֹךְ חֲמָתְךָ אֶל הַגּוֹיִם אֲשֶׁר לֹא יְדָעוּךָ וְעַל מַמְלָכוֹת אֲשֶׁר בְּשִׁמְךָ לֹא קָרָאוּ: כִּי אָכַל אֶת יַעֲקֹב וְאֶת נָוֵהוּ הֵשַׁמּוּ: שְׁפָךְ עֲלֵיהֶם זַעְמֶךָ וַחֲרוֹן אַפְּךָ יַשִּׂיגֵם: תִּרְדֹּף בְּאַף וְתַשְׁמִידֵם מִתַּחַת שְׁמֵי יְהֹוָה:

Pour out Your wrath upon the nations

It is an ancient custom to say these verses as part of the Haggadah, as an introduction to the second half of *Hallel*, over which we drink the fourth and final cup. In some communities, additional verses are said at this point, all having the same message — God executing judgments on those who have oppressed us. Various explanations are

*Before the blessing over the third cup,
some say:*

*Here I am, ready and willing to fulfill the mitzvah of drinking
the third cup of the Four Cups.*

***B**LESSED ARE YOU, Hashem our God, King of the Universe,
Creator of the fruit of the vine.*

*Everyone drinks the cup. One should drink the whole cup, or
at least most of it, without pausing in the middle, while reclining on the left side. Have in mind that this is the mitzvah of
the third of the four cups.
Some now pour the fourth cup of wine, before saying "Pour
out Your wrath." Others wait, and pour the fourth cup only
after "Pour out Your wrath" and immediately before reciting
the second half of Hallel. An extra cup — that of Eliyahu — is
poured now, although some pour the Cup of Eliyahu at the
beginning of the Seder.*

*One of the Seder participants now opens the front door of the
house, and everyone says, "Pour out Your wrath."
(Some stand to say this.)*

POUR OUT YOUR WRATH *upon the nations that do not recognize You, upon the kingdoms that do not call in Your Name. For they have devoured Yaakov and laid waste to his abode. Pour out Your fury on them, and have Your indignation consume them. Pursue them in anger, and remove them from under the skies of Hashem.*

given for this custom.
Up until now, we have spoken of the redemption from Egypt, and said *Hallel* about it. In the process, we spoke about the judgments that God executed upon Pharaoh and his servants, before He liberated us and brought us to the Land of Israel. Now we turn to the war with Gog and Magog, our oppressors of the future, and the part of

Hallel which is about Israel's future redemption, when Gog and Magog will be defeated. We introduce this part of *Hallel* with verses about God's execution of justice, for just as in the past, God redeemed Israel only after first meting out punishments to Egypt, so, too, will the future redemption come about only after He pours out His wrath on those who have *devoured Yaakov and laid waste to his abode*.

It follows that the enemies that arose against us after we left Egypt should receive harsh punishments. After all, Egypt received such punishments, though we grew to a great nation within her borders, and everything that the Egyptians did in order to harm us, was done there. By contrast, the enemies that came upon us afterwards attacked us while we were living in peace in our own land! They destroyed our Temple, devoured the best that we had, and made our blood flow like rivers. They persist in their evil even today. Thus all the more so will God repay them with His wrath and fury!

And even if they have "built their nests in rock" (*Bemidbar* 24:21) they will not escape these punishments, and God will utterly destroy them, leaving no trace of them whatsoever under the heavens. On His People, the remnant that survives the attacks of the nations, God will have mercy, and He will not allow them to be harmed again.

Even if at that time we will not have sufficient merits, God will redeem us for the sake of His Name, for we are identified with Him. With all our hearts, we pray now that He redeem us so that His Name be magnified and glorified, because our sole desire is that His name not be desecrated. We ask for salvation not for our sake, but for His, as the second part of the *Hallel* begins: *Not to us, Hashem! Not to us, but to Your Name shall honor be given!* And this is the way we finish the Seder.

As we come before our Redeemer with our prayer for the Final Redemption, we consciously prepare ourselves to experience this redemption immediately, opening wide the doors of our homes, ready to go out and meet the *Mashiach*, and say "Welcome!" to Eliyahu the Prophet, who will announce his coming.

Below are some additional explanations — from the wisdom of our

Sages — of why we open the door to the house when we say *Pour our Your wrath*, why we say this prayer before the second half of *Hallel*, and other related matters:

As noted, the Jerusalem Talmud says that the four cups of wine that we drink at the Seder correspond to the four kingdoms that subjugated Israel after Egypt. We drink the four cups to symbolize how God will make those nations drink four bitter cups of punishment. Thus, when the fourth cup is poured, we hint at this, saying, *Pour out Your wrath* (*Meiri, Ran* on *Pesachim*, Tenth Chapter).

First we say, *Pour our Your wrath* and then we say, *Not to us* and the remainder of *Hallel*, which speaks of our desire for the Ultimate Redemption. This is a reflection of a general principle — that the righteous cannot be uplifted until the wicked are brought low. (*Vilna Gaon*)

Because we are about to ask of God: *Not us! Not us!* — that is to say, "Please do not include us in the war with Gog and Magog"— we precede our request with yet another one, that God pour His wrath out on Gog and Magog and eliminate them in some other way, but not by involving us in their downfall. (*Haggadah of Darmstadt*)

Up to now, we have mentioned Pharaoh and Egypt many times this night, and he who mentions the names of the wicked must immediately afterwards say a curse on them. Therefore, we say, *Pour out Your wrath*. (*Or Zarua*)

We open the door of the house to remind ourselves that the Seder night is a night of "guarding," when Hashem provides us with special protection from all harm. In the merit of our faith in this, *Mashiach* will come and pour out Hashem's wrath on the nations. We open the door also to demonstrate our faith that *Mashiach* can come at any moment, even though he has delayed so long. In the merit of this act, we hope that he will come immediately, and take Hashem's vengeance on the nations. (*Mateh Moshe*)

We ate and then blessed Hashem, while they *devour Yaakov* and shout blasphemy against Hashem. (*Meiri*, in the name of an anonymous commentator)

Even though all the suffering that comes upon Israel is decreed by God, in order to provide us with the atonement we need for our sins, the nations who oppress us also have their own evil and selfish motivations in mind.

In the days of the Temple, as noted, the meat of each Pesach offering could be eaten only at night, in groups, and only by those who already were "counted" on the offering at the time it was slaughtered, the afternoon before the Seder. Thus, in the days when the Temple stood, the doors of our homes were locked on the Seder night, so that those who were not "counted" on each particular group's offering could not come in off the street and partake of it. When the meat of the offering had been completely consumed, the people would unlock their doors and open them wide, to make up for what they had done, and give honor to passersby. Thus, we observe the practice of opening the door at the end of the meal, too, as a remembrance of this ancient practice, and we do so after completing the *Afikoman*, which actually is in remembrance of the Pesach offering.

When Yaakov *Avinu* came before Yitzchak *Avinu* in order to receive the blessing which Yitzchak *Avinu* intended to give to Esav, it was the Seder night, and Yaakov came with two kid goats, representing the *Chagigah* and the Pesach offering. He also brought his father wine, alluding to the mitzvah of the four cups. Afterwards, as Esav arrived, in hope of receiving the blessing, Yitzchak was reciting, *Pour out Your wrath*. When Esav opened the door, Yaakov hid behind it and slipped out quickly as Esav passed by him, so that Esav never saw him. Perhaps this is why we say *Pour out Your wrath* as we open the door of the house. (*Minchas Tziyon*)

During the many epochs when Jews were wantonly murdered, because of blood libels and other slanders, another reason was found for observing the practice of opening our doors on the night of the Seder. Often, in former times, while the Seder was in process, non-Jews would be listening from outside, hoping to hear something that would enable them to slander the Jews and inform on them to the authorities. When the Jews opened their doors wide, however, it would be a clear indication that they in fact had nothing to hide. Or, with the doors open, the informers outside would be able to hear clearly that we were praying to God, and that He, and not us, would be the One to pour out wrath.

Many had the custom of sending one of the Seder participants outside, after the Grace after Meals, where he would stand at the door and lean against it. As soon as everyone started to say, *Pour out Your wrath*, someone inside the house would open the door, causing the one outside to immediately burst through the doorway! This was to signify that — especially on Pesach, the night of our first redemption — we have complete faith that the Final Redemption is waiting to come, and can "burst upon us" at any moment. *(Yosef Ometz)*

Perhaps this is why we open the door when we say, *Pour out Your wrath* — to demonstrate our faith that the Redemption to Come will be different from the redemption from Egypt. That is, when God brought the last punishing plague on Egypt — the slaying of their firstborn — the Jews remained locked behind closed doors, inside their homes, and were not allowed to see the downfall of their enemies, as the verse states *(Shemos 12:22): And you shall not go out from the door of your house, not any one of you, until the morning.* Before we say the second half of *Hallel*, about the Ultimate Redemption, we open the door and say *Pour out Your wrath*, to demonstrate our faith that regarding the future, we will be allowed to see the punishments that God metes out to our enemies, for then Hashem will take His vengeance in public. *(Sefas Emes)*

Pour out your wrath upon the nations that do not recognize You, upon the kingdoms that do not call in Your Name. For they have devoured Yaakov, and laid waste to his abode —As long as the Nation of Israel dwelled in its own land, and our Holy Temple stood, all the other nations of the world recognized God, as well, and so too did they "call in [speak] His Name," even though they did not really wish to do so. The verse says *(Tehillim 145:21): My mouth shall declare the praise of the Lord, so that all flesh shall bless His holy Name.* This is to say that the praises of God that are uttered by Israel have the power to awaken other nations to praise God, too. Therefore, when it came to be that the nations *devoured Yaakov and laid waste to his abode*, the nations ceased to recognize God, and no longer did they "call in His Name."

הַלֵּל

If the fourth cup was not poured yet, pour it now, and say the second half of Hallel over it. The door of the house is now closed.

לֹא לָנוּ יְהֹוָה, לֹא לָנוּ, כִּי לְשִׁמְךָ תֵּן כָּבוֹד, עַל חַסְדְּךָ עַל אֲמִתֶּךָ: לָמָה יֹאמְרוּ הַגּוֹיִם, אַיֵּה נָא אֱלֹהֵיהֶם: וֵאלֹהֵינוּ בַשָּׁמָיִם, כֹּל אֲשֶׁר חָפֵץ עָשָׂה: עֲצַבֵּיהֶם כֶּסֶף וְזָהָב מַעֲשֵׂה יְדֵי אָדָם: פֶּה לָהֶם וְלֹא יְדַבֵּרוּ, עֵינַיִם לָהֶם וְלֹא יִרְאוּ: אָזְנַיִם לָהֶם וְלֹא יִשְׁמָעוּ, אַף לָהֶם וְלֹא יְרִיחוּן: יְדֵיהֶם וְלֹא יְמִישׁוּן, רַגְלֵיהֶם וְלֹא יְהַלֵּכוּ, לֹא יֶהְגּוּ בִּגְרוֹנָם: כְּמוֹהֶם יִהְיוּ עֹשֵׂיהֶם, כֹּל אֲשֶׁר בֹּטֵחַ בָּהֶם: יִשְׂרָאֵל בְּטַח בַּיהֹוָה, עֶזְרָם וּמָגִנָּם הוּא: בֵּית אַהֲרֹן בִּטְחוּ בַיהֹוָה, עֶזְרָם

Not to us, Hashem. Not to us — That is, "Not for our sake." We are telling God: You need not even do Your kindnesses to us for our sake, nor be faithful to us for our sake. Rather, everything that comes from Your Hand should be only for the honor of Your Name. To what can this be compared? To a poverty-stricken man who had a daughter to marry off, and his wealthy brother gave him a huge sum of money for the sake of his niece's dowry. The poor brother, however, went and spent it all on himself. Afterwards, he asked his wealthy brother for more money, saying "Not for me! Don't even put the money into my hand! Just put out enough so that it will be a nice wedding, so that you will not be embarrassed." (*Maggid of Dubno*)

📖

Why should the nations say, "Where is their God?" — Here, in the Hebrew (*Tehillim* 115:2), the nations are quoted as saying, *Where is their God?* with the word *na*, which connotes a request, meaning "Where, please…" Elsewhere in *Tehillim* (79:10) we find the same ex-

Hallel

If the fourth cup was not poured yet, pour it now, and say the second half of Hallel over it. The door of the house is now closed.

NOT TO US, HASHEM. *Not to us, but to Your Name shall honor be given, for Your kindness and faithfulness. Why should the nations say, "Where is their God?" when our God is in Heaven and does anything He pleases! Their disgusting idols are silver and gold, the work of men's hands. They have a mouth but will not speak, eyes but will not see. They have ears but they will not hear, a nose but they will not smell. Their hands do not feel, and their feet do not walk. There is no sound in their throats. Those who make them will become like them! So, too, all who trust in them! Israel must trust in Hashem! He is their*

act verse, except that the word *na* is left out! This hints at the significance of the word *na*. When the nations have success in shedding our blood, they poke fun, saying sarcastically, "Please show us their God!" On the other hand, there will come a time when the nations themselves will tire of the killing, and even they will want to see God's Strong Hand evident in the world, so that the bloodshed will stop. Then the time will come when they say "please" seriously. (*Chasam Sofer*)

Their disgusting idols are silver and gold — That is, even after the manufacturer finishes making them, they remain simply *silver and gold*, and do not gain a new name. Were the newly shaped forms to serve a new purpose of some sort, a new name would be appropriate. However, *They have a mouth but will not speak...* Thus, nothing has changed. (*Alshich*)

Israel must trust in Hashem! He is their Help and Shield — When it

וּמָגִנָּם הוּא: יִרְאֵי יְהֹוָה בִּטְחוּ בַיהֹוָה, עֶזְרָם וּמָגִנָּם הוּא:

יְהֹוָה זְכָרָנוּ יְבָרֵךְ, יְבָרֵךְ אֶת בֵּית יִשְׂרָאֵל, יְבָרֵךְ אֶת בֵּית אַהֲרֹן: יְבָרֵךְ יִרְאֵי יְהֹוָה, הַקְּטַנִּים עִם הַגְּדֹלִים: יֹסֵף יְהֹוָה, עֲלֵיכֶם וְעַל בְּנֵיכֶם: בְּרוּכִים אַתֶּם לַיהֹוָה עֹשֵׂה שָׁמַיִם וָאָרֶץ: הַשָּׁמַיִם שָׁמַיִם לַיהֹוָה, וְהָאָרֶץ נָתַן לִבְנֵי אָדָם: לֹא הַמֵּתִים יְהַלְלוּ יָהּ, וְלֹא כָּל יֹרְדֵי דוּמָה: וַאֲנַחְנוּ נְבָרֵךְ יָהּ, מֵעַתָּה וְעַד עוֹלָם, הַלְלוּיָהּ:

אָהַבְתִּי כִּי יִשְׁמַע יְהֹוָה אֶת קוֹלִי תַּחֲנוּנָי: כִּי הִטָּה אָזְנוֹ לִי וּבְיָמַי אֶקְרָא: אֲפָפוּנִי חֶבְלֵי מָוֶת, וּמְצָרֵי שְׁאוֹל מְצָאוּנִי, צָרָה וְיָגוֹן אֶמְצָא: וּבְשֵׁם יְהֹוָה אֶקְרָא, אָנָּה יְהֹוָה מַלְּטָה נַפְשִׁי: חַנּוּן יְהֹוָה וְצַדִּיק, וֵאלֹהֵינוּ מְרַחֵם: שֹׁמֵר פְּתָאיִם יְהֹוָה, דַּלּוֹתִי וְלִי יְהוֹשִׁיעַ: שׁוּבִי נַפְשִׁי לִמְנוּחָיְכִי, כִּי יְהֹוָה גָּמַל עָלָיְכִי: כִּי חִלַּצְתָּ נַפְשִׁי מִמָּוֶת, אֶת עֵינִי

appears that Hashem is helping the 39 evil nations who oppress us, Israel should reflect: Here are these nations who go against Hashem's Will, causing Him only anger, and their whole existence has one sole purpose — to provide Israel with atonement for its sins. Yet look — Hashem helps them, shields them, and does good for them! If this is what He does for such nations, then for us, who are Hashem's ser-

Help and Shield. The House of Aharon must trust in Hashem. He is their Help and Shield. Those who fear Hashem must trust in Hashem. He is their Help and Shield.

Hashem has been mindful of us, He will send blessing. He will bless the House of Israel. He will bless the House of Aharon. He will bless those that fear Hashem, the small with the great. May Hashem add to your blessing, to yours and to your children's. You are blessed by Hashem, Creator of Heaven and earth. The heaven? The heaven is Hashem's, but the earth He has given to mankind. Not do the dead praise Him, not those who descend into silence. But we will bless God, from now to eternity. Praise God!

I have had love [for Hashem] for He listens to my voice and my pleadings, for He bends His ear to hear me, and I shall call to Him all my days. I have been gripped by death pangs, and the clutches of the grave found me. Pain and sorrow were upon me, but I will call in the Name of Hashem, "Please, Hashem, deliver my soul!" Hashem is kind and just. Our God shows mercy, Hashem protects the simple. Though I had fallen low, He saved me. Return, my soul, and be at rest, for Hashem has been good to you. For You delivered my soul from death, my ears from tears,

vants, whose only desire is to do His Will — surely the Source of Life will help, shield, and do good for us, for we are the nation that regards Him as King! (*Alshich*)

Hashem protects the simple — Rabbi Akiva said, "The small children of the evil ones of Israel will still merit the World to Come, for the

מִן דִּמְעָה, אֶת רַגְלִי מִדֶּחִי: אֶתְהַלֵּךְ לִפְנֵי יְהֹוָה, בְּאַרְצוֹת הַחַיִּים: הֶאֱמַנְתִּי כִּי אֲדַבֵּר, אֲנִי עָנִיתִי מְאֹד: אֲנִי אָמַרְתִּי בְחָפְזִי, כָּל הָאָדָם כֹּזֵב:

מָה אָשִׁיב לַיהֹוָה, כָּל תַּגְמוּלוֹהִי עָלָי: כּוֹס יְשׁוּעוֹת אֶשָּׂא, וּבְשֵׁם יְהֹוָה אֶקְרָא: נְדָרַי לַיהֹוָה אֲשַׁלֵּם, נֶגְדָה נָּא לְכָל עַמּוֹ: יָקָר בְּעֵינֵי יְהֹוָה הַמָּוְתָה לַחֲסִידָיו: אָנָּה יְהֹוָה כִּי אֲנִי עַבְדֶּךָ, אֲנִי עַבְדְּךָ בֶּן אֲמָתֶךָ, פִּתַּחְתָּ לְמוֹסֵרָי: לְךָ אֶזְבַּח זֶבַח תּוֹדָה, וּבְשֵׁם יְהֹוָה אֶקְרָא: נְדָרַי לַיהֹוָה אֲשַׁלֵּם, נֶגְדָה נָּא לְכָל עַמּוֹ: בְּחַצְרוֹת בֵּית יְהֹוָה, בְּתוֹכֵכִי יְרוּשָׁלָיִם, הַלְלוּיָהּ:

הַלְלוּ אֶת יְהֹוָה כָּל גּוֹיִם, שַׁבְּחוּהוּ כָּל הָאֻמִּים:
כִּי גָבַר עָלֵינוּ חַסְדּוֹ,
וֶאֱמֶת יְהֹוָה לְעוֹלָם,
הַלְלוּיָהּ:

verse says, *Hashem protects the simple. Though I had fallen low, He saved me.* (*Sanhedrin* 110b)

📖

I will walk in God's Presence in the land of the living — If this means, "in the Land of Israel," why call it the land of "the living"? That is, people do live there, but people also die there! What does this phrase mean? The answer is that King David is indeed referring to the Land of Israel — for after *Mashiach* comes, when the time arrives for the Resurrection of the Dead, the Jews who are buried there will be the first ones to be brought back to life, *in the land of the living.* (*Pesikta Ravti*, Chapter One) *my feet from stumbling. I will walk in God's Presence in the land of the living. I trust in Him, even when I say, "I am suffering greatly," even when I say in my haste, "All people are deceivers."*

What can I give in return to Hashem for all the good He has bestowed on me? I will lift up the cup of salvation and I will call in the Name of Hashem. I will pay my vows to Hashem in the presence of His entire nation. How grevious in the eyes of Hashem is the death of His righteous ones! With gratitude, Hashem, I am Your servant, and son of Your handmaid. You have untied my shackles. I will slaughter an offering of thanks, and will call in the Name of Hashem. I will pay my vows to Hashem in the presence of His entire nation, in the courtyards of the House of God, in the midst of Jerusalem. Praise God!

*Praise Hashem, all nations! Laud Him, all peoples!
For great is the kindness that He has shown us
and Hashem's Truth endures forever.
Praise God!*

I will lift up the cup of salvation — Regarding Avraham and his newborn son, Yitzchak, we read in the Torah (*Bereshis* 21:8): *And the child grew, and was weaned. And Avraham made a great feast on the day that Yitzchak was weaned.* Because the Hebrew root ג-מ-ל connotes both "wean" and "bestow," our Sages taught the following, based on this verse:

So, too, will Hashem make a great feast for his righteous ones, on the day that He will bestow a special kindness upon the descendants of Yitzchak — when He brings the Final Redemption.

After the meal, they will want to honor Avraham, by giving him the cup of wine which is held by the one who leads the Grace after

Meals. Avraham will say to them: "Thank you, but I cannot accept, because Yishmael issued from me."

Next, they will say to Yitzchak, "You take the cup, and lead us in the Grace after Meals." He will say to them: "Thank you, but I cannot accept, because Esav issued from me."

Next, they will say to Yaakov, "You take the cup and lead us." He will say to them: "Thank you, but I cannot accept, because I married two sisters while both were still living, which is something that the Torah would later prohibit."

Next, they will say to Moshe *Rabbenu*, "You take the cup and lead us." He will answer them: "Thank you, but I cannot accept, because I never merited to enter the Land of Israel, not while I was alive and not after I died."

Next, they will say to Yehoshua, "You take the cup and lead us." He will answer: "Thank you, but I cannot accept, because I did not merit to have a son."

Finally, they will say to David, "You take the cup and lead us." He will say to them: "Thank you, I will, for it is fitting that I lead the blessing since I wrote, *I will lift up the cup of salvation, and I will call in the Name of Hashem.*" (*Pesachim* 119a)

How grevious in the eyes of Hashem is the death of His righteous ones! — Hashem said, "It is difficult for Me to decree death upon these righteous ones, and were it not for the fact that they decreed death on themselves, I would not let them die!" Avraham said, *I am destroyed* (*Bereshis* 15:2). Yitzchak said, *That I may bless you before I die* (*Bereshis* 27:4). Moshe said, *For I am going to die* (*Devarim* 4:22). (*Yalkut Shimoni, Tehillim* 874)

I am Your servant, and son of Your handmaid — A slave that You would buy in the market is not the same as one born in Your home, of Your own maidservant. And I am a grandson of Ruth, who called herself (*Megillas Ruth, Chapter Three*) *Your maidservant.* (*Yalkut Shimoni, Tehillim* 875)

You have untied my shackles — Although this is the literal meaning, the Hebrew word "shackles" here is very closely related to the word for "prohibition," for essentially, a prohibition "ties" or "shackles" a person. King David is saying that God untied one prohibition which would have forbidden the union between Yehudah and Tamar, and another that would have forbidden the union between Boaz and Ruth. What greater "shackle" could there be? If God had not "untied" these two prohibitions, our King David would never have even been born!

Rava expounds that King David was not referring to God's "untying" a possible prohibition on the union between Yehudah and Tamar. Rather, the second prohibition that God "untied" was one that might have forbidden the marriage of King Shelomo, David's son, to Na'amah, who came from the nation of Ammon. That is, one might think that Na'amah from Ammon, and Ruth from Moav, could not convert and marry into Israel, for the Torah says (*Devarim 23:4*): *No Ammonite or Moavite may come into Hashem's congregation* (that is, Israel cannot accept converts from these nations). Doubt could arise over whether the prohibition applies both to the men and to the women of these nations, or just to the men.

The Torah, however, gives a reason: *Because they did not offer you bread as you traveled*, a criticism which applies only to the men. As a result, women converts from these nations are allowed. Thus, Boaz was able to marry Ruth, David would be born, and later, Shelomo was able to marry Na'amah, and carry on David's line, the line of *Mashiach*. (*Ibid*)

📖

Praise Hashem, all nations — Those that were involved in subjugating Israel.

Laud him, all peoples — Those that did not subjugate Israel. Those nations that did not subjugate us saw that even the nations who did, were praising Hashem. They said to themselves, "All the more so should we praise Hashem!" Then they said, *For great is the kindness that He has shown us*. (*Ibid*)

The leader of the Seder says each of the next four lines out loud, and everyone answers him after each line with "Thank Hashem, for He is good, for His kindness endures forever."

הוֹדוּ לַיהֹוָה כִּי טוֹב　　כִּי לְעוֹלָם חַסְדּוֹ:

יֹאמַר נָא יִשְׂרָאֵל　　כִּי לְעוֹלָם חַסְדּוֹ:

יֹאמְרוּ נָא בֵית אַהֲרֹן　　כִּי לְעוֹלָם חַסְדּוֹ:

יֹאמְרוּ נָא יִרְאֵי יְהֹוָה　　כִּי לְעוֹלָם חַסְדּוֹ:

מִן הַמֵּצַר קָרָאתִי יָּהּ, עָנָנִי בַמֶּרְחָב יָהּ: יְהֹוָה לִי לֹא אִירָא מַה יַּעֲשֶׂה לִי אָדָם: יְהֹוָה לִי בְּעֹזְרָי, וַאֲנִי אֶרְאֶה בְשֹׂנְאָי: טוֹב לַחֲסוֹת בַּיהֹוָה, מִבְּטֹחַ בָּאָדָם: טוֹב לַחֲסוֹת בַּיהֹוָה מִבְּטֹחַ בִּנְדִיבִים: כָּל גּוֹיִם סְבָבוּנִי, בְּשֵׁם יְהֹוָה כִּי אֲמִילַם: סַבּוּנִי גַם סְבָבוּנִי, בְּשֵׁם יְהֹוָה כִּי אֲמִילַם: סַבּוּנִי כִדְבֹרִים דֹּעֲכוּ כְּאֵשׁ קוֹצִים, בְּשֵׁם יְהֹוָה כִּי אֲמִילַם: דָּחֹה דְחִיתַנִי לִנְפֹּל, וַיהֹוָה עֲזָרָנִי: עָזִּי וְזִמְרָת יָהּ, וַיְהִי לִי לִישׁוּעָה: קוֹל רִנָּה וִישׁוּעָה בְּאָהֳלֵי צַדִּיקִים, יְמִין יְהֹוָה

It is good to take shelter in Hashem, rather than rely on princes — The Hebrew "to take shelter" implies that the person enters on his own, even without hearing any promise that he will find protection. By contrast, the word "rely" implies that a promise, in fact, has been given. Thus, we are taught here that rather than rely on promises from men — even from "princes" who truly want to keep their word — it is better to take shelter in God, even in the absence of a promise. (*Vilna Gaon*)

The leader of the Seder says each of the next four lines out loud, and everyone answers him after each line with "Thank Hashem, for He is good, for His kindness endures forever."

Thank Hashem, for He is good,   for His kindness endures forever.

Let Israel say that   His kindness endures forever.

Let the House of Aharon say that   His kindness endures forever.

Let those who fear Hashem say that   His kindness endures forever.

FROM DISTRESSFUL CONSTRICTION I called to Hashem. Hashem answered me with expansive freedom! Hashem is with me, I shall not fear. What could a mere man do to me? Hashem is with me to help me, and I will face my enemies. It is good to take shelter in Hashem, rather than trust in man. It is good to take shelter in Hashem, rather than rely on princes. All the nations encircle me; in the Name of Hashem I will cut them down. They truly surround me; in the Name of Hashem I will wipe them out. They swarm about me like bees; in the Name of Hashem I will make them vanish, like a brush fire is extinguished. You pushed and pushed me, to try to make me fall, but Hashem helped me! Hashem is my Strength and Song, and this has been my salvation. There are voices of rejoicing and salvation in the tents of the

---

You pushed and pushed me, to try to make me fall — The redundant language is used because King David is actually speaking about man's evil inclination, and how it constantly stands in wait, trying to make each of us fall spiritually. If one of its tactics fails, it always has another one to try. Thus, our Sages say (*Sukkah 52a*), *A person's evil inclination strengthens itself over him every day, trying to kill him, and if it were not for the Holy One's assistance, a person would not be able to stand the onslaught.* (*Maharal, quoting the Zohar*)

עָשָׂה חָיִל: יְמִין יְהֹוָה רוֹמֵמָה, יְמִין יְהֹוָה עָשָׂה חָיִל: לֹא אָמוּת כִּי אֶחְיֶה, וַאֲסַפֵּר מַעֲשֵׂי יָהּ: יַסֹּר יִסְּרַנִּי יָּהּ, וְלַמָּוֶת לֹא נְתָנָנִי: פִּתְחוּ לִי שַׁעֲרֵי צֶדֶק אָבֹא בָם אוֹדֶה יָהּ: זֶה הַשַּׁעַר לַיהֹוָה צַדִּיקִים יָבֹאוּ בוֹ:

אוֹדְךָ כִּי עֲנִיתָנִי, וַתְּהִי לִי לִישׁוּעָה: אוֹדְךָ כִּי עֲנִיתָנִי, וַתְּהִי לִי לִישׁוּעָה: אֶבֶן מָאֲסוּ הַבּוֹנִים, הָיְתָה לְרֹאשׁ פִּנָּה: אֶבֶן מָאֲסוּ הַבּוֹנִים, הָיְתָה לְרֹאשׁ פִּנָּה: מֵאֵת יְהֹוָה הָיְתָה זֹּאת, הִיא נִפְלָאת בְּעֵינֵינוּ: מֵאֵת יְהֹוָה הָיְתָה זֹּאת, הִיא נִפְלָאת בְּעֵינֵינוּ: זֶה הַיּוֹם עָשָׂה יְהֹוָה, נָגִילָה וְנִשְׂמְחָה בוֹ: זֶה הַיּוֹם עָשָׂה יְהֹוָה, נָגִילָה וְנִשְׂמְחָה בוֹ:

There are voices of rejoicing and salvation in the tents of the righteous — We see that this is the sequence of things regarding wars which are fought by the righteous: Before entering battle, they raise their *voices* in prayer. Immediately afterwards, as they enter the fray, they *rejoice* for they are certain that Hashem will hear their prayers, and help them to destroy the evil. Finally, there comes *salvation*, complete victory. (Vilna Gaon)

From Hashem this came; it is a miracle in our eyes — This refers to the verse in *Shir haShirim* (3:6): *Who is this coming out of the wilderness...perfumed with myrrh and frankincense?* For so long, we had been slaves, toiling day in and day out with brick and mortar. Now we were in the desert, and suddenly we were organized into four mighty camps, surrounding an ark containing the tablets of God! We wondered to ourselves, "Is this really us?" A Divine Voice answered, righteous: "Hashem's right Hand does valiantly! Hashem's right Hand is triumphant! Hashem's right Hand does valiantly!" No, I will not be killed. For I will live to recount the deeds of Hashem. Hashem has surely chastened me with suffering, but He has not given me over to death. Open for me the gates of righteousness, and I will enter them and thank Hashem. This is the Gate of Hashem! The righteous shall come through it!

I GIVE THANKS to You, for You have answered me, and this has been salvation. I give thanks to You, for You have answered me, and this has been salvation. The stone that the builders rejected became the cornerstone. The stone that the builders rejected became the cornerstone. From Hashem this came; it is a miracle in our eyes. From Hashem this came; it is a miracle in our eyes. This day is a creation of Hashem. Let us be glad and rejoice in Him! This day is a creation of Hashem. Let us be glad and rejoice in Him!

From Hashem this came! (*Yalkut Shimoni, Tehillim 876*)

This day is a creation of Hashem. Let us be glad and rejoice in Him! — All the past redemptions were followed by exiles and subjugations, but *this day* — the day of the Final Redemption — will be different. (*Ibid*)

This day — The day of the Ultimate Redemption, the day of our rejoicing.
Is a creation of Hashem — Hashem made it long ago, and has had it waiting in front of Him ever since, for everything miraculous, everything that supercedes the bounds of nature, was created when the world itself was created! (*Maharal*)

If there are at least three males of bar-mitzvah age at the Seder, the leader first says the first of the following lines by himself, and the others repeat after him. So, too, the second, third, and fourth line. If there are not three males of this age, each person says each of the four lines twice:

אָנָּא יְהֹוָה הוֹשִׁיעָה נָּא:

אָנָּא יְהֹוָה הוֹשִׁיעָה נָּא:

אָנָּא יְהֹוָה הַצְלִיחָה נָּא:

אָנָּא יְהֹוָה הַצְלִיחָה נָּא:

בָּרוּךְ הַבָּא בְּשֵׁם יְהֹוָה, בֵּרַכְנוּכֶם מִבֵּית יְהֹוָה: בָּרוּךְ הַבָּא בְּשֵׁם יְהֹוָה, בֵּרַכְנוּכֶם מִבֵּית יְהֹוָה: אֵל יְהֹוָה וַיָּאֶר לָנוּ, אִסְרוּ חַג בַּעֲבֹתִים, עַד קַרְנוֹת הַמִּזְבֵּחַ: אֵל יְהֹוָה וַיָּאֶר לָנוּ, אִסְרוּ חַג בַּעֲבֹתִים, עַד קַרְנוֹת הַמִּזְבֵּחַ: אֵלִי אַתָּה וְאוֹדֶךָּ, אֱלֹהַי אֲרוֹמְמֶךָּ: אֵלִי אַתָּה וְאוֹדֶךָּ, אֱלֹהַי אֲרוֹמְמֶךָּ: הוֹדוּ לַיהֹוָה כִּי טוֹב, כִּי לְעוֹלָם חַסְדּוֹ: הוֹדוּ לַיהֹוָה כִּי טוֹב, כִּי לְעוֹלָם חַסְדּוֹ:

Thank Hashem for He is good

This psalm contains praises to Hashem for many different things — for the wonders of nature that He created, how He sustains and nourishes everything in His world, and how He does wonders which run counter to the "fixed" laws of nature. Because the psalm praises God from so many perspectives, it is called *Hallel haGadol* — the "Great" *Hallel*. Twenty-six times, the verse says: *For His kindness endures forever*; and twenty-six is the numerical equivalent of the four-letter name of Hashem!

If there are at least three males of bar-mitzvah age at the Seder, the leader first says the first of the following lines by himself, and the others repeat after him. So, too, the second, third, and fourth line. If there are not three males of this age, each person says each of the four lines twice:

We plead to You, Hashem, save us!

We plead to You, Hashem, save us!

We plead to You, Hashem, grant us success!

We plead to You, Hashem, grant us success!

BLESSED BE THE ONE who comes in Hashem's Name. We bless you from the House of Hashem! Blessed be the one who comes in Hashem's Name. We bless you from the House of Hashem! Hashem is All-Mighty, and He will bring us light. Tie the festival offering with ropes until the corners of the altar! Hashem is All-Mighty, and He will bring us light. Tie the festival offering with ropes until the corners of the altar! You are my God, and I will thank You. You are my God, and I will extol You! You are my God, and I will thank You. You are my God, and I will extol You! Thank Hashem for He is Good, for His kindness endures forever! Thank Hashem for He is Good, for His kindness endures forever!

R. Yochanan explained (*Pesachim* 118a) that the name *Hallel ha-Gadol* actually means "*Hallel* to the Great One." Why is this psalm called *Hallel haGadol*? R. Yochanan said, "Because it states: *He Who gives bread to all flesh...* the Holy One sits on high and sends an appropriate portion of nourishment to every creature."

Hallel haGadol was put into the Haggadah primarily because the *Gaonim* proposed a fifth cup of wine, to correspond to the fifth promise that God made to the Jews in Egypt (*Shemos* 6:8): *And I will bring you into the land.* Stated after the four other expressions of redemption, this promise is tied intimately to the fact that God *gives bread to*

הוֹדוּ לַיהוָה כִּי טוֹב	כִּי לְעוֹלָם חַסְדּוֹ:
הוֹדוּ לֵאלֹהֵי הָאֱלֹהִים	כִּי לְעוֹלָם חַסְדּוֹ:
הוֹדוּ לַאֲדֹנֵי הָאֲדֹנִים	כִּי לְעוֹלָם חַסְדּוֹ:
לְעֹשֵׂה נִפְלָאוֹת גְּדֹלוֹת לְבַדּוֹ	כִּי לְעוֹלָם חַסְדּוֹ:

all flesh, for the Nation's sustenance was to be supplied specifically from the Land of Israel, the land that was aflow with "milk and honey."

In truth, the praise that we give to Hashem for His feeding all His creations is higher and greater than the praise that we give Him for sending us the redemption; sustaining "all flesh" is a continual accomplishment and feat, while the redemption was begun and completed just once, over a limited span of time. Therefore, true to the pattern of speaking in which we say, "Not only this, but also that," the psalm mentions first the smaller praise: *And delivered us from our oppressors*. Afterwards, it "builds up" to the higher praise: *Who gives bread to all flesh.*

Our Sages taught, in fact, that providing a person with his sustenance is, so to speak, more "difficult" for God than saving the person from trouble. An indication of this comes from what Yaakov *Avinu* said on his deathbed, regarding being saved from troubles throughout his life: told his son Yosef that an "angel" of God was able to do this for him (*Bereshis* 48:16). As for having his sustenance provided for him all his life, Yaakov *Avinu* said that this, only God Himself was able to do! (*Ibid*) Sustenance, provided constantly for the whole world, comes from a "higher" place, being sent by God alone, Whose four-letter Name connotes "Was, Is, and Always Will Be" — *His kindness endures forever [constantly]*!

Our custom is to say *Hallel haGadol* over the fourth cup. On the other hand, we do acknowledge the opinion of the *Gaonim*, for we say *Hallel haGadol* over a fifth cup, as well — the cup of the Prophet Eliyahu. According to tradition, Eliyahu is actually Pinchas *haKohen*, who did not really die, having received a "covenant of peace and life"

Thank Hashem for He is Good,   *for His kindness endures forever.*
Thank the God of gods,   *for His kindness endures forever.*
Thank the Master of masters,   *for His kindness endures forever.*
Who does great wonders on
His own,   *for His kindness endures forever.*

as a reward for his courageous act for the sake of Heaven. In his merit, may we, too, be sustained with abundant blessing, and may we merit continuing life in prosperity and peace.

📖

Thank Hashem for He is Good, for His kindness endures forever — Rabbi Yehoshua ben Levi said: Thank the One Who collects His debts from us in kindness (i.e., in such a way that the payments are not too difficult to make). [That is, if someone sins and must suffer a financial loss in order to gain atonement, then] someone wealthy pays with his ox, the less wealthy with his sheep, the widow with her hen, the orphan with his egg.

He also said, "It says specifically twenty-six times: *for His kindness endures forever.* Why? Because He did not give His Torah until twenty-six generations has passed since He created the world. All those generations were sustained only because *His kindness endures forever. (Pesachim* 118a)

📖

Who does great wonders on His own — The words *on His own* would seem to be superfluous, for Hashem does not need anyone's assistance to do anything! Rather, the intention is that He does great wonders without anyone else knowing. For example, someone is lying in bed. Although he is totally unaware of it, a snake is coiled on the ground below him. He starts to get out of bed, and suddenly, as if for no reason, the snake slithers away in fear! The person never even sees the snake! Who knows that there was a miracle? Only Hashem! Even the beneficiary of the miracle does not appreciate it, for it is written, *He Who does great wonders on His own. (Yalkut Shimoni, Tehillim* 883)

לְעֹשֵׂה הַשָּׁמַיִם בִּתְבוּנָה	כִּי לְעוֹלָם חַסְדּוֹ:
לְרוֹקַע הָאָרֶץ עַל הַמָּיִם	כִּי לְעוֹלָם חַסְדּוֹ:
לְעֹשֵׂה אוֹרִים גְּדֹלִים	כִּי לְעוֹלָם חַסְדּוֹ:
אֶת הַשֶּׁמֶשׁ לְמֶמְשֶׁלֶת בַּיּוֹם	כִּי לְעוֹלָם חַסְדּוֹ:
אֶת הַיָּרֵחַ וְכוֹכָבִים לְמֶמְשְׁלוֹת בַּלָּיְלָה	כִּי לְעוֹלָם חַסְדּוֹ:
לְמַכֵּה מִצְרַיִם בִּבְכוֹרֵיהֶם	כִּי לְעוֹלָם חַסְדּוֹ:
וַיּוֹצֵא יִשְׂרָאֵל מִתּוֹכָם	כִּי לְעוֹלָם חַסְדּוֹ:
בְּיָד חֲזָקָה וּבִזְרוֹעַ נְטוּיָה	כִּי לְעוֹלָם חַסְדּוֹ:
לְגֹזֵר יַם סוּף לִגְזָרִים	כִּי לְעוֹלָם חַסְדּוֹ:
וְהֶעֱבִיר יִשְׂרָאֵל בְּתוֹכוֹ	כִּי לְעוֹלָם חַסְדּוֹ:

Who struck the Egyptians with their firstborn — Egypt had prior warning about the tenth plague, for Moshe *Rabbenu* had told Pharaoh himself (*Shemos* 11:4-5), in Hashem's Name, *Approximately at midnight...every firstborn will die.* Immediately, the firstborn of Egypt went to plead before their fathers, "Everything that Moshe has said thus far has come to be! Don't you want us to live? Come, let us get those Jews out of our midst, for if not we are going to die!"

The fathers replied, "Even if we all die, the Jews are not going out!"

What did the firstborn do? They went in and faced Pharaoh, and pleaded to him, "We beg of you, let that nation leave Egypt now, lest evil befall us and you!" Pharaoh would not listen, however, and commanded his servants, "Throw these insolent ones out, and take a strap to their backs!"

The firstborn ran out. Each one gathered a sword in his hand and slew his own father, as is written, *Who struck the Egyptians with their*

Who, with wisdom, makes the heavens,	for His kindness endures forever.
Who stretches the land upon the waters,	for His kindness endures forever.
Who makes the great lights,	for His kindness endures forever.
The sun, to reign in the day,	for His kindness endures forever.
The moon and the stars to reign at night,	for His kindness endures forever.
Who struck the Egyptians with their firstborn,	for His kindness endures forever.
And took Israel out from their midst,	for His kindness endures forever.
With a strong Hand and an outstretched Arm,	for His kindness endures forever.
Who cut the Sea of Reeds into slices,	for His kindness endures forever.
And crossed Israel through it,	for His kindness endures forever.

firstborn. It does not say, "Who struck the firstborn of Egypt," although Hashem did that, too! Rather, 600,000 Egyptians were slain by their own firstborn! (*Yalkut Shimoni, Tehillim*)

Who cut the Sea of Reeds into slices — The Midrash says that God carved twelve separate pathways into the sea, in order that each of the Twelve Tribes would have a path of its own. Why did Hashem perform the miracle this way? To teach us that each tribe was important enough that the sea should be made to split for its sake alone! Moreover, each individual Jew was important enough! Thus, it says in *Tehillim* (74:13): *You with Your Power crumbled the sea to pieces* — as every crumb is part of the whole, every Jew had a part in the miracle! And God has blessed the Jewish People, that we be as "the stars in the heavens" and "the sands of the seas." That is, each Jew has been blessed to have his own portion in the land, the sea, and also the heavens, and these three comprise all the creation! (*Sefas Emes*)

וַיְנַעֵר פַּרְעֹה וְחֵילוֹ בְיַם סוּף	כִּי לְעוֹלָם חַסְדּוֹ:
לְמוֹלִיךְ עַמּוֹ בַּמִּדְבָּר	כִּי לְעוֹלָם חַסְדּוֹ:
לְמַכֵּה מְלָכִים גְּדֹלִים	כִּי לְעוֹלָם חַסְדּוֹ:
וַיַּהֲרֹג מְלָכִים אַדִּירִים	כִּי לְעוֹלָם חַסְדּוֹ:
לְסִיחוֹן מֶלֶךְ הָאֱמֹרִי	כִּי לְעוֹלָם חַסְדּוֹ:
וּלְעוֹג מֶלֶךְ הַבָּשָׁן	כִּי לְעוֹלָם חַסְדּוֹ:
וְנָתַן אַרְצָם לְנַחֲלָה	כִּי לְעוֹלָם חַסְדּוֹ:
נַחֲלָה לְיִשְׂרָאֵל עַבְדּוֹ	כִּי לְעוֹלָם חַסְדּוֹ:
שֶׁבְּשִׁפְלֵנוּ זָכַר לָנוּ	כִּי לְעוֹלָם חַסְדּוֹ:
וַיִּפְרְקֵנוּ מִצָּרֵינוּ	כִּי לְעוֹלָם חַסְדּוֹ:
נֹתֵן לֶחֶם לְכָל בָּשָׂר	כִּי לְעוֹלָם חַסְדּוֹ:
הוֹדוּ לְאֵל הַשָּׁמָיִם	כִּי לְעוֹלָם חַסְדּוֹ:

Who struck down great kings...and slew mighty rulers...Sichon, king of the Emorites...and Og, king of Bashan...and gave their land as an inheritance...an inheritance for Israel, His servant — The Chida qoutes the Maharash Primo's explanation of these verses:

WHO STRUCK DOWN GREAT KINGS — The kings of Ammon.

AND SLEW MIGHTY RULERS — The kings of Moav. Hashem accomplished this, by means of:

SICHON, KING OF THE EMORITES...AND OG, KING OF BASHAN.

AND GAVE THEIR LAND — The land of Ammon and Moav.

AS AN INHERITANCE — To Sichon and Og. Only afterwards, this land was passed to the Jews:

AN INHERITANCE FOR ISRAEL, HIS SERVANT — That is, Israel could not have taken land from Ammon or Moav through warfare, for

Who flung Pharaoh and his army into the Sea of Reeds,	for His kindness endures forever.
Who led His people through the desert,	for His kindness endures forever.
Who struck down great kings,	for His kindness endures forever.
And slew mighty rulers,	for His kindness endures forever.
Sichon, king of the Emorites,	for His kindness endures forever.
And Og, king of Bashan,	for His kindness endures forever.
And gave their land as an inheritance,	for His kindness endures forever.
An inheritance for Israel, His servant,	for His kindness endures forever.
Who remembered us in our lowest moments,	for His kindness endures forever.
And delivered us from our oppressors,	for His kindness endures forever.
Who gives bread to all flesh,	for His kindness endures forever.
Gives thanks to God in Heaven,	for His kindness endures forever!

God had forbidden this explicitly, saying (*Devarim* 2:18): *Do not harass them or contend with them.* Land which originally belonged to Ammon and Moav was "purified" for Israel when Hashem had it fall to Sichon and Og. Afterwards Hashem gave Sichon and Og into Israel's hand, and the land went to Israel, too!

Sichon, king of the Emorites...and Og, king of Bashan — Our Sages say that Sichon and Og each were mightier than Pharaoh and his armies. Thus, just as the Jews sang at the sea after the drowning of Egypt, they also should have sung after the fall of Sichon and Og. Therefore, King David came along later and sang, *Sichon, king of the Emorites...and Og....*(*Yalkut Shimoni, Tehillim* 883)

נִשְׁמַת כָּל חַי תְּבָרֵךְ אֶת שִׁמְךָ יְהֹוָה אֱלֹהֵינוּ, וְרוּחַ כָּל בָּשָׂר תְּפָאֵר וּתְרוֹמֵם זִכְרְךָ מַלְכֵּנוּ תָּמִיד. מִן הָעוֹלָם וְעַד הָעוֹלָם אַתָּה אֵל. וּמִבַּלְעָדֶיךָ אֵין לָנוּ מֶלֶךְ גּוֹאֵל וּמוֹשִׁיעַ, פּוֹדֶה וּמַצִּיל וּמְפַרְנֵס וְעוֹנֶה וּמְרַחֵם בְּכָל עֵת צָרָה וְצוּקָה. אֵין לָנוּ מֶלֶךְ עוֹזֵר וְסוֹמֵךְ אֶלָּא אָתָּה. אֱלֹהֵי הָרִאשׁוֹנִים וְהָאַחֲרוֹנִים, אֱלוֹהַּ כָּל בְּרִיּוֹת, אֲדוֹן כָּל תּוֹלָדוֹת, הַמְהֻלָּל בְּרֹב הַתִּשְׁבָּחוֹת, הַמְנַהֵג עוֹלָמוֹ בְּחֶסֶד וּבְרִיּוֹתָיו בְּרַחֲמִים. וַיהֹוָה עֵר, הִנֵּה לֹא יָנוּם וְלֹא יִישָׁן, הַמְעוֹרֵר יְשֵׁנִים, וְהַמֵּקִיץ נִרְדָּמִים, וְהַמֵּשִׂיחַ אִלְּמִים וְהַמַּתִּיר אֲסוּרִים, וְהַסּוֹמֵךְ נוֹפְלִים, וְהַזּוֹקֵף כְּפוּפִים, וְהַמְפַעֲנֵחַ נֶעְלָמִים. וּלְךָ לְבַדְּךָ אֲנַחְנוּ מוֹדִים. וְאִלּוּ, פִּינוּ מָלֵא שִׁירָה כַיָּם, וּלְשׁוֹנֵנוּ רִנָּה כַּהֲמוֹן גַּלָּיו, וְשִׂפְתוֹתֵינוּ

From Nishmas until the drinking of the Fourth Cup: Birkas haShir

After *Hallel haGadol* we recite a praise called *Nishmas*, followed by another called *Yishtabach*. These two praises also are said in the morning prayer service on Shabbos (and on holidays), as a final blessing after *Pesukei d'Zimra* — the songs of *Tehillim*, and the Song of the Sea. Because of where they are found in the Shabbos service, the two together are called *Birkas haShir*, which means "the Blessing of the Song." Both on Shabbos and on the Seder night, first *Nishmas* is said, and then *Yishtabach*.

However, *Birkas haShir* on the Seder night differs slightly from *Birkas haShir* on Shabbos. On Shabbos, the second part — *Yishtabach* — ends with, *He Who chooses songs of praise, King, Life of the universe*, while on the Seder night, a different ending is used — the normal ending of *Hallel*: *King Who is extolled with praises*.

The Haggadah uses this particular wording because of a dispute in the Talmud. Accordingly, based on how different commen-

*T*HE SOUL OF *every living thing shall bless Your Name, Hashem, our God; and the spirit in all flesh shall ever glorify and exalt the remembrance of You, our King. From eternity to eternity You are the All-Powerful, and besides You we have no king, redeemer, or savior, to deliver us, save or support us, who has mercy at all times of stress and sorrow. We have no King other than You. God of the first ones and the last ones, You are Lord of all creations, Master of all the generations, extolled with multitudes of praises, Who manages His world with kindness and treats its creatures with mercy. Hashem neither dozes nor sleeps. He awakens sleepers, arouses slumberers, gives speech to the mute, freedom to those in fetters. He upholds those who would fall, straightens the bowed and bent. To You alone do we give thanks!*

tators explain the dispute, the only way to fulfill one's obligation according to all opinions is to say *Birkas haShir* as the Haggadah prescribes. The formula has been generally accepted throughout the generations. (See *Shulchan Aruch, Orach Chayim* 486, *Beis Yosef, Bach* and *Taz*)

Also, one should note that on the Seder night, *Birkas haShir* follows not only *Hallel haGadol*, but also *Hallel*, the former being very similar to *Pesukei d'Zimra*. Thus, it is fitting that *Birkas haShir* end not only with *Yishtabach*, which is the normal ending of *Pesukei d'Zimra*, but also with *King Who is extolled with praises*, which is the normal ending of *Hallel*.

In truth, there are differing opinions on the matter. For example, the Vilna Gaon would take the normal ending of *Hallel*, which is placed, by the Haggadah, at the very end of *Birkas haShir*, and say that ending after *Hallel*, and before *Hallel haGadol*, leaving out the final line, which is a blessing containing Hashem's Name. After *Hallel haGadol*, he would say *Nishmas*, just as the Haggadah prescribes, but he would say *Yishtabach* afterwards in its entirety, just as the two are said on Shabbos. Many, in fact, follow the custom of the Vilna Gaon.

Birkas haShir — the blessing of the song

Birkas haShir is said at three different times: in the weekday morning prayer service; in the prayer service of Shabbos morning; and on the Seder night, as part of the Haggadah. However, each time it is said in a slightly different way. Compared to weekdays, the form that *Birkas haShir* takes on Shabbos is more exalted, and on the Seder night it is found in the most exalted form of all.

On weekdays, *Birkas haShir* which follows *Pesukei d'Zimra* and the Song of the Sea, and is actually a blessing on them, consists only of *Yishtabach*, and ends by saying of Hashem that *He chooses songs of praise*.

On Shabbos, as well, *Birkas haShir* is an afterblessing on *Pesukei d'Zimra* and the Song of the Sea, and its ending is the same as on weekdays. However, it is more than doubled in length, and also is much more exalted, for it contains the sublime praise of *Nishmas*, prior to *Yishtabach*.

On the Seder night, *Birkas haShir* is in the same form as on Shabbos, except for one change which elevates its sanctity even more: Near the end of *Yishtabach*, the blessing deletes the normal ending of *Yishtabach* and uses in its stead the normal ending of *Hallel* — *King Who is extolled with praises*.

We can provide a very satisfying explanation for these changes in *Birkas haShir* — the Blessing of the Song. Really, all human beings should sing praises to Hashem, every day, as the angels do. Unfortunately, however, the nations of the world do not recognize Hashem as King, Creator, and Sustainer of everything. The Egypt of long ago was brought to recognize Hashem, as it is written (*Shemos* 14:18): *And Egypt shall know that I am Hashem*.

Nevertheless, many generations have passed since the Exodus, and the Egyptians have forgotten what happened to their forefathers. The same is true of other nations whose forefathers saw the Hand of Hashem. What was once known has become forgotten, so that the only nation that remains who recognizes Hashem is Israel. During the week, however, Israel is preoccupied with having to make a living, and we cannot trouble them to say their praises to

Hashem at length, and certainly we cannot ask them to bring along others to join in the praise that they say.

Shabbos, however, is a day of rest, and there is time to praise God, as is fitting. Thus, in the morning prayer, we add *Nishmas*, inviting the souls of all living things to join us. It is appropriate that all living things should sing praises to God on Shabbos, for Shabbos commemorates the Creation, that in six days God created everything that exists, and on the Seventh Day, He "rested." Should not every creation praise its Creator? On the other hand, the ending of *Yishtabach* is the same as on weekdays — *He Who chooses songs of praise* — for still, almost the entire world is living in error, and even among those who do sing praises to Hashem, not all hearts are one, and there is a great variation in sincerity. Thus, even on Shabbos, *Birkas haShir* says that Hashem "chooses" which songs of praise are pleasing to Him — which ones will actually come before Him, and which ones will not.

The Seder night is also called "Shabbos," for we see in the Torah (*Vayikra* 23:11) that the second day of Pesach is called *the day after the Shabbos*. What is more, the Seder night is the centerpiece of Pesach — the night that shines as day, which is why *Hallel* can be said at the Seder, even though normally *Hallel* is said only during the daylight hours. This is the night of the tenth plague, which completed the redemption of our People from Egypt. This is the night when every Jew and every Egyptian had clear knowledge of Hashem, and all recognized that there is none other like Him, He is One, and that thanks and praise are to be given to Him. On this night, all hearts were one regarding this, and thus all the praises that were said to Him were equally sincere and pleasing to Hashem, and all were accepted before Him.

In remembrance of that night, we conclude *Birkas haShir* just the way that *Hallel* is concluded — for *Hallel* is about the redemption of the future, when all hearts will achieve understanding, and every mouth will speak the truth. The ending of *Hallel* is *King Who is extolled with praises* — for then, it will not be necessary to "choose" between one person's praise and another's, since every creature's recognition of Hashem will be complete, and all praise for Him will be pure and will be accepted.

In the bright future that awaits us, *Birkas haShir* always will be said this way, even on weekdays, by every nation of the world — the way we say it on the Seder night, over the fourth cup of wine. We say it after *Hallel*, which speaks about the Future Redemption. We say it after *Pour out Your wrath*, where we ask Hashem to speed us that Redemption!

On this night, *Birkas haShir* is a blessing to the *King Who is extolled with praises* for although the *Mashiach* and Eliyahu have not yet come, we feel in our hearts that they are here, as if the Redemption had already arrived!

The soul of every living thing — Each human being has a "soul of life" in him, given to him by God, and this allows him to know God "by Name." Thus, *The soul of every living thing shall bless Your Name*.

And the spirit in all flesh — All other live creatures have "spirit," but they are lacking the "soul of life." As a result, they cannot recognize Your "Name," but they are able to possess a remembrance of You — and know that You created them, as well as keep them alive and give them their sustenance. Therefore, they glorify and exalt *the remembrance of You*.

From eternity — Before anything was created.

Until eternity — And after everything is gone.

And besides You, we have no King, redeemer, or savior — That is, though Your existence is not at all dependent upon ours, our existence is totally dependent upon Yours.

We have no King other than You — Even should You decide not to provide all our needs.

God of the first ones — The first man and woman, who did not have parents to praise You or speak of You.

And the last ones — The world's final generation, which will not bear children to praise You or speak of You. Nevertheless, the first ones praised You themselves, and so will the last ones! All the more so do we, for we have heard our fathers speak of Your powers and Your wonders, and so, too, shall we speak of these things to our children — such are the words of *the soul of every living thing*.

Lord of all creations — At the time that all the animal species were first formed, they did not yet have offspring.

Master of all the generations — Up to the last generation of animals, which, as the first generation, also will not have offspring. Still, they, too, will praise Your "remembrance." Certainly, then, do we, the animals of all the generations in between praise You, for we are offspring who have offspring, and thus we recognize the greatness of Your deeds — Your "remembrance" — even more — such are the words of *the spirit of all flesh*.

📖

Extolled with multitudes of praises — Not only do all the multitudes praise him, but also, each creation and each person himself has a multitude of praises to say to Hashem! All say that Hashem *manages His world* — which itself has neither sins nor merits — *with kindness*, and *treats His creatures*, even those that sin, *with mercy*, as a father has mercy on his children, for they are his making. This, in fact, is His greatest kindness — for even though they anger Him, He does not reject them or cut them off, even for a moment. Rather, He continues to sustain them, at all times, and awaits their return to Him.

📖

Hashem neither dozes nor sleeps — For if, God forbid, Hashem were to not "pay attention" to the world for even a split second — that is, if He were to "fall asleep" — all existence would revert to nothingness, as if nothing had ever existed at all. Also, Hashem *awakens sleepers, arouses slumberers* — He renews the creation every moment.

📖

To You alone do we give thanks — And not to any angel, seraph, or any other spiritual being among Your hosts in heaven. Even though we know that our thanks are inadequate, and we are not able to sing as would be fitting, we nevertheless want to thank you and praise you appropriately, for even *were our mouths as full of song as the sea...were our eyes to shine like the sun...* — from the song bursting from our hearts and mouths; *were our arms outspread as the wings of eagles* — in thanks; *were our feet as swift as gazelles'* — to skip and dance before You; *we still would not be able to thank You sufficiently* — for what You did for us in the past. All the more so is it impossible for us to start to thank You for the great kindnesses that You have promised us for the future.

שֶׁבַח כְּמֶרְחֲבֵי רָקִיעַ, וְעֵינֵינוּ מְאִירוֹת כַּשֶּׁמֶשׁ וְכַיָּרֵחַ, וְיָדֵינוּ פְרוּשׂוֹת כְּנִשְׁרֵי שָׁמַיִם, וְרַגְלֵינוּ קַלּוֹת כָּאַיָּלוֹת. אֵין אֲנַחְנוּ מַסְפִּיקִים לְהוֹדוֹת לְךָ יְהֹוָה אֱלֹהֵינוּ וֵאלֹהֵי אֲבוֹתֵינוּ, וּלְבָרֵךְ אֶת שִׁמְךָ מַלְכֵּנוּ עַל אַחַת מֵאֶלֶף אֶלֶף אַלְפֵי אֲלָפִים וְרִבֵּי רְבָבוֹת פְּעָמִים, הַטּוֹבוֹת נִסִּים וְנִפְלָאוֹת שֶׁעָשִׂיתָ עִם אֲבוֹתֵינוּ וְעִמָּנוּ. מִלְּפָנִים מִמִּצְרַיִם גְּאַלְתָּנוּ יְהֹוָה אֱלֹהֵינוּ וּמִבֵּית עֲבָדִים פְּדִיתָנוּ, בְּרָעָב זַנְתָּנוּ וּבְשָׂבָע כִּלְכַּלְתָּנוּ, מֵחֶרֶב הִצַּלְתָּנוּ וּמִדֶּבֶר מִלַּטְתָּנוּ, וּמֵחֳלָיִים רָעִים וְרַבִּים וְנֶאֱמָנִים דִּלִּיתָנוּ. עַד הֵנָּה עֲזָרוּנוּ רַחֲמֶיךָ וְלֹא עֲזָבוּנוּ חֲסָדֶיךָ יְהֹוָה אֱלֹהֵינוּ וְאַל תִּטְּשֵׁנוּ יְהֹוָה אֱלֹהֵינוּ לָנֶצַח.

עַל כֵּן אֵבָרִים שֶׁפִּלַּגְתָּ בָּנוּ, וְרוּחַ וּנְשָׁמָה שֶׁנָּפַחְתָּ בְּאַפֵּנוּ, וְלָשׁוֹן אֲשֶׁר שַׂמְתָּ בְּפִינוּ, הֵן הֵם יוֹדוּ וִיבָרְכוּ וִישַׁבְּחוּ

📖

Please do not forsake us! Forever! — That is to say, *forever* will we be indebted to You Hashem, our God. Never will we be able to repay You for even a fraction of what You have done for us. Thus, what actual difference exists between the inadequate thanks coming from our small lips, and the thanks that come from angels? Neither can come close to reaching the truth!

📖

Therefore — Therefore we will not seek to thank and praise You in a way that is beyond us. What little we can do, however, is also something, and it is better that we know that it is only a little, than for us to imagine that we are meeting our obligation. It really is impossible for

Were our mouths as full as the sea with song, and were our tongues as full of music as its multitude of waves; were our lips opened with praise as wide as the sky, were our eyes to shine like the sun and the moon; were our arms outspread like the wings of eagles, were our feet as swift as gazelles'; we still would not be able to thank You sufficiently, Hashem our God, God of our fathers, and we could not fittingly bless Your Name, for even one thousandth of the countless millions of favors that You have done for our fathers and for us! You redeemed us from Egypt, Hashem our God, and You delivered us from the house of bondage. When there was hunger, You fed us. When there was plenty, You sustained us. You rescued us from the sword, led us in escape from pestilence, and spared us from serious and lasting illness. Until now, Your mercy has always helped us, and Your kindness has never abandoned us. Hashem, our God, please do not forsake us! Forever!

Therefore, with the limbs that you have allotted us, and the soul and spirit that You have breathed into our nostrils, and with the

us to give You the praise and thanks that You deserve, but small as we are, we can do our best.

📖

Therefore, with the limbs that You have allotted us — Even the smallest of them. All of our parts, down to the tiniest hairs that are found on our bodies, will be full of praise and thanks for You, which will reach them from our hearts, as life-giving water flows from the source of a river to all the tiny tributaries! This is as it should be, for You have allotted us our limbs, even the smallest ones!

And the soul and spirit — As they are, for we did not make them, but:
That You have breathed into our nostrils — You gave us these!

וִיפָאֲרוּ וִישׁוֹרְרוּ וִירוֹמְמוּ וְיַעֲרִיצוּ וְיַקְדִּישׁוּ וְיַמְלִיכוּ אֶת שִׁמְךָ מַלְכֵּנוּ תָּמִיד. כִּי כָל פֶּה לְךָ יוֹדֶה, וְכָל לָשׁוֹן לְךָ תִשָּׁבַע, וְכָל עַיִן לְךָ תְצַפֶּה, וְכָל בֶּרֶךְ לְךָ תִכְרַע, וְכָל קוֹמָה לְפָנֶיךָ תִשְׁתַּחֲוֶה. וְכָל הַלְּבָבוֹת יִירָאוּךָ, וְכָל קֶרֶב וּכְלָיוֹת יְזַמְּרוּ לִשְׁמֶךָ. כַּדָּבָר שֶׁכָּתוּב, כָּל עַצְמֹתַי תֹּאמַרְנָה יְהֹוָה מִי כָמוֹךָ. מַצִּיל עָנִי מֵחָזָק מִמֶּנּוּ וְעָנִי וְאֶבְיוֹן מִגֹּזְלוֹ. שַׁוְעַת עֲנִיִּים אַתָּה תִשְׁמַע צַעֲקַת הַדַּל תַּקְשִׁיב וְתוֹשִׁיעַ. מִי יִדְמֶה לָּךְ וּמִי יִשְׁוֶה לָּךְ וּמִי יַעֲרָךְ לָךְ. הָאֵל הַגָּדוֹל הַגִּבּוֹר וְהַנּוֹרָא אֵל עֶלְיוֹן קֹנֵה שָׁמַיִם וָאָרֶץ: נְהַלֶּלְךָ וּנְשַׁבֵּחֲךָ וּנְפָאֶרְךָ וּנְבָרֵךְ אֶת שֵׁם קָדְשֶׁךָ. כָּאָמוּר, לְדָוִד, בָּרְכִי נַפְשִׁי אֶת יְהֹוָה וְכָל קְרָבַי אֶת שֵׁם קָדְשׁוֹ:

And with the tongue that You have put in our mouths — simply with these shall we thank You and bless You — For these are the work of Your Hands! Therefore, we are not ashamed to use them to praise and thank You.

For every — Even though everything about us is inadequate to the task, nevertheless, this is what we have, and we give "everything" to You — *every mouth* — and all of one's mouth; *every tongue* — and all of one's tongue; *every knee* — and all of one's knee; *and all hearts* —

tongue that You have put in our mouths — simply with these shall we thank You and bless You, and praise, glorify, extol and revere, hallow and pay homage to Your Name, our King. For every mouth shall one day thank You, every tongue shall swear in Your Name. Every knee shall bend to You, and every person shall bow to the ground. And all hearts shall have fear and awe of You, and the innermost being of all men shall sing praises to Your Name, as it is written, "All my being shall say, O Lord, Who is like You?" (Tehillim 35:10), Who saves the poor from the one who is stronger, the poor and needy from the one who would rob them. Who resembles You? Who could be like You? Who could even compare to You — O Great, Mighty and Revered God, Supreme Lord, Master of the heavens and earth! We shall praise You, glorify You and laud You, and bless Your holy Name, as is said by David, "Bless Hashem, O my soul. Let my entire being bless His holy Name" (Tehillim 103:1).

our good inclination is one "heart" and our evil inclination is our second "heart." Both hearts will be given over completely to You, in fear and awe!

And the innermost being of all men — Nothing will be held back! Each part of us, in its entirety, *shall sing praises to Your Name, as it is written: All my being shall say* — until the living waters shall reach to even the smallest "tributaries" of our being! Thus, *All my being shall say, O, Lord, Who is like You? Who saves the poor...* — Our entire constitution expresses praise and gratitude!

הָאֵל בְּתַעֲצֻמוֹת עֻזֶּךָ, הַגָּדוֹל בִּכְבוֹד שְׁמֶךָ, הַגִּבּוֹר לָנֶצַח וְהַנּוֹרָא בְּנוֹרְאוֹתֶיךָ. הַמֶּלֶךְ הַיּוֹשֵׁב עַל כִּסֵּא רָם וְנִשָּׂא:

שׁוֹכֵן עַד מָרוֹם וְקָדוֹשׁ שְׁמוֹ. וְכָתוּב, רַנְּנוּ צַדִּיקִים בַּיהוָה לַיְשָׁרִים נָאוָה תְהִלָּה: בְּפִי יְשָׁרִים תִּתְרוֹמָם: וּבְשִׂפְתֵי צַדִּיקִים תִּתְבָּרַךְ: וּבִלְשׁוֹן חֲסִידִים תִּתְקַדָּשׁ: וּבְקֶרֶב קְדוֹשִׁים תִּתְהַלָּל:

וּבְמַקְהֲלוֹת רִבְבוֹת עַמְּךָ בֵּית יִשְׂרָאֵל בְּרִנָּה יִתְפָּאֵר שִׁמְךָ מַלְכֵּנוּ בְּכָל דּוֹר וָדוֹר, שֶׁכֵּן חוֹבַת כָּל הַיְצוּרִים, לְפָנֶיךָ יְהוָה אֱלֹהֵינוּ וֵאלֹהֵי אֲבוֹתֵינוּ, לְהוֹדוֹת לְהַלֵּל לְשַׁבֵּחַ לְפָאֵר לְרוֹמֵם לְהַדֵּר לְנַצֵּחַ לְבָרֵךְ לְעַלֵּה וּלְקַלֵּס עַל כָּל דִּבְרֵי שִׁירוֹת וְתִשְׁבְּחוֹת דָּוִד בֶּן יִשַׁי עַבְדְּךָ מְשִׁיחֶךָ:

וּבְכֵן, יִשְׁתַּבַּח שִׁמְךָ לָעַד מַלְכֵּנוּ הָאֵל הַמֶּלֶךְ הַגָּדוֹל וְהַקָּדוֹשׁ בַּשָּׁמַיִם וּבָאָרֶץ. כִּי לְךָ נָאֶה יְהוָה אֱלֹהֵינוּ וֵאלֹהֵי אֲבוֹתֵינוּ. שִׁיר וּשְׁבָחָה הַלֵּל וְזִמְרָה עֹז וּמֶמְשָׁלָה נֶצַח גְּדֻלָּה וּגְבוּרָה תְּהִלָּה וְתִפְאֶרֶת קְדֻשָּׁה וּמַלְכוּת. בְּרָכוֹת וְהוֹדָאוֹת לְשִׁמְךָ הַגָּדוֹל וְהַקָּדוֹשׁ, וּמֵעוֹלָם וְעַד עוֹלָם אַתָּה אֵל:

The All-Mighty God, in the magnitude of Your Strength; the Great One, in the glory of Your Name; the forever Powerful, Instiller of fear through Your awesome deeds — the King, Who sits on high on an exalted throne.

He Who Lives Forever, Holy and Exalted Is His Name! And it is written, "Rejoice, O righteous, in Hashem. It is fitting for the upright to give praise" (Tehillim 33:1). By the mouth of the upright You are praised. With the words of the righteous You are blessed. By the tongues of the faithful You are extolled. And among Your holy ones You are sanctified.

And by the assemblies of Your people, in the tens of thousands, shall Your Name, our King, be glorified in song, by the House of Israel, throughout the generations. For all things that You created have this duty towards You, our God and God of our forefathers, to thank and praise, glorify and laud, extol and honor, bless, exalt and celebrate You, even beyond all the words of song and praise said by David, son of Yishai, Your servant, Your anointed one.

PRAISED BE Your Name forever, our King, great and holy God and King, in heaven and earth; for to You, Hashem our God and God of our fathers, is fitting song and praise, glorification and hymns, strength and dominion, victory, greatness and might, renown and glory, holiness and kingship, blessings and thanks to Your great and holy Name, because for all eternity You are Lord.

יְהַלְלוּךָ יְהֹוָה אֱלֹהֵינוּ כָּל מַעֲשֶׂיךָ, וַחֲסִידֶיךָ צַדִּיקִים עוֹשֵׂי רְצוֹנֶךָ, וְכָל עַמְּךָ בֵּית יִשְׂרָאֵל, בְּרִנָּה יוֹדוּ וִיבָרְכוּ וִישַׁבְּחוּ וִיפָאֲרוּ וִישׁוֹרְרוּ וִירוֹמְמוּ וְיַעֲרִיצוּ וְיַקְדִּישׁוּ וְיַמְלִיכוּ אֶת שִׁמְךָ מַלְכֵּנוּ תָּמִיד. כִּי לְךָ טוֹב לְהוֹדוֹת וּלְשִׁמְךָ נָאֶה לְזַמֵּר, כִּי מֵעוֹלָם וְעַד עוֹלָם אַתָּה אֵל: בָּרוּךְ אַתָּה יְהֹוָה מֶלֶךְ מְהֻלָּל בַּתִּשְׁבָּחוֹת:

The blessing over wine is said for the last time this night.
Then everyone drinks the fourth cup of wine, leaning
on the left side. Some say:

הִנְנִי מוּכָן וּמְזוּמָן לְקַיֵּם מִצְוַת כּוֹס רְבִיעִי שֶׁל אַרְבַּע כּוֹסוֹת.

בָּרוּךְ אַתָּה יְהֹוָה אֱלֹהֵינוּ מֶלֶךְ הָעוֹלָם בּוֹרֵא פְּרִי הַגָּפֶן:

All Your works shall praise You, Hashem our God — That is, all the nations of the world.

And Your pious ones — The pious of Israel, and the pious of the other nations. Afterwards, the verse says *and the righteous*, but here it is not "the" but "Your" pious ones — for their good deeds are known only to You, as our Sages say, "Who is considered pious? He who does kindness with His Creator," i.e., alone — without the involvement or knowledge of anyone else.

ALL YOUR WORKS shall praise You, Hashem our God; and Your pious ones, and the righteous who do Your Will. So, too, Your entire nation, the House of Israel, will joyfully thank and bless You, laud and honor You, exalt, revere, sanctify and pay homage to Your Name, our King. For it is good to thank You, and fitting to sing praises to Your Name, because for all eternity You are Lord. Blessed are You, Hashem, King Who is extolled with praises.

The blessing over wine is said for the last time this night. Then everyone drinks the fourth cup of wine, leaning on the left side. Some say:

Here I am, ready and willing to fulfill the mitzvah of drinking the fourth cup of the Four Cups.

*B*LESSED ARE YOU, Hashem our God, King of the universe, Who creates the fruit of the vine.

All Your works shall praise You...So, too, Your entire nation, the House of Israel, will joyfully thank and bless You, laud and honor You, exalt, revere, sanctify, and pay homage to Your Name, our King. For it is good to thank You, fitting to sing praises to Your Name — This ending of *Birkas haShir* contains ten different expressions of praise and thanks. The Maharal points out that in the Haggadah text, after we finish telling the story of the Exodus, before we begin the first part of *Hallel*, the same expressions are used: *Therefore, it is our duty to laud,*

After drinking the fourth cup, the following blessing is said:

בָּרוּךְ אַתָּה יְהֹוָה אֱלֹהֵינוּ מֶלֶךְ הָעוֹלָם עַל הַגֶּפֶן וְעַל פְּרִי הַגֶּפֶן וְעַל תְּנוּבַת הַשָּׂדֶה וְעַל אֶרֶץ חֶמְדָּה טוֹבָה וּרְחָבָה שֶׁרָצִיתָ וְהִנְחַלְתָּ לַאֲבוֹתֵינוּ לֶאֱכֹל מִפִּרְיָהּ וְלִשְׂבֹּעַ מִטּוּבָהּ. רַחֶם נָא יְהֹוָה אֱלֹהֵינוּ עַל יִשְׂרָאֵל עַמֶּךָ וְעַל יְרוּשָׁלַיִם עִירֶךָ וְעַל צִיּוֹן מִשְׁכַּן כְּבוֹדֶךָ וְעַל מִזְבְּחֶךָ וְעַל הֵיכָלֶךָ. וּבְנֵה יְרוּשָׁלַיִם עִיר הַקֹּדֶשׁ בִּמְהֵרָה בְיָמֵינוּ וְהַעֲלֵנוּ לְתוֹכָהּ וְשַׂמְּחֵנוּ בְּבִנְיָנָהּ וְנֹאכַל מִפִּרְיָהּ וְנִשְׂבַּע מִטּוּבָהּ וּנְבָרֶכְךָ עָלֶיהָ בִּקְדֻשָּׁה וּבְטָהֳרָה. (בשבת: וּרְצֵה וְהַחֲלִיצֵנוּ בְּיוֹם הַשַּׁבָּת הַזֶּה) וְשַׂמְּחֵנוּ בְּיוֹם חַג הַמַּצּוֹת הַזֶּה. כִּי אַתָּה יְהֹוָה טוֹב וּמֵטִיב לַכֹּל וְנוֹדֶה לְּךָ עַל הָאָרֶץ וְעַל פְּרִי הַגָּפֶן: בָּרוּךְ אַתָּה יְהֹוָה עַל הָאָרֶץ וְעַל פְּרִי הַגֶּפֶן (בא"י: גַּפְנָהּ):

praise, thank, honor, exalt, etc. In both cases, the ten different expressions correspond to the ten different ways in which psalms are begun in the *Book of Tehillim*.

The matter is understood if we note that, in essence, the *Book of Tehillim* is one great praise and thanks to *the King Who is extolled with praises*. *Hallel* is the same, but much shorter. Thus, by ending *Hallel* with the ten expressions, and by using this ending here in the Haggadah, we state our hope that every *Hallel* we say, including the Seder night's, shall rise up and be accepted before our King, as if we have said all the praises and thanks given by the sweet singer of Israel

After drinking the fourth cup, the following blessing is said:

𝑩LESSED ARE YOU, Hashem our God, King of the Universe, for the vine and for the fruit of the vine, and for the produce of the field, and for the desirable, goodly, and expansive land that pleased You to give as an inheritance to our forefathers, to eat of its fruit and be satiated through its good. Have mercy, Hashem our God, on Your People Israel, on Your city Jerusalem, on Zion the dwelling-place of Your Glory, on Your altar and Your Sanctuary. Rebuild Your holy city Jerusalem, soon, in our days. And allow us to go up to it, and rejoice in its reconstruction. And we will eat of its fruit, and be satiated through its good, and we will bless You for it in holiness and purity. [*On Shabbos add:* May it be Your Will to give us strength on this Shabbos.] And we will rejoice over this Festival of Matzos, for You are Hashem, Who is good and does good to all, and we thank You for the Land and for the fruit of the vine. Blessed are You, Hashem, for the Land and for the fruit of the vine. [*If the wine was made in the Land of Israel, then say:* for the Land and for the fruit of its vines.]

in the the entire *Book of Tehillim*!

For it is good to thank You — Good for us, that is. You, however, have no need at all for our thanks, for the concept of "needs" is not even pertinent to You.

Fitting to sing praises to Your Name — And as we sing them, we distinguish between You and us, making it clear that *for all eternity You are Lord*, while we are but a passing shadow! Still, You grant us permission to sing Your praises, and thereby we have some connection to Your Eternal Self and Your blessing. *Blessed are You, Hashem, King who is extolled with praises!*

נִרְצָה

חֲסַל סִדּוּר פֶּסַח כְּהִלְכָתוֹ כְּכָל מִשְׁפָּטוֹ וְחֻקָּתוֹ. כַּאֲשֶׁר זָכִינוּ לְסַדֵּר אוֹתוֹ. כֵּן נִזְכֶּה לַעֲשׂוֹתוֹ. זָךְ שׁוֹכֵן מְעוֹנָה. קוֹמֵם קְהַל עֲדַת מִי מָנָה. בְּקָרוֹב נַהֵל נִטְעֵי כַנָּה. פְּדוּיִים לְצִיּוֹן בְּרִנָּה:

Three times:

לְשָׁנָה הַבָּאָה בִּירוּשָׁלָיִם:

Next year in Jerusalem! — Only twice a year does the nation of Israel say this prayer. Both times we say it in unison, in a loud and joyous voice — now, at the end of the holy night of the Seder, and also at the end of the holiest day of the year — Yom Kippur, after the *Ne'ilah* service. We are sworn to remind ourselves of Jerusalem at times of great happiness, as it is written (*Tehillim* 137:6): *May my tongue cling to the roof of my mouth if I do not remember you, if I do not set Jerusalem above my highest joy.*

For the nation as a whole, never is there greater happiness than on the Seder night and on Yom Kippur. At the Pesach Seder, we rejoice both that we were redeemed from our enslavement, and that we escaped Egypt's impurity. So, too, at the close of Yom Kippur, it is redemption that causes us joy — redemption from our sins and transgressions, for Hashem has cleansed us of all of them, and has removed from us all the impurities that stem from them.

Really, the joy that flows from the sanctity of the Seder night is greater than that which comes from Yom Kippur, for on Yom Kippur we attain our holy state by forcibly separating ourselves from food, drink, and from all other needs of the body. On the Seder night, how-

Nirtzeh — Acceptance

ENDED IS THE ORDER of the Pesach Seder, as its laws require — in accordance with all of its statutes and ordinances. Just as we were found worthy to arrange it tonight, may we also be found worthy to do it (i.e., to actually bring the Pesach offering in the future). O Pure One, Who dwells on High, Whose congregation cannot be numbered — cause Your congregation to stand once more! Take in hand the offspring of Your plantings, soon, and lead them back to Zion, redeemed, in joyous song.

Three times:

Next year in Jerusalem!

ever, there is no need for such "forcing." On the contrary, the food and drink themselves bring us to a holy state, for along with the words that we speak about the Exodus — every word being a mitzvah — and together with the songs of praise that we sing, the eating and drinking also are for the sake of mitzvos, and the lack of "forcing" causes our hearts and souls to rejoice even more over our liberation.

By the time each of these two holy days has come to a close, we truly feel ourselves in a state of spiritual ecstasy. It is just at this moment that we take hold of the joy that stems from our souls' redemption, and redirect it, turning it to remember our greatest hope and desire — Jerusalem, the Holy City. If we did not merit the rebuilding of Jerusalem and the Temple this year, we look forward to next year, hoping that then, we will be able to partake of the Pesach offering itself in Jerusalem! So, too, at the end of Yom Kippur, we hope that next year we will merit to again have a *Kohen Gadol* who will perform the entire Yom Kippur service as it used to be performed, when we had the Temple and the Holy of Holies! Next year, may we merit all of this, in Jerusalem!

Outside of the Land of Israel where two Seders are held, this song is sung on the first night:

וּבְכֵן וַיְהִי בַּחֲצִי הַלָּיְלָה

אָז רֹב נִסִּים הִפְלֵאתָ בַּלַּיְלָה.
בְּרֹאשׁ אַשְׁמוֹרֶת זֶה הַלַּיְלָה.
גֵּר צֶדֶק נִצַּחְתּוֹ כְּנֶחֱלַק לוֹ לַיְלָה.
וַיְהִי בַּחֲצִי הַלָּיְלָה:

דַּנְתָּ מֶלֶךְ גְּרָר בַּחֲלוֹם הַלַּיְלָה.
הִפְחַדְתָּ אֲרַמִּי בְּאֶמֶשׁ לַיְלָה.
וַיָּשַׂר יִשְׂרָאֵל לְמַלְאָךְ וַיּוּכַל לוֹ לַיְלָה.
וַיְהִי בַּחֲצִי הַלָּיְלָה:

זֶרַע בְּכוֹרֵי פַתְרוֹס מָחַצְתָּ בַּחֲצִי הַלַּיְלָה.
חֵילָם לֹא מָצְאוּ בְּקוּמָם בַּלַּיְלָה.
טִיסַת נְגִיד חֲרֹשֶׁת סִלִּיתָ בְּכוֹכְבֵי לַיְלָה.
וַיְהִי בַּחֲצִי הַלָּיְלָה:

And now — This is a phraseology used in the prayers of the High Holidays, on Rosh Hashanah and Yom Kippur: *And now, place fear of You...* Regarding the Seder night, we mean to say: Now that all the foregoing is true, and it is just past midnight, let us say all the praises to God that are connected to night-time!

It was then — This is a song to Pesach night, counting out eleven different miracles that Hashem performed, many of them on Pesach itself, in different historical periods, either for chosen individuals or for the Jewish nation as a whole. In the original Hebrew, the first word of

Outside of the Land of Israel where two Seders are held, this song is sung on the first night:

Uv'chen vaYehi baChatzi haLaylah
(*And Now, It Happened at Midnight*)

It was then that You did many wondrous miracles	at night.
At the start of this watch	at night.
To the righteous convert You gave victory	
when his camp he divided	at night.
It happened at midnight!	
You judged the King of Gerar in a dream	at night.
You frightened the Aramean earlier	at night.
And Israel wrestled the angel and bested him	at night.
It happened at midnight!	
You crushed Egypt's firstborn at half of	the night.
They did not find their wealth when they arose	at night.
You dispelled Sisera's armies with the stars	of night.
It happened at midnight!	

the first line begins with the Hebrew letter *aleph*. The first word of the second line begins with the letter *beis* and so on, throughout, so that the entire song is set in the acrostic of the twenty-two letters of the Hebrew alphabet.

The eleven miracles are as follows:

    1. The military victory won by Avraham *Avinu* over Nimrod-Amraphel and the three kings who were allied with him.

    2. The punishment of Avimelech, King of Gerar, for his having caused anguish to Sarah *Immenu*.

    3. Hashem's revealing Himself to Lavan in a dream, and warning him not to harm Yaakov *Avinu*.

יָעֵץ מְחָרֵף לְנוֹפֵף אִוּוּי הוֹבַשְׁתָּ פְגָרָיו בַּלַּיְלָה.
כָּרַע בֵּל וּמַצָּבוֹ בְּאִישׁוֹן לַיְלָה.
לְאִישׁ חֲמוּדוֹת נִגְלָה רָז חֲזוֹת לַיְלָה.
וַיְהִי בַּחֲצִי הַלַּיְלָה:

מִשְׁתַּכֵּר בִּכְלֵי קֹדֶשׁ נֶהֱרַג בּוֹ בַּלַּיְלָה.
נוֹשַׁע מִבּוֹר אֲרָיוֹת פּוֹתֵר בִּעֲתוּתֵי לַיְלָה.
שִׂנְאָה נָטַר אֲגָגִי וְכָתַב סְפָרִים בַּלַּיְלָה.
וַיְהִי בַּחֲצִי הַלַּיְלָה:

עוֹרַרְתָּ נִצְחֲךָ עָלָיו בְּנֶדֶד שְׁנַת לַיְלָה.
פּוּרָה תִדְרֹךְ לְשׁוֹמֵר מַה מִלַּיְלָה.
צָרַח כַּשּׁוֹמֵר וְשָׂח אָתָא בֹקֶר וְגַם לַיְלָה.
וַיְהִי בַּחֲצִי הַלַּיְלָה:

קָרֵב יוֹם אֲשֶׁר הוּא לֹא יוֹם וְלֹא לַיְלָה.
רָם הוֹדַע כִּי לְךָ הַיּוֹם אַף לְךָ הַלַּיְלָה.
שׁוֹמְרִים הַפְקֵד לְעִירְךָ כָּל הַיּוֹם וְכָל הַלַּיְלָה.
תָּאִיר כְּאוֹר יוֹם חֶשְׁכַת לַיְלָה.
וַיְהִי בַּחֲצִי הַלַּיְלָה:

4. Yaakov's victorious struggle with the angel of Esav.
5. The slaying of Egypt's firstborn, and the loss of their wealth.
6. Hashem's use of the stars to defeat the army of Sisera.
7. Hashem's sending a plague and slaying the entire invading force when Sancheriv raised his hand against Jerusalem and sent an army to destroy it, under Ravshakay, who said blasphemy.
8. The incident in which Hashem broke Bel, the idol of Nevuchadnezer, King of Babylonia, and also destroyed its base.

Sancheriv shook his fist at Jerusalem,	
and his dead You made wither	at night.
The idol Bel and its pedestal You broke in the dark	of night.
To Daniel, Your treasure, You revealed secrets	at night.
It happened at midnight!	

He who got drunk with the holy vessels was killed	at night.
You saved from the lions' den the one who interpreted the fearful	at night.
The Aggagite bore hate and wrote his letters	at night.
It happened at midnight!	

You began his defeat by disturbing sleep	at night.
You will work the wine-press for those who watch	from night.
Shout as a watchman saying: Comes morning and also	night.
It happened at midnight!	

Bring the day that is day and not	night.
Show, Most High, that Yours is the day and	night.
Appoint watchmen for Your city, for all the day and	night.
Light up as day the darkness	of night.
It happened at midnight!	

9. Hashem's helping Daniel to interpret Nevuchadnezer's dream.

10. Hashem's causing Balshazar, Nevuchadnezer's grandson, to be killed when he used the vessels of the Temple for revelry, immediately after Daniel had interpreted the writing on Nevuchadnezer's wall.

11. Hashem's causing Achashverosh to be sleepless, to save the Jews from Haman.

In countries where two Seders are held, this song is sung on the second night:

וּבְכֵן וַאֲמַרְתֶּם זֶבַח פֶּסַח

בְּפֶסַח.   אֹמֶץ גְּבוּרוֹתֶיךָ הִפְלֵאתָ
פֶּסַח.   בְּרֹאשׁ כָּל מוֹעֲדוֹת נִשֵּׂאתָ
פֶּסַח.   גִּלִּיתָ לְאֶזְרָחִי חֲצוֹת לֵיל
וַאֲמַרְתֶּם זֶבַח פֶּסַח:

בְּפֶסַח.   דְּלָתָיו דָּפַקְתָּ כְּחֹם הַיּוֹם
בְּפֶסַח.   הִסְעִיד נוֹצְצִים עֻגוֹת מַצּוֹת
פֶּסַח.   וְאֶל הַבָּקָר רָץ זֵכֶר לְשׁוֹר עֵרֶךְ
וַאֲמַרְתֶּם זֶבַח פֶּסַח:

בְּפֶסַח.   זֹעֲמוּ סְדוֹמִים וְלֹהֲטוּ בָּאֵשׁ
פֶּסַח.   חֻלַּץ לוֹט מֵהֶם וּמַצּוֹת אָפָה בְּקֵץ
בְּפֶסַח.   טִאטֵאתָ אַדְמַת מֹף וְנֹף בְּעָבְרְךָ
וַאֲמַרְתֶּם זֶבַח פֶּסַח:

פֶּסַח.   יָהּ רֹאשׁ כָּל אוֹן מָחַצְתָּ בְּלֵיל שִׁמּוּר
פֶּסַח.   כַּבִּיר עַל בֵּן בְּכוֹר פָּסַחְתָּ בְּדַם
בְּפֶסַח.   לְבִלְתִּי תֵּת מַשְׁחִית לָבֹא בִּפְתָחַי
וַאֲמַרְתֶּם זֶבַח פֶּסַח:

This song is written in the same style as the previous one, but mentions several additional incidents that took place on Pesach:
- *To Avraham You revealed Yourself* — To tell him that Yitzchak would be born.
- The overturning of S'dom and Amorah was on Pesach.

In countries where two Seders are held, this song is sung on the second night:

VaAmartem Zevach Pesach
(*And You Shall Say, "It Is a Pesach Offering!"*)

You displayed Your great power   on Pesach.
You raised up above all festivals   Pesach.
To Avraham You revealed Yourself at midnight   of Pesach.
    And you shall say, "It is a Pesach Offering!"

You knocked on his door at the heat of the day   on Pesach.
You fed fiery angels matzah cakes   on Pesach.
And to the cattle he ran, to choose a remembrance
    of the beast that is offered   on Pesach.
    And you shall say, "It is a Pesach Offering!"

Sodomites angered You and were
    consumed by fire   on Pesach.
Lot was rescued, having made matzah cakes
    for the angels at the close   of Pesach.
You swept clean Moph and Noph [Egyptian cities]
    when You passed over Egypt   on Pesach.
    And you shall say, "It is a Pesach Offering!"

Hashem, You struck down their firstborn
    on the night that is guarded   Pesach.
Mighty One, You spared our firstborn
    in the merit of the blood of   the Pesach.
You refused the destroyer permission to come
    through our doors   on Pesach.
    And you shall say, "It is a Pesach Offering!"

- The city of Jericho was besieged just after Pesach started.
- Gideon defeated Midyan on Pesach, after being encouraged by a dream, where he saw a barley cake rolling into the Midyan camp — barley being an offering brought on Pesach.

מִסְגֶּרֶת סֻגָּרָה בְּעִתּוֹתֵי	פֶּסַח.
נִשְׁמְדָה מִדְיָן בִּצְלִיל שְׂעוֹרֵי עֹמֶר	פֶּסַח.
שׂוֹרְפוּ מִשְׁמַנֵּי פּוּל וְלוּד בִּיקַד יְקוֹד	פֶּסַח.

וַאֲמַרְתֶּם זֶבַח פֶּסַח:

עוֹד הַיּוֹם בְּנֹב לַעֲמֹד עַד גָּעָה עוֹנַת	פֶּסַח.
פַּס יָד כָּתְבָה לְקַעֲקֵעַ צוּל	בְּפֶסַח.
צָפֹה הַצָּפִית עָרוֹךְ הַשֻּׁלְחָן	בְּפֶסַח.

וַאֲמַרְתֶּם זֶבַח פֶּסַח:

קָהָל כִּנְּסָה הֲדַסָּה צוֹם לְשַׁלֵּשׁ	בְּפֶסַח.
רֹאשׁ מִבֵּית רָשָׁע מָחַצְתָּ בְּעֵץ חֲמִשִּׁים	בְּפֶסַח.
שְׁתֵּי אֵלֶּה רֶגַע תָּבִיא לְעוּצִית	בְּפֶסַח.
תָּעֹז יָדְךָ וְתָרוּם יְמִינֶךָ כְּלֵיל הִתְקַדֶּשׁ חַג	פֶּסַח.

וַאֲמַרְתֶּם זֶבַח פֶּסַח:

כִּי לוֹ נָאֶה. כִּי לוֹ יָאֶה

אַדִּיר בִּמְלוּכָה. בָּחוּר כַּהֲלָכָה. גְּדוּדָיו יֹאמְרוּ לוֹ: לְךָ וּלְךָ. לְךָ כִּי לְךָ. לְךָ אַף לְךָ. לְךָ יְהֹוָה הַמַּמְלָכָה.

כִּי לוֹ נָאֶה. כִּי לוֹ יָאֶה:

דָּגוּל בִּמְלוּכָה. הָדוּר כַּהֲלָכָה. וָתִיקָיו יֹאמְרוּ לוֹ: לְךָ וּלְךָ. לְךָ כִּי לְךָ. לְךָ אַף לְךָ. לְךָ יְהֹוָה הַמַּמְלָכָה.

כִּי לוֹ נָאֶה. כִּי לוֹ יָאֶה:

The different parts of this song's refrain ("To You and to You," etc.) all are taken from Scriptural verses, and abbreviate them.

- **To You and to You** (Tehillim 65:2): *To You, [our] silence is a praise [for there is no end to Your praise]...and to You are vows paid.*

Jericho was besieged during their fears	of Pesach.
Midyan was destroyed by Gideon's *omer* of barley	on Pesach.
Sancheriv's army led by Pul and Lud was burned	on Pesach.

And you shall say, "It is a Pesach Offering!"

Sancheriv threatened to be at Nob, but retribution came to him at the time	of Pesach.
The hand wrote on the wall of Bavel's fall	on Pesach.
Balshazar's watchmen set the festive table	on Pesach.

And you shall say, "It is a Pesach Offering!"

Esther gathered the people to fast three days	on Pesach.
The heir of Amalek was hung on the gallows	on Pesach.
Double misfortune will You bring upon Edom	on Pesach.
May Your Hand be strong, Your right upraised, as the night You sanctified the festival	of Pesach.

And you shall say, "It is a Pesach Offering!"

Ki Lo Na'eh
(*Because to Him It Is Fitting*)

Mighty in His Kingship, truly Supreme. His companies of angels say to Him: To You and to You; To You because it is to You; To You and only to You; To You, Hashem, is the Kingship.
Because to Him it is fitting. Because to Him it is due.

Celebrated in His Kingship, truly Glorious. His faithful say to Him: To You and to You; To You because it is to You; To You and only to You; To You, Hashem, is the Kingship.
Because to Him it is fitting. Because to Him it is due.

- **To You because it is to You** (*Divrei Hayamim I* 29:11): *To You, O Lord, is the greatness, power and glory, the victory and the majesty; because all that is in heaven and earth is Yours; to You is the Kingship.*

זַכַּאי בִּמְלוּכָה. חָסִין כַּהֲלָכָה. טַפְסְרָיו יֹאמְרוּ לוֹ: לְךָ וּלְךָ. לְךָ כִּי לְךָ. לְךָ אַף לְךָ. לְךָ יְיָ הַמַּמְלָכָה.

כִּי לוֹ נָאֶה. כִּי לוֹ יָאֶה:

יָחִיד בִּמְלוּכָה. כַּבִּיר כַּהֲלָכָה. לִמּוּדָיו יֹאמְרוּ לוֹ: לְךָ וּלְךָ. לְךָ כִּי לְךָ. לְךָ אַף לְךָ. לְךָ יְיָ הַמַּמְלָכָה.

כִּי לוֹ נָאֶה. כִּי לוֹ יָאֶה:

מוֹשֵׁל בִּמְלוּכָה. נוֹרָא כַּהֲלָכָה. סְבִיבָיו יֹאמְרוּ לוֹ: לְךָ וּלְךָ. לְךָ כִּי לְךָ. לְךָ אַף לְךָ. לְךָ יְיָ הַמַּמְלָכָה.

כִּי לוֹ נָאֶה. כִּי לוֹ יָאֶה:

עָנָו בִּמְלוּכָה. פּוֹדֶה כַּהֲלָכָה. צַדִּיקָיו יֹאמְרוּ לוֹ: לְךָ וּלְךָ. לְךָ כִּי לְךָ. לְךָ אַף לְךָ. לְךָ יְיָ הַמַּמְלָכָה.

כִּי לוֹ נָאֶה. כִּי לוֹ יָאֶה:

קָדוֹשׁ בִּמְלוּכָה. רַחוּם כַּהֲלָכָה. שִׁנְאַנָּיו יֹאמְרוּ לוֹ: לְךָ וּלְךָ. לְךָ כִּי לְךָ. לְךָ אַף לְךָ. לְךָ יְיָ הַמַּמְלָכָה.

כִּי לוֹ נָאֶה. כִּי לוֹ יָאֶה:

תַּקִּיף בִּמְלוּכָה. תּוֹמֵךְ כַּהֲלָכָה. תְּמִימָיו יֹאמְרוּ לוֹ: לְךָ וּלְךָ. לְךָ כִּי לְךָ. לְךָ אַף לְךָ. לְךָ יְיָ הַמַּמְלָכָה.

כִּי לוֹ נָאֶה. כִּי לוֹ יָאֶה:

- **To You, and only to You** (Tehillim 74:16): *To You is the day, and also to You is the night,* and (Tehillim 89:12): *To You are the skies, and also to You is the land.*

Pristine in His Kingship, truly Powerful. His princely angels say to Him:
To You and to You; To You because it is to You;
To You and only to You; To You, Hashem, is the Kingship.
Because to Him it is fitting. Because to Him it is due.

Alone in Kingship, truly Mighty. His disciples say to Him:
To You and to You; To You because it is to You;
To You and only to You; To You, Hashem, is the Kingship.
Because to Him it is fitting. Because to Him it is due.

Ruler in Kingship, truly Awesome. Those around Him say:
To You and to You; To You because it is to You;
To You and only to You; To You, Hashem, is the Kingship.
Because to Him it is fitting. Because to Him it is due.

Humble in Kingship, truly a Redeemer. His righteous ones say to Him:
To You and to You; To You because it is to You;
To You and only to You; To You, Hashem, is the Kingship.
Because to Him it is fitting. Because to Him it is due.

Holy in Kingship, truly merciful. His choruses of angels say to Him:
To You and to You; To You because it is to You;
To You and only to You; To You, Hashem, is the Kingship.
Because to Him it is fitting. Because to Him it is due.

Powerful in Kingship, truly Sustaining. His perfect ones say to Him:
To You and to You; To You because it is to You;
To You and only to You; To You, Hashem, is the Kingship.
Because to Him it is fitting. Because to Him it is due.

Because these verses proclaim Hashem's many wonders and greatness, we make a chorus of them and repeat the chorus after each stanza of the song.

אַדִּיר הוּא

אַדִּיר הוּא יִבְנֶה בֵּיתוֹ בְּקָרוֹב. בִּמְהֵרָה בִּמְהֵרָה בְּיָמֵינוּ בְּקָרוֹב.
אֵל בְּנֵה אֵל בְּנֵה. בְּנֵה בֵיתְךָ בְּקָרוֹב:

בָּחוּר הוּא. גָּדוֹל הוּא. דָּגוּל הוּא. יִבְנֶה בֵּיתוֹ בְּקָרוֹב. בִּמְהֵרָה בִּמְהֵרָה בְּיָמֵינוּ בְּקָרוֹב.
אֵל בְּנֵה אֵל בְּנֵה. בְּנֵה בֵיתְךָ בְּקָרוֹב:

הָדוּר הוּא. וָתִיק הוּא. זַכַּאי הוּא. חָסִיד הוּא. יִבְנֶה בֵּיתוֹ בְּקָרוֹב. בִּמְהֵרָה בִּמְהֵרָה בְּיָמֵינוּ בְּקָרוֹב.
אֵל בְּנֵה אֵל בְּנֵה. בְּנֵה בֵיתְךָ בְּקָרוֹב:

טָהוֹר הוּא. יָחִיד הוּא. כַּבִּיר הוּא. לָמוּד הוּא. מֶלֶךְ הוּא. יִבְנֶה בֵּיתוֹ בְּקָרוֹב. בִּמְהֵרָה בִּמְהֵרָה בְּיָמֵינוּ בְּקָרוֹב.
אֵל בְּנֵה אֵל בְּנֵה. בְּנֵה בֵיתְךָ בְּקָרוֹב:

נוֹרָא הוּא. שַׂגִּיב הוּא. עִזּוּז הוּא. פּוֹדֶה הוּא. צַדִּיק הוּא. יִבְנֶה בֵּיתוֹ בְּקָרוֹב. בִּמְהֵרָה בִּמְהֵרָה בְּיָמֵינוּ בְּקָרוֹב.
אֵל בְּנֵה אֵל בְּנֵה. בְּנֵה בֵיתְךָ בְּקָרוֹב:

קָדוֹשׁ הוּא. רַחוּם הוּא. שַׁדַּי הוּא. תַּקִּיף הוּא. יִבְנֶה בֵּיתוֹ בְּקָרוֹב. בִּמְהֵרָה בִּמְהֵרָה בְּיָמֵינוּ בְּקָרוֹב.
אֵל בְּנֵה אֵל בְּנֵה. בְּנֵה בֵיתְךָ בְּקָרוֹב:

Victorious is He — In his commentary on the *Shulchan Aruch*, the Chasam Sofer substituted this for "Wise is He," since he felt such a description was inappropriate.

Adir Hu
(*Mighty Is He*)

Mighty is He; May He build His House soon.
Speedily, speedily, in our days. Soon! Build O God, build!
Build O God, build! Build Your House! Soon!

Supreme is He; Great is He; Celebrated is He;
May He build His House soon. Speedily, speedily, in our days. Soon!
Build O God, build!
Build O God, build! Build Your House! Soon!

Splendid is He; Faithful is He; Just is He; Righteous is He;
May He build His House soon. Speedily, speedily, in our days. Soon!
Build O God, build!
Build O God, build! Build Your House! Soon!

Pure is He; Unique is He; Mighty is He; Victorious is He;
King is He; Awesome is He; May He build His House soon.
Speedily, speedily, in our days. Soon! Build O God, build!
Build O God, build! Build Your House! Soon!

Sublime is He; Strong is He; a Redeemer is He; Upright is He;
Holy is He; Merciful is He; Unlimited is He; Powerful is He:
May He build His House soon. Speedily, speedily, in our days. Soon!
Build O God, build!
Build O God, build! Build Your House! Soon!

אֶחָד מִי יוֹדֵעַ

אֶחָד אֲנִי יוֹדֵעַ. אֶחָד אֱלֹהֵינוּ שֶׁבַּשָּׁמַיִם וּבָאָרֶץ:

שְׁנַיִם מִי יוֹדֵעַ. שְׁנַיִם אֲנִי יוֹדֵעַ. שְׁנֵי לוּחוֹת הַבְּרִית. אֶחָד אֱלֹהֵינוּ שֶׁבַּשָּׁמַיִם וּבָאָרֶץ:

שְׁלֹשָׁה מִי יוֹדֵעַ. שְׁלֹשָׁה אֲנִי יוֹדֵעַ. שְׁלֹשָׁה אָבוֹת. שְׁנֵי לוּחוֹת הַבְּרִית. אֶחָד אֱלֹהֵינוּ שֶׁבַּשָּׁמַיִם וּבָאָרֶץ:

אַרְבַּע מִי יוֹדֵעַ. אַרְבַּע אֲנִי יוֹדֵעַ. אַרְבַּע אִמָּהוֹת. שְׁלֹשָׁה אָבוֹת. שְׁנֵי לוּחוֹת הַבְּרִית. אֶחָד אֱלֹהֵינוּ שֶׁבַּשָּׁמַיִם וּבָאָרֶץ:

חֲמִשָּׁה מִי יוֹדֵעַ. חֲמִשָּׁה אֲנִי יוֹדֵעַ. חֲמִשָּׁה חֻמְשֵׁי תוֹרָה. אַרְבַּע אִמָּהוֹת. שְׁלֹשָׁה אָבוֹת. שְׁנֵי לוּחוֹת הַבְּרִית. אֶחָד אֱלֹהֵינוּ שֶׁבַּשָּׁמַיִם וּבָאָרֶץ:

שִׁשָּׁה מִי יוֹדֵעַ. שִׁשָּׁה אֲנִי יוֹדֵעַ. שִׁשָּׁה סִדְרֵי מִשְׁנָה. חֲמִשָּׁה חֻמְשֵׁי תוֹרָה. אַרְבַּע אִמָּהוֹת. שְׁלֹשָׁה אָבוֹת. שְׁנֵי לוּחוֹת הַבְּרִית. אֶחָד אֱלֹהֵינוּ שֶׁבַּשָּׁמַיִם וּבָאָרֶץ:

שִׁבְעָה מִי יוֹדֵעַ. שִׁבְעָה אֲנִי יוֹדֵעַ. שִׁבְעָה יְמֵי שַׁבַּתָּא. שִׁשָּׁה סִדְרֵי מִשְׁנָה. חֲמִשָּׁה חֻמְשֵׁי תוֹרָה. אַרְבַּע אִמָּהוֹת. שְׁלֹשָׁה אָבוֹת. שְׁנֵי לוּחוֹת הַבְּרִית. אֶחָד אֱלֹהֵינוּ שֶׁבַּשָּׁמַיִם וּבָאָרֶץ:

Who Knows One? — This ancient, well-known song appears to be very simple and straightforward, as if it were nothing more than a kind of memory game. In truth, however, commentators throughout the ages have found that *Who Knows One?* contains a host of subtle messages that are particularly connected to the Seder night.

For example, one commentator explains that the song intentionally reaches the number thirteen to symbolize the ten plagues plus

Echad Mi Yode'a
(*Who Knows One?*)

Who knows one? I know one: One is our God Who is in Heaven and earth.

Who knows two? I know two: two Tablets of the Covenant; One is our God Who is in Heaven and earth.

Who knows three? I know three: three Fathers, two Tablets of the Covenant; One is our God Who is in Heaven and earth.

Who knows four? I know four: four Mothers, three Fathers, two Tablets of the Covenant; One is our God Who is in Heaven and earth.

Who knows five? I know five: five Books of the Chumash, four Mothers, three Fathers, two Tablets of the Covenant; One is our God Who is in Heaven and earth.

Who knows six? I know six: six Orders of the Mishnah, five Books of the Chumash, four Mothers, three Fathers, two Tablets of the Covenant; One is our God Who is in Heaven and earth.

Who knows seven? I know seven: seven days in a Shabbos [week], six Orders of the Mishnah, five Books of the Chumash, four Mothers, three Fathers, two Tablets of the Covenant; One is our God Who is in Heaven and earth.

the three memory aids of Rabbi Yehudah. Now that we have completed the Seder according to all of its laws and statutes, we again deal with the number thirteen, to make it clear that Israel lives and flourishes — but not because of the plagues that Hashem dealt to Pharaoh. No, Israel's life and prosperity depend only upon our fulfillment of the Torah — upon complete dedication to our rich heritage — some of the components of which are listed in the song.

שְׁמוֹנָה מִי יוֹדֵעַ. שְׁמוֹנָה אֲנִי יוֹדֵעַ. שְׁמוֹנָה יְמֵי מִילָה. שִׁבְעָה יְמֵי שַׁבַּתָּא. שִׁשָּׁה סִדְרֵי מִשְׁנָה. חֲמִשָּׁה חֻמְשֵׁי תוֹרָה. אַרְבַּע אִמָּהוֹת. שְׁלֹשָׁה אָבוֹת. שְׁנֵי לוּחוֹת הַבְּרִית. אֶחָד אֱלֹהֵינוּ שֶׁבַּשָּׁמַיִם וּבָאָרֶץ:

תִּשְׁעָה מִי יוֹדֵעַ. תִּשְׁעָה אֲנִי יוֹדֵעַ. תִּשְׁעָה יַרְחֵי לֵדָה. שְׁמוֹנָה יְמֵי מִילָה. שִׁבְעָה יְמֵי שַׁבַּתָּא. שִׁשָּׁה סִדְרֵי מִשְׁנָה. חֲמִשָּׁה חֻמְשֵׁי תוֹרָה. אַרְבַּע אִמָּהוֹת. שְׁלֹשָׁה אָבוֹת. שְׁנֵי לוּחוֹת הַבְּרִית. אֶחָד אֱלֹהֵינוּ שֶׁבַּשָּׁמַיִם וּבָאָרֶץ:

עֲשָׂרָה מִי יוֹדֵעַ. עֲשָׂרָה אֲנִי יוֹדֵעַ. עֲשָׂרָה דִבְּרַיָּא. תִּשְׁעָה יַרְחֵי לֵדָה. שְׁמוֹנָה יְמֵי מִילָה. שִׁבְעָה יְמֵי שַׁבַּתָּא. שִׁשָּׁה סִדְרֵי מִשְׁנָה. חֲמִשָּׁה חֻמְשֵׁי תוֹרָה. אַרְבַּע אִמָּהוֹת. שְׁלֹשָׁה אָבוֹת. שְׁנֵי לוּחוֹת הַבְּרִית. אֶחָד אֱלֹהֵינוּ שֶׁבַּשָּׁמַיִם וּבָאָרֶץ:

אַחַד עָשָׂר מִי יוֹדֵעַ. אַחַד עָשָׂר אֲנִי יוֹדֵעַ. אַחַד עָשָׂר כּוֹכְבַיָּא. עֲשָׂרָה דִבְּרַיָּא. תִּשְׁעָה יַרְחֵי לֵדָה. שְׁמוֹנָה יְמֵי מִילָה. שִׁבְעָה יְמֵי שַׁבַּתָּא. שִׁשָּׁה סִדְרֵי מִשְׁנָה. חֲמִשָּׁה חֻמְשֵׁי תוֹרָה. אַרְבַּע אִמָּהוֹת. שְׁלֹשָׁה אָבוֹת. שְׁנֵי לוּחוֹת הַבְּרִית. אֶחָד אֱלֹהֵינוּ שֶׁבַּשָּׁמַיִם וּבָאָרֶץ:

שְׁנֵים עָשָׂר מִי יוֹדֵעַ. שְׁנֵים עָשָׂר אֲנִי יוֹדֵעַ. שְׁנֵים עָשָׂר שִׁבְטַיָּא. אַחַד עָשָׂר כּוֹכְבַיָּא. עֲשָׂרָה דִבְּרַיָּא. תִּשְׁעָה יַרְחֵי לֵדָה. שְׁמוֹנָה יְמֵי מִילָה. שִׁבְעָה יְמֵי שַׁבַּתָּא. שִׁשָּׁה סִדְרֵי מִשְׁנָה. חֲמִשָּׁה חֻמְשֵׁי תוֹרָה. אַרְבַּע אִמָּהוֹת. שְׁלֹשָׁה אָבוֹת. שְׁנֵי לוּחוֹת הַבְּרִית. אֶחָד אֱלֹהֵינוּ שֶׁבַּשָּׁמַיִם וּבָאָרֶץ:

שְׁלֹשָׁה עָשָׂר מִי יוֹדֵעַ. שְׁלֹשָׁה עָשָׂר אֲנִי יוֹדֵעַ. שְׁלֹשָׁה עָשָׂר מִדַּיָּא. שְׁנֵים עָשָׂר שִׁבְטַיָּא. אַחַד עָשָׂר כּוֹכְבַיָּא. עֲשָׂרָה דִבְּרַיָּא. תִּשְׁעָה יַרְחֵי לֵדָה. שְׁמוֹנָה יְמֵי מִילָה. שִׁבְעָה יְמֵי שַׁבַּתָּא. שִׁשָּׁה סִדְרֵי מִשְׁנָה. חֲמִשָּׁה חֻמְשֵׁי תוֹרָה. אַרְבַּע אִמָּהוֹת. שְׁלֹשָׁה אָבוֹת. שְׁנֵי לוּחוֹת הַבְּרִית. אֶחָד אֱלֹהֵינוּ שֶׁבַּשָּׁמַיִם וּבָאָרֶץ:

Who knows eight? I know eight: eight days until a *Bris,* seven days in a Shabbos, six Orders of the Mishnah, five Books of the Chumash, four Mothers, three Fathers, two Tablets of the Covenant; One is our God Who is in Heaven and earth.

Who knows nine? I know nine: nine months until a birth, eight days until a *Bris,* seven days in a Shabbos, six Orders of the Mishnah, five Books of the Chumash, four Mothers, three Fathers, two Tablets of the Covenant; One is our God Who is in Heaven and earth.

Who knows ten? I know ten: ten Commandments, nine months until a birth, eight days until a *Bris,* seven days in a Shabbos, six Orders of the Mishnah, five Books of the Chumash, four Mothers, three Fathers, two Tablets of the Covenant; One is our God Who is in Heaven and earth.

Who knows eleven? I know eleven: eleven stars [in Yosef's dream], ten Commandments, nine months until a birth, eight days until a *Bris,* seven days in a Shabbos, six Orders of the Mishnah, five Books of the Chumash, four Mothers, three Fathers, two Tablets of the Covenant; One is our God Who is in Heaven and earth.

Who knows twelve? I know twelve: twelve tribes, eleven stars, ten Commandments, nine months until a birth, eight days until a *Bris,* seven days in a Shabbos, six Orders of the Mishnah, five Books of the Chumash, four Mothers, three Fathers, two Tablets of the Covenant; One is our God Who is in Heaven and earth.

Who knows thirteen? I know thirteen: thirteen *Middos* [HaKadosh Baruch Hu's attributes of mercy], twelve tribes, eleven stars, ten Commandments, nine months until a birth, eight days until a *Bris,* seven days in a Shabbos, six Orders of the Mishnah, five Books of the Chumash, four Mothers, three Fathers, two Tablets of the Covenant; One is our God Who is in Heaven and earth.

חַד גַּדְיָא

חַד גַּדְיָא, חַד גַּדְיָא. דְּזַבִּין אַבָּא בִּתְרֵי זוּזֵי.
חַד גַּדְיָא, חַד גַּדְיָא.
וְאָתָא שׁוּנְרָא, וְאָכְלָה לְגַדְיָא, דְּזַבִּין אַבָּא בִּתְרֵי זוּזֵי.
חַד גַּדְיָא, חַד גַּדְיָא.
וְאָתָא כַלְבָּא, וְנָשַׁךְ לְשׁוּנְרָא, דְּאָכְלָה לְגַדְיָא, דְּזַבִּין אַבָּא בִּתְרֵי זוּזֵי.
חַד גַּדְיָא, חַד גַּדְיָא.
וְאָתָא חֻטְרָא, וְהִכָּה לְכַלְבָּא, דְּנָשַׁךְ לְשׁוּנְרָא, דְּאָכְלָה לְגַדְיָא, דְּזַבִּין אַבָּא בִּתְרֵי זוּזֵי.
חַד גַּדְיָא, חַד גַּדְיָא.

One kid — Although it is similar in style to the previous two songs, this ancient tune is perhaps even more well-known. In addition, it is much more mysterious, and possesses its own particular charm. Thus, it has attracted a great number of commentators, each striving to reveal its secrets and uncover what he can of its hidden messages. The song is clearly one of great sanctity, and even the Vilna Gaon offered several explanations. Below, we shall quote, in brief, one of the Vilna Gaon's interpretations:

📖

One kid, one kid — These represent the two kid goats that Rivkah told Yaakov *Avinu* to bring to her, which she prepared as a meal that Yaakov served to Yitzchak *Avinu* on Pesach night. By means of the two kids, Yaakov received both Yitzchak's blessing and the birthright of Esav. Thus the two kids initiated mitzvos for all the generations — the Pesach offering and the accompanying *Chagigah* offering. In turn, Yaakov passed his birthright and the blessing of Yitzchak to Yosef.

Chad Gadya
(*One Kid*)

One kid, one kid, that my father bought for two zuzim.
One kid, one kid.

Then came a cat and ate the kid my father bought for two zuzim.
One kid, one kid.

Then came a dog and bit the cat that ate the kid
my father bought for two zuzim.
One kid, one kid.

Then came a stick and hit the dog that bit the cat that ate the kid
my father bought for two zuzim.
One kid, one kid.

Then came a cat — This represents the jealousy that the brothers had of Yosef, which led them to sell him as a slave to traders on their way to Egypt — all in order to deprive Yosef of the birthright and the blessing.

Then came a dog — This represents Pharaoh, for so did the Sages refer to the King of Egypt. The tribes, who had been jealous, were oppressed by Pharaoh, and this helped atone for their sin.

Then came a stick — This represents the staff of Moshe *Rabbenu*, which he and Aharon used in Egypt to perform all the signs and wonders there. This staff was passed down to Yehoshua, and afterwards, through all the generations including that of King David, and until the destruction of the First Temple, all the wonders and miracles that were done for Israel's sake against her enemies, were done with this staff, the same staff that was used against Pharaoh.

וְאָתָא נוּרָא, וְשָׂרַף לְחֻטְרָא, דְּהִכָּה לְכַלְבָּא, דְּנָשַׁךְ לְשׁוּנְרָא, דְּאָכְלָה לְגַדְיָא, דְּזַבִּין אַבָּא בִּתְרֵי זוּזֵי.

חַד גַּדְיָא, חַד גַּדְיָא.

וְאָתָא מַיָּא, וְכָבָה לְנוּרָא, דְּשָׂרַף לְחֻטְרָא, דְּהִכָּה לְכַלְבָּא, דְּנָשַׁךְ לְשׁוּנְרָא, דְּאָכְלָה לְגַדְיָא, דְּזַבִּין אַבָּא בִּתְרֵי זוּזֵי.

חַד גַּדְיָא, חַד גַּדְיָא.

וְאָתָא תוֹרָא, וְשָׁתָה לְמַיָּא, דְּכָבָה לְנוּרָא, דְּשָׂרַף לְחֻטְרָא, דְּהִכָּה לְכַלְבָּא, דְּנָשַׁךְ לְשׁוּנְרָא, דְּאָכְלָה לְגַדְיָא, דְּזַבִּין אַבָּא בִּתְרֵי זוּזֵי.

חַד גַּדְיָא, חַד גַּדְיָא.

וְאָתָא הַשּׁוֹחֵט, וְשָׁחַט לְתוֹרָא, דְּשָׁתָה לְמַיָּא, דְּכָבָה לְנוּרָא, דְּשָׂרַף לְחֻטְרָא, דְּהִכָּה לְכַלְבָּא, דְּנָשַׁךְ לְשׁוּנְרָא, דְּאָכְלָה לְגַדְיָא, דְּזַבִּין אַבָּא בִּתְרֵי זוּזֵי.

חַד גַּדְיָא, חַד גַּדְיָא.

וְאָתָא מַלְאַךְ הַמָּוֶת, וְשָׁחַט לְשׁוֹחֵט, דְּשָׁחַט לְתוֹרָא, דְּשָׁתָה לְמַיָּא, דְּכָבָה לְנוּרָא, דְּשָׂרַף לְחוּטְרָא, דְּהִכָּה לְכַלְבָּא, דְּנָשַׁךְ לְשׁוּנְרָא, דְּאָכְלָה לְגַדְיָא, דְּזַבִּין אַבָּא בִּתְרֵי זוּזֵי.

חַד גַּדְיָא, חַד גַּדְיָא.

Then came fire — This represents the fire of the evil inclination, by means of which came the destruction of the First Temple, for the evil inclination for idol-worship caused Jews to bring a graven image into the Temple itself, and this nullified the power of the staff.

Then came water — This represents the Torah scholarship of the Men of the Great Assembly, which was able to rid Israel of the evil inclination for idol-worship.

Then came fire and burned the stick that hit the dog that bit the cat
that ate the kid my father bought for two zuzim.
One kid, one kid.

Then came water and put out the fire that burned the stick
that hit the dog that bit the cat that ate the kid
my father bought for two zuzim.
One kid, one kid.

Then came a bull and drank the water that put out the fire
that burned the stick that hit the dog that bit the cat
that ate the kid my father bought for two zuzim.
One kid, one kid.

Then came the *shochet* and slaughtered the bull that drank
the water that put out the fire that burned the stick that hit the dog
that bit the cat that ate the kid my father bought for two zuzim.
One kid, one kid.

Then came the Angel of Death and slaughtered the *shochet*
who slaughtered the bull that drank the water that put out the fire that
burned the stick that hit the dog that bit the cat
that ate the kid my father bought for two zuzim.
One kid, one kid.

Then came a bull — This is the kingdom of Edom, whose emblem is a bull. Besides destroying the Temple, Edom caused other great suffering in Israel by legislating harsh decrees to uproot the Torah, and break the nation's allegiance to it.

📖

Then came the shochet — This is *Mashiach* ben Yosef, who will make war on Edom.

📖

Then came the Angel of Death — For before the ultimate victory, *Mashiach* ben Yosef will be killed.

וְאָתָא הַקָּדוֹשׁ בָּרוּךְ הוּא, וְשָׁחַט לְמַלְאַךְ הַמָּוֶת דְּשָׁחַט לְשׁוֹחֵט, דְּשָׁחַט לְתוֹרָא, דְּשָׁתָה לְמַיָּא, דְּכָבָה לְנוּרָא, דְּשָׂרַף לְחוּטְרָא, דְּהִכָּה לְכַלְבָּא, דְּנָשַׁךְ לְשׁוּנְרָא, דְּאָכְלָה לְגַדְיָא, דְּזַבִּין אַבָּא בִּתְרֵי זוּזֵי.

חַד גַּדְיָא, חַד גַּדְיָא.

Then came the Holy One, blessed is He — Who will cause an end to death, when in His mercy, He brings the Ultimate Redemption, which will be permanent salvation for us, may this come soon, speedily in our days!

📖

In *Maasei Nissim* we find a different explanation of this song:

Then came a cat (in the song's Aramaic, *shunra*) — This refers to Nevuchadnezer, king of Babylonia, who was called by our Sages a *soneh ra* — "an evil hater," the most evil of those who hated our People. Nevuchadnezer came and destroyed the Temple.

📖

Then came a dog — This refers the Persian King Koresh (Cyrus) who, as an infant, was said to have nursed from a dog. Koresh came and conquered Babylonia.

📖

Then came a stick — This is Greece, which yielded a powerful staff, conquering the world and winning control over the entire Persian empire.

📖

Then came fire — This represents the Hasmoneans, *Kohanim* who would tend the fires of the Temple altar and also would offer incense, who defeated the Greeks, and were able to kindle the Temple menorah, whose light lasted eight days through the miracle of the burning oil.

📖

Then came water — This is evil Edom, symbolized by the roar of the waves of the ocean, which crash with great force and violence all the world over. Edom came and overthrew the Hasmonean Kingdom.

Then came the Holy One, blessed is He and slaughtered
the Angel of Death that slaughtered the *shochet*
who slaughtered the bull that drank the water that put out the fire
that burned the stick that hit the dog that bit the cat
that ate the kid my father bought for two zuzim.
One kid, one kid.

Then came a bull — This represents Yishmael, who, according to the Midrash, will conquer Edom.

Then came the Angel of Death — Who will take the life of *Mashiach* ben Yosef.

Then came the Holy One — Who will put an end to death, once and for all!

In *Chayim Sha'al*, a collection of the Chida's responsa, we find the following: It once happened that a certain Jew was attending a Seder, and when the participants began to sing *Chad Gadya*, he started to ridicule them. Although singing this song on the holy night of the Seder had long been a custom in Ashkenazic communities, this Jew made fun of the custom and laughed out loud at the entire idea. The other participants strongly objected to his behavior, and in response, one of them rose and declared a *nidui* upon him — a type of excommunication. The question came before the *Chida*: Was the imposed *nidui* justified, and actually in effect?

This is the Chida's answer:

> *This person is clearly guilty of brazen insolence, for he has mocked and ridiculed a custom that has been followed by tens of thousands of Jews in Poland, Germany, and other Ashkenazic communities. He has scoffed at them and at all those who are associated with them. He has made fun of what has been held sacred in Israel since ancient times — something that has been sacred in the eyes of the gedolei olam — the Holy Ones of God, the wise men of all the generations. Even today, Israel is not an orphan. We have many roshei*

yeshivos and geonim — may Hashem protect them — who have said this piyut in the past, and will continue to say it in the future! As a result, this evil mocker has derided tens of thousands of Jews, as well as the great Torah scholars who lead them — heads of the battei dinim [courts], and the world's geonim. He has inflicted a mortal wound on himself, for he must be put into nidui... Even today nidui is the punishment for ridicule of a Torah scholar, whether the scholar has passed away, or is one of the contemporary geonim and holy ones, May Hashem give them life and protect them! In this case, the statement was made that anyone who said or says this piyut is a fool, and is involving himself in nonsense. Thus it is clear without any doubt at all that the one who made this statement must be put into nidui.

The reply of the Chida continues:

My dear friend, I now will repeat what has already been said, so that you will appreciate this well. Commentators have found that this piyut lends itself to many different interpretations — some of which have been published, and some which are found only in manuscript. I have even heard that one of the geonim of the present day has produced more than twenty explanations of this piyut, expounding it on all four levels of interpretation — simple meaning, hints, derash, and secrets — and all twenty of these explanations are pleasing and sweet. Thus, there is no question about it. Chad Gadya is definitely not nonsense. What is more, it has long been very well-known that the songs and piyutim which are customary in Ashkenazic communities are founded upon true wisdom, as was stated by the Ari, z"l, in his holy words. It also has been written in the name of our teacher, the Mahara from Garmizah author of Sefer haRoke'ach, that all matters of the piyutim, and what can be inferred from them, is ancient wisdom that has been passed down through the generations, from one man's mouth to another, from one teacher to another.

These are the words of the Chida.

Appendices

Appendix One

Shir haShirim — The Song of Songs

It is customary to read *Shir haShirim* on the first night of Pesach, at the end of the Seder. In some communities of the Diaspora, where the Seder is repeated on the second night of Pesach, part of *Shir haShirim* is said on the first night, and the rest on the second night. However, the more common custom in the Diaspora is to read all of *Shir haShirim* on both nights.

In Ashkenazic communities, *Shir haShirim* also is read publicly on the Shabbos of *Chol haMo'ed*, the intermediate days of Pesach, during the morning service in the synagogue before the reading of the Torah. In some communities, the public reading is from a hand-written parchment scroll, and the reader recites two blessings: "Who has commanded us on the reading of the Megillah," and *Shehecheyanu*. In many places, however, an ordinary printed book of Scriptures is used, in which case no blessings are said, and everyone reads *Shir haShirim* on his own.

Why is *Shir haShirim* read on Pesach? *Machzor Vitry* gives two reasons: First, Pharaoh is mentioned in *Shir haShirim* explicitly (1:9). Second, its theme throughout is Israel's repetitious history of exile and redemption, and Hashem's continuing love for His nation, even in times when He seems distant.

Similarly, the *Zohar* explains that *Shir haShirim* "includes the entire Torah within it," including the story of the exile in Egypt and our redemption from there, as well as all our other exiles and redemptions. Thus, on Pesach night, this reading is itself a sort of fulfillment of the mitzvah of telling the story of the exile and redemption from Egypt.

Moreover, *Shir haShirim* is a love song between Israel and God, and historically, Pesach was the time that Israel expressed this love. It was then that the nation entered a covenant of "marriage" with God, becoming "betrothed" to Him, by following Him out of Egypt into the barren desert, as a young bride follows her husband (see *Yechezkel* 16).

Shelomo haMelech and Israel — "Kissed" by God

The author of *Shir haShirim* was King Solomon — *Shelomo haMelech*. Verses in Scripture testify (*Melachim I*, 5:11-12) that the wisdom of Shelomo was greater than that of "all men," even that of Avraham *Avinu*, and even that of Moshe *Rabbenu* (*Bava Basra* 15a).

Melachim, or the *Book of Kings*, penned by the Prophet Yirmeyahu, contains praise for Shelomo for the magificent works which actually became a part of the Holy Scriptures (*Ibid* 5:12): *And he (Shelomo) said three thousand analogies, and his song was five and one thousand.*

Yirmeyahu's first reference to the *three thousand analogies* is to *Mishlei*, the *Book of Proverbs*, which is divided into three sections and in which no verse deals with fewer than two or three different ideas, comparing and contrasting them. However, Yirmeyahu wrote that it is not *Mishlei* that represents the peak of Shelomo's God-given wisdom. The writing which embodies his most sublime wisdom is what the Prophet refers to in his second phrase — *his song* — Shir haShirim — *of five and one thousand.* What is the meaning of this name?

In *Shir haShirim*, Shelomo speaks allegorically of the ways of love between a man and a woman, to describe his own love for God. Shelomo felt the love of God in its fullest force during the five times that he was granted prophecy. When he wrote *Shir haShirim*, guided by Divine inspiration, Shelomo became elevated to where he saw all of Israel's history before his eyes, and he was shown a parallel between himself and Israel as a whole, so that *Shir haShirim* is not only about Shelomo's love for Hashem, but also about our People's love for Hashem (and Hashem's love for us), from our birth as a nation until the end of time — from the day that we entered the covenant with Him at Mount Sinai, until when *the world shall be filled with the knowledge of God (Yeshayahu* 11:9) and *The Temple Mount shall be the highest of all the peaks* (2:2).

That is, Shelomo had prophecy five times, and the Jewish nation also can be seen as having five distinct periods when we, too, enjoy particular nearness to God, wherein God's promise that (*Shemos* 25:8) *I shall dwell in their midst* is fulfilled. In terms of the analogy, the four periods which interrupt between these times of closeness — times when the nations separate Israel from her Beloved — these are passing times when the Husband is temporarily apart from His loved one. In the End of Days, however, He will be reunited with her, and He then will hold her close to Him forever.

In the very beginning of *Shir haShirim* (1:2), Shelomo alludes to the five occasions when he was elevated to prophecy and supreme knowledge, saying that these were times that he was *kissed with the kisses of His Mouth* — for prophecy is the greatest level of nearness to God that is possible for a human being. For their part, the Scriptures explicitly enumerate the five times that Shelomo enjoyed such closeness and intimacy with God:

1. *At Givon God appeared to Shelomo* (*Melachim I*, 3:5).

2. *And God gave Shelomo wisdom, and much understanding, and a heart as wide as the sand by the sea...and Shelomo's wisdom multiplied...and he became the wisest of all men* (*Ibid* 5:9).

3. *And the word of God came to Shelomo saying, This House that you will build... and I will dwell in the midst of the Children of Israel* (*Ibid* 6:12). That is, all the details of how the "House" — the Temple — would be built, were revealed through prophecy, as David said (*Divrei Hayamim I*, 28:19): *The entire plan, everything written by the Hand of God, I was given to understand.* The design of the Temple incorporated sublime wisdom about the creation of heaven and earth itself. This wisdom, transmitted through prophecy, was given to Shelomo, too.

4. *And Shelomo stood before the altar of God, opposite the entire congregation of Israel, and he lifted his hands on the heavens* (*Melachim I, 8:35*) — Note that it is not written "to the heavens," but rather, "on the heavens," as if, while he was saying his prayer, Shelomo was holding on to God, refusing to let Him go

until He agreed to his request!

5. *And God appeared to Shelomo again, as He had appeared to him at Givon (Ibid 9:2).*

Corresponding to the five "kisses" listed above, the five periods of great intimacy and closeness between Israel and God are as follows:

1. *And the cloud covered the Tent of the Meeting, and the Glory of God filled the Tabernacle (Shemos 40:34).* God, as it were, "left" his legions in heaven, and established His Place of Abode below, on earth, in the *Mishkan* that was built for Israel's travels in the wilderness.

2. *And the Kohanim were unable to serve because of the Cloud, for the Glory of God filled the House of God (Melachim I 8:11).* God established a more permanent residence in the lower world, by resting His Presence in the First Temple, where It remained for four hundred and ten years, until the First Temple was destroyed and the Divine Presence departed.

3. The third intimacy between God and His People was manifested during the days of the Second Temple, built by Ezra, which housed God's Presence for four hundred and twenty years, until it was defiled by the Greeks, causing the Divine Presence to depart again.

4. The fourth special closeness came about when the Hasmoneans defeated the Greeks and repurified the Temple, so that God's Presence returned to His People.

5. The fifth period will be when the Third Temple is built, which will stand forever.

To allude to these five times of intimacy between God and Israel, Shelomo writes the following verses:

1. *[But] my Beloved was to me [as if He gave me] a pocket of myrrh; He would [nevertheless] reside between my breasts (Shir haShirim* 1:13) — A reference to the two poles of the *Aron haKodesh,* where the Tablets lay, and above which God's Voice was heard in the *Mishkan.*

2. *[I remember how] His left hand was [placed] under my head, and His right hand would embrace me (Ibid 2:6)* — A reference to the First Temple.

3. *Shortly after I left them, I found Him Whom my soul loves. I took hold of Him and would not let Him go, until I brought Him to my mother's House and to the Room of the one who bore me (Ibid 3:4)* — A reference to the Divine Presence that dwelled in the Second Temple.

4. *[God continues:] I entered My garden, My sister, the bride. I picked My myrrh with My perfume (Ibid 5:1)* — A reference to God coming back to His "garden," to again rest His Presence on the Second Temple, when the Hasmoneans drove away the Greeks.

5. *His left hand is [placed] under my head, and His right hand embraces me (Ibid 8:3)* — [Although the words are like those in 2:6, this is] a reference to the Third Temple, which will stand forever, may it be built soon in our days. When that time comes, never again will the nations be able to separate Israel from her Beloved. The construction of the Third Temple is guaranteed, for as to the love between God and Israel, Shelomo writes (Ibid 8:7): *Great amounts of water could not extinguish [my] love [for You], nor could rivers wash it away,* for it is a love that is *as strong as death (Ibid 8:6),* i.e., it cannot be compromised.

Thus, the Prophet Yirmeyahu calls Shelomo's *Shir haShirim* "his song of five." Yirmeyahu, added however, that *Shir haShirim* is Shelomo's song of five and one thousand. We understand why "five," but where does "one thousand" come in?

According to the Malbim, the last six verses in *Shir haShirim* (8:8-14) are a book in their own right, and in two of those verses — 11 and 12 — Shelomo mentions the number "one thousand." According to Rashi, these verses would be roughly understood as follows:

> *Shelomo [Hashem] had a vineyard [the People of Israel] in Jerusalem. He handed the vineyard over to guards [Babylonia, Persia, Greece, and Rome]. Each man [i.e., each of these four kingdoms thus] had fruit that would bring one thousand*

pieces of silver [i.e., the kingdoms could collect taxes from this "fruit"]. (verse 11)

[At the End of Days, the Holy One will say,] My vineyard [the People of Israel] lies before Me [i.e., although I put them into your hands, they are My People. And I see all that you have done to them, all that you have grabbed from them. You took the vineyard's fruit!] The thousand [pieces are] yours, Shelomo [the oppressors admit their guilt, and say to "Shelomo" (i.e., to God) that they will pay the thousand back to Him] and two hundred to the watchmen of His fruit [i.e., the nations that oppressed Israel also say that they shall add two hundred pieces of silver from their own pockets, in addition to the thousand that they will pay to God, and they will hand over the extra payment to Israel's leaders, the wise men who are Israel's true guards and watchmen, who actually do help God take care of the "vineyard"]. (verse 12)

According to the Malbim's interpretation of these verses, the translation will vary slightly, for the Malbim maintains that the name *Shelomo* actually means Shelomo and the allegory that is intended is completely different. These verses, however, help explain the words of Yirmeyahu (in *Melachim I*) — that Shelomo wrote *Mishlei*, and also *his song was five and one thousand* (based on *Malbim, Melachim I*, 5:12).

Translator's note: Perhaps this "Song of One Thousand" is actually a part of the "Song of Five." That is, as mentioned above, *Shir haShirim* is essentially a love song spanning the entire history of our Nation. Shelomo's masterpiece speaks of five "kisses" — five periods of intimacy between Israel and God — concluding with the final "reunion" between the two "lovers," at the End of Days.

Great amounts of water could not extinguish [my] love — The Temple will be rebuilt, never to be destroyed again, and the "lovers" will be together forever. Just as the Ultimate Redemption is the concluding episode of *Shir haShirim* as a whole — which is based on the number five — the Ultimate Redemption also is the concluding episode of the short song of "one thousand" at the end of *Shir haShirim*! God will "collect" from all the kingdoms that oppressed us! Thus, the Prophet Yirmeyahu aptly refers to Shelomo's *Shir haShirim* as: *his song was five and one thousand.*

The Parable of the Lovers

Shir haShirim is unlike the rest of the Holy Scriptures, for not once does it mention any one of God's Names, and neither is there any direct reference to God. (*The Book of Esther* also does not explicitly mention any of God's Names, but one verse can be seen as referring to one of His Names: *Relief and salvation shall stand up for the Jews from a different place* [*Megillas Esther* 4:14], for our Sages teach that God is the "Place" of the universe.)

As noted, all of *Shir haShirim* is parable, comparing the love relationship between the Holy One and Israel, to the relationship of love between a man and a woman. True, none of God's Names are mentioned, but the Holy One is certainly there, "between the lines" of the parables. In fact, our Sages add that every time in *Shir haShirim* that the name *Shelomo* is written, it is sacred (that is, it is considered as a Name of Hashem) for it signifies the One Who is the Source of *shalom* — peace.

According to one opinion in the Talmud (*Shevuos* 35b), there is only one exception to this rule — the verse (8:12): *My vineyard is Mine...Master of Peace [Shelomo]! The thousand to You...* [*Translator's note:* See above, about the "Song of One Thousand," that Rashi does not follow this opinion, for in his commentary on this very verse, Rashi explains that the name *Shelomo* means "God," even there! It is God Who is being paid "the thousand"! The Malbim, however, agrees with the above opinion, that the "thousand" is going to Shelomo himself, and according to the Malbim, this opinion in effect is stating that this verse is separate from *Shir haShirim*, for it is part of the "Song of One Thousand," which is a "song" in its own right.]

In the Midrash (*Shir haShirim Rabbah*, Chapter 1), the Sages say:

> *The world was never as worthy of having been created as it*

was on the day when Shir haShirim was given to Israel, for all of Scripture is holy, but Shir haShirim is the holiest of all things holy.

Holiness is achieved when man is able to raise himself from his lowly state, separate himself from worldly matters, and sanctify himself by denying himself that which is permitted so that he becomes bonded to the Higher sanctity. The highest degree of holiness, however, is achieved by one who reaches an even greater level of sanctity: to him all corporeal matters are transformed into acts of sanctity. He eats and drinks, he walks and finds pleasure, he engages in his livelihood and finds enjoyment. He does not separate himself from anything that is permitted — and the *Shechinah* manifests Its Presence in all that he does. He is like the wooden *aron* which became the repose for the Master of all the worlds, the site where He came after leaving all of His other worlds and where He established His major Presence. This is the highest degree of holiness.

When man reaches this level, he does not need to mention God's Name explicitly. Like Shelomo himself, every action of his, all that he did, invokes God's Presence in the world.

Man's preoccupation with the mundane affairs of this world is liable to separate him from God; if he is capable of investing all of his ordinary actions with spirituality so that they all strengthen his bond to God, then those very actions become more sanctified than all others. To the same degree that his actions bring him physical pleasures, so too can they be transformed into a vessel that holds God's blessings.

This is why our Sages referred to *Shir haShirim* as the "Holy of Holies" — the most sacred of all the Holy Writings — for it is built on an analogy to physical feelings of love between a man and a woman, the strongest physical feelings that people experience for one another, the greatest earthly desire that exists. This physical phenomenon is used for the sake of holiness, to describe Israel's bond with Hashem and Hashem's bond with Israel. The two "lovers" are eternally bound together, in boundless affection, so that any separation between them is only temporary, and eventually, they will embrace each other forever.

Reading Shir haShirim on Pesach

Shir haShirim shows us that all earthly desires are merely a metaphor to enable us to understand the love that we should have for God. This is alluded to in the name of the work — *Shir haShirim* — Song of Songs — that is, the song that is the sum of all songs. It is the melody of overwhelming joy that finds its ultimate expression when man speaks of his love for his Creator.

And yet, not everyone is capable of understanding the allegorical message of this song nor is every hour suitable for its expression. When man immerses himself solely in the parable — i.e., in the material world — he is not able to understand the higher message that the parable conveys.

On Pesach, however, the time of our freedom, one can learn the Will of the Almighty from nature and all the material world that surrounds him. The spiritual essence of the material world is then revealed before us. Pharaoh and his army, horse and rider, the sea and its tempest, the earth and all of creation, all were subordinate to the Will of God. It is by means of this revelation that Israel attained redemption.

The metaphor of *Shir haShirim* is especially relevant, therefore, on Pesach when we are all freed from the slavery of Egypt and the slavery to our evil inclination. At this time we are most apt to understand the song of love between God and His people: the Song of all Songs! (*Sefas Emes*)

Comments from the Zohar on Shir haShirim

R. Yosei said: Shelomo was inspired to write this "love song" at the time that he completed the building of the First Temple. This structure incorporated all the different "worlds" that comprise the creation, the upper ones and the lower ones, bringing all the "worlds" together into one entity. When the Temple — God's "Home" on earth — was completed, the joy before God was no less than the joy before Him on the day that He created the universe!

Shir haShirim — The Song of Songs

As the *Beis haMikdash* on earth was completed, a spiritual *Beis haMikdash* was completed on high, which permeated all the worlds and gave them light. On earth, a beautiful fragrance entered the atmosphere, wafting over the entire surface of the globe, as windows in heaven were opened to allow in the light from the Temple above. This was the greatest happiness that all the worlds had ever seen. At that moment, the heavens and earth burst into song — *Shir haShirim*, the song of the singers, those who sing praises to the Holy One.

David *haMelech* had sung his *Song of Ascents*, while it was Shelomo *haMelech* who merited to sing *Song of Songs*. But do not the songs resemble one another? Yes! In fact, they are One. It was only that in David's time, the Temple had not yet been built. Therefore, all the beings in all the different worlds who would sing their praises to God were not affixed yet in their proper places, and thus they could not yet sing the greatest song of all. Only when the song could be sung on earth, in the Temple, could the song be sung on high, for all is one, and these depend upon these.

When the Temple was finally completed, however, all the singers found their places, and a new light that never existed before began to shine. At this point, a new song was established to sing in honor of the Holy One — a song more sublime than any that had preceded it.

The day that this song was revealed on earth, a new "wholeness" entered creation, a wholeness and peace which derived from the very Source of Wholeness and Peace.

The day that this song was revealed on earth, the impurity from the snake in the Garden of Eden lost its effect on mankind, though it had infected our species since the days of Adam and Eve.

The day that this song was revealed on earth, the Divine Presence — the *Shechinah* — descended to earth, as it is written: *And the Kohanim were unable to serve because of the Cloud, for the Glory of God filled the House of God* (Melachim I, 8:11). Shelomo merited this song through Divine inspiration. And what is the nature of this song? All of the Torah is incorporated in it, and all the secrets about how God created the heavens and the earth, and everything that is contained within them. The lives of the Patriarchs are included therein, as well as all that happened to our forefathers in Egypt, and how they were redeemed. The Song that they sang after the splitting of the sea is included, as well as the Ten Commandments, the covenant that was made at Mount Sinai, how our forefathers traveled in the desert, how they entered the Land of Israel, and everything up to the construction of the Temple. *Shir haShirim* includes the Crown that is made of His Holy Name, with all of His Name's sanctity, love, and joy. It contains all our People's exiles among the nations, as well as the redemptions from those exiles, the coming resurrection of the dead, and the Ultimate Shabbos to Hashem. Everything that was, is, and will be in the future is included in this song!

Therefore, our Sages tell us: *Were anyone to take even one verse out of Shir haShirim, and say it aloud in a tavern or at a party, where wine is being drunk in levity, the Torah would dress in sackcloth and ascend to the Holy One to complain: Your children are making a mockery of Me!*

This being so, every one of us must be extremely careful about each word of *Shir haShirim*, and we must lay a crown upon each word, before we actually emit it from our lips.

שִׁיר הַשִּׁירִים

א א שִׁיר (ש׳ רבתי) הַשִּׁירִים אֲשֶׁר לִשְׁלֹמֹה: ב יִשָּׁקֵנִי מִנְּשִׁיקוֹת פִּיהוּ כִּי־טוֹבִים דֹּדֶיךָ מִיָּיִן: ג לְרֵיחַ שְׁמָנֶיךָ טוֹבִים שֶׁמֶן תּוּרַק שְׁמֶךָ עַל־כֵּן עֲלָמוֹת אֲהֵבוּךָ: ד מָשְׁכֵנִי אַחֲרֶיךָ נָּרוּצָה הֱבִיאַנִי הַמֶּלֶךְ חֲדָרָיו נָגִילָה וְנִשְׂמְחָה בָּךְ נַזְכִּירָה דֹדֶיךָ מִיַּיִן מֵישָׁרִים אֲהֵבוּךָ: ס ה שְׁחוֹרָה אֲנִי וְנָאוָה בְּנוֹת יְרוּשָׁלִָם כְּאָהֳלֵי קֵדָר כִּירִיעוֹת שְׁלֹמֹה: ו אַל־תִּרְאוּנִי שֶׁאֲנִי שְׁחַרְחֹרֶת שֶׁשְּׁזָפַתְנִי הַשָּׁמֶשׁ בְּנֵי אִמִּי נִחֲרוּ־בִי שָׂמֻנִי נֹטֵרָה אֶת־הַכְּרָמִים כַּרְמִי שֶׁלִּי לֹא נָטָרְתִּי: ז הַגִּידָה לִּי שֶׁאָהֲבָה נַפְשִׁי אֵיכָה תִרְעֶה אֵיכָה תַּרְבִּיץ בַּצָּהֳרָיִם שַׁלָּמָה אֶהְיֶה כְּעֹטְיָה עַל עֶדְרֵי חֲבֵרֶיךָ: ח אִם־לֹא תֵדְעִי לָךְ הַיָּפָה בַּנָּשִׁים צְאִי־לָךְ בְּעִקְבֵי הַצֹּאן וּרְעִי אֶת־גְּדִיֹּתַיִךְ עַל מִשְׁכְּנוֹת הָרֹעִים: ס ט לְסֻסָתִי בְּרִכְבֵי פַרְעֹה דִּמִּיתִיךְ רַעְיָתִי: י נָאווּ לְחָיַיִךְ בַּתֹּרִים צַוָּארֵךְ בַּחֲרוּזִים: יא תּוֹרֵי זָהָב נַעֲשֶׂה־לָּךְ עִם נְקֻדּוֹת הַכָּסֶף: יב עַד־שֶׁהַמֶּלֶךְ בִּמְסִבּוֹ נִרְדִּי נָתַן רֵיחוֹ: יג צְרוֹר הַמֹּר ׀ דּוֹדִי לִי בֵּין שָׁדַי יָלִין: יד אֶשְׁכֹּל הַכֹּפֶר ׀ דּוֹדִי לִי בְּכַרְמֵי עֵין גֶּדִי: ס טו הִנָּךְ יָפָה רַעְיָתִי הִנָּךְ יָפָה עֵינַיִךְ יוֹנִים: טז הִנְּךָ יָפֶה דוֹדִי אַף נָעִים אַף־עַרְשֵׂנוּ רַעֲנָנָה: יז קֹרוֹת בָּתֵּינוּ אֲרָזִים רַחִיטֵנוּ (רַהִיטֵנוּ ק׳) בְּרוֹתִים:

Shir haShirim

1

¹THE SONG OF [ALL] SONGS, which is [dedicated] to [God,] the Master of Peace. ²[Yisrael, in exile, says to God:] If only He would kiss me with the kisses of His Mouth, for Your love is better [for me] than wine [and all wordly pleasures]. ³On account of the fragrance of Your fine oils, Your fame is [now like] poured [aromatic] oil; therefore young maidens fell in love with You. ⁴[You sent messengers to] draw me [to You, but I responded,] "We shall run after You!" The King brought me to His [private] rooms, [and even now] we are ecstatic and rejoice [that we were once close] to You. We recall Your love [more] than wine [and all wordly pleasures]; [we] loved You with an unrestrained love. ⁵[Yisrael then says to the nations:] I am blackened but of beautiful figure, daughters of Yerushalayim. [Though I am now black] like the tents of the Kedarim, [I can be easily cleansed to be] like the hangings of the Master of Peace. ⁶Do not look at me [disparagingly] because I am deep black, for the sun tanned me. My mother's sons enticed me, [until] they placed me as keeper of the vineyards. My own vineyard, [however,] I did not guard. ⁷[Yisrael then says to God:] Tell me, You Whom my soul loves! How could You pasture [Your flock like this]?! How could You have [them] crouch in the heat of the day?! For why let me be like one shrouded [in mourning over my sheep], alongside the flocks of Your colleagues? ⁸[God responds:] The most beautiful among women! If you do not know [where to lead your sheep], go out [and follow] the tracks of the flock, and [then you will be able to] pasture your kid goats [even] among the dwellings of the [other] shepherds. ⁹Through My troop of horses among Par'oh's chariots, I silenced you, My dear one. ¹⁰Your cheeks were beautified with rows [of jewelry]; your neck, with strings [of precious stones]. ¹¹[I and My Heavenly Court decided] We would make rows of gold [jewelry] for you, besides the engraved articles of silver. ¹²[Yisrael responds:] [Even] while the King was still at His [wedding] feast my spikenard spoiled its fragrance. ¹³[But] my Beloved was to me [as if He gave me] a pocket of myrrh; He would [nevertheless] reside between my breasts. ¹⁴My Beloved was to me [as if He gave me] a kofer cluster from among the vineyards of Ein Gedi. ¹⁵[God consoles Yisrael:] You are indeed beautiful, My dear one; you are indeed beautiful, [for] your eyes are [like those of] doves. ¹⁶[Yisrael responds:] It is You, my Beloved, who are indeed beautiful [and] also pleasant, [and thus] our bed, too, is flourishing. ¹⁷The walls of our House are of cedar wood; our furnishings, of cypress wood.

Shir haShirim

ב א אֲנִי֙ חֲבַצֶּ֣לֶת הַשָּׁר֔וֹן שֽׁוֹשַׁנַּ֖ת הָעֲמָקִֽים: ב כְּשֽׁוֹשַׁנָּה֙ בֵּ֣ין הַחוֹחִ֔ים כֵּ֥ן רַעְיָתִ֖י בֵּ֥ין הַבָּנֽוֹת: ג כְּתַפּ֨וּחַ֙ בַּעֲצֵ֣י הַיַּ֔עַר כֵּ֥ן דּוֹדִ֖י בֵּ֣ין הַבָּנִ֑ים בְּצִלּוֹ֙ חִמַּ֣דְתִּי וְיָשַׁ֔בְתִּי וּפִרְי֖וֹ מָת֥וֹק לְחִכִּֽי: ד הֱבִיאַ֙נִי֙ אֶל־בֵּ֣ית הַיָּ֔יִן וְדִגְל֥וֹ עָלַ֖י אַהֲבָֽה: ה סַמְּכ֙וּנִי֙ בָּאֲשִׁישׁ֔וֹת רַפְּד֖וּנִי בַּתַּפּוּחִ֑ים כִּי־חוֹלַ֥ת אַהֲבָ֖ה אָֽנִי: ו שְׂמֹאלוֹ֙ תַּ֣חַת לְרֹאשִׁ֔י וִימִינ֖וֹ תְּחַבְּקֵֽנִי: ז הִשְׁבַּ֨עְתִּי אֶתְכֶ֜ם בְּנ֤וֹת יְרֽוּשָׁלִַ֙ם֙ בִּצְבָא֔וֹת א֖וֹ בְּאַיְל֣וֹת הַשָּׂדֶ֑ה אִם־תָּעִ֧ירוּ | וְאִם־תְּעֽוֹרְר֛וּ אֶת־הָאַהֲבָ֖ה עַ֥ד שֶׁתֶּחְפָּֽץ: ס ח ק֣וֹל דּוֹדִ֔י הִנֵּה־זֶ֖ה בָּ֑א מְדַלֵּג֙ עַל־הֶ֣הָרִ֔ים מְקַפֵּ֖ץ עַל־הַגְּבָעֽוֹת: ט דּוֹמֶ֤ה דוֹדִי֙ לִצְבִ֔י א֖וֹ לְעֹ֣פֶר הָֽאַיָּלִ֑ים הִנֵּה־זֶ֤ה עוֹמֵד֙ אַחַ֣ר כָּתְלֵ֔נוּ מַשְׁגִּ֙יחַ֙ מִן־הַֽחֲלֹּנ֔וֹת מֵצִ֖יץ מִן־הַֽחֲרַכִּֽים: י עָנָ֥ה דוֹדִ֖י וְאָ֣מַר לִ֑י ק֥וּמִי לָ֛ךְ רַעְיָתִ֥י יָפָתִ֖י וּלְכִי־לָֽךְ: יא כִּֽי־הִנֵּ֥ה הַסְּתָ֖ו עָבָ֑ר הַגֶּ֕שֶׁם חָלַ֖ף הָלַ֥ךְ לֽוֹ: יב הַנִּצָּנִים֙ נִרְא֣וּ בָאָ֔רֶץ עֵ֥ת הַזָּמִ֖יר הִגִּ֑יעַ וְק֥וֹל הַתּ֖וֹר נִשְׁמַ֥ע בְּאַרְצֵֽנוּ: יג הַתְּאֵנָה֙ חָֽנְטָ֣ה פַגֶּ֔יהָ וְהַגְּפָנִ֥ים | סְמָדַ֖ר נָ֣תְנוּ רֵ֑יחַ ק֥וּמִי לָ֛ךְ (לָךְ ק) רַעְיָתִ֥י יָפָתִ֖י וּלְכִי־לָֽךְ: ס יד יוֹנָתִ֞י בְּחַגְוֵ֣י הַסֶּ֗לַע בְּסֵ֙תֶר֙ הַמַּדְרֵגָ֔ה הַרְאִ֙ינִי֙ אֶת־מַרְאַ֔יִךְ הַשְׁמִיעִ֖ינִי אֶת־קוֹלֵ֑ךְ כִּי־קוֹלֵ֥ךְ עָרֵ֖ב וּמַרְאֵ֥יךְ נָאוֶֽה: ס טו אֶֽחֱזוּ־לָ֙נוּ֙ שֽׁוּעָלִ֔ים שֽׁוּעָלִ֥ים קְטַנִּ֖ים מְחַבְּלִ֣ים כְּרָמִ֑ים וּכְרָמֵ֖ינוּ סְמָדַֽר: טז דּוֹדִ֥י לִי֙ וַאֲנִ֣י ל֔וֹ הָרֹעֶ֖ה בַּשּׁוֹשַׁנִּֽים: יז עַ֤ד שֶׁיָּפ֙וּחַ֙ הַיּ֔וֹם וְנָ֖סוּ הַצְּלָלִ֑ים סֹב֩ דְּמֵה־לְךָ֨ דוֹדִ֜י לִצְבִ֗י א֛וֹ לְעֹ֥פֶר הָאַיָּלִ֖ים עַל־הָ֥רֵי בָֽתֶר: ס ג א עַל־מִשְׁכָּבִי֙ בַּלֵּיל֔וֹת בִּקַּ֕שְׁתִּי אֵ֥ת שֶׁאָהֲבָ֖ה נַפְשִׁ֑י בִּקַּשְׁתִּ֖יו וְלֹ֥א מְצָאתִֽיו: ב אָק֙וּמָה נָּ֜א וַאֲסוֹבְבָ֣ה בָעִ֗יר בַּשְּׁוָקִים֙ וּבָ֣רְחֹב֔וֹת אֲבַקְשָׁ֕ה אֵ֥ת שֶׁאָהֲבָ֖ה נַפְשִׁ֑י בִּקַּשְׁתִּ֖יו וְלֹ֥א מְצָאתִֽיו: ג מְצָא֙וּנִי֙ הַשֹּׁ֣מְרִ֔ים הַסֹּבְבִ֖ים בָּעִ֑יר אֵ֥ת שֶׁאָהֲבָ֛ה נַפְשִׁ֖י רְאִיתֶֽם: ד כִּמְעַט֙ שֶׁעָבַ֣רְתִּי מֵהֶ֔ם עַ֣ד שֶֽׁמָּצָ֔אתִי אֵ֥ת שֶׁאָהֲבָ֖ה נַפְשִׁ֑י אֲחַזְתִּיו֙ וְלֹ֣א

2 ¹[Y ISRAEL THEN SAYS:] I am [like] the rose of Sharon; [even like] the lush rose of the valleys. ²[God responds:] Like a rose amidst the thorns, so is My dear one amidst the [other] maidens. ³[Yisrael replies:] Like an apple tree among the trees of the forest, so is my Beloved among the [other] young men. I yearned for His shade and sat [under it], and His fruit is sweet to my palate. ⁴He brought me to the banqueting house, and [my] attraction to Him [still arouses in] me [feelings of] love. ⁵[So now,] sustain me with flasks [of nutrients and] spread [fragrant] apples around me, for I am lovesick. ⁶[I remember how] His left hand was [placed] under my head, and His right hand would embrace me. ⁷I hold you to oath, daughters of Yerushalayim, [that you will be punished to be like] the deer or the gazelles of the field, if you cause hatred or challenge the love [between me and my Beloved] while it is still strongly desired. ⁸[Yisrael then reminisces about the redemption from Mitzrayim:] It is the sound of my Beloved. He is coming right now, leaping over the mountains [and] springing over the hills. ⁹My Beloved is like a stag or gazelle fawn. He is there, standing behind our wall, gazing from the windows [and] looking in from the casements. ¹⁰My Beloved called out and said to me, "Arise, My dear one, My fair one, and go on your [way]! ¹¹For winter has now passed; the rain has disappeared and gone away. ¹²The blossoms have appeared in the land, the season of the birds' song has arrived, and the sound of the turtle-dove is heard in our land. ¹³The fig-tree has sprouted its [yet] unripe fruit, and the vines, young grapes; they have produced a fragrance. Arise, My dear, My fair one, and go on your [way]! ¹⁴My dove is in the clefts of the rock, in the nooks of the stairs! Show Me [now] your [true] image, [and] let Me hear your voice, for your voice is sweet, and your appearance, beautiful." ¹⁵[We called out,] "Seize for us the foxes, [even] the small foxes, those that damaged the vineyards while our vineyards were [still] unripe." ¹⁶My Beloved [relied upon] me and I [relied upon] Him, the One Who pastures [His flock] among the roses. ¹⁷[This was] until the day sweltered and the shadows disappeared. [You then] turned around, my Beloved, as if You were like a stag or gazelle fawn upon remote mountains.

3 ¹[WHILE LYING] UPON MY BED AT NIGHTS, I searched for Him Whom my soul loves; I searched for Him but did not find Him. ²Let me now arise and go around the city, among the streets and plazas, [and] seek Him Whom my soul loves! I searched for Him but did not find Him. ³The guards who patrol the city found me. [I asked them,] "Have you seen Him Whom my soul loves?" ⁴Shortly after I left them I found Him Whom my soul loves. I took hold of Him and

אֲרָפֶּנּוּ עַד־שֶׁהֲבֵיאתִיו אֶל־בֵּית אִמִּי וְאֶל־חֶדֶר הוֹרָתִי: ה הִשְׁבַּעְתִּי אֶתְכֶם בְּנוֹת יְרוּשָׁלִַם בִּצְבָאוֹת אוֹ בְּאַיְלוֹת הַשָּׂדֶה אִם־תָּעִירוּ ׀ וְאִם־תְּעוֹרְרוּ אֶת־הָאַהֲבָה עַד שֶׁתֶּחְפָּץ: ס ו מִי זֹאת עֹלָה מִן־הַמִּדְבָּר כְּתִימֲרוֹת עָשָׁן מְקֻטֶּרֶת מֹר וּלְבוֹנָה מִכֹּל אַבְקַת רוֹכֵל: ז הִנֵּה מִטָּתוֹ שֶׁלִּשְׁלֹמֹה שִׁשִּׁים גִּבֹּרִים סָבִיב לָהּ מִגִּבֹּרֵי יִשְׂרָאֵל: ח כֻּלָּם אֲחֻזֵי חֶרֶב מְלֻמְּדֵי מִלְחָמָה אִישׁ חַרְבּוֹ עַל־יְרֵכוֹ מִפַּחַד בַּלֵּילוֹת: ס ט אַפִּרְיוֹן עָשָׂה לוֹ הַמֶּלֶךְ שְׁלֹמֹה מֵעֲצֵי הַלְּבָנוֹן: י עַמּוּדָיו עָשָׂה כֶסֶף רְפִידָתוֹ זָהָב מֶרְכָּבוֹ אַרְגָּמָן תּוֹכוֹ רָצוּף אַהֲבָה מִבְּנוֹת יְרוּשָׁלִָם: יא צְאֶינָה ׀ וּרְאֶינָה בְּנוֹת צִיּוֹן בַּמֶּלֶךְ שְׁלֹמֹה בָּעֲטָרָה שֶׁעִטְּרָה־לּוֹ אִמּוֹ בְּיוֹם חֲתֻנָּתוֹ וּבְיוֹם שִׂמְחַת לִבּוֹ: ס

ד א הִנָּךְ יָפָה רַעְיָתִי הִנָּךְ יָפָה עֵינַיִךְ יוֹנִים מִבַּעַד לְצַמָּתֵךְ שַׂעְרֵךְ כְּעֵדֶר הָעִזִּים שֶׁגָּלְשׁוּ מֵהַר גִּלְעָד: ב שִׁנַּיִךְ כְּעֵדֶר הַקְּצוּבוֹת שֶׁעָלוּ מִן־הָרַחְצָה שֶׁכֻּלָּם מַתְאִימוֹת וְשַׁכֻּלָה אֵין בָּהֶם: ג כְּחוּט הַשָּׁנִי שִׂפְתוֹתַיִךְ וּמִדְבָּרֵיךְ נָאוֶה כְּפֶלַח הָרִמּוֹן רַקָּתֵךְ מִבַּעַד לְצַמָּתֵךְ: ד כְּמִגְדַּל דָּוִיד צַוָּארֵךְ בָּנוּי לְתַלְפִּיּוֹת אֶלֶף הַמָּגֵן תָּלוּי עָלָיו כֹּל שִׁלְטֵי הַגִּבֹּרִים: ה שְׁנֵי שָׁדַיִךְ כִּשְׁנֵי עֳפָרִים תְּאוֹמֵי צְבִיָּה הָרוֹעִים בַּשּׁוֹשַׁנִּים: ו עַד שֶׁיָּפוּחַ הַיּוֹם וְנָסוּ הַצְּלָלִים אֵלֶךְ לִי אֶל־הַר הַמּוֹר וְאֶל־גִּבְעַת הַלְּבוֹנָה: ז כֻּלָּךְ יָפָה רַעְיָתִי וּמוּם אֵין בָּךְ: ס ח אִתִּי מִלְּבָנוֹן כַּלָּה אִתִּי מִלְּבָנוֹן תָּבוֹאִי תָּשׁוּרִי ׀ מֵרֹאשׁ אֲמָנָה מֵרֹאשׁ שְׂנִיר וְחֶרְמוֹן מִמְּעֹנוֹת אֲרָיוֹת מֵהַרְרֵי נְמֵרִים: ט לִבַּבְתִּנִי אֲחֹתִי כַלָּה לִבַּבְתִּנִי באחד (בְּאַחַת ק) מֵעֵינַיִךְ בְּאַחַד עֲנָק מִצַּוְּרֹנָיִךְ: י מַה־יָּפוּ דֹדַיִךְ אֲחֹתִי כַלָּה מַה־טֹּבוּ דֹדַיִךְ מִיַּיִן וְרֵיחַ שְׁמָנַיִךְ מִכָּל־בְּשָׂמִים: יא נֹפֶת תִּטֹּפְנָה שִׂפְתוֹתַיִךְ כַּלָּה

would not let Him go, until I brought Him to my mother's House and to the Room of the one who bore me. ⁵I held you to oath, daughters of Yerushalayim, [that you would be punished to be like] the deer or the gazelles of the field, if you caused hatred or challenged the love [between me and my Beloved] while it was still strongly desired. ⁶[The nations exclaimed,] "Who is This coming up from the desert like erect columns of smoke, fumed with myrrh and frankincense, [and] with all the powders of the perfume vendor?" ⁷Look! The Bed of the Master of Peace [has] sixty mighty men around it, of the mighty warriors of Yisrael. ⁸All are girded with swords [and] trained for battle; each man has his sword at his thigh, out of fear [of what will be] in the nights. ⁹The King, Master of Peace, made for Himself a canopy out of Levanon wood. ¹⁰Its pillars He made of silver, His couch of gold, [and] its hangings, of purple [wool]. Its interior was furnished with [furnishings of] love from the daughters of Yerushalayim. ¹¹Women of distinction! Go out and observe the King, Master of Peace, with the crown with which His mother adorned Him on the day of His wedding and on the day His heart rejoiced.

4

¹[GOD THEN PRAISES YISRAEL:] You are indeed beautiful, My dear one, you are indeed beautiful; your image is [like] a dove. Under your snood, your hair is like [that of] the goat flock that descends from Mount Gil'ad, leaving it exposed. ²Your teeth are [fine and white] like the flock of selected [ewes] which came up from the bathing pool, which are all perfect with no defect among them. ³Your lips are like a scarlet thread, and your diction is beautiful; your upper cheek is like a section of pomegranate, under your snood. ⁴Your neck is like the Tower of David built as a model. A thousand shields hang on its [walls, with] all the quivers of the mighty warriors. ⁵Your two breasts are like two [identical] fawns, twins [born of] a hind, that pasture among the roses. ⁶[This was] until the sun sweltered and the shadows disappeared. [I then said,] "I will go away to the mountain of myrrh and the hill of frankincense." ⁷[There,] My dear one, you were completely beautiful and there was no blemish on you. ⁸[When you will be exiled] from Levanon [it will be] with Me, O bride, [and] with Me, [Who has been with you] since Levanon, you will return. Contemplate the beginnings of [your] faith, [until you came to] the peaks of Senir and Chermon, the lions' lairs [and] leopards' mountains. ⁹You drew My heart to you, My sister, the bride; you endeared Me to you with [even] one of your [fine] images, with [even] one link of your necklace. ¹⁰How beautiful are your affections, My sister, the bride. How much more pleasing than wine are your affections, and the fragrance of your oil, than all perfumes. ¹¹[From] your lips flows sweetness, O bride. Honey and

Shir haShirim

דְּבַשׁ וְחָלָב֙ תַּ֣חַת לְשׁוֹנֵ֔ךְ וְרֵ֥יחַ שַׂלְמֹתַ֖יִךְ כְּרֵ֥יחַ לְבָנֽוֹן: ס יב גַּ֥ן ׀ נָע֖וּל אֲחֹתִ֣י כַלָּ֑ה גַּ֥ל נָע֖וּל מַעְיָ֥ן חָתֽוּם: יג שְׁלָחַ֨יִךְ֙ פַּרְדֵּ֣ס רִמּוֹנִ֔ים עִ֖ם פְּרִ֣י מְגָדִ֑ים כְּפָרִ֖ים עִם־נְרָדִֽים: יד נֵ֣רְדְּ ׀ וְכַרְכֹּ֗ם קָנֶה֙ וְקִנָּמ֔וֹן עִ֖ם כָּל־עֲצֵ֣י לְבוֹנָ֑ה מֹ֣ר וַאֲהָל֔וֹת עִ֖ם כָּל־רָאשֵׁ֥י בְשָׂמִֽים: טו מַעְיַ֣ן גַּנִּ֔ים בְּאֵ֖ר מַ֣יִם חַיִּ֑ים וְנֹזְלִ֖ים מִן־לְבָנֽוֹן: טז ע֤וּרִי צָפוֹן֙ וּב֣וֹאִי תֵימָ֔ן הָפִ֥יחִי גַנִּ֖י יִזְּל֣וּ בְשָׂמָ֑יו יָבֹ֤א דוֹדִי֙ לְגַנּ֔וֹ וְיֹאכַ֖ל פְּרִ֥י מְגָדָֽיו:

ה א בָּ֣אתִי לְגַנִּי֮ אֲחֹתִ֣י כַלָּה֒ אָרִ֤יתִי מוֹרִי֙ עִם־בְּשָׂמִ֔י אָכַ֤לְתִּי יַעְרִי֙ עִם־דִּבְשִׁ֔י שָׁתִ֥יתִי יֵינִ֖י עִם־חֲלָבִ֑י אִכְל֣וּ רֵעִ֔ים שְׁת֥וּ וְשִׁכְר֖וּ דּוֹדִֽים: ס ב אֲנִ֥י יְשֵׁנָ֖ה וְלִבִּ֣י עֵ֑ר ק֣וֹל ׀ דּוֹדִ֣י דוֹפֵ֗ק פִּתְחִי־לִ֞י אֲחֹתִ֤י רַעְיָתִי֙ יוֹנָתִ֣י תַמָּתִ֔י שֶׁרֹּאשִׁי֙ נִמְלָא־טָ֔ל קְוֻצּוֹתַ֖י רְסִ֥יסֵי לָֽיְלָה: ג פָּשַׁ֨טְתִּי֙ אֶת־כֻּתָּנְתִּ֔י אֵיכָ֖כָה אֶלְבָּשֶׁ֑נָּה רָחַ֥צְתִּי אֶת־רַגְלַ֖י אֵיכָ֥כָה אֲטַנְּפֵֽם: ד דּוֹדִ֗י שָׁלַ֤ח יָדוֹ֙ מִן־הַחֹ֔ר וּמֵעַ֖י הָמ֥וּ עָלָֽיו: ה קַ֥מְתִּֽי אֲנִ֖י לִפְתֹּ֣חַ לְדוֹדִ֑י וְיָדַ֣י נָֽטְפוּ־מ֗וֹר וְאֶצְבְּעֹתַי֙ מ֣וֹר עֹבֵ֔ר עַ֖ל כַּפּ֥וֹת הַמַּנְעֽוּל: ו פָּתַ֤חְתִּֽי אֲנִי֙ לְדוֹדִ֔י וְדוֹדִ֖י חָמַ֣ק עָבָ֑ר נַפְשִׁי֙ יָֽצְאָ֣ה בְדַבְּר֔וֹ בִּקַּשְׁתִּ֙יהוּ֙ וְלֹ֣א מְצָאתִ֔יהוּ קְרָאתִ֖יו וְלֹ֥א עָנָֽנִי: ז מְצָאֻ֧נִי הַשֹּׁמְרִ֛ים הַסֹּבְבִ֥ים בָּעִ֖יר הִכּ֣וּנִי פְצָע֑וּנִי נָשְׂא֤וּ אֶת־רְדִידִי֙ מֵֽעָלַ֔י שֹׁמְרֵ֖י הַחֹמֽוֹת: ח הִשְׁבַּ֥עְתִּי אֶתְכֶ֖ם בְּנ֣וֹת יְרוּשָׁלָ֑͏ִם אִֽם־תִּמְצְאוּ֙ אֶת־דּוֹדִ֔י מַה־תַּגִּ֣ידוּ ל֔וֹ שֶׁחוֹלַ֥ת אַהֲבָ֖ה אָֽנִי: ט מַה־דּוֹדֵ֣ךְ מִדּ֔וֹד הַיָּפָ֖ה בַּנָּשִׁ֑ים מַה־דּוֹדֵ֣ךְ מִדּ֔וֹד שֶׁכָּ֖כָה הִשְׁבַּעְתָּֽנוּ: י דּוֹדִ֥י צַח֙ וְאָד֔וֹם דָּג֖וּל מֵרְבָבָֽה: יא רֹאשׁ֖וֹ כֶּ֣תֶם פָּ֑ז קְוֻצּוֹתָיו֙ תַּלְתַּלִּ֔ים שְׁחֹר֖וֹת כָּעוֹרֵֽב: יב עֵינָ֕יו כְּיוֹנִ֖ים עַל־אֲפִ֣יקֵי מָ֑יִם רֹֽחֲצוֹת֙ בֶּֽחָלָ֔ב יֹשְׁב֖וֹת עַל־מִלֵּֽאת: יג לְחָיָו֙ כַּעֲרוּגַ֣ת הַבֹּ֔שֶׂם מִגְדְּל֖וֹת מֶרְקָחִ֑ים שִׂפְתוֹתָיו֙ שֽׁוֹשַׁנִּ֔ים נֹטְפ֖וֹת מ֥וֹר עֹבֵֽר: יד יָדָיו֙ גְּלִילֵ֣י זָהָ֔ב מְמֻלָּאִ֖ים

milk are under your tongue, and the fragrance of your garments is like the fragrance of Levanon. ¹²My sister, the bride, is [like] a locked garden; a plugged wellspring, a sealed fountain. ¹³[Even] your arid fields [are as abundant as] a pomegranate orchard, with luscious fruit; kofers with spikenards. ¹⁴Spikenard, saffron, spice cane and cinnamon, with all [kinds of] frankincense wood; myrrh and aloes, with all the choicest perfumes. ¹⁵A garden fountain; a well of fresh water that flows from Levanon. ¹⁶North wind, be aroused, and south wind, come! Blow across My garden [so that] its perfumes flow forth. [Yisrael responds:] Let my Beloved enter His garden and eat His luscious fruit.

5

¹[GOD CONTINUES:] I entered My garden, My sister, the bride. I picked My myrrh with My perfume; I [even] ate My honey cane with My honey, [and] drank My [red] wine with My milk[-like white wine]. Eat, dear ones! Drink and become intoxicated, beloved ones! ²[Yisrael then says:] I was asleep, but my Heart was awake. The voice of my Beloved is knocking [and saying,] "Open for Me, My sister, My dear one, My dove, My sincere one, for My head is filled with dew; My [matted] locks of hair, [with] heavy raindrops of the night." ³I have removed my robe. How can I put it on [again]? I have washed my feet. How can I make them dirty? ⁴My Beloved stretched His hand through the gap [of the door], and [on seeing it,] my innards churned [in yearning] for Him. ⁵I rose to open for my Beloved, while myrrh dripped from my hands, and strong-scented myrrh [dripped] from my fingers onto the handles of the lock. ⁶I opened [the door] for my Beloved, but my Beloved had disappeared [and] gone. My soul left [me] when He declared, ["I will not enter."] I searched for Him but did not find Him; I called Him but He did not answer me. ⁷The guards who patrol the city found me; they beat me [and] wounded me. The guards of the walls removed my fine jewelry from me. ⁸I hold you to oath, daughters of Yerushalayim, [that] if you find my Beloved, what you will testify to Him [is] that I am lovesick. ⁹[The nations ask Yisrael:] The most beautiful among women! In what way is your Beloved [different] from any [other] friend? In what way is your Beloved [different] from any [other] friend, that you hold us to oath like this? ¹⁰[Yisrael responds:] My Beloved is white but [of] ruddy [complexion], escorted by tens of thousands [of soldiers]. ¹¹His head [shines like] a fine gold jewel; His locks of hair hang in curls, black as a raven. ¹²His eyes are like [those of] doves, [when they look out] on pools of water; [they are] bathed in milk [and] positioned in [their] proper settings. ¹³His cheeks are like a plant-bed of perfume spices [where] plants of fragrance blends [grow]. His lips are [like] roses, dripping strong-scented myrrh. ¹⁴His hands are

Shir haShirim

בַּתַּרְשִׁישׁ מֵעָיו עֶשֶׁת שֵׁן מְעֻלֶּפֶת סַפִּירִים: טו שׁוֹקָיו עַמּוּדֵי שֵׁשׁ מְיֻסָּדִים עַל־אַדְנֵי־פָז מַרְאֵהוּ כַּלְּבָנוֹן בָּחוּר כָּאֲרָזִים: טז חִכּוֹ מַמְתַקִּים וְכֻלּוֹ מַחֲמַדִּים זֶה דוֹדִי וְזֶה רֵעִי בְּנוֹת יְרוּשָׁלָם:

ו א אָנָה הָלַךְ דּוֹדֵךְ הַיָּפָה בַּנָּשִׁים אָנָה פָּנָה דוֹדֵךְ וּנְבַקְשֶׁנּוּ עִמָּךְ: ב דּוֹדִי יָרַד לְגַנּוֹ לַעֲרוּגוֹת הַבֹּשֶׂם לִרְעוֹת בַּגַּנִּים וְלִלְקֹט שׁוֹשַׁנִּים: ג אֲנִי לְדוֹדִי וְדוֹדִי לִי הָרֹעֶה בַּשּׁוֹשַׁנִּים: ס ד יָפָה אַתְּ רַעְיָתִי כְּתִרְצָה נָאוָה כִּירוּשָׁלָם אֲיֻמָּה כַּנִּדְגָּלוֹת: ה הָסֵבִּי עֵינַיִךְ מִנֶּגְדִּי שֶׁהֵם הִרְהִיבֻנִי שַׂעְרֵךְ כְּעֵדֶר הָעִזִּים שֶׁגָּלְשׁוּ מִן־הַגִּלְעָד: ו שִׁנַּיִךְ כְּעֵדֶר הָרְחֵלִים שֶׁעָלוּ מִן־הָרַחְצָה שֶׁכֻּלָּם מַתְאִימוֹת וְשַׁכֻּלָה אֵין בָּהֶם: ז כְּפֶלַח הָרִמּוֹן רַקָּתֵךְ מִבַּעַד לְצַמָּתֵךְ: ח שִׁשִּׁים הֵמָּה מְלָכוֹת וּשְׁמֹנִים פִּילַגְשִׁים וַעֲלָמוֹת אֵין מִסְפָּר: ט אַחַת הִיא יוֹנָתִי תַמָּתִי אַחַת הִיא לְאִמָּהּ בָּרָה הִיא לְיוֹלַדְתָּהּ רָאוּהָ בָנוֹת וַיְאַשְּׁרוּהָ מְלָכוֹת וּפִילַגְשִׁים וַיְהַלְלוּהָ: ס י מִי־זֹאת הַנִּשְׁקָפָה כְּמוֹ־שָׁחַר יָפָה כַלְּבָנָה בָּרָה כַּחַמָּה אֲיֻמָּה כַּנִּדְגָּלוֹת: יא אֶל־גִּנַּת אֱגוֹז יָרַדְתִּי לִרְאוֹת בְּאִבֵּי הַנָּחַל לִרְאוֹת הֲפָרְחָה הַגֶּפֶן הֵנֵצוּ הָרִמֹּנִים: יב לֹא יָדַעְתִּי נַפְשִׁי שָׂמַתְנִי מַרְכְּבוֹת עַמִּי־נָדִיב:

ז א שׁוּבִי שׁוּבִי הַשּׁוּלַמִּית שׁוּבִי שׁוּבִי וְנֶחֱזֶה־בָּךְ מַה־תֶּחֱזוּ בַּשּׁוּלַמִּית כִּמְחֹלַת הַמַּחֲנָיִם: ב מַה־יָּפוּ פְעָמַיִךְ בַּנְּעָלִים בַּת־נָדִיב חַמּוּקֵי יְרֵכַיִךְ כְּמוֹ חֲלָאִים מַעֲשֵׂה יְדֵי אָמָּן:

[like] golden wheels inset with tarshish-stone. His innards are [like] a mass of ivory adorned with sapphires. ¹⁵His thighs are [like] marble pillars supported on fine gold bases. His appearance is [tall like the cedars of] Levanon. [He is] distinguished [among young men], like cedars [are among trees]. ¹⁶His palate [emits] sweet [words], and His whole Being is [made of] precious things. This is my Beloved and this is my Dear One, daughters of Yerushalayim!

6 ¹[THE NATIONS TAUNT YISRAEL:] The most beautiful among women! Where has your Beloved gone? To where has your Beloved turned, that we may search for Him with you?! ²[Yisrael responds:] My Beloved has gone down to His garden, to the beds of perfume spices, to pasture [His flock] among the gardens and to pick roses. ³I belong to my Beloved — the One Who pastures [His flock] among the roses — and my Beloved is mine. ⁴[God then says:] You are beautiful, My dear one, when you are pleasing [to Me], [and] lovely [now] as [you were before in] Yerushalayim. [You are] dreaded like cohorts of soldiers. ⁵Turn your eyes away from facing Me, for they have stimulated pride in Me. Your hair is like [that of] the goat flock that descends from Mount Gil'ad, leaving it exposed. ⁶Your teeth are [fine and white] like the flock of ewes which came up from the bathing pool, which are all perfect with no defect among them. ⁷Your upper cheek is like a section of pomegranate, under your snood. ⁸There are sixty queens, eighty concubines, and a countless number of maidens. ⁹[But only] one is My dove, My sincere one. She is united [in purpose] for her [congregation, and] complete for the one who bore her. Maidens saw her and gave her acclaim; queens and concubines praised her, [saying,] ¹⁰"Who is this who looks down [upon us] like the morning dawn, as beautiful as the moon, as bright as the sun, [and] dreaded like cohorts of soldiers?" ¹¹I went down to the nut-orchard to observe the first-ripening plants of the brook; to see if the vine had blossomed [and] the pomegranate trees budded. ¹²[Yisrael then says:] I did not know [how to behave, and thus] imposed upon myself [to become like] chariots [for] a nation of nobility.

7 ¹[THE NATIONS SAID TO YISRAEL:] Turn away, turn away, perfectly faithful one! Turn away, turn away, and we will appoint you to high positions! [Yisrael answered them:] What high positions can you offer the perfectly faithful one, that compare to [even the banners of] the encirclement of the [desert] encampments? ²[The nations responded:] How beautiful are your steps in [perfectly fitting] shoes, daughter of nobility! The hidden parts of your thighs are like arrays of jewelry made by a craftsman. ³Your navel is [like] a round bowl [that] never

שָׁרְרֵךְ֙ אַגַּ֣ן הַסַּ֔הַר אַל־יֶחְסַ֖ר הַמָּ֑זֶג בִּטְנֵךְ֙ עֲרֵמַ֣ת חִטִּ֔ים סוּגָ֖ה בַּשּׁוֹשַׁנִּֽים: ד שְׁנֵ֥י שָׁדַ֛יִךְ כִּשְׁנֵ֥י עֳפָרִ֖ים תָּאֳמֵ֥י צְבִיָּֽה: ה צַוָּארֵ֖ךְ כְּמִגְדַּ֣ל הַשֵּׁ֑ן עֵינַ֜יִךְ בְּרֵכ֣וֹת בְּחֶשְׁבּ֗וֹן עַל־שַׁ֙עַר֙ בַּת־רַבִּ֔ים אַפֵּךְ֙ כְּמִגְדַּ֣ל הַלְּבָנ֔וֹן צוֹפֶ֖ה פְּנֵ֥י דַמָּֽשֶׂק: ו רֹאשֵׁ֤ךְ עָלַ֙יִךְ֙ כַּכַּרְמֶ֔ל וְדַלַּ֥ת רֹאשֵׁ֖ךְ כָּאַרְגָּמָ֑ן מֶ֖לֶךְ אָס֥וּר בָּרְהָטִֽים: ז מַה־יָּפִית֙ וּמַה־נָּעַ֔מְתְּ אַהֲבָ֖ה בַּתַּֽעֲנוּגִֽים: ח זֹ֤את קֽוֹמָתֵךְ֙ דָּֽמְתָ֣ה לְתָמָ֔ר וְשָׁדַ֖יִךְ לְאַשְׁכֹּלֽוֹת: ט אָמַ֙רְתִּי֙ אֶעֱלֶ֣ה בְתָמָ֔ר אֹֽחֲזָ֖ה בְּסַנְסִנָּ֑יו וְיִֽהְיוּ־נָ֙א שָׁדַ֜יִךְ כְּאֶשְׁכְּל֣וֹת הַגֶּ֗פֶן וְרֵ֥יחַ אַפֵּ֖ךְ כַּתַּפּוּחִֽים: י וְחִכֵּ֕ךְ כְּיֵ֥ין הַטּ֛וֹב הוֹלֵ֥ךְ לְדוֹדִ֖י לְמֵישָׁרִ֑ים דּוֹבֵ֖ב שִׂפְתֵ֥י יְשֵׁנִֽים: יא אֲנִ֣י לְדוֹדִ֔י וְעָלַ֖י תְּשׁוּקָתֽוֹ: יב לְכָ֤ה דוֹדִי֙ נֵצֵ֣א הַשָּׂדֶ֔ה נָלִ֖ינָה בַּכְּפָרִֽים: יג נַשְׁכִּ֙ימָה֙ לַכְּרָמִ֔ים נִרְאֶ֞ה אִם־פָּֽרְחָ֤ה הַגֶּ֙פֶן֙ פִּתַּ֣ח הַסְּמָדַ֔ר הֵנֵ֖צוּ הָרִמּוֹנִ֑ים שָׁ֛ם אֶתֵּ֥ן אֶת־דֹּדַ֖י לָֽךְ: יד הַדּֽוּדָאִ֣ים נָֽתְנוּ־רֵ֗יחַ וְעַל־פְּתָחֵ֙ינוּ֙ כָּל־מְגָדִ֔ים חֲדָשִׁ֖ים גַּם־יְשָׁנִ֑ים דּוֹדִ֖י צָפַ֥נְתִּי לָֽךְ:

ח א מִ֤י יִתֶּנְךָ֙ כְּאָ֣ח לִ֔י יוֹנֵ֖ק שְׁדֵ֣י אִמִּ֑י אֶֽמְצָאֲךָ֤ בַחוּץ֙ אֶשָּׁ֣קְךָ֔ גַּ֖ם לֹא־יָב֥וּזוּ לִֽי: ב אֶנְהָֽגֲךָ֗ אֲבִֽיאֲךָ֛ אֶל־בֵּ֥ית אִמִּ֖י תְּלַמְּדֵ֑נִי אַשְׁקְךָ֙ מִיַּ֣יִן הָרֶ֔קַח מֵעֲסִ֖יס רִמֹּנִֽי: ג שְׂמֹאלוֹ֙ תַּ֣חַת רֹאשִׁ֔י וִֽימִינ֖וֹ תְּחַבְּקֵֽנִי: ד הִשְׁבַּ֥עְתִּי אֶתְכֶ֖ם בְּנ֣וֹת יְרֽוּשָׁלִָ֑ם מַה־תָּעִ֧ירוּ ׀ וּֽמַה־תְּעֹֽרְר֛וּ אֶת־הָאַהֲבָ֖ה עַ֥ד שֶׁתֶּחְפָּֽץ: ס ה מִ֣י זֹ֗את עֹלָה֙ מִן־הַמִּדְבָּ֔ר מִתְרַפֶּ֖קֶת עַל־דּוֹדָ֑הּ תַּ֤חַת הַתַּפּ֙וּחַ֙ עֽוֹרַרְתִּ֔יךָ שָׁ֚מָּה חִבְּלַ֣תְךָ אִמֶּ֔ךָ שָׁ֖מָּה חִבְּלָ֥ה יְלָדַֽתְךָ: ו שִׂימֵ֙נִי כַחוֹתָ֜ם עַל־לִבֶּ֗ךָ כַּֽחוֹתָם֙ עַל־זְרוֹעֶ֔ךָ כִּֽי־עַזָּ֤ה כַמָּ֙וֶת֙ אַהֲבָ֔ה קָשָׁ֥ה כִשְׁא֖וֹל קִנְאָ֑ה רְשָׁפֶ֕יהָ

lacks prepared drink. Your womb is [like] a pile of wheat fenced off by roses. ⁴Your two breasts are like two [identical] fawns, twins of a hind. ⁵Your neck is [erect] like an ivory tower. Your eyes are [like] the reservoirs in Cheshbon, at the gateway of [the city of] multitudes. Your forehead is like the tower of Levanon that looks out on Damesek. ⁶Your head [adornment] upon you is [awesome] like [Mount] Carmel, and the braids of your hair are [as beautiful] as [twined] purple wool. [The Name of] the King is bound [to your head] with tresses. ⁷How beautiful are you [in every respect], and how delightful it is [to feel] a true, pleasurable love for you. ⁸This was your stature [that you were] comparable to a date-palm, and your breasts [were comparable] to grape clusters. ⁹[God then says to Yisrael in exile:] I said [to the Heavenly legions], "I shall be exalted through [Yisrael who is like] a date-palm, [and] I shall grasp its branches." So let now your breasts be like the grape clusters of the vine, and the fragrance of your forehead be like [the fragrance of] apples. ¹⁰And [let the utterances of] your palate [be] like the best wine, [so that you may say, "From it] flows forth to my Beloved to [show Him my] unrestrained love," [thus] arousing speech in the lips of the sleeping ones. ¹¹[Yisrael responds:] I belong to my Beloved, and His desire is for me. ¹²Come, my Beloved, we shall go out to the fields; let us stay the night in the villages. ¹³Let us arise early [to go] to the vineyards, [and] see if the vine has blossomed, the young grapes have begun to appear, [and] the pomegranates have matured. There, I shall show [the extent of] my love for You. ¹⁴The pots [of figs] have produced a fragrance, and on our doorsteps are all [kinds of] sweet delicacies, both new and old. My Beloved! I treasured [them] for You.

8

¹IF ONLY YOU WERE LIKE a brother to me, nursing from my mother's breasts. I shall find You outside [and] kiss You; [I] even [know people] will not disgrace me. ²I shall lead You [and] bring You to my mother's House; teach me [there]! I shall give You to drink from the blended wine, from the sweet wine of my pomegranate tree. ³His left hand is [placed] under my head and His right hand embraces me. ⁴[Yisrael then says to the nations:] I hold you to oath, daughters of Yerushalayim. What hatred could you cause, and in what way can you challenge the love [between my and my Beloved] while it is still strongly desired? ⁵[God and His Heavenly Court then says about Yisrael:] Who is this coming up from the desert, uniting herself with her Beloved? [She says,] "I awakened You under the apple tree. There, Your mother had birth pangs for You; there, she who gave birth to You was in labor. ⁶Place me [firmly] like a seal upon Your heart [and] like a seal upon Your arm. [See] that [my] love [for You] is so strong as [to accept] death [for You], [and] the zeal

רִשְׁפֵּי אֵשׁ שַׁלְהֶבֶתְיָה: ז מַיִם רַבִּים לֹא יוּכְלוּ לְכַבּוֹת אֶת־הָאַהֲבָה וּנְהָרוֹת לֹא יִשְׁטְפוּהָ אִם־יִתֵּן אִישׁ אֶת־כָּל־הוֹן בֵּיתוֹ בָּאַהֲבָה בּוֹז יָבוּזוּ לוֹ: ס ח אָחוֹת לָנוּ קְטַנָּה וְשָׁדַיִם אֵין לָהּ מַה־נַּעֲשֶׂה לַאֲחוֹתֵנוּ בַּיּוֹם שֶׁיְּדֻבַּר־בָּהּ: ט אִם־חוֹמָה הִיא נִבְנֶה עָלֶיהָ טִירַת כָּסֶף וְאִם־דֶּלֶת הִיא נָצוּר עָלֶיהָ לוּחַ אָרֶז: י אֲנִי חוֹמָה וְשָׁדַי כַּמִּגְדָּלוֹת אָז הָיִיתִי בְעֵינָיו כְּמוֹצְאֵת שָׁלוֹם: יא כֶּרֶם הָיָה לִשְׁלֹמֹה בְּבַעַל הָמוֹן נָתַן אֶת־הַכֶּרֶם לַנֹּטְרִים אִישׁ יָבִא בְּפִרְיוֹ אֶלֶף כָּסֶף: יב כַּרְמִי שֶׁלִּי לְפָנָי הָאֶלֶף לְךָ שְׁלֹמֹה וּמָאתַיִם לְנֹטְרִים אֶת־פִּרְיוֹ: יג הַיּוֹשֶׁבֶת בַּגַּנִּים חֲבֵרִים מַקְשִׁבִים לְקוֹלֵךְ הַשְׁמִיעִנִי: יד בְּרַח ׀ דּוֹדִי וּדְמֵה־לְךָ לִצְבִי אוֹ לְעֹפֶר הָאַיָּלִים עַל הָרֵי בְשָׂמִים:

[of the nations against me] is as harsh as the grave. The burning coals of [my love] are [like] the fiery coals of the Godly flame [of Gehenna]. ⁷*Great amounts of water could not extinguish [my] love [for You], nor could rivers wash it away. If a man would give the entire wealth of his household [to depose this] love, [people] would greatly despise him."* ⁸*We have a little sister, but she does not [yet] have breasts. What shall We do for Our sister on the day she is spoken of [by the nations to be eliminated]?* ⁹*If she is [like] a wall, We shall build upon her a stronghold of silver, but if she is [like] a door, We shall protect her with [only] boards of cedar wood.* ¹⁰*[Yisrael responds:] I am [like] a wall, and my breasts are like towers. Then, [when I said this,] He regarded me as one who is found to be perfect.* ¹¹*The Master of Peace had a vineyard in the plain of the masses. He gave over the vineyard to the watchmen, [and] each of them gathered a thousand [coins] of its produce.* ¹²*[On the Day of Reckoning He will say to them,] "My vineyard is Mine, [and what you took from it is reckoned] before Me." [They will answer,] "Master of Peace! The thousand [coins we shall return] to You, [and also give] two hundred to those who guard its produce."* ¹³*[God then says to Yisrael: You,] who sit in the gardens! [Your] associates are listening to your voice. Let Me hear [it]!* ¹⁴*[Yisrael responds:] Flee, my Beloved, and make Yourself like a stag or gazelle fawn, on the spice mountains.*

Appendix Two

The Miracles in Egypt
A Compendium of Midrashim

Was Egypt any different from the other nations in history that have subjugated our People? And in that particular historical epoch, why was Israel enslaved specifically to Egypt, as opposed to another nation?

When Moshe *Rabbenu* lived, Egypt had become a world empire, and was the most powerful nation on the face of the earth. On the other hand, the land of Egypt was steeped in sin and transgression. No nation in the world committed immorality as Egypt did, and its people engaged in every variety of idol-worship.

Our Sages teach: All those who oppress Israel are made powerful, in order that no one will be able to say that Hashem handed over His People to a lowly nation. Thus, the degenerate nation of Egypt actually became so powerful only because earlier, God had decreed that Israel would be enslaved there!

And so writes the *Zohar*:

> Come and see how all the different nations of the world, all the different kingdoms, acquired their might only for the sake of Israel! Egypt became a world power only after the Children of Israel entered her borders. The same is true of Babylonia and Edom, who at first were insignificant. When Israel was given over to them, they became great empires.

In this way, there is similarily between Egypt and our other oppressors.

Moreover, God sent Israel specifically down into degenerate Egypt, as a test — to see whether His holy nation would resist the many temptations in the land where they were held, whether they would refuse to follow in Egypt's ways.

Come, Let Us Be Clever with Him

The Jewish People had multiplied greatly within Egypt's borders, until Pharaoh said (*Shemos* 1:10): *Come, let us be clever with him, lest he grow too numerous, and should a war come, he might ally himself to our enemies, and fight us and leave the country.*

Pharaoh was not the first to say *Come*. We find that thus said the "generation of the dispersion" (*Bereshis* 11:3-4): *Come, let us build a city and tower*. So, too, was that generation punished with *Come*, for in response, Hashem told His angels (11:7): *Come, let us go down and confuse their language*. Similarly, they built their city and their tower, saying, *Lest we be scattered* but, as the Torah states: *And Hashem scattered them* (11:8).

And this is how it went in Egypt as well. They said first, *Let us be clever with him* — *lest he grow too numerous*, but, as the Torah states, *The more that they afflicted them* — *the more numerous they became* (*Shemos* 1:12).

Yes, in response to Pharaoh Hashem also used the word "come" (whose Hebrew letters have the numerical value of twelve). Hashem told the Egyptians: They were only twelve brothers when they first came to you, and look how many they are now!

Let us be clever with him — To attack Israel with the sword was not possible for Pharaoh, for the whole world would shout, "Injustice! First you invite them to dwell within your borders, and then you attack them with the sword?"

"No," said Pharaoh, "that we cannot do. Let us instead impose harsh taxes upon them. It is common knowledge that the taxes paid to the King by foreign residents in his land are higher than those paid by his native subjects. This way, when they cannot pay we will punish them, and in the eyes of the world our hands will be clean!"

Let us be clever with him — R. Berachyah said in the name of R. Levi: Cursed are the evil ones who have plotted against Israel, each one boasting, "My plot is better than yours!" Esav said, "What a fool Cain was for killing Abel while their father still had many years to live, for Shes was born afterwards. I will not be like Cain. Rather, (Bereshis 27:41) *when the days of mourning for my father shall come, I shall kill Yaakov, my brother*, and that way I will inherit everything!" Came Pharaoh and said, "What a fool Esav was for waiting to kill Yaakov, for in the meantime Yaakov had many children. I will not be like Esav. Rather, I will kill the Children of Israel as soon as they are born, and I will make their lives so miserable for them, they will not even want to have children!" We will conquer them only if we are clever with them!

Lest he grow too numerous — Even more than he has already!

And should a war come — It was a specific war that Pharaoh feared — a war with the nations of Canaan. During the great famine in the days of Yosef, when only Egypt had grain, Egypt had shown no mercy upon the nations of Canaan, for when they sold the Canaanite nations grain, they milked them of all their wealth. Now, Pharaoh feared that the Canaanite nations would take revenge for this. What is more, the Jewish nation was in Egypt, and Pharaoh knew that the Jews had a teaching that they would inherit the lands of Canaan, and drive out the Canaanites. Pharaoh feared that the Jews would see the Canaanites invading Egypt, *he might ally himself to our enemies* — to increase the tumult and confusion — *and fight us* — so that the Canaanites succeed in conquering Egypt. Then the Jews would be able do as they wanted, *and leave the country* — to go and conquer Canaan, which had long been their desire. Therefore, Pharaoh said, *Come, let us be clever*.

📖

And the more they afflicted them, the more numerous they became, and the more they abounded — This is the way the Hebrew is normally understood. If so, however, the Torah should have used the verbs in the past tense and not the present. From this we understand that a Divine Voice would speak to them, all through their long days of misery, promising and encouraging them: "Because of this [terrible affliction] you will become numerous! Because of this [terrible oppression] you will abound!"

Pharaoh fought against Israel by isssuing four harsh decrees, and in the end, each one actually served to help bring salavation for the Jews! The first decree was: *And they put taskmasters over him* (*Shemos* 1:11). What happened? *And the more they afflicted them, the more numerous they became* (1:12).

The second decree was: *And they embittered their lives with hard labor* (*Shemos* 1:14). What happened? Hashem started to set the stage for Moshe *Rabbenu* — Israel's redeemer. Moshe's older sister was born — Miriam, whose name contains the Hebrew letters that connote "bitterness."

The third decree was: *If the child is a boy, you shall kill him* (*Shemos* 1:16). Pharaoh had been told by his astrologers that the time had come for Israel's redeemer to be born. In response, he issued this decree in an attempt to discourage the Jews from having children. What happened? Hashem caused Moshe *Rabbenu*'s older brother to be born — Aharon, whose name contains the Hebrew letters that can connote "pregnancy." Afterwards, Pharaoh commanded his entire nation: *Every newborn son shall be cast into the river* (*Shemos* 1:22). It was then that Moshe *Rabbenu* was born, who was named after the water — *because out of the water I drew him* (*Shemos* 2:10) — the connotation of the Hebrew letters in his name.

Pharaoh's fourth decree, addressed to his taskmasters, was the following: *You shall give them no straw to make the bricks* (*Shemos* 5:7). What happened? The Jews complained to Moshe and Aharon, and Hashem immediately sent them to stand before Pharaoh, to announce that the next day, all the water in Egypt would be turned to blood. From that day forth, our forefathers in Egypt no longer had to do any hard labor at all!

Every son that is born shall be cast into the river — R. Chanan taught: What did the virtuous and modest women of Israel do when they heard this evil decree? They took their newborn sons and hid them in crawl spaces under their houses. The children were discovered, however, because the wicked Egyptians would burst into the Jewish homes carrying their own children, and would pinch the children in order to make them cry. When the Jewish infants heard the crying, they would start to cry, too, and the Egyptians would snatch them from their hiding places and cast them into the river.

It was then that the Holy One, blessed is He, commanded His ministering angels, "Go down and see how the children of My beloved ones — Avraham, Yitzchak, and Yaakov — are being thrown into the river!" The angels hastily descended, and waded into the water up to their knees, plucked the Jewish children out, and placed them on the rocks by the water. Then the Holy One, blessed is He, formed mother's breasts from the rocks, and gave the infants to nurse.

And God Heard Their Cries

And Moshe was shepherding the flocks of Yisro.... and the Lord called to Him from within the bush (Shemos 3:1-4) — So said the Holy One, blessed is He, to Moshe: Can you see that I am suffering, just as Israel is suffering? Look at the place from where I speak — from amidst sharp thorns! From this you should realize that I, too, feel pain!

From within the bush — R. Yosei taught: Why did He speak to Moshe from such a place? Because it is the way of a bush to have its thorns pointing down, so that if a person puts his hand in, he is not injured. Only when he tries to remove his hand is he injured by the thorns. Similarly, when Israel first went down into Egypt, they were welcomed, as the Torah quotes Pharaoh telling Yosef: *The land of Egypt is before you. Settle your father and brothers on the best land of Egypt (Bereshis 47:6).* However, when the Jews later wanted to leave, the Egyptians grabbed them and would not let them go, as Pharaoh said: *And I shall not allow Israel to go (Shemos 5:2).*

And so taught R. Pinchas *haKohen*, son of R. Chama: What do we know about such a bush? A man inserts his hand into it and does not feel anything, but when he extracts his hand he is scratched. So, too, when Israel entered into Egypt, no one sensed anything bad about the Egyptians. When Israel was taken out, though, it was through signs, wonders, and battle.

📖

And take this staff in your hand, with which you will perform the signs (Shemos 4:17) — R. Levi said: Hashem created this staff between the six and seventh day of the creation of the world, and gave it into the hand of Adam, in Gan Eden. Adam passed it on to Chanoch, who passed it on to Shem. Shem gave it over to Avraham *Avinu*, who gave it to Yitzchak, Yitzchak to Yaakov, and Yaakov to Yosef. When Yosef died, all of his possessions were put into Pharaoh's palace, where Yisro, an adviser to Pharaoh, spotted it and greatly desired it, for he was attracted by the inscriptions that he saw carved in it. Yisro took the staff and planted it as a tree in his garden in Midyan, and no man was able to approach it. When Moshe came to Yisro's home and saw the staff standing in the garden, he went up to it, read the inscriptions and lifted it into his hand. Yisro saw and said, "This is the one who is destined to redeem Israel from Egypt." He therefore gave Moshe his daughter Tzipporah as a wife.

📖

And their pleadings rose to God from their work [avodah] (Shemos 2:23) — What work was this? They began to serve their God!* When the ministering angels saw that Israel's cries were being heard, the angels burst forth in praise to God, "Blessed is He Who listens to prayer!"

The *Zohar* says: What does the Torah mean when it says: *And the king of Egypt died, and the Children of Israel groaned...and they cried out. And their pleadings rose to God (Shemos 2:23-24)*? Had they not groaned and cried beforehand? But this "king" of Egypt was Egypt's appointed angel in heaven, whom Hashem cast down and humiliated. Once this angel's power had been crushed, Hashem remembered His nation and heard their prayers.

R. Yehudah said: Come and see how it was, that all the while that their appointed angel was given rule over Israel, the prayers of Israel were not heeded. Once Egypt's appointed angel fell, as it is written, *And the king of Egypt died* — immediately the Children of Israel groaned from their servitude and they cried out. And their pleadings rose to God, for until then, their prayers were not answered, despite their crying!

📖

Israel was redeemed from Egypt because of five things: Their time had come, they were suffering, they were crying, they had the merit of their ancestors, and they repented.

THEIR TIME HAD COME — for it is written: *And it was, after many days had passed* (Shemos 2:23).

THEY WERE SUFFERING — as it says: *And the Children of Israel groaned from their servitude, and cried out* (Ibid), because of the suffering.

THEY WERE CRYING — for it is written: *And God heard their cries* (Ibid 24).

THEY HAD THE MERIT OF THEIR FOREFATHERS — as it says: *And God remembered His covenant* (Ibid) — because of the merit of their forefathers.

THEY REPENTED — for it is written: *God saw the Children of Israel* (Ibid 25) — because they repented.

📖

And Hashem said, I have seen, I have surely seen the suffering of My people who are in Egypt (Shemos 3:7) — The seeming redundancy indicates that Hashem saw two things: [I see] that the Egyptains are drowning newborn boys in the river, and [I see] that they are using the bodies as filler in the bricks of the buildings that the Jews have to build. Therefore [Hashem said], "I see fit to bestow kindness upon the Jews, and I see fit to take revenge upon their oppressors."

I have seen, I have surely seen — Another interpretation: "I see them as they will come to accept My Torah, and I see them as they will come to sin with the golden calf" [when God will say:] *I have seen this people, and behold, it is a stiff-necked people* (Shemos 32:9).

---

* The Hebrew *avodah* connotes labor, servitude, and worship.

And their cry I have heard — Even though they are undeserving.

By reason of their taskmasters — I was only slightly angry with them, but the Egyptians were vicious in their anger.

For I know their pains — Even though I know what pains they will cause Me, in the desert and in the Land of Israel (see *Tehillim* 78:40-1), still, none of this will stop me from redeeming them.

📖

Go and gather together the elders of Israel, and say unto them, "Hashem, the God of your forefathers, has appeared to me...saying: I have surely remembered you" — For you are the descendants of holy ancestors.

And what is being done to you — For I detest viciousness.

I have surely remembered you — Yosef had taught them that this would be the key phrase by which their true redeemer would be recognized. Interestingly, the Hebrew root פ-ק-ד connotes not only "remember," "designate," or "appoint," but it also connotes a "lacking," or that something is "missing," as it is written (*Bemidbar* 31:49) about the number of Jewish soldiers who returned from the war against Midyan: *Not one man was missing*. Once we realize that the numerical equivalent of these letters is 190, we see that God commanded Moshe *Rabbenu* to tell the elders, "One hundred and ninety years are missing from the four hundred years that were decreed in the Covenant between the Pieces." Moshe *Rabbenu* was to say, in Hashem's Name, "Although this 190 is missing, I am remembering you now, and bringing you the redemption early!"

📖

And I shall give this nation favor in the eyes of the Egyptians (*Shemos* 3:21) — So that afterwards, when the Egyptians regret the favor they show you, they will feel even more that their teeth have been knocked out!

And when you shall go out, you shall not go out empty-handed (*Ibid*) — Hashem here stated a negative prohibition, thereby actually forbidding the Jews to go out empty-handed, for He wanted it to be very clear that the Egyptians had to be utterly broken and humiliated.

But each [Jewish] woman shall ask of her [Egyptian] neighbor silver, etc. — Here, Hashem stated His command in the positive, as well, so that the women of Israel, in fact, were ordered to go and ask the Egyptian women for these things.

You might ask, Why did Israel have to ask to borrow these items? After all, legally they could have claimed these items as theirs, as wages for their labor over all those years, and as compensation for all their property that they had to leave behind! Hashem, however, told the Jewish women to ask for these expensive items, as if they were only borrowing them, so that the Egyptians would think that their gold and silver was coming back to them, and that there was no need to chase after the Jews in an attempt to get everything back. This also was a good way to create a great and lasting separation between the two nations, for when the Egyptians saw that the Jews were not coming back, they would hate them forever for the trick they had played on them.

But each woman shall ask of her neighbor — For an entire year this trick that they were to play on the Egyptians was kept a secret among them. For that whole time, not one Jew went to an Egyptian to tell him, "Tomorrow, so-and-so is going to do such-and-such to you!" From here we see that among the Jews there were no informers or talebearers.

📖

Before Moshe returned to Egypt from Midyan, the Jewish slaves in Egypt were allowed rest from their labors on Shabbos. Soon after Moshe returned, he and Aharon stood before Pharaoh, and told Pharaoh in God's Name that the Jews now must be set free. Pharaoh refused, and in the Torah, he is quoted as telling his taskmasters: *And the labor of these people shall be made heavier...and they shall do [on] it* (Shemos 5:9). Then, he added, *And do not speak [play] of [with] false things*.

The Midrash tells us that we derive from this verse that on Shabbos, when the Jews were able to rest, their leaders would expound to them from written scrolls about Hashem's redeeming them, and the Jews would speak together about the promised redemption. Pharaoh, in response to the demands of Moshe and Aharon, told his taskmasters that Israel now would have to work *on it* — on Shabbos. He then told Moshe and Aharon that thereby, the slaves would no longer have time on Shabbos to *play* and amuse themselves by speaking lies about the redemption.

The Signs

And Aharon cast down his staff...and it became a serpent (Shemos 7:10) — The Torah says that at the burning bush, when Moshe's staff became a serpent, Moshe fled from it. Pharaoh, by contrast, did not even flinch when the same thing happened to Aharon's staff. It was not that Pharaoh had more courage than Moshe; as far as Pharaoh was concerned, Aharon had simply performed an everyday magic trick.

Moreover, our Sages tell us that Pharaoh started to dance like a rooster and make fun of Moshe and Aharon. "These are the signs of your great God? It is the way of the world that someone who has goods to sell only brings them to places where they are needed — to places where there is a shortage of what he is selling. But who brings fish brine to Spain? What trader exports fish to Acco? Have you not heard that Egypt already has every type of magic that exists?!"

Pharaoh immediately sent for some Egyptian schoolchildren, and they, too, turned walking staffs into serpents! Then he sent for his wife, and she, too, repeated the feat. Finally, Pharaoh sent for some four and five-year-olds, and even they were able to do it! This is what the Torah says: *And Pharaoh also called to wise men and to sorcerers, and so, also, did the magicians of Egypt do by means of their secret arts* (Shemos 7:11). The word *also* is used twice — once to reflect that also Pharaoh's wife was able to do the trick, and once to reflect that so, too, the small children.

After a short while, all the serpents turned back into staffs, even that of Aharon. Suddenly, as the Torah relates: *Aharon's staff swallowed up their staffs* (Ibid 12). Hashem said: If Aharon's serpent had swallowed up your serpents, you would have been able to say, "One snake swallows others. This is the way of the world." But it was a wooden staff that swallowed your "serpents"!

R. Eliezer said, "It was a miracle within a miracle!"

Seeing this, Pharaoh became fearful, and he said in his heart: What if they tell the staff to swallow me and my throne? In a minute I will be swallowed, too!

R. Chama ben Chanina said: There was another miracle here, for Aharon's staff swallowed not one Egyptian staff, or two...no, it was a great number — enough to make ten piles of staffs! Nevertheless, after they all were swallowed, Aharon's staff looked exactly as it had beforehand, so that everyone recognized whose it was, and declared, "That is the staff of Aharon!"

The Plague of Blood

And there shall be blood throughout the land of Egypt (Shemos 7:19) — Even stagnant water that was lying in ditches, holes, and caves would turn to blood.

And in wood and stone — So, too, the drawn water in cups, pots, and other vessels, whether the vessels were made of wood or stone. However, water that was in metal vessels did not turn to blood.

Another interpretation: Blood would spew from their idols, which the Egyptians made of wood and stone. Even saliva from an Egyptian's mouth would turn to blood!

And the fish which were in the river died, and the river became foul — The dead fish rotted.

And the Egyptians could not drink water from the river — They wanted to drink what already had been drawn from the river, but this, too, had turned to blood, whether it was in vessels or in the ground.

And the blood was throughout all the land of Egypt — R. Avin haLevi taught: Through the plague of blood, Israel became wealthy. How did this come about? If a Jew and an Egyptian lived in the same building, they would have a common barrel full of drinking water. If the Egyptian went to fill a flask, the water in it would turn to blood, while the Jew was able to drink water from the barrel. The Egyptian would say to the Jew: "Draw a little water for me with your hand." The Jew would draw it and give it to him, but it would turn to blood! The Egyptian would say, "Come, let us drink from the same flask." The Jew would drink water while the Egyptian would drink blood, but if the Egyptian would pay the Jew for the water, it would remain water. In this way, the Jews became wealthy.

The Plague of Frogs

And you [Moshe] shall say to him [Pharaoh]: "Let my people go...and if you refuse to let them go, behold I shall smite all your borders with frogs (Shemos 7:26-7) — The Hebrew root of the word for "smite" here — נ-ג-פ — also connotes "a plague of fatal sickness." As a result of the frogs, many Egyptians fell ill and died. This also happened as a result of the plague of blood. In fact, of the ten times that Hashem struck Egypt, every single time fatal illness among the Egyptians was a result!

With frogs — These frogs were a new, aggressive species that was created only now, for the purpose of punishing the Egyptians. Afterwards, this species remained in the waters of the Nile, where it grew and developed until it became a much larger reptile — the crocodile which is found in the Nile today as a remembrance of the second plague.

Other commentators say that the "frogs" mentioned here were from an unknown species of small creatures which simply croaked like frogs. This seems to be the view of the Sages in the Midrash.

And the river shall swarm with frogs — That very day the water became absolutely filled with them, though on the previous day there were none there at all.

And they shall go up and come into your house — The biggest and the mightiest frogs shall go up into the house of Pharaoh. The more important the Egyptian, the bigger would be the frogs that entered his house. But this was not all:

And upon you — And even into your internal organs.

And into your people and all of your servants — Regarding the frogs simply entering the Egyptian houses, the houses of Pharaoh's "servants," i.e., close aides, are mentioned before the houses of his "people." Here, however, regarding the frogs croaking from inside the very bodies of the Egyptians, Pharaoh's "people" are mentioned first. Why? Because first it was the masses who stood as taskmasters over the Jewish slaves, shouting as they forced the Jews to work, and thus it was Pharaoh's "people" who first heard the frogs shouting from their bellies.

One verse about Hashem's command (*Shemos* 8:1) is stated in the plural — *And bring up the frogs*, while another, (*Ibid* 2) is in the singular — *And the frog came up*. Rabbi Akiva explained: One frog came out of the river, and the Egyptians started beating it with sticks. As a result, it started splitting and dividing into many frogs, until they filled the land of Egypt. Rabbi Elazar ben Azaryah explained: At first, one frog came out of the river, but then he called to his comrades to follow after him.

It was one frog that came out first, and he quickly proceeded to the house of Pharaoh, which was situated near to the riverbank. As soon as this happened, the frogs in Egypt multiplied, and covered the entire country. In every place where there was water, even a single drop, there was immediately a frog. They filled the homes of the wealthy just as they filled the homes of the poor. The homes of the wealthy had marble floors, but the stones cracked, allowing the frogs to enter from the ground underneath. They swarmed through all the rooms and into the stomachs of the people who lived there, croaking loudly all the while. Many of the wealthy Egyptians could not cope with this suffering, and died on the spot.

Hashem told Moshe to tell Pharaoh that the frogs would even go into the kneading troughs and ovens of the Egyptians (*Shemos* 7:28). If the dough was on a counter or a table, waiting to be put into the oven, the frogs would jump onto it and squash themselves together in it until it was completely ruined. Even if the dough was already baking, the frogs would enter the firey ovens and die in the dough, or cling to the hot oven walls, where they were burned alive, which also spoiled the bread baking in the oven.

Chananyah, Misha'el and Azaryah took example from the frogs, so that later in history, they, too, entered fire to sanctify the Name of God. They deduced: Frogs are not commanded to give up their lives to sanctify God's Name, but in Egypt, this is what they did when they entered the fire. We Jews, in fact, are commanded to sanctify God's Name, so all the more so we should enter the fire!

Pharaoh eventually asked Moshe to take the frogs away. Moshe agreed, saying: *And the frogs shall depart from you and your houses, from your servants and your people* (Shemos 8:7) — In the same order that they came upon Egypt, so shall they leave Egypt, beginning with Pharaoh.

Only in the river shall they remain — As a remembrance and praise to Hashem, and also to remind Egypt of God's punishments. Around Egypt's neck these creatures would hang forever. The Egyptians would see them in the Nile, and be afraid: "Are they going to come up and attack us again?"

They remained for an additional reason as well: A trick of magic is not lasting. When the trick is over, things return to normal. Here, the frogs would remain always, to remind the Egyptians that the second plague was an act of God — the One Who created everything, creates anew, and sustains whatever He wants, for as long as He wants!

The Plague of Lice

This plague came without warning, for Hashem warns a person once, and then a second time, but after that there is no need to warn him again. So, too, regarding the sixth plague and the ninth — each "third" plague came without any warning.

And they [Moshe and Aharon] did so, and there were lice upon man and beast... throughout all the land of Egypt (Shemos 8:13) — The plague of lice differed from all the others, for there were lice also affecting the Jews in Goshen, and they even were on the bodies of the Jews.

All the dust of the earth became lice — Even the dust of Goshen, but the lice there were benign, and the Jews hardly noticed them. This is a teaching that we have by tradition from our Sages.

This plague was extremely humiliating for the Egyptians. Even after it passed, many lice still remained, so much so that the dust of Egypt was filled with them. This was Hashem's Will. The land of Egypt had to be made disgusting, so that the Jewish people would have no desire to stay there.

What is more, our Sages teach us that from the time of the third plague onwards, no longer did the Jews have to work making bricks. There were so many lice remaining in the Egyptian earth, that there was no way to use it for brickmaking!

The Plague of Mixed Beasts

This plague was brought upon the Egyptians because although the Jews no longer had to make bricks, their masters still forced them to do other things. They commanded them, "Go into the wilderness and bring us back bears and lions, so that we can make circuses and entertain ourselves." As a punishment for this, Hashem sent the wild beasts out of the wilderness, to entertain themselves on the Egyptians.

The Plague of Pestilence

See, the Hand of Hashem is on your herds in the fields (Shemos 9:3) — But not the animals that have been brought indoors.

On your horses and donkeys, on your camels, oxen and sheep — Five different species, as if Hashem sent one "finger" against each species — for against all of them together came *the Hand of Hashem*.

And the Lord shall make a division between the flocks of Israel and the flocks of Egypt — This phrase about making a "division" also is used with respect to both the plague of mixed beasts and the slaying of the firstborn. In all three of these plagues, Moshe and Aharon played no role. Rather, Hashem alone brought forth the plague. Thereby, Hashem sent Moshe and Aharon a subtle message: Although all creatures are the work of My hands, and I show mercy to all of them, between Israel and Egypt I make a distinction.

And behold, from the herds of Israel, not one thing died — Even where a Jew had agreed to sell an Egyptian one of his animals, and had accepted payment, so that on the morrow, only one thing remained to be done — to hand the animal over — the animal was saved from the plague, simply because it still was in the hands of the Jew.

If an Egyptian and Jew were co-owners of an animal, then even if the animal were in the hands of the Egyptian, it survived the plague, though all the Egyptian's other animals perished. This let him know that the one animal survived only because it was primarily "Jewish." Even if the Egyptian and Jew had equal partnership, the animal survived the plague.

The Plague of Boils

And Hashem said to Moshe and Aharon, "Take for yourselves handfuls of soot from a furnace" (*Shemos* 9:8) — There were miracles within miracles in this plague. For one, only Moshe tossed the soot upwards, yet beforehand, each filled his two hands with soot. Thus, when Aharon gave his handfuls to Moshe, Moshe's hands were able to hold them, despite the fact that Moshe hands were full already!

When a man throws an arrow up into the air, it does not reach higher than a hundred feet or so, yet Moshe threw soot from a furnace into the air — something of practically no substance at all — yet it reached over the heavens, to the Throne of God!

And it became boils, breaking out into sores on man and beast — R. Yehoshua ben Levi said: The boils that Hashem sent upon Egypt were wet on the outside and dry on the inside. It is understood that people could be punished this way, for people sin. But what wrong did the animals of Egypt do? However, the verse says: *Hashem's angel is encamped around those who fear Him* (*Tehillim* 34:8) — even those around the righteous are afforded protection. Thus, happy are the righteous, and all those associated with them, and woe to the wicked, and all those associated with them!

And Hashem hardened the heart of Pharaoh (Shemos 9:12) — Before that, Pharaoh on his own was able to harden his heart and not let the plagues affect him. He wanted to keep his slaves, and on his own he refused to let the plagues force him to free them. However, once the plague of the boils struck him, Pharaoh's heart on its own was no longer strong enough to remain impervious. Then Hashem intervened, to "harden" Pharaoh's heart so that he could remain stubborn. Hashem strengthened him, enabling him to continue to refuse to let the Jews go, as long as this truly was his heart's desire.

The Plague of Hail

Hashem commanded Moshe to tell Pharaoh, *Behold, I will cause to rain down, about this time tomorow* (Shemos 9:18) — Moshe made a scratch for Pharaoh on the wall of Pharaoh's house, tracing the line on a place where the sun was shining, and below there was shade. Moshe said, "When the sun shall reach this point on the wall tomorrow, and will be shining in the sky and lighting up your house, suddenly, there will rain down *a very heavy hail.*

Upon every man and beast that shall be found in the field, and shall not be brought home, the hail shall fall, and they shall die — The hail was decreed on Egypt only for the sake of destroying what was growing in the their gardens, fields, orchards, and vineyards. The Egyptians were given the chance, however, to save their animals, for again, just as regarding the pestilence, any animals that would be inside the Egyptians' houses would not be killed. Surely, though, the reason the animals would be saved was not that the houses kept the hail out. After all, the hail destroyed mighty trees, reducing them to nothing, and the roofs that the Egyptians built for their houses were not nearly as strong as these trees. Rather, it was simply a decree from Heaven, that the hail would fall only upon Egypt's open spaces. Wherever a house stood, no hail fell at all.

Come and see how great is the mercy of Hashem! Even at a time when He shows anger toward the evil ones, He has mercy — both on them and on their property — for He sent the hail only to destroy the crops of Egypt, and He sent warning to the Egyptians, so that they and their animals would not be harmed.

And now, send and hurry in your herds — As regarding all of the plagues, Pharaoh sent for Moshe and Aharon to ask them to put a stop to the hail, but in his request, it was only regarding the hail that he said, *Hashem is the righteous One!* This is understood, for when someone seeks to make war on someone else, in order to kill him and take all that he has, he will attack suddenly, and try to take his enemy by surprise. What did Hashem do? He warned Pharaoh: *And now, send and hurry in your herds!* Therefore, Pharaoh declared, *Hashem is the righteous One!*

Among the servants of Pharaoh, he who feared the word of God made his servants and flocks flee into the houses (Shemos 9:20) — From here, Rabbi Shimon bar Yochai used to say: The best non-Jew — kill him; the best snake — squash his head! For it is written [later on]: *And he [Pharaoh] took six hundred prize [horse-drawn] chariots [to chase after the Jews].*

Where did they get the horses? If you say, from the Egyptian army — that cannot be, for the Torah already writes [regarding the plague of the pestilence], *And all of Egypt's animals died.* If you say, they were Pharaoh's — that cannot be either, for the Torah already writes [also regarding the pestilence], *See, the Hand of Hashem is on your herds.* And if you say, these horses belonged to Israel — that cannot be either, as it is written: *And all of our animals shall go [out of Egypt], too!* Whose horses were they then? They belonged to the Egyptians *who feared the word of God!* Because of these very Egyptians, Israel later found itself in danger of death!

And Hashem said to Moshe, "Stretch forth your hand on the heavens, and there shall be — immediately — **hail throughout the land of Egypt, upon man and upon beast** — The Egyptians could have saved themselves and their animals, but simply to spite God, they did not do so. Therefore, the hail struck them first, and only afterwards struck *every herb of the field*.

Only in the land of Goshen, where the Children of Israel were, was there no hail — As a result, any Egyptians who were in Goshen also were saved, out of Hashem's mercy, for the whole purpose of this plague was to open everyone's eyes, to see that *the earth belongs to Hashem* (Shemos 3:29).

There was no hail — But there was thunder and lightning, even in Goshen, in order to put the fear of Heaven into everyone who was there. Thunder, in fact, was created for this purpose — for fear of Heaven straightens the crookedness in a person's heart, and it was necessary for Israel, too, to have fear of Heaven.

The Plague of Locusts

The miracles in Egypt actually served two purposes: To bring Pharaoh to submission before Hashem, and to fortify the hearts of those Jews in Egypt who lacked faith in Hashem. In verses about the plague of locusts, both purposes are mentioned: *In order that I may place these signs of Mine inside him [i.e., in the heart of Pharaoh], and in order that you may tell of it into the ears of your son, and your son's son* (Shemos 10:1-2).

Further on in the Torah, however, after the plague of darkness, when Hashem states the purpose of the slaying of Egypt's firstborn, this second purpose is not mentioned. Rather, the tenth plague was simply *in order to multiply My wonders in the land of Egypt* (Shemos 11:9). By then, all the Jews of no faith had perished, in the first three days of the darkness, and the Jews who remained did not need fortification of their faith.

The verse about the plague of locusts continues: *And you shall know that I am Hashem*. This is said to the Jews who, in fact, would leave Egypt. Until the Exodus, there were among them some who had erred, having put stock in the idols of Egypt.

"However," God said, "after seeing what you saw in Egypt, no longer is there any room for such error. Such idol-worship should be uprooted from your hearts, because you saw that their idols were powerless."

Locusts are edible. In fact, the Egyptians regarded them as a delicacy. Usually they were scarce in Egypt, and when some were seen, the Egyptians would be happy, and they would set out to trap them, in order to salt and pickle them, and serve them at meals as appetizers.

"Locust" is a general term for the species, but there are eight general types of locust, and one of these eight is itself called "locust." Our Sages said that in each one of the eight groups are one hundred "sub-species," and when Hashem brought the locusts upon Egypt, He brought all eight types and every sub-species!

Rabban Gamliel said: What is unique about an attack of locusts, as opposed to other types of suffering? It demonstrates man's smallness and powerlessness. Man can eat locusts, yet when he sins and angers God, his own food comes to punish him! And God has even stronger executioners at His disposal! How many lions and bears does He have? And how many leopards and other wild beasts?

When the locust swarms over the land, even if all the people of the world were to come and take up swords and lances against him, and encircle him with fire, he still will achieve what he wants, and will not be defeated. Is it any wonder that in the Name of Hashem, the Prophet Yoel calls the locust *My great warrior (Yoel 2:25)*?

And when it was morning a wind from the east carried the locusts (Shemos 10:13) — Lifting them from where they had been resting.

And the locusts rose over all the land of Egypt — During the first three days they remained aloft, for if they had alighted on the land and its people immediately, Egypt would have been destroyed completely. Rather, they flew in the air above Egypt, until Shabbos. Then, on Shabbos:

And they came to rest throughout all the borders of Egypt

The Miracles in Egypt: A Compendium of Midrashim

— *And it became clear that it was very grievous. Before them, never were there locusts like them, and after them there would never be such* — All the species and sub-species together. There was a plague of locusts in the days of Yoel, as well, *the likes of which there never was* (Yoel 2:2). All the species and sub-species were there, too, but only one after another, and not all together.

After the Shabbos rest was over, the locusts again took to the air *and they covered the eye of the land* — that is, the sun — *and the land became dark*. Over the remaining days of the plague, *they ate every herb*. Finally, Pharaoh asked Moshe and Aharon to ask Hashem to remove the locusts.

And Hashem turned — He turned the wind that had brought the locusts from the east, and had continued blowing strong all the while — Hashem turned that wind's direction and made it a *tremendously strong west wind, which lifted up the locusts, and propelled them to the Sea of Reeds* — as a man propels a stone to the ground, and makes it stick there.

Why does the Torah call the wind from the west *tremendously strong*, while this is not said regarding the wind from the east? The reason is that the miracle that took the locusts away was greater than the miracle that brought them. That is, Heaven gives, but once having done so, it rarely takes the thing back. This is a principle that we have as tradition. Moreover, when the locusts first appeared, many Egyptians thought they were a blessing, and were happy, for they saw them as a source of food: "We will gather them, cook them, salt them and pickle them, and store them in barrels for years!"

The Holy One said, "This plague that I have brought upon you to punish you — you are happy with it!?" Immediately, He brought a *tremendously strong wind* and took the locusts away from them.

Not one locust was left in all the borders of Egypt — Even those that already had been cooked, salted and pickled, and were in barrels, or still were cooking in pots! The live locusts came and picked up the dead ones, and the wind carried all of them away. Since, however, Hashem deprived the Egyptians of this "good" thing, He gave them something else in its stead: Never would locusts harm Egypt again. Moshe prayed to Hashem to rid Egypt of the destroying locusts, and the prayer stands answered to this very day.

The Plague of Darkness

Moshe *Rabbenu* did not explicitly warn Pharaoh about the advent of the plague of darkness, but by now, at the end of the month of Adar, Pharaoh and his subjects should have been expecting that some sort of terror was about to strike them at any moment. The darkness was to be the ninth plague, and twice previously, Hashem had sent two plagues with prior warning, followed by a third plague that struck without any warning. This pattern began the previous year, on the first of the month of Av. Now that the locusts, the second plague in the third set of three, were gone, and things had been quiet for twenty-two days, Pharaoh and Egypt should have been living in apprehension and fear. But no, life went on as if none of them had been paying any attention whatsoever to what had transpired in the past.

And Hashem said to Moshe (Shemos 10:21) — Slightly before nightfall of *Rosh Chodesh* Nisan.

Stretch forth your hand on the heavens — From where the earth's light comes, from the sun, moon, and stars.

That there be darkness on the land of Egypt — He Who told the great lights to shine down, also shall tell them not to shine down.

Darkness that shall be felt — The Midrash explains that this darkness actually had substance to it, so that literally it could be "felt"! It was a "double" darkness that actually blocked out the light, for it had "thickness" to it, as the width of a gold coin. Even if the Egyptians had brought in all the candles and torches in the world, it would have been impossible for them to receive any light thereby. The flames would be extinguished, or the "thick" darkness would spread over each flame, surrounding it like a curtain, so that none of its light could escape. In effect, every light that Egypt could hope to see was felt "out" by this darkness.

That there be darkness — The Malbim explains: These are the first three days of the darkness, when the Egyptians still were able to move and walk about.

Darkness that shall be felt — These are the last three days of the darkness, when the Egyptians could not budge even one of their limbs, due to the thick darkness that weighed heavily all around them. Thus, in its account of how the plague started, the Torah writes: *And Moshe stretched forth his hand on the heavens, and there was a thick darkness in all the land of Egypt, three days (Shemos* 10:22) — i.e., during these first three days, if someone who was sitting wanted to stand up, he could, and someone who was standing could sit down.

During the first three days, as they remained in their houses, the Egyptians would have frightening visions, for they could hear the voices of their Jewish neighbors, and they could make out their shadows, as the Jews entered the Egyptian homes to search out all the hiding places where the silver and gold and other valuables were kept. The Jews were surrounded in light, which allowed them to see everything, while the Egyptian homeowners, shrouded in blackness, could not see, but only hear. Why did Hashem have the Jews enter the Egyptian homes and walk about this way? So that the Egyptians would not think for a moment that the Jews, too, were suffering in darkness. Nevertheless, the Jews left everything in its place. They did not take even a shoelace.

And during those first three days, the "dough" of Israel was purified of all its *chametz*. The many Jews who were not worthy of redemption died during this time, and the Egyptians, sitting in darkness, were oblivious to the entire incident. The Jews who did merit to leave Egypt busied themselves all three days quietly burying the bodies. It is said: "One man did not see his fellow," even if the two Egyptians were in the same room in the same house. All the more so were they unable to see what the Jews were doing outside.

Once these three days passed, the Egyptians were faced with an even worse darkness — *and no man was able to stand up from his seat for three days* — three days more. When these last days started, one who had been sitting could not stand. One who had been standing could not sit. No one who was bent could straighten up, and no one standing erect could lie down. If one's fist was clenched, it remained clenched. If one's hand was open, it remained open.

Really, the plague of darkness was to last for seven days, as all the other plagues, but Hashem subtracted one day for the darkness that the Egyptians would suffer in the future, when they chased after the Jews into the sea. It is written there: *And there was the cloud and the darkness [for the Egyptians], and it lit the night [for the Jews]* (Shemos 14:20). So, too, while they still were in Egypt, during the plague of darkness, the Torah says: *But for all the children of Israel, there was light in every one of their dwelling places* (Shemos 10:23) — If a Jew came and sat down at any given place, there would be light that would come along with him. If he got up and left, the light, too, would leave.

The Fourteenth of Nisan in Egypt

The fourteenth of Nisan arrived. That afternoon, the Pesach offering would be slaughtered. In all the Jewish settlements in Egypt, there had been great activity since *Rosh Chodesh*, in order to prepare for this important mitzvah. Four days earlier, on the tenth of Nisan, all the Jews who had survived the plague of darkness had done as Hashem had commanded: *And they shall take for themselves, each man, a lamb* (Shemos 12:3).

Hashem also had told Moshe and Aharon to tell the people that there was a certain condition attached to this mitzvah: *This is the law of the Pesach offering* (Shemos 12:43). Men, as well as their sons and servants (when they would have servants) would not be able to have any portion in the Pesach offering unless they were circumcised. No "foreigner" can eat of the Pesach, Moshe had told the people: *And any servant that a man may have, as a monetary possession, you shall circumcise him, and [only] then he shall eat of it.* As soon as the nation heard Hashem's decree, they happily rose and, singing praises to Hashem, they quickly circumcised everyone among them who was lacking this mitzvah. Hashem also helped, and He caused every circumcision to heal immediately.

To what can this be compared? A great king made an elaborate feast for all those who were close to him. He commanded, however, "Anyone who is not properly dressed will not be allowed to enter." So, too, it was with Hashem, Who made a great feast for the Jewish People, serving roasted meat with matzah and *maror*, in honor of the redemption from Egypt. Hashem stipulated, however, "He whose flesh does not bear the sign of the covenant that I made with Avraham, shall not have a taste!" Immediately, all the Jews who were born in Egypt who lacked this "sign" consented to be circumcised. About them it can be said: *Gather for Me My devoted ones, who fulfill My covenant at the time of the offering (Tehillim 50:5).*

Also, a great multitude of Egyptians had asked to be circumcised, in order to become converts, as did a large number of people from other lands who were in Egypt during the plagues. Many of the most famous Egyptian sorcerers also converted, notably Yanos and Yimbros. They, too, would be able to eat of the Pesach offering, as long as they were "counted" on a lamb at the time that it was slaughtered.

The feelings of anticipation were heightened by yet another phenomenon. The tenth plague — the slaying of the Egyptian firstborn — had already been announced, and many of the common people of Egypt had been bringing their firstborn to the Jews, begging the Jews to hide them in their homes, believing that this would save them from being killed. The Jews did not refuse the request, though in the end, the tactic of the Egyptians failed. [If, in fact, the Egyptian was a firstborn, he died on the night of the tenth plague (see further on) even if he was fast asleep in the same bed with a Jewish firstborn. Actually, the Egyptians made it worse for themselves by hiding their firstborn in Jewish homes, for when the destroyer came to an Egyptian house and found that the firstborn was not there, he took the life of the next oldest in the house!]

As Hashem had commanded them, the Jews had gone to Egyptian homes as well, asking to borrow silver and gold vessels, and also clothing. Knocking on the doors, the Jews would ask for just a few things, but the Egyptians, who wanted Israel to leave as soon as possible, would give them much more than they really wanted, and actually forced the valuable goods on them, not caring that they were left with practically nothing for themselves.

The time to slaughter the Pesach offering finally came. All those who had been circumcised and also had circumcised the members of their household, slaughtered their lambs. They now were ready for the night-time, when there would be many other mitzvos to perform. However, there were still many among them who had not consented to have the "sign of the covenant" put in their flesh.

Hashem told Moshe to slaughter his Pesach lamb. Then, He commanded the four winds of the world to rush to Gan Eden, and blow about with the breezes that are there, and then return to Moshe's lamb, carrying Gan Eden's sweet fragrances with them. The winds complied, and the aromas from Gan Eden mixed and blended with the lovely fragrance emitting from Moshe's offering. Then Hashem commanded the four winds to leave the place of the offering, and carry the enchanting aromas in every direction as far as a man can walk in forty days.

It did not take long for all of Israel to gather around Moshe with a request: "Please, Moshe, let us eat of your Pesach offering!" They had been captivated by the aroma, which drained them of their strength. Moshe told them, "But Hashem has said that if you are not circumcised you cannot eat."

Immediately, they gave themselves over to circumcise their flesh, and the blood of the mitzvah of the *Pesach* mixed with the blood of this other holy mitzvah. Came Hashem and kissed each one of them, giving them a blessing, as it is written (Yechezkel 16:7): *And I passed over, and saw you rolling in your blood. And I said to you, "Through your blood you shall live! Through your blood you shall live!"* The phrase is said twice — once for life that comes from the blood of the Pesach offering, and once for life that comes from the blood of the circumcision.

The Miracles in Egypt: A Compendium of Midrashim

And all that night, there was light for Israel, as strong as the light of day — light that arose from having done the mitzvos of Pesach and circumcision. Meanwhile, in the homes of the Egyptians, there was only darkness — darkness arising from the fear in their hearts, and soon it would be midnight.

And It Came to Pass, at Midnight

And Moshe said, Thus says Hashem: At about midnight, I shall go out in the midst of Egypt (Shemos 11:4) — In the Talmud (*Berachos* 4a), our Sages explained that Moshe did not say simply "at midnight," but rather "at about midnight," because he was afraid that Egypt's astrologers would not really know the exact moment when midnight would arrive. If they were told that the plague was coming "at midnight," and they would think, mistakenly, that midnight had already arrived and the plague had not yet struck, they would say, "Moshe is a liar." Therefore, Moshe said "at about midnight."

One might ask, "Why should Moshe care if the astrologers said he was a liar? Let them say so, for in another moment's time, they will see that really they are the liars!" From here we learn that the evil that arises from the desecration of God's Name is greater than the good that arises from His Name's sanctification. Desecration of God's Name cannot be allowed even for a moment, even in the eyes of those who are not Jewish, and even in the eyes of one person alone!

And it came to pass at midnight, and Hashem struck every firstborn of Egypt, from the firstborn of Pharaoh, who sat on his throne, down to the firstborn of the captives who were in the dungeons, and all firstborn animals (Shemos 12:29) — This is the meaning of the verse: *At midnight, I will rise to thank You for Your righteous judgments (Tehillim 119:62)* — For You brought justice to the Egyptians, and performed kindness to us.

When Moshe first gave the warning: *And every firstborn shall die (Shemos 11:5)*, some of the Egyptians were frightened, and some were not. The ones who were frightened took their firstborn sons to the homes of the Jews and begged, "Please take him and let him stay with you!" When midnight came, the Holy One killed all the Egyptian firstborn, even the ones that were staying with the Jews. If an Egyptian firstborn was sleeping in the same bed with a Jewish firstborn, God stepped between them, and took the life of the Egyptian only. In the morning, when the Jews awoke and saw the Egyptians lying dead beside them, they broke out in a song of praise, saying *At midnight, I will rise to thank You*, for You brought justice to the Egypians and performed kindnesses to us.

R. Yochanan said: Even though He struck them a fatal blow at midnight, their souls were not extinguished until the morning. The Torah records that when the plague first hit, the Egyptians ran to try to hasten the Jews out of Egypt, saying: *All of us are dying* (*Shemos* 12:33). This shows that those who were struck by the plague did not die immediately.

Hashem said, "How can I inform My son of the silent death of those who have hated him? I shall keep the Egyptians alive until morning, and My son shall see them die!"

And it came to pass at midnight, and Hashem struck — R. Elazar said: Every time that the verse says *and Hashem*, it means "Hashem and His executioner." First, Hashem and His court sat to deliberate on the matter of the Egyptian firstborn. They decided on death, and issued the decree, and it was then that the plague struck.

Every firstborn — Not only the firstborn sons, but also the firstborn daughters; not only the firstborn of the father, but also the firstborn of the mother. R. Abba said: If in any given house, there was no firstborn present, then whoever was oldest was killed.

From the firstborn of Pharaoh — Pharaoh himself was a firstborn, but Hashem saved him from the tenth plague so that Pharaoh would be able to tell the world about Hashem's greatness. Also, Hashem intentionally did not destroy "Baal Tzafon," the principle idol worshiped in Egypt. This was to lead the Egyptians to think that Hashem was not All-Powerful, so that later, after the Jews had left, they would not be afraid to chase after God's People, and Hashem then would drown the Egyptians in the sea.

R. Avun said in the name of R. Yehudah ben Pazi: The daughter of Pharaoh, Basyah, also was a firstborn, but Moshe *Rabbenu* prayed for her, and in this merit, she, too, survived the tenth plague.

Down to the firstborn of the captives — One might ask, "Why were they killed? What sin did they commit?" They died to stop the captives from saying, "It was our god that brought the suffering on Egypt. Our god is strong, and stands alone — so powerful, the plagues had no effect on him!"

Another explanation: It was because the captives sinned by being pleased with Pharaoh's evil decrees, and by being happy about how the Egyptians oppressed the Jews. Not only were the captives like this; so were the maidservants and other slaves that the Egyptians possessed, as it is written: *down to firstborn of the maidservant (Shemos* 11:5).

Down to the firstborn of the captives — Another interpretation: These were the nobles and princes from foreign lands, who were captives in Egypt, and were being held by Pharaoh for ransom.

And all firstborn animals — What sin did they commit, that they were killed? They died so that the Egyptians, who worshiped sheep, would not be able to say, "It was our god who brought this suffering upon us. Look at the great power of our god, that he brought us such suffering! Our god stands strong, and the plagues had no effect on him!"

Arise, and leave — R. Levi said: Just as Moshe's voice was given extra strength, so too was Pharaoh's. Pharaoh was heard through the entire land of Egypt, the distance of a forty-day walk. And what was he saying? *Arise, and leave from amidst my people! (Shemos* 12:31). "In the past, you were my slaves. Now you are the slaves of Hashem!" It was then that the Jews broke out in song: *Praise God! Give thanks, servants of Hashem (Tehillim* 113:1) for no longer are we servants of Pharaoh!

And bless me also — Pharaoh told the Jews to leave, and he also made a request of them: *And bless me also (Shemos 12:32);*

that is, "Please pray that the suffering stop!"

At this point, what Hashem had wanted all along was finally achieved. Pharaoh knew that he had no more plagues to fear, but nevertheless, he was letting the Jews go! Willingly he was freeing them, without having to be coerced! Legally, this made his statement valid and effective, as if an official writ of emancipation had been issued: "Arise, former slaves, and leave from amidst my people!"

Only in the hearts of the Egyptian masses was there still fear, as the Torah states: *And the Egyptians were urgent upon the people, hastening to send them out, for they said* (*Shemos* 12:33) — a complaint against Moshe: You told us that only *every firstborn shall die*, but in fact, *all of us are dying!* The Egyptian men thought that if a family had four or five children, then only one would die in the tenth plague — the oldest of them. Little did they know that their wives had been unfaithful, and the other children in the house that died that night all were firstborn of different men! What their wives had done in secret Hashem made known!

Taking Spoils from Egypt

And the people picked up their dough before it would rise, [along with] their leftovers tied in their clothes on their shoulders. And the Children of Israel did according to what Moshe had said, and they asked the Egyptians for jewels and vessels of silver, jewels and vessels of gold, and clothing. And Hashem gave the people favor in the eyes of the Egyptians, so that they lent to them, and they emptied Egypt (*Shemos* 12:34-36).

During the first half of the night, the Jews were occupied with their Pesach offering, roasting it and then eating it along with matzah and *maror*, being careful to not leave any of it over. However, there was no prohibition on keeping matzah and *maror* as leftovers, and since these were their very first mitzvos, and thus were very dear to them, they saved the matzah and *maror* that was left over from the night's meal, and tied it in their clothes, as a man wraps up a precious jewel so that it will not get lost.

The Miracles in Egypt: A Compendium of Midrashim

During the second half of the night, the Jews were occupied with praises and songs of thanks to God, for their redemption from slavery and for the salvation of their souls. As a result, they did not attend to getting ready for the actual Exodus from Egypt, and prepared no food for the trip, neither for themselves nor for their children. They were rejoicing in Hashem, with complete trust in Him, and soon they would follow after Him, into the desert — *a land that was not sown*.

When day came, they began to prepare food for the way, kneading dough that would give them bread for one day. The Egyptians came and interrupted, however, putting great pressure on them to speed things up and leave immediately. Moshe *Rabbenu* also urged them to hurry: "The time has come for us to leave here!"

The result — *And the people picked up their dough before it would rise.* At the time of the Exodus, the prohibition of *chametz* to Israel for the seven days of Pesach was not in effect yet. There only was a command to eat matzah, either for all seven days or for only the first day, but the Jews also could eat *chametz*, all seven days. On the other hand, they had already heard that, in the future, they would be prohibited from eating and even possessing *chametz*, all seven days — and even now they wanted to bake their dough before it rose, and eat only matzah on Pesach!

However, they were not given time to bake at all, for the Egyptians chased them out, as the Torah writes [see further on], *They could not wait.* What did they do? Regarding this, too, they had trust in God, that their dough would not rise. They tied it amidst their clothes and carried it on their shoulders, along with *their leftovers* — the precious matzah and *maror* that remained over from the Seder night.

Tied in their clothes on their shoulders — This was their preparation for their journey, for they had no chance at all to do one other thing for themselves!

At that moment, many of them remembered, "How can we leave without having complied with what Moshe *Rabbenu* told us to do? If we do not do so now, when will we have the chance?" Immediately:

And the Children of Israel — The best of them — *did according to what Moshe had said.* — The Torah testifies that they acted only in order to fulfill the request of Moshe *Rabbenu*, and not because they sought wealth for themselves.

Did according to what Moshe had said — They asked no questions as to the necessity of what they were doing.

If, in fact, they had stopped to think about what Moshe asked them to do, there is no doubt that they would have refused to do it! At that moment, the firstborn of Egypt were lying dead before them. This was a time to go asking the Egyptians for jewelry? Moreover, the Jews knew that the Egyptians wanted Israel out of Egypt forever, so how could they ask to "borrow" anything? How would they be able to return what they borrowed! Furthermore, everywhere there was tumult then. Things were happening so fast that there was no time to even bake their dough! And now they were supposed to take the time to go asking around for jewelry?

The best of Israel did what they did only because it was *what Moshe had said*. Their dough was yet on their shoulders, along with their leftovers from the Seder, but off they went to ask for *silver...gold, and clothing*.

The verse also speaks about *the people* — the ones who did not merit to be among the best of the Jews. That is, many Jews did not ask the Egyptians for anything, for they were certain that their request would be refused. However, Hashem wanted to fulfill His promise to Avraham, that the nation would go out of Egypt *with great wealth*. Therefore —

And Hashem gave the people favor in the eyes of the Egyptians, so that they lent to them — Even without their asking!

And they lent to them — R. Yosei the Galilean said: Because the Jews had shown themselves to be honest during the plague of darkness, the Egyptians believed that the Jews would return everything. The Egyptians reasoned, "If during the darkness, when they were inside our houses and could have taken everything, they nevertheless were honest, why should we not trust them now?"

The Miracles in Egypt: A Compendium of Midrashim

So that they lent to them — R. Eliezer ben Yaakov said: When the Jews stood at the doorways of the Egyptian houses, the Divine Spirit rested upon them. Therefore, they were able to say, "Lend me such-and-such — you will find it lying in such-and-such place." The Egyptian would go and check, and seeing that the Jew was correct, he would fulfill his request.

So that they lent to them — R. Nasan said: There is no need to say this except to tell us that the Egyptians gave them even more than they requested. The Jew would say, "Please lend me this." The Egyptian would answer, "Take it, and here is another one like it!" The Jews would tell them, "If we return, you will get all these things back. If not, you can collect payment for them from the fields and vineyards that we are leaving behind!"

And they emptied Egypt — R. Yehudah said in the name of Shemuel: [Long ago, during the years of famine] all the gold and silver in the world had come to Egypt, on account of Yosef [who interpreted Pharaoh's dream and subsequently managed Egypt's grain sales]. Now, as the Jews left Egypt, they took all this wealth with them.

R. Elazar said: You could not find one Jew who was not leading out sixty donkeys completely laden with silver and gold.

"With a Soft Mouth" — Measure for Measure

The matter is a wonderment: Certainly, it would not have been too much for Hashem to command His faithful servant Moshe to speak harshly to Pharaoh in His Name, and tell him, "The time for Israel's redemption has come. Send My People out with all their belongings, and pay them all the wages that you cheated them of — wages that are due them for the work that they did for you all these years! Give them all of your wealth, for this is no less than what you owe them. Then they will leave your country and they will never see your face again!"

Do you think that Pharaoh and his people would have refused? Without question they would have agreed! Pharaoh and Egypt would have complied in full! Moreover, was Israel to go upon the way that they would travel only if Egypt were willing to do them a favor? Israel was leaving on the strength of the Hand of Hashem! And now that they were timidly approaching the Egyptians with a request, asking to leave only for a three-day journey, one might say — God forbid — that Hashem did not have the power to redeem them!

Rather, Hashem was paying Pharaoh back for what Pharaoh had done, long ago, when he used a "soft mouth" — *peh rach* — to get the Jews to do hard work — *parech* — for him. Pharaoh did not speak harshly, ordering the Jews to work for him. Instead, he tied around his own neck the mold employed for making bricks, as if he, too, would take part in the project, and then he softly asked they Jews, "Do me a favor, work with me for just one day." Israel said, "For the honor of Pharaoh, we shall toil with him for one day with all our strength." Afterwards, however, Pharaoh had the Egyptians tally the number of bricks that the Jews had made, and then he commanded them that every day afterwards, they were to produce the same number of bricks that they produced that first day!

When would Hashem repay Pharaoh for the great pain and shame that he caused Israel through his "soft mouth"? Now! Now, as the Jews were about to leave Egypt, Hashem would repay him, measure for measure. Pharaoh said to himself, "What harm is there in it? They are asking to go only for three days!" After he had done them this "favor," however, he was told that the Jews had fled for good. It caused his teeth to ache, just as Israel's teeth had ached the day after they had done the "favor" he had asked of them!

What is more, Hashem saw fit that it should be this way, so that the Jews would never have any desire to return to the impurities of Egypt. They always would know that in the chronicles of Egypt, Israel is written down as Egypt's slave, who is guilty of fleeing under false pretenses, and who deserves punishment for this. The Jews, therefore, would always be afraid to go back there.

We find therefore, that through the "soft mouth" that

Hashem used to repay Pharaoh, Israel became separated from Egypt forever, and so, too, did Pharaoh and Egypt become separated from Israel. Israel would always feel shame for leaving Egypt with deceit and trickery — taking wages that were due them, but as if they simply were borrowing. They could have claimed what they took, saying, "All this is ours!" And whenever Egypt would recall what Israel did, anger and hatred would well up in the Egyptians, so that never would Egypt seek any ties or any closeness with them. As Hashem freed His nation from the Egyptian bondage, this was the very thing that He wanted — to separate the two peoples, for all time.

The "Spoils" that Moshe Rabbenu Took from Egypt

At that time, what was Moshe *Rabbenu* taking from Egypt? Our Sages taught: Come and see how Moshe *Rabbenu* treasured the mitzvos! While all the rest of Israel was occupied in taking gold, silver, and other wealth out of Egypt, he was engaged in a different type of taking, as it is written: *And Moshe took the bones of Yosef with him (Shemos 13:19).*

How did Moshe know where Yosef was buried? Our Sages said: One person from that generation who was still alive was Sarach, daughter of Asher. Moshe went to her and asked, "Do you know where Yosef is buried?" She told him, "The Egyptians made a metal coffin for him and submerged it in the Nile, so that the river's waters would be blessed. Also, Pharaoh's sorcerers told him, "Do you want to make sure that Israel never leaves Egypt? See to it that they cannot find the bones of Yosef, for they will never leave without them!"

Moshe went to the riverbank and cried out, "Yosef, Yosef! Hashem swore to redeem His people, and the time has come for Him to fulfill His oath! You made Israel swear that they would take you with them from here when the time to leave came! For the Honor of Hashem, the God of Israel! The *Shechinah* is waiting for you! Israel and the Clouds of Glory are waiting for you! If you show yourself, everything will be fine, but if not, we will be held back by the oath that we swore to you!" Immediately, the coffin began to totter back and forth. It loosened itself from its place at the bottom of the river and floated to the surface of the water like a piece of bamboo, so that Moshe was able to take it.

R. Nasan said: Yosef had been buried as all Egyptian kings were buried. Moshe *Rabbenu* went to the place where the Egyptians buried their kings, and cried out, "Yosef, Yosef! Hashem swore..." Immediately, a coffin began to shake. Moshe knew that it was Yosef's, and he took it.

Some say that Yosef was buried in the same tomb as the Egyptain kings, and Moshe could not recognize which bones were Yosef's. There was another old woman who still remained alive from that generation — Yocheved, Moshe's mother. She told her son, "I will show you which bones you want." They went together, and when Yocheved looked at the bones that were Yosef's, she smelled the aroma of Gan Eden in them. The two then knew that these were what they sought, and Moshe took the bones away with him in a coffin.

On the Wings of Eagles

And the Children of Israel traveled from Raamses towards Sukkos, about six hundred thousand men on foot, aside from the little ones (*Shemos* 12:37) — Later, before giving them the Torah, Hashem would remind them of how it had been seven weeks earlier: *You saw what I did to the Egyptians, and how I bore you on eagle's wings* (*Shemos* 19:4).

When did He bear them on eagle's wings? The Jews settled in Egypt, not only all over the land of Goshen, but throughout all the other parts of the vast land of Egypt as well. Nevertheless, when the time of the redemption arrived, Hashem quickly gathered everyone together in Goshen. From Goshen, they all went together to Raamses, and arrived there in practically no time at all. Then—

And the children of Israel traveled from Raamses — It was in Raamses that Pharaoh had spoken softly to them about working for Egypt, as a "favor," and it was in that very Raamses that they went out into freedom:

Towards Sukkos — Which received this name because there Hashem enveloped His People in Seven Clouds of Glory, so that their camp was under a *sukkah* for shade, and beneath a wedding canopy for honor. At each of the four directions a cloud stood to protect them from the elements. So, too, above their heads — to shield them from the burning sun, and from rain and hail. Beneath them was a sixth cloud, spread out as a soft carpet, to protect their feet from thorns, stones, snakes and scorpions. The seventh cloud stood in front of the camp, and when the Jews traveled, it smoothed and straightened the way before them, eliminating the holes and ditches, flattening hills, so that it would be easy to walk and camp.

About six hundred thousand men — It says "about" because one was missing, but Hashem's Presence made up for him. This was as before, when Yaakov went down to Egypt. Then, too, there were only sixty-nine souls, but Hashem's Presence made it seventy.

And also a great mixed multitude went up [from Egypt] with them — There were about one hundred and twenty thousand men numbered in this group — all of them already circumcised when they left Egypt. Therefore, their original nationalities are not mentioned.

And flocks and herds and a great many cattle — Those of Israel and those of the mixed multitude. Hashem brought all of them to one place in Goshen, all of these people and all of these animals, though both had been scattered throughout the land of Egypt. He quickly brought them to Raamses, and after Raamses they came to Sukkos in virtually no time at all (though Raamses and Sukkos were about 120 miles apart). This was a feat that the eye could not imagine, and the ear could not hear, were it not written in the Torah.

Realize, that the dough that the Jews prepared in Egypt, on the morning of the Exodus, did not have time to rise, for they were rushed out of their homes by the Egyptians and by Moshe *Rabbenu*. All of a sudden they all were in Goshen and Raamses, and then they all were in Sukkos. Where, in fact, did they bake this dough? They baked it in Sukkos. You would think that by then the dough would have risen. However, the Torah tells us otherwise, in the very next verse (*Shemos* 12:39):

And they baked the dough that they brought out of Egypt, unleavened cakes — The dough of our forefathers did not have time to rise when suddenly, the King of kings, the Holy One, appeared to them, rushed them out of Egypt and brought them into His Clouds of Glory in Sukkos. It was there that they baked the dough, and even by then the dough had not had the time to rise!

Because it did not ferment — It did not have time to ferment! On eagle's wings they were brought to Sukkos, in less than a third of an hour!

And neither had they prepared any food for the way — This is to let us know that Israel was to be praised for not saying to Moshe, "How can we set out for the wilderness? We have no provisions for the way!" No, they believed him, that Hashem would provide for them. They followed the leadership of Moshe *Rabbenu*. About that generation the Prophet says explicitly (Yirmeyahu 2:2): *Go, call in the ears of Jerusalem and say: Thus says Hashem, I remember to your favor, the devotion of your youth, how you loved Me as a bride, and followed Me into the desert, into a land that was not sown.* And what was their reward? They became His Nation, *Holy to Hashem* (Ibid).

The Secret Is Finally Revealed

The Jewish People did not know when the redemption from Egypt would be, until it actually came about. The date was hidden from all the generations until then, and kept as a secret under the *sukkah* of their King's Clouds of Glory.

The wording of the Covenant between the Pieces was as follows: *Know for certain that your seed shall be strangers in a land that is not theirs. And they [the native people] will work them as slaves, and will oppress them* (Bereshis 15:13).

The Torah then places a pause (*esnachta*) in the verse, and says, for *four hundred years*.

Four hundred years — The Jews wondered: What were

The Miracles in Egypt: A Compendium of Midrashim

these years, and from when were they numbered? Did the count start from the day that Hashem first made His covenant with Avraham, or perhaps only from when Avraham first had a child? Did all four hundred have to be years of being a "stranger" and years of slavery and oppression, or perhaps some years would be one way and others would be another way? To those generations, the details of the Covenant between the Pieces were veiled in mystery.

Many from the tribe of Ephraim calculated the four hundred years from the day that the Covenant was made. On this assumption, they took up arms and tried to leave Egypt by force, thirty years too early, and the Egyptians killed them in battle.

Many of the Jews had given up hope of seeing the redemption, even though they calculated the four hundred years from the birth of Yitzchak. They assumed that all four hundred years had to be years of estrangement, slavery, and oppression. They said, "As for estrangement, our years in Egypt, away from our homeland, number only two hundred and ten. As for enslavement and oppression, this has been our lot for only eighty-six years, since the day *a new king arose over Egypt*. The rest of our years in Egypt were years of comfort and honor." As a result, they did not think that they would see the redemption in their lifetimes.

However, Hashem had His own way of determining when the redemption would be, as He had told Avraham. Now that Avraham's descendants were out of Egypt, camped in Sukkos under their Redeemer's protective care, the Torah states Hashem's calculation (*Shemos* 12:40):

Now the dwelling of the Children of Israel that dwelled in Egypt — This completed the four hundred years.

Was thirty years — This was from the day of the Covenant between the Pieces until Yitzchak was born, for regarding Yitzchak, Hashem said, *Your seed shall be strangers*.

And four hundred years — From Yitzchak's birth until now.

The Attribute of Justice might try to complain: How was the decree of estrangement fulfilled in Yitzchak? Yitzchak never left Canaan all his life and never was in Egypt at all! The answer is simple — the Covenant was that Avraham's seed would be strangers *in a land that is not theirs* — and though Canaan would eventually be inherited by the Jews, it did not belong to them while Yitzchak lived there!

The Attribute of Justice might try to complain further: The decree in the Covenant was not only estrangement for four hundred years, it also was to be slavery and oppression for four hundred years! Is this not the simple meaning of the words that Hashem spoke in the Covenant?

The Egyptians had already enslaved and oppressed them much more harshly than the decree, however, so that the decree had been fulfilled that much more quickly. For this reason, Hashem told Moshe: *I know their pains* (Shemos 3:7) — I know exactly how much they were being hurt more than the decree, which made up for the missing years.

The appointed angels of the nations of the world might also complain, saying: It is stated officially on paper that Israel must be enslaved to Egypt for four hundred years. How can this nation go free before the time has expired? Already, however, Pharaoh himself set Israel free, for he said: *Arise, and leave from amidst my people!* (Shemos 12:31).

One might say, "But the decree was they would be *in a land that is not theirs*, so that they were slaves to all of Egypt, and not just to to Pharaoh, and all of Egypt did not free them!" Long ago, however, Yosef had arranged that the Egyptian people all would sell themselves as slaves to Pharaoh, so that if Pharaoh freed Israel, who was left in Egypt with the right to complain? Moreover, it already is written: *For they were chased out of Egypt...and the Egyptians were urgent on the nation, to hasten them out of their land* (Shemos 12:33,39).

This is what Hashem had intended from the very beginning — that the redemption would be four hundred and thirty years from the day of the Covenant, and the estrangement would be only four hundred years. Thus, if Yitzchak's birth had been moved up within the thirty years after the Covenant, the redemption would have remained four hundred and thirty years from the time of the Covenant, but the estrangement would have ended earlier. In truth, Yitzchak was born thirty years after the Covenant, so that the end of the four hundred and thirty years and the end of the four hundred years of estrangement exactly coincided with one another. Therefore (*Shemos* 12:41):

And it came to pass, at the end of four hundred and thirty years, and it was on this selfsame day — The fifteenth of Nisan, the day the Covenant was made, the day Yitzchak was born, and the day Yaakov descended into Egypt.

That all of the hosts of Hashem left the land of Egypt — Who were the hosts of Hashem? — Israel.

All — The converts who joined them.

Come and see two parallel constructions that are written in the Torah: Hashem said to Avraham at the Covenant between the Pieces, after He told him that he would bear children: *I am Hashem, your God, Who took you out of Ur Kasdim* (*Bereshis* 15:7). Later, at Mount Sinai, Hashem said to the entire Jewish Nation: *I am Hashem, your God, Who took you out of the land of Egypt* (*Shemos* 20:2).

Between these two similar statements some four hundred and thirty years had passed, but when Hashem took the Children of Israel out of Egypt, He took their fathers out as well — Avraham, Yitzchak, and Yaakov. The Patriarchs and their descendants were redeemed from Egypt together, and thereby Hashem gave the souls of His People eternal freedom — from every oppression and every exile that they ever would suffer in the future.

Appendix Three

Those Who Would Devour Yaakov: Persecution and Blood Libels

And Esav ran to greet him and he fell upon his neck and he kissed him (Bereshis 33:4). According to tradition, the Hebrew word for *he kissed him* in this verse is written with dots placed above each letter. The Sages (*Yalkut Shimoni* 133) comment that this teaches us that the wicked Esav said to himself: "I will not kill Yaakov with a bow and arrow, but with my mouth and my teeth I will kill him...." Do not read, *And he kissed him*; read, *And he bit him*. [The Hebrew root נ-ש-ק — "kiss" — resembles the root נ-ש-ך — "bite."]

From the time that Edom [the descendants of Esav] became a world power and swallowed up the great kingdoms — Babylonia, Persia, and Greece — that had preceded her, she assumed their role as persecutors of Israel. Edom destroyed the Temple, burned Jerusalem and the cities of Yehudah, mercilessly killing many of our nation, abandoning them as prey for the vultures of the skies. The remnant was exiled and dispersed to the four corners of the earth. Ever since Edom's ascendancy, we have had neither peace nor rest and there has not been a day that has not been marred by trouble and sorrow.

The wicked descendants of Esav subjected us to tortures that her predecessors had never considered, for Edom is a base nation lacking honor even compared to the earlier kingdoms. The sword and spear were not sufficient for her; bows and arrows brought her no satisfaction. Rather, she sought to sink her teeth into our nation like a wild animal, to destroy us with her mouth as well.

It was during the reign of Edom/Rome that the calumny of the blood libel was first raised. A nation soaked in blood, who thirsted for blood, raised a nefarious accusation against a nation that detests blood, claiming that we slaughter her children so as to use their blood in preparing the matzos used on Pesach.

As a result of this libel, rivers of blood have been shed through the long years of our exile. Esav sought to transform our Festivals into days of mourning. Precisely at those times when Israel sought to release herself from the shackles of her physical bondage in the Diaspora by celebrating the Festival of her freedom, her heart was terror-stricken as she wondered what Edom — the most abject of nations — was plotting.

Nevertheless, our Festival was not canceled nor was the joy of the commemoration of our freedom marred. On this night that is guarded, we posted extra guards to foil their plots. And when they were nevertheless successful, we ascended the stake, accepting the tortures that they inflicted, and still our Festival was not abandoned.

Turei Zahav, in his commentary to the laws of Pesach (*Orach Chayim* 472) writes: *In our times we refrain from using red wine [for the four cups] because of the false libels that are raised due to our many sins.*

Many times, God broke the fangs of the vicious dogs, saving us from them, and causing our accusers to retract in shame. But many times, their fangs were broken only after they had managed to bite Yaakov/Israel, destroying his dwelling places in the lands of his dispersion. The libels spread from land to land, reaching even the Arab countries. The bloodthirstiness of Edom flowed through the veins of every nation as all peoples sought to destroy us in unison. Few in number were those among them who arose in opposition to their own people.

They chose the Festival of Pesach — specifically the night of the Seder — as the time to unleash their calumny. They invited everyone to join in consuming our flesh — young and old, wise and foolish, kings and ministers, priests and cardinals, and the rabble. Very few were the voices of sanity who were willing to stand up and expose their pernicious slander for what it really was. *Remember, God, what they sought to do and remain not silent over our [spilled] blood!*

The Jealousy of Slaves toward Free Men

The nations of the world with their kings, ministers, cardinals, and priests; Rome, Greece, England, Italy, France, Germany, Poland, and the rest of Europe; Syria, Egypt, and even the [gentile] authorities in Hebron and Jerusalem; their high station and wealth made no difference in their character, for in essence they were only slaves at heart and their souls were denigrated. The efforts that they directed against the remnant of Israel in their midst were in vain, attempts to afflict and impoverish, to humiliate and crush were of no avail. Israel remained free despite the bondage that they sought to impose. She remained exalted and proud despite her constraints and those who oppressed her and tormented her were consumed with envy.

This was especially true at Pesach time, for it was then that God had redeemed Israel from bondage and made her truly free. Israel's enemies could afflict only her body; her soul was eternally beyond reach. Israel needed only to switch her glance from her immediate predicament for a moment and remind herself of the Exodus from Egypt. The shackles of her servitude fell away when she sat at the Seder table like royalty, her face radiant with the joy of freedom and redemption, her entire being declaring God's glory and splendor.

When the soul of Israel tasted once again true freedom and redemption, the kings and rulers who had never known such an experience were driven into jealous frenzy. But that short moment of Israel's pleasure was sufficient for her to be able to withstand the bitter herbs that she might eat all year, for the taste of the freedom of Pesach lingered in her mouth together with the pleasure of the anticipation of the coming Pesach.

Among the kings and governments that envied Israel, jealousy was rife. Freedom for one meant enslavement for another. They eyed each other suspiciously, plotting continuously as one fell and another took its place. Only Israel stood apart; the freedom of one Jew never adversely affected his brother. The more who were free, the greater the total freedom of the nation. It is for this reason that Israel invites all to share in her freedom — every man and nation who foreswears the use of the sword is called to join with Israel. Freedom is offered to all mankind and the soul of every living thing thanks God for this gift.

At the beginning of the Seder, Israel announces: *Whoever is hungry, let him come and eat! Whoever is in need, let him come and join in the Pesach!* It is this very declaration that makes us guilty in the eyes of the nations. It forms the basis of their hatred and from it their jealousy and calumny take root.

Because jealousy is the origin of their slanderous claims against us, even the wise and enlightened of the nations are guilty of spreading this poison. In fact, they were often the most rabid initiators of these claims and charted the paths that others followed. Wisdom, when unlinked to a soul that is truly free, is even more prone to envy and animosity than is ignorance and foolishness.

The First Libels

The first known instances of libels regarding the riual slaughter of human beings are to be found among the "wise men" of ancient Greece. As the powers of the Greeks declined after they were soundly defeated by the Hasmoneans, they began to spread this slander. The Romans, who followed Greece and inherited her role as the world's major power, carried forth this libel to all the lands where their sovereignty extended.

Josephus, in his work *Contra Apionem*, quotes a contemporary report sent by one of the Greek residents of Jerusalem:

> *Antiochus, upon entering the Sanctuary, discovered a man reclining on a couch with a table spread with delicacies before him. He was eating sea fish and fowl. It is the custom of the Jews, at a set time every year, to capture a Greek, feed him and fatten him and then murder him. He is then offered as a sacrifice according to their custom with much pomp and ceremony after which his corpse is thrown into one of the wells.*

Democritus, an early Greek philosopher, wrote: *Once every*

seven years, the Jews capture a heathen and offer him as a sacrifice, cutting his flesh into pieces.

Even Socrates makes reference to a supposed Jewish custom of ritual murder, writing: *On Purim, drunken Jews seized a heathen and hung him on a tree in place of [an effigy of] Haman.*

As the fire of hatred spread throughout the world and the libels increased year by year in every country, historians tired of recording individual episodes. The libels were spread against Jews wherever they lived. Since it would be impossible to record every instance of libels spread against Jews, we shall recount only some of the more famous ones.

In the year 4904 [1144 C.E.], Theobald of Cambridge — a renegade Jew — testified that it was the practice of the Jews to sacrifice a Christian child on Pesach and that the town chosen for that year's sacrifice was Norwich. The anti-Semitic heads of the church seized upon this "evidence" and when a Christian child was found dead in the town, they canonized him as St. William. This libel spread quickly throughout Europe, and two year later, as the Second Crusade began, it was used as an excuse to justify the slaughter of Jews wherever the Crusaders marched.

Three years after the libel of Norwich, in the year 4907 [1107 C.E.], the body of a Christian who had drowned in the river in Wurzburg, Germany on the 22nd of Adar, was discovered. The Jews of the area were accused of ritual murder and after three days of indiscriminate slaughter in Wurzburg, the Crusaders spread the slaughter to other cities. A massacre took place on *chol ha-mo'ed* Pesach and outbreaks of violence continued until Shavuos. In the *piyut* recited in some communities on the Shabbos of *chol ha-mo'ed* Pesach, the liturgical poet R. Yitzchak ben Shalom writes:

> *God, who is like You among the silent,*
> *The oppressor struck in darkness,*
> *On the twentieth of the first month.*

Twenty-four years later the fires of hatred spread to France, to the area where the Tosafists lived. In Lyon, the entire

Jewish community was destroyed because of a blood libel, sanctifying the Name of Heaven as they perished.

R. Efrayim ben Yaakov of Bonn, in a contemporary account of the travails of the period, writes:

> The oppressors decreed [that the Jews be murdered] and they took R. Yechiel ben R. David, R. Yekusiel ben R. David, who were Kohanim and students of Rabbenu Shemuel, as well as R. Yehudah ben R. Aharon. They were bound with ropes at the stake and a fire was lit which burned the ropes that bound them. Then the three men told the servants of the oppressor: "The fire has not harmed us. Why should we not be set free?" But the oppressors replied: "We swear that you shall not escape." They murdered them with the sword and cast their bodies into the fire, the three of them along with thirty-one fellow Jews. As the blade cut them down and their souls departed, they lifted their voices in songs of praise to God. The heathens present commented: "We hear your song but do not understand it. We have heard no song like this before." The praise that they sang was "Aleinu Leshabe'ach.

In the year 4981 [1221 C.E.], a new libel was spread in Erfurth, Germany. An contemporary historian wrote:

> When non-Jewish merchants came to the town and saw that the Jews were prospering, they were filled with jealousy. They spread the slander that the Jews had captured a gentile, and after killing him, had drunk his blood. The oppressors seized upon the opportunity and set the local synagogue on fire, killing all those who were praying there.

In the registry of the Mainz Jewish community, we find the following account of Jews who died as a result of a blood libel:

> R. Shem Tov haLevi, who killed himself in front of the holy ark; Madrona and her sister Rachel, young maidens who threw themselves into the fire; Yosef, a young Levi who threw himself into the fire. Those who were accused were given the chance to "purify" themselves by converting. But these holy souls spurned the offer and ascended the stake to sanctify the Name of Heaven.

In 4995 [1235 C.E.] in Fulda, Germany, Crusaders murdered five Christian children and sent witnesses to testify in the court of Frederik II that they had seen "how the Jews had left this house [where the bodies of the children were discovered] carrying leather flasks full of blood." The town was in an uproar and the bodies were brought before the emperor. After investigating the charges, he banished those who had brought the libel, ordering that the corpses be buried. He further issued a "writ of acquittal" in which he declared that the blood libel was without any foundation. However, this very writ became a weapon in the hands of our enemies who sought to shed Jewish blood, for they claimed that the Jews had bribed the emperor.

On Pesach in the year 5024 [1264 C.E.], the blood libel was renewed in England and pogroms spread throughout most of the local communities. In London alone, some one thousand five hundred Jews were killed. The remnant of the community fled to safety, but their homes and property were plundered. Jewish life was made intolerable, until finally an expulsion order was issued in the year 5051 [1291 C.E.] ordering the Jews to leave England and never return.

In the year 5027 [1267 C.E.], the Jews of Forzheim in the German province of Baden were accused of slaughtering a Christian girl, to use her blood for ritual purposes. Three of the local rabbis were arrested and subjected to inhuman torture in order to exact a confession admitting the crime. When the three realized that they would be unable to withstand the tortures, they committed suicide. Their memory is commemorated in the registry of the Mainz community, and two *selichos* — recited in the penitential prayers of the Worms community — were written in their memory.

During this same period, there are records of blood libels in the communities of Sinzach on the Rhine, Wiesenberg, Mainz, Munich, and Bachrach. These communities were all destroyed. The local church officials offered to save the Jews through conversion, but their offers were rejected out of hand. Our saintly ancestors spurned the opportunity given them and slew themselves, together with their wives and children, rather than fall into the clutches of their oppressors.

The greatest havoc of this period took place in Prague, on the last day of Pesach in the year 5149 [1389 C.E.]. A rabid mob murdered thousands of Jews and despite the offer of protection given to those who would convert, not a single Jew accepted and all willingly went to the stake.

In his book *Emek haBacha* — "Vale of Tears" — R. Yosef haKohen writes:

> On the twenty-second day of Nisan, the heathens of Prague surrounded the vineyard of God, the House of Israel. The people came with their axes, and like woodcutters, they slaughtered thousands, burning many at the stake, turning over the graves of those who sleep in the dust, and destroying their tombstones. There was no escape from them on the day of God's anger.

A special memorial poem, composed by R. Avigdor Kara, was inserted into the *Minchah* prayer of Yom Kippur recited according to the custom of the Prague community, to commemorate the slaughter.

Many years later, when the Maharal served as rabbi of Prague, there were again blood libels against the Jewish community. Many popular legends have come down to us about how the Maharal used his mystical powers to defeat the slanderers, including tales of the golem that he fashioned to thwart Israel's enemies.

In Jerusalem, there is a legend about R. Kalonymus *Ba'al haNes* who is buried at the foot of the Mount of Olives near the grave of the Prophet Zecharyah. Using his mystical knowledge, R. Kalonymus thwarted the libel of the local Arabs who had killed one of their own children and thrown his body into the courtyard of the synagogue in an attempt to libel the Jews. Although this took place on Shabbos, R. Kalonymus wrote an amulet which he placed on the forehead of the dead child, who thereupon stood up and pointed out who had murdered him. Although it was permitted to write for the sake of saving the lives of the Jews, R. Kalonymus nevertheless passed sentence upon himself for having desecrated the Shabbos; he asked that after his death, all those who passed his grave throw stones at it. The people of Jerusalem carried out his wishes, and it became the custom that whoever passed there added a stone to the heap on his grave.

At the end of the Middle Ages, the period of the Renaissance for many, blood libels spread to Turkey, Egypt, Syria, and even to Hebron in the Land of Israel. The calumny respected to boundaries. While the enemies of the Jews in Arab lands copied the wickedness of the Christians in Europe in slandering the Jews with this bestial claim, it was nevertheless mainly in the Christian world that this slander took root and spread, flourishing especially in the period of the Renaissance with the active encouragement of the Church.

One of the worst episodes concerns a Christian child — Simon of Trieste, Italy. He was two or three years old when he disappeared from his home on the first day of Pesach. His body was discovered in a stream near the home of a Jew. By the order of the local bishop, the leaders of the Jewish community were arrested and subjected to terrible tortures until they "confessed" that the child had been killed so that his blood could be used. Reports of the ritual murder spread throughout Italy and Germany, where Jews were subsequently arrested, tortured, and burned at the stake. Among those arrested was the Rabbi of Regensburg, one of the leading Halachic authorities of the period, whose life was miraculously saved. Even today, if you travel through Central Europe, you will likely come across churches and monasteries bearing the name St. Simon, for the child was canonized and declared a saint by the Church.

The cruel persecutions to which the Jews of Germany and Italy were subjected led many of them to flee to Poland, but there too they were not safe from the hatred of their enemies. In Poland and Russia, blood libels were not spread secretly, but were publicized amid much pomp and ceremony with kings and princes taking part. Throughout these lands, defenseless Jews were dragged to the gallows after "confessions of guilt" had been extracted from them.

In the year 5358 [1598 C.E.], the body of a young child was discovered in a marsh near Lublin. Five Jews were arrested and were forced to "confess" that they "drank wine mixed with Christian blood that they had taken from the body of the child." They were then forced to admit that this blood had been mixed into the dough used to bake matzos. The high court in Lublin found them guilty of murder and a death cell was constructed in the courtyard of the Great Synagogue. They were put to death and their bodies were cut into pieces and sent to be displayed in the four corners of the city. The child was declared a saint and was buried in the local cathedral.

One hundred years later, a blood libel took place in Sandomircz, Poland. The bishop of Cracow ordered the investigating tribunal in Lublin to conduct their inquiry using all the methods of the Inquisition — orders that were carried out to the letter.

In 5356 [1596 C.E.], two brothers — R. Moshe and R. Yehudah, the sons of R. Yekusiel — were accused of ritual murder and were tortured until they "confessed." They died on the fourteenth and eighteenth of Iyar. Their martyrdom is commemorated in one of the *Selichos* prayers recited according to the Lithuanian custom.

> *They spoke lies about me and accused me falsely,*
> *Their mouths uttered falsehood and they testified untruthfully,*
> *Moshe and Yehudah, sons of Yekusiel, fell into the snare. In sanctification of the Great and Awesome Name they gave their lives.*
> *Both of their souls departed with great torture and their honor was desecrated.*
> *They tied them like horses and dragged them like dogs.*
> *They buried them among the wicked after crucifying them like thieves.*
> *They nailed them up with their hands and legs spread.*
> *They were consumed by fire and their image was destroyed.*

By the beginning of the eighteenth century, the slander of the blood libel was so widespread in Poland that Kittowitz, a contemporary writer, could tell his readers that there was no such thing as matzah without Christian blood.

The cruelty of those who spread this slander extended to all — even to those whose deaths served as an excuse for propagating a libel, when their bodies were discovered.

In 5456 [1696 C.E.], the body of a Christian child was discovered near the town of Posen. In the communal register, the following details are recorded:

A pupil was killed in the forest, a short distance from our community, and it was not known who had murdered him. Not only had he been killed, but he was also brutally tortured — in a manner that had never been seen before. His eyes had been gouged out, his hands and legs amputated, and his heart removed.

During this period, Augustus II, king of Poland, made the following heinous declaration: The unbelieving Jews shed the blood of Christian children for use on the festival of matzos, as has been testified by one of them.

From that time on, there was hardly a town or village in Russia, Poland, Lithuania, and Galicia — wherever Jews lived — where the Christians did not kindle the fire of hatred. They trained their children to fear the Jews, and urged them to beware, warning them: "Look! The Jew is coming. He will slaughter you to drink your blood on Pesach!" The priests used their pulpits to encourage the populace to cause trouble for the Jews. Slaughter as a result of these libels was the order of the day — slaughter to a population already reeling from the horrors of the Chmielnicki pogroms of 1648-49 and the terror unleashed by Petlura and Heller.

There was no escape — neither through petitions nor bribes, nor even the pleas made to those Jews who had abandoned their faith and enjoyed positions of influence within the various governments and who were sometimes willing to try to help. Emissaries were dispatched to Rome to plead before

Those Who Would Devour Yaakov: Persecution and Blood Libels

the Pope, but even these efforts provided no more than temporary respite for the victims — and this at enormous cost.

All knew that the slander was baseless and that it was no more than a vile attempt to provide a reason to persecute the Jews. But this fact did not prevent our fathers from being tortured through every type of cruelty that man is capable of devising. Entire families and communities were destroyed, with no one left alive to mourn them.

As if our numerous enemies were not enough, there were others who joined forces with them, as the Prophet had foretold: *Those who destroy you and overthrow you will come from your midst* (Yeshayahu 49:17). In the middle of the eighteenth century, Jacob Frank declared that he was the *Mashiach*. Together with many of the followers whom he had duped into believing this, he converted to Christianity and aligned himself with our enemies. The Church leaders used them as an instrument to destroy the remnant of our people, and there were no more trying times in the European exile than this period. The Frankists, at the urging of the Church, issued written testimony in which they declared that all of the Jews who follow the Talmud are required to slaughter Christians in order to use their blood for making matzos on Pesach. They went so far as to claim that the Hebrew acronym used as a mnemonic for the ten plagues recounted at the Seder was in reality a secret code that stated: We all require blood in the manner that was done to "that man" by the Sages in Jerusalem.

The Church, which in this period enjoyed almost unlimited power, compelled the Jews of Poland to participate in a public debate with the Frankists. Although they knew that the purpose of this debate was not to establish the truth but rather to compromise the Jewish leaders, they had no alternative but to agree. Two outstanding Rabbis of the period were sent: R. Chayim *haKohen* Rapaport and R. Yisrael Baal Shem Tov. Legend has it that on the day of the debate, R. Chayim wore burial shrouds beneath his clothing, for he was convinced that he would not return alive. But God came to their assistance in their time of need and they returned from the debate with great honor while the evil designs of their enemies were foiled.

The following story is told of R. Yechezkel Landau, author of the famous responsa *Noda b'Yehudah* and Rabbi of Prague in the latter half of the eighteenth century. Once, on the night before Pesach, he was sitting in his room with the door bolted shut. Around midnight he heard the sounds of an unruly mob approaching his home. God enlightened him and made him realize that the mob's arrival portended a blood libel. He quickly searched through his study — and found a flask of blood which someone had hidden among his books!

Realizing that there was no escape from this desperate situation, he quickly took the flask, drank its contents, and then washed it out with the water that he kept in his study for washing his hands. When he opened the door, the leaders of the mob burst into the room and went directly to the shelf where they had hidden the flask. When they found it empty they had no choice but to shamefacedly take leave, acknowledging that it had been the hand of God that had saved the Rabbi and his community.

The calumny of ritual slaughter continued to spread throughout Europe. Infamous episodes of this slander took place in Damascus in 1840, in Hungary, in Poland, and wherever Jewish communities were to be found. The calumny of ritual murder continued into the twentieth century, the most notable example being the Beilis case in the years before the outbreak of the First World War.

The last was the most serious of all. During the years 5671 [1911] through 5673 [1913] all Jews under Russian rule were siezed with terror because of the blood libel brought against Mendel Beilis. This was brought before a jury with the avowed intention of declaring to the world that the Jews ate human blood. The Russian government was even asked to consider ways and means of stopping religious murders being carried out by Jews.

World Jewry rose to the challenge and even found some support from a few honest and upright non-Jews who recoiled from these falsehoods. Russia's enemies had a hand in confusing the Russian leaders on this matter, hoping to divert their attention from the preparations for war against her. The evil Russian plan was foiled for the time being — and then the First World War broke out, bringing fresh disasters to the Jewish People. This was followed, twenty years later, by the Second World War when Hitler, the chief slaughterer, rose against us.

In these immortal words from *Tehillim*, King David spoke for all Jews, in every generation and in every place:

> *Arise, God, let not man prevail. Let the nations be judged in Your presence (9:20).*
>
> *My heart was hot within me; while I was pondering, the fire burned. Then I spoke with my tongue (39:4).*
>
> *With no fault of mine, they run and prepare themselves. Arise to help me and see (59:5).*
>
> *Pour out Your fury on them and let Your fierce anger overtake them (69:25).*
>
> *Pour out Your wrath upon the nations which do not recognize You, upon the kingdoms that do not call in Your Name. For they have devoured Yaakov and laid waste to his abode (79:6).*
>
> *How long, God? Will You forever be angry? Will Your wrath burn like fire? (89:5).*
>
> *O God, our God, You answer them. You are a God Who forgives and Who avenges their deeds (99:9).*
>
> *For they have opened the mouth of wickedness and deceit against me. They have spoken against me with the tongue of falsehood (109:2).*
>
> *How many are the days of Your servant? When will You execute judgment against those who persecute me? (119:84).*

Appendix Four

A Night that Is Guarded

Within the space of a single verse, the Torah twice refers to the night of the Seder as *leil shimurim* — "a night that is guarded": *It is a night that is guarded by God to take them [Israel] out of Egypt. This night remains to God a night that is guarded for all the Children of Israel for all their generations* (Shemos 12:42). Our Sages offered a number of explanations of this phrase.

A night that is guarded — A night of anticipation and waiting, for God guarded and anticipated this night when He would fulfill His promise to take them out of the land of Egypt. (*Rashi*)

A night that is guarded — A night that is specially set aside for a two-fold redemption: for God and for His Nation. [This explanation is based on the use of the plural *shimurim*.] We see that throughout the period of bondage, it is as if the Divine Presence were also enslaved in Egypt. Moreover, we find that whenever Israel went into exile, the *Shechinah* went with them in their exile. (*Yalkut Shimoni, Shemos* 210)

A night that is guarded — A night that is reserved for the future redemption. Why is the word *shimurim* repeated in this verse? Because on this night [in other times and places] God did great things for the righteous, just as He had done for Israel in Egypt. On this night He saved Chizkiyahu from Sancheriv and his armies; on this night He saved Chananyah, Misha'el, and Azaryah; on this night He save Daniel from the lion's den; and on this night Eliyahu and *Mashiach* are made great (*Shemos Rabbah* 18). This is why the verse ends with the words: *It is a night that is guarded for all the Children of Israel for all their generations.*

A night that is guarded — A night on which there is protection from harmful elements. For this reason we do not recite the entire *Shema* and the other prayers asking for God's protection that are usually said before going to sleep. We read only

A Night that Is Guarded

the first paragraph of the *Shema* because on this night we enjoy special protection from God. (*Shulchan Aruch, Orach Chayim* 481)

The Talmud (*Pesachim* 109b) notes that although drinking the four cups of wine at the Seder has a potentially deleterious effect, we may do so because this is *a night that is guarded*.

Maaseh Roke'ach notes that he heard of a great Sage who would never lock the doors of his house on this night. He adds that it has become customary to leave the doors open so that we may out to greet Eliyahu without delay, for it is written that Israel is destined to be redeemed on the night of Pesach. It is a night that has been guarded and reserved for redemption, ever since Creation. Magen Avraham, quoting Maharil, writes that while one should not bolt the doors, he may close them, since a person should not rely on a miracle for protection.

A night that is guarded — Ibn Ezra writes that this means a night of guarding, of wakefulness, for it is customary to refrain from sleeping so that we might occupy ourselves with praises of God and relate His mighty deeds when He brought us out of Egypt. The Haggadah mentions the Sages of Bnei Brak who remained awake until it was time for the recital of the morning *Shema*.

Four Nights

As noted, the word *shimurim* is the plural form, and it is mentioned twice in the above verse. Our Sages say that this could connote a total of four nights, which would correspond to the four references to *this night* in *Shemos* 12:

> *And they shall eat the meat on this night (v. 8).*
> *And I shall pass through Egypt on this night (v. 12).*
> *And it was in the middle of this night (v. 29).*
> *This night remains to God (v. 42).*

The *Targum*, ascribed to Yonasan ben Uziel, and the *Targum Yerushalmi* explain that the four mentions of *this night* allude to four special, guarded nights in our history. The first is an allusion to the time when God revealed Himself at Creation:

The earth was chaos and darkness was on the face of the abyss (Bereshis 1:2). It was then that His light filled His world and He called it "night" rather than "darkness."

The second night is an allusion to the night of Yitzchak's birth, when God revealed Himself to Avraham, who was 100 years old, and to Sarah, who was 90, to fulfill His promise.

The third night alludes to the night when God appeared to the Egyptians at midnight, His right hand slaying the firstborn of the Egyptians while His left saved the firstborn of Israel.

The fourth night will come in the future, when the time arrives for the world to be redeemed. The power of the wicked will be severed and their might will be broken. Moshe *Rabbenu* will emerge from the wilderness and *Mashiach* will descend from Above. They will lead the Nation together and the voice of God will be heard as they walk together. *This night remains to God a night that is guarded for all the Children of Israel for all their generations (Ibid 12:41).*

All of these special nights — from Creation until the Days to Come — are guarded and set aside for Israel alone.